GEORGE CATLIN
LETTERS AND NOTES ON THE
NORTH AMERICAN
INDIANS

G. Catlin.

GEORGE CATLIN
LETTERS AND NOTES ON THE
NORTH AMERICAN INDIANS

EDITED AND WITH AN INTRODUCTION
BY MICHAEL MACDONALD MOONEY

In One Volume

 Clarkson N. Potter, Inc./Publisher   NEW YORK

DISTRIBUTED BY CROWN PUBLISHERS, INC.

We are grateful to the following for their kind permission to use illustrations on the pages listed:

Thomas Gilcrease Institute: xviii, 15, 57, 324

Smithsonian Institution, Washington, D.C.: 4, 5, 14, 17, 20, 23, 24, 25, 28, 29, 33, 38, 39, 40, 41, 50, 51, 52, 53, 56, 58, 62, 63, 72, 78, 86, 96, 116, 123, 130, 132, 140, 149, 150, 154, 161, 164, 165, 170, 210, 230, 239, 240, 252, 253, 256, 263, 265, 269, 270, 276, 278, 288, 291, 292, 294, 296, 304, 320, 322, 329, 330, 332, 348. Color Plates I, II, III, V, VI, VIII, following page 270.

Hirschl & Adler Galleries, Inc., New York: 12, 16

The New-York Historical Society: 13

The New York Public Library: 44–45

The Kennedy Galleries, New York: 34, 344

Collection of Mr. and Mrs. Paul Mellon: 70, 71

American Museum of Natural History: 268. Color Plate IV, following page 270.

Fort Leavenworth Museum, Fort Leavenworth, Kansas: 282

From "Western Wagons," by Stephen Vincent Benét, from *A Book of Americans,* by Rosemary and Stephen Vincent Benét. Copyright 1933, Rosemary and Stephen Vincent Benét. Copyright renewed 1961 by Rosemary Carr Benét. Holt, Rinehart and Winston, Inc., New York. Reprinted by permission of Brandt & Brandt, New York.

Printed in the United States of America
Published simultaneously in Canada
by General Publishing Company Limited.
Inquiries should be addressed to Clarkson N. Potter, Inc.,
419 Park Avenue South, New York, N.Y. 10016.
First Edition
Designed By Shari de Miskey

Library of Congress Cataloging in Publication Data

Catlin, George, 1796–1872.
Letters and notes on the North American Indians.

Original work, published in 1841 under title: Letters and notes on the manners, customs,
and condition of the North American Indians,
has been condensed and rearranged by the editor.
Bibliography: p.
Includes index.
1. Indians of North America. 2. Indians of North America—The West.
I. Mooney, Michael Macdonald, 1930-   ed. II. Title.
E77.c38 1975   977   75–4615
ISBN 0-517-52016-8

Preface

Letters and Notes on the Manners, Customs, and Condition of the North American Indians, by George Catlin, was first published in London in 1841. Those two volumes were then, and are today, an astonishing work by an extraordinary reporter. What I have done is to edit Catlin's report to a more convenient one volume; to choose sketches, illustrations, and portraits; to provide an introductory essay.

The essay examines briefly Catlin's amazing talent, his life and circumstances, and why his reports of the Plains Indians are so singular.

In editing Catlin I have taken unusual liberties with his original text, shortening and condensing as well as rearranging some parts and sections—all of which will surely offend some scholars. I took these liberties to attract the general reader; the scholar, after all, has the opportunity to consult the original. The introductory essay explains the changes.

In editing, in preparing the essay, in selecting the illustrations, and in tracking Catlin's paths across the plains, I am indebted to a long list of contributors. My acknowledgments, and a selected bibliography, follow the main Catlin text.

What engendered my own enthusiasm for Catlin's work—both his paintings and his reporting—was his unique position as a deliberate eyewitness of the Indian societies at their last moment of glory. By editing his work to one volume, I hope to pass on to the general reader Catlin's history of those lost tribes.

Michael M. Mooney

Contents

INTRODUCTION

Beyond the frontier, 1832–1836—American ethnology begins with Catlin—In some instances he is the only reporter of lost tribes.

The pot of gold—First academician in Philadelphia—Society portraits—Indians a subject worthy of his lifetime.

The geography and history of the Great Blank Space on the maps—A frontier town—Trade—The Missouri River system—Spanish, French, Americans—The fur trade companies.

Painting General Clark—The fur trade aristocracy—Three routes west—Catlin goes beyond the frontier, 1832–1836.

LETTERS AND NOTES ON THE NORTH AMERICAN INDIANS

by George Catlin

from St. Louis to Fort Union—The prairies—The commotion made by the Big Thunder Canoe—Mr. McKenzie's Fort—A rendezvous of tribes.

the Sioux—A theory on cholera—The death of Four Bears—The Mandans extinct.

Under the white flag—Plenty of buffalo meat—Wild horses—
Taken with the lasso—Arrival at Comanchee village.

List of Illustrations

xv

Map of Indian localities in 1833. Drawn by George Catlin.

INTRODUCTION

George Catlin's 1824 self-portrait hid a long tomahawk scar running down his left cheek.

I
Catlin's Achievements

> *. . . You shall name him Ismael . . . and he shall live at odds with all his kinsmen.*
>
> —Genesis 16:12

THE YEARS between 1832 and 1836 were the last years before the flood of American civilization was to sweep across the unmeasured lands west of the Mississippi. The frontier, that boundary zone between two cultures, was still lapping along the river's banks. To the west, out on the Great Plains, up in the valleys beyond the Rockies, the Indian societies believed they were still secure. The missionaries, the Army, and the real estate speculators had not yet fanned out to claim the plains as their own. The effects of whiskey, trade, and smallpox had not yet ruined the tribes. The buffalo still followed the long grass, God still held title to the land, and the rains still came in response to the dances of the chiefs.

Out there, out west beyond the boundary zone, out beyond the corruptions of the frontier, an extraordinary man—adventurer, promoter, painter, reporter—described what was to be the last high afternoon of glory for the American Indian. He was George Catlin. His task, he said, was to rescue "from oblivion the looks and customs of the vanishing races of native men in America." It was, he said, "worthy the life-time of one man."

And Catlin devoted his life to the task. Because he saw the frontier advancing behind him, he worked with the fever of the possessed. His travels, the number of his paintings and sketches, the volume of his notes, were prodigious. He had to record every

detail he could, he said, for it would all soon be lost. American ethnology begins with Catlin.

He was the first professional painter of the West, and perhaps the most important. He was the first to paint the Indians of the plains: the first to paint the Arikara of the northern plains, the various Sioux, the Omaha, the Osage, the legendary Mandans; the first to paint the Caddo of the southern plains, the Wichita, the horsemen of the Comanche. No other artist ever painted as many pictures of the trans-Mississippi West. He was the first professional to paint the Indians in their own country, in their native costumes. He pictured their occupations, their dances, their games, their great Medicines, their feasts and ceremonies. He was the first to paint portraits of their principal citizens and personalities. He painted and reported on twenty-three tribes of the lakes and woodlands, and twenty-six tribes of the plains. In some cases he was the *only* one to portray them because, after Catlin, they were extinct.

He was the first to paint and describe the Sioux sun dance. He was the first white man to visit and describe the holy pipestone quarries—the single source of the Indian ceremonial pipes. Indeed, he was the first to analyze the peculiar red claystone from which the sacred pipes were made—and it is still called "catlinite" after him. He accompanied the first permanent cavalry regiment in the U.S. Army on its first expedition west to the Comanche

2

territories, an expedition that was virtually wiped out by sickness. Catlin survived by riding back to St. Louis alone. He reported the disaster in the Arkansas Territories. He was in the Oklahoma Territory as the civilized tribes—the Choctaw, Chickasaw, Cherokee, and Creeks—were being resettled from the South, and his reports ached with injustice. He reported on the Seminole War, and went to paint Os-ce-o-la five days before that cursing hero died of a broken heart.

He was the first and the last eyewitness and invited participant at the O-kee-pah—the Mandan initiation ceremonies of torture. In fact, he is virtually our only source on the fantastic Mandans, the legendary descendants, it was said, of lost Welsh tribes or perhaps even the Vikings—because many Mandans had red hair and blue eyes. In 1837 the Mandan villages were wiped out by smallpox.

He was the first to paint the buffalo herds, buffalo hunting, buffalo dances, buffalo feasts. His artistic conventions of the buffalo became, by the imitation of his successors, our artistic conventions. He was the first to paint the fantastic lands of the Upper Missouri: the weird castled domes, the endless ocean of prairie, the huge scale of a chase for wild horses, the strange bluffs of grass, the scenes of wolf and bear and bighorn sheep and prairie dog, the awful sweep of prairie fire and the practical details of how best to escape its terror. He described a land unimaginable in either scale or detail to the people of the sheltered coves and copses of the woodland East. And his influence was immense and permanent.

Generations of artists knew Catlin. Shortly after his shows traveled the eastern cities, the great western migrations began. Then, in every city along the Atlantic coast, lithographers and illustrators could barely meet the demand for pictures of the promised land across the wide Missouri. The American imagination was hungry for details—first of Oregon, then of California, but always of the plains, the mythical "Wild West." The printers turned to Catlin in the original, and if not in the original, then in illustrations and lithographs by others who perhaps had not been out west but had Catlin to guide them. The picture books of Manifest Destiny were colored from Catlin's palette.

Yet today most of his work is stored away, inaccessible and unseen. Because he went broke in midlife, he was eventually forced to copy his own works, to copy quickly and from memory, to borrow money or to buy firewood. His copies were often poor. Sometimes copies of Catlin by Catlin are displayed as his "originals," or unfortunately believed to be representative of his work. Even if the originals are reexamined, even if we should finally grant him his rightful place among our greatest portraitists, even if we might finally award him—a bit late—the respect and wonder we should grant his extraordinary life, and rescue from obscurity his due as our first ethnologist, we would still be in his debt for his amazing instinct of being in the right place at the right time. Although the volume and skill of his work now seems astounding, his timing was even more singular. He went out there beyond the frontier in the nick of time: at the last moment.

In 1836, as Catlin returned East to serve as promoter and advocate of the Indian cause, the first wagon train for Oregon was crossing the plains and threading its way over South Pass to the Wyoming basin. The first white women ever to travel through the pass, Narcissa A. P. Whitman and Eliza H. Spaulding, were the wives of missionaries sent in

"Big Bend," on the Upper Missouri, 1900 miles above St. Louis, was part of a landscape beyond the frontier unknown and unimagined by the peoples of sheltered copse and cove back east.

response to the requests of Nez Percé ambassadors for "The White Medicine." In the tracks of those women's blessed wagons, the great migrations were soon to follow. Missionaries went first, of course, bringing the Good News of Redemption to the poor tribes, and the idea that God had given the earth to man for his increase. The first thing to do, therefore, was to subdivide, to start a garden, and then send East for skilled mechanics and carpenters to do the Lord's work. Although no white women had crossed the plains before 1836, white men—Spanish, French, English, and finally American explorers and trappers—had been there for nearly three hundred years. But such men were allies of Indian societies, and they were often husband and father in Indian lodges. They might own traps, but not land.

   After 1836 a different kind of white man appeared on the Indian horizon: the white man of the frontier—more preachers and their wives, then soldiers and ranchers and farmers. With them came the paraphernalia of civilization: the righteousness of Redemption, the whiskey stores, the district courts always prepared to issue a writ enforcing the claim of a real estate agent. As the frontier advanced, fur traders—the legendary mountain men—and the Indians backed away together. For both, the frontier was an advancing zone of corruption,

In 1832 the frontier had reached only to the Mississippi. The Indian nations still believed they were secure. War parties marched the endless grass, and God still held title to the land.

disease, and despair. After 1836 the frontier began to sweep up the Missouri and Platte valleys, then through the mountain passes west to the Pacific. Not until just before the Civil War would the Indians resist. And it would take sixty years before the flood would inundate every hill and canyon, and the historians would mark the frontier as "closed." Only in the last thirty years would there be relentless war between Indians and settlers—the romantic war of cavalry and Indian extinction in a legendary West. Yet the tide started to flood west beginning July 4, 1836, when the anointed authorities of "White Medicine," the Reverends Whitman and Spaulding, took their wives with them through South Pass.

The year after Catlin had gone East, smallpox swept through the tribes, destroying some completely, decimating others. Catlin had described and painted societies—some of them exotic—exquisitely balanced between glory and extinction. In some tribes the women or the Medicine Chiefs had objected to Catlin's portraiture because, they explained, if he could capture a man's likeness so exactly, he might easily capture his spirit for eternity. The Medicine Chiefs were proved right. After the smallpox epidemic of 1837, many of Catlin's models existed only on his canvases, and the Nations they represented were forever shattered.

5

Working beyond the frontier in the years 1832 to 1836, Catlin knew he had precious little time. He could see the floodwaters of immigration rising behind him. Moved by what he saw, he was the first to propose a National Park to preserve for the Nations some corner of an unspoiled West against the ravages of civilization. He could not get anyone to listen. He was the first to propose a National Museum of Indian Arts and Crafts. At his own expense he collected an Indian Museum, a *Gallery unique* he called it, the first Wild West show, and an authentic one. He offered it to the Government of the United States. The House passed the appropriation, but in the Senate, despite the advocacy of Daniel Webster, the proposal lost by a margin of one vote.

With his Indian artifacts, costumes, and teepees, with his sketchbooks, descriptions, and paintings, he went on a lecture tour—Philadelphia, Boston, New York, and Washington. He served as promotion man, press agent, the prototype of P. T. Barnum and Buffalo Bill, but always as the advocate of the Indian cause. He imagined he would lobby Congress into Indian reforms. His audiences were charmed, but he did not succeed. Because he deemed the United States insufficiently interested, he set sail with his museum for London and Paris. He thought if Europe raved, perhaps America could be shamed into acting.

Europe was charmed and made a celebrity of Catlin, then grew bored. In Paris, at fifty-seven years of age, Catlin went bankrupt. He would still go on to explore and paint the Indians of South America, but he never really recovered. Nevertheless, he had recorded the Indians of North America at their last moment of glory. After 1836, as the frontier swept west, as missionaries, smallpox, and whiskey settled in, gradually at first but then with increasing velocity, the buffalo dwindled, God relinquished title to the land to the heirs, successors, and assigns of real estate promoters, and the rain began to fall in answer to white men's prayers. Catlin understood exactly that his paints and pencils were his only weapons against the mists of oblivion for the Nations. Before attending his *Letters and Notes* then, let us sketch his life and circumstance.

II

Catlin's Life to Age Thirty-four

And the history and customs of such a people, preserved by pictorial illustrations, are themes worthy the life-time of one man, and nothing short of the loss of my life, shall prevent me from visiting their country, and of becoming their historian.

—George Catlin, *Letters and Notes on the North American Indians*

GEORGE CATLIN was born July 26, 1796, in Wilkes-Barre, Pennsylvania, and he died, at seventy-six, in Jersey City, New Jersey, December 23, 1872.

When Catlin died Ulysses S. Grant had already been elected to his second term as the eighteenth President of the United States, despite charges that artful Republicans had given away millions of acres of choice western lands to the railroad companies. The companies replied that the frontier lands were fair and just compensation; that as a direct result they were able to offer tickets, New York to San Francisco, six days and twenty hours, for $75 cash or credit, regularly scheduled service.

When Catlin was born, George Washington was ending his second term as President of the United States. Wilkes-Barre was a riverfront town on the Susquehanna, a town then famous as the site of the atrocious Wyoming Valley massacre during the Revolutionary War. In Wilkes-Barre the West was unknown territory, and the frontier began around the corner from the Catlin family barn.

George was the fifth child of fourteen children: Charles, Henry, Clara, Juliette, George, Eliza, James, Mary, Julius, Lynde, Sally, Richard, John, and Francis. His father, Putnam Catlin, had been born in Litchfield, Connecticut, April 5, 1764. He enlisted in the

Revolutionary Army at thirteen, in 1777; served as the regimental fife-major for eight years; returned to Litchfield to study law; moved to Wilkes-Barre in 1789 at twenty-five to establish his practice. He married nineteen-year-old Miss Polly Sutton the same year.

Polly Sutton was born September 30, 1770, the daughter of early settlers in Pennsylvania's Wyoming Valley. The valley was then a strategic alley of war between the Delawares, who claimed it as their own, and the Iroquois, allies of England's King George. The Iroquois had been selling it to colonial speculators and settlers. During the Revolutionary War, in July 1778, in the valleys north of Wilkes-Barre, American settlers and their Delaware allies battled Butler's Tory Rangers and St. Leger's Loyal Greens, and their Iroquois, Seneca, and Oneida allies. The Americans and Delawares were routed. A massacre of the settlers followed.

Polly Sutton's father escaped by swimming the Susquehanna, but Polly and her mother were captured. The colonials regrouped, sent punitive expeditions north under General John Sullivan, chased the Iroquois and their allies into central New York. Polly and her mother were released unharmed, but atrocity stories from the guerrilla wars between Indians and settlers were part of the lore of the valley as young George Catlin grew up.

A year after George was born, Squire Putnam Catlin moved his family to a farm in the forest about forty miles from town, to a site on the banks of the Susquehanna. The valley of the Susquehanna was one of the trails west, and young George grew up hearing not only the tales of the Wyoming Valley settlers, but of the Indian fighters, trappers, hunters, and explorers who stopped at the farm on their way from the old Northwest Territories—from the Ohio Valley and Illinois and the lands of the mysterious Mississippi still farther west.

By the time George Catlin was ten, Kentucky, Tennessee, and Ohio had joined the original thirteen states, President Jefferson had negotiated the Louisiana Purchase from Napoleon Bonaparte, and Lewis and Clark had returned from the far West to report there was no Northwest passage but there was an immense new land out there. Americans were beginning to realize they had won not only a War of Independence, they had won a continent. The geography of the continent was a mystery, but wherever the land might be—to the west, farther west—they would surely populate it.

Examined rationally, the idea was preposterous. Who was going to populate it? By what means? The national government, barely founded, was fragile. The nation lacked industry, wealth, ships, or arms; it was eyed greedily by mature empires in Europe with every means to subdue it. But the idea of "The West" as a national birthright was a commonplace of American self-consciousness. It was something that was ours, just as Putnam Catlin's wilderness farm was his.

Preposterous: Contrary to every rational expectation, a lawyer trained in the classics, used to discoursing on the politics of Plato's *Republic,* abandoned his law practice and moved his family from town to a tract by the river's bank. He cleared the land, planted corn and wheat. Despite his ignorance of husbandry, despite Indians, fearful winters, recurrent plagues, he assumed he and his family would prosper. He also assumed his children would have a classical education, and in the natural course of things the children would probably settle farther west. In fact, the art of agriculture was wasteful and primitive on a settler's farm.

8

Without game to supplement it, the diet would have been mean. But quail, coon, and turkey crowded the woods. The river teemed with fish. And the meat of scrawny cattle could be supplemented with deer. Hunting was a necessity. It was also fun. By the time he was ten, George Catlin could handle a long smoothbore rifle, if the weight of its long barrel was propped up on a rest.

At dusk one summer evening George took an older brother's gun and set out for deer. He hid near the ruins of the Old Saw Mill, waiting, watching a salt spring lick. In time, a big buck arrived.

Too excited at first, the boy took a while to get a rest for his barrel, took time to steady down his front sight and draw his bead. When he was ready to squeeze off his shot, he took a deep breath, let out half, and held it. Then, from his left, another rifle cracked. The buck dropped.

Though startled, he had the sense to stay hidden. He watched as an Indian appeared from the bush, trailing a rifle in his left hand and drawing a knife with his other from the sheath in the hollow of his back. The Indian slit the deer's throat, then hung the animal by its hind legs from a tree to let it bleed.

Indian and boy would both have to wait. The Indian drew and lit his pipe. The boy was flush with fear: "If he sees me, I'm lost. He will scalp me, and my mother will never know what became of me!"

The Indian's back and shoulders were turned toward the boy. Young George thought: "My rifle is leveled and I am now perfectly cool. A bullet would put an end to all my fears." Then the Indian turned around and moved his eyes over and about the ledge where the boy was hidden. Years later George Catlin said: "I saw then—though a child—in the momentary glance of that face, what infant human nature could not fail to see, and none but human nature could express. I saw humanity."

George snuck away. Once clear, he ran for home to report an Indian at the Old Saw Mill lick. At dawn the next day, with his father as an armed escort, George found the Indian camped, with his wife and ten-year-old daughter, cooking the venison he had shot the night before. The settlers sat with him. He said his name was On-o-gong-way, which means The Great Warrior. They passed the pipe, and smoked, and talked.

Young George told how he had his bead drawn the night before, how surprised he was by The Great Warrior's shot. The Great Warrior said he would share the venison with the boy, it should be half his.

He said he was from the Oneida, that his tribe now lived between the Oneida and Cayuga lakes in New York. When he was a boy, his father had been one of the warriors in the battle of Wyoming. They had been victorious.

After the battle his father's party had been driven, with many battles and great slaughter, up the Susquehanna and across the mountains to the lakes where they now lived. During their retreat his father made him carry many heavy things they had taken from the white people. The most valuable of these things, and the most difficult to carry, was a big kettle of gold.

But white soldiers trapped them on the banks of the creek on which the Old Saw

Mill was built. His father and mother buried the kettle of gold, with other things, before they had to flee. Now he had made a great journey to retrieve it. But he could see the fields had since been plowed, that things were changed, and that it would be useless now.

Perhaps not, said Putnam Catlin. He asked how big the kettle was.

The Great Warrior made a circle the full reach of his arms: "About this large, and as much as I could lift. It must be of great value."

Putnam Catlin sent George to the house for a little brass kettle that had been turned up when the field was ploughed a few years before.

When the boy returned to camp with the kettle, The Great Warrior turned it over and over in his hands. He tried his knife two or three times on the rim of it, laid it down, and drawing a deep breath through his pipe, said he had no doubt it was the same kettle. Two things troubled him: It was not a kettle of gold, and the kettle was now so small.

Putnam Catlin suggested that a good brass kettle had its uses too. The Great Warrior and his family should keep it, and make good use of it. In any case, they could stay at their camp, fish the streams, and hunt. In the meantime he would attempt to arrange a secure route home for them. It was a long journey, and an Indian family traveling alone might be in great danger.

They stayed while Squire Catlin attempted to make safe travel arrangements. Each day young George would go over to the Indian's camp. George had a whole cabinet of Indian implements he had picked up, and he brought them to be repaired and to learn their uses and their Medicine.

The Great Warrior made a hickory bow plumed with woodpecker feathers for the boy. He shafted and feathered the boy's flint arrowheads. From the skin of a deer he made a quiver for his arrows. The boy had found a rusty iron pipe-tomahawk. The Great Warrior replaced the old handle with a new one of hickory and demonstrated how to throw it, how to sink its blade into the bark of a target tree. The boy promised to practice.

Fall was coming. Despite the dangers of the route home, The Great Warrior and his family slipped away one night. On a hook of the woodhouse he left a saddle of venison with an eagle quill set in it as a farewell.

A few days later he was found dead no more than ten miles from the Catlins' farm. He had been shot twice. No one ever learned what became of his wife and daughter. There was no sign of the pot of gold.

Young George Catlin promised himself again to practice. The tomahawk with the new hickory handle was polished and sharpened to a razor's edge and buried deep into the bark of target trees, though perhaps the targets no longer represented the traditional settler's enemies—the howling savages of the Wyoming massacres.

At times he practiced with neighborhood boys, each taking their turn. In one attack on an old tree, a bad throw glanced from the bark and cut into George's left cheekbone, scarring him for life.

Despite the long scar down his cheek, he grew to be handsome. By the time he was twenty-one he was about 5 feet, 8 inches tall, thin and wiry, weighing about 135 pounds. He had a dark complexion and a shock of black hair, but straight, quick, blue eyes. Later, when he had weathered, he liked to think that, except for the blue eyes, he might pass for an Indian. He always said he was George Catlin from Wyoming, Pennsylvania. He had spent his youth, he said, "with books reluctantly held in one hand, and a rifle or fishing pole firmly and affectionately grasped in the other."

In 1817, at twenty-one, he entered the law school of Reeve and Gould in Litchfield, Connecticut. It was America's most unusual law school, conducted on the parlor floors of the white Federal house of Judge Tapping Reeve. The judge was somewhat of a legend. He lectured on the sacredness of the law in a failed voice that required him to speak in whispers, yet his students could hear him well enough. They came from all the states, and from the wealthiest and most aristocratic families of the new Republic.

It was said that old Judge Reeve helped Miss Sarah Pierce set up her Female Academy in Litchfield, the first such school for young ladies. In fact, the way to compliment any young woman in the former colonies was to say "she could pass on Litchfield Hill." It was said that Judge Reeve liked pretty young women; he said he never saw a bad one.

His partner, James Gould, polished the manners of the young law students by his example: precise, widely read in the classics, exact in rhetoric. Before 1833 the two tutors, Reeve and his successor, Gould, had trained two Vice Presidents, six Cabinet members, thirty-seven Federal and State Supreme Court judges, 129 senators and congressmen, twenty-four governors and lieutenant governors, and hundreds of successful lawyers, teachers, and financiers. The continental empire needed trained men.

At Litchfield, George Catlin learned more than law. Although the young ladies and young gentlemen attended separate lectures for their studies, they roomed and took their meals together in the town's handsome Yankee houses. Catlin could hear the worldly talk of the politics of the new Republic, take lessons not only in the thoughtful metaphors of Plato or the stoicism of Marcus Aurelius but in the quick banter, the confident accents of Yankee misses and Southern belles. The ladies studied history, composition, literature. They learned to sketch. They worked with watercolors. George Catlin tried his hand.

He had a cousin, Grove Catlin, who kept the tavern on Litchfield Green. Grove's daughter, Flora, was considered the belle of Litchfield. She was a drawing mistress in Miss Pierce's Academy. Another cousin, Dr. Abel Catlin, had adopted a daughter, Mary Peck. She too was a drawing mistress at the academy. For artistic examples, Litchfield had Anson Dickinson miniatures, and portraits by Ralph Earle. Catlin produced a portrait of Judge Reeve. It was much admired.

He passed his bar exams and returned to Lucerne County, Pennsylvania, to practice law. He had few cases and plenty of time. He sketched the courtroom characters. He practiced sketching himself in the mirror. He sketched impressions, as he called them, of rage, joy, wonder, ecstasy. Late in 1820 he sold his law library, moved to Philadelphia, took a modest studio, and hung out his shingle: "George Catlin, Miniature Painter."

In March 1821 his father wrote him from the farm on the banks of the Susquehanna: "My dear George . . . I am pleased that you have at length resolved to attempt portraits, though you had me convinced last fall that miniatures were as valuable. Most painters of eminence have worked at portraits and history. . . . I have set down the names of

In Philadelphia, Catlin won immediate recognition. He painted society miniatures, like this watercolor on ivory of Midshipman Joseph Stallings, and his work was exhibited by The Academy.

the Artists in your line. . . ." Four pages of catalogue follow, listing the great European painters to study from the fifteenth and sixteenth centuries, in the minute and careful hand of the lawyer, classics scholar, and settler in the Wyoming Valley.

In Philadelphia, George Catlin was at work in the new Republic's Athens—or so its citizens hoped it would be. Each May the Pennsylvania Academy of Art gave young artists an exhibition. A committee of senior artists selected the entries. They chose four Catlin miniatures in May 1821, then six in 1822.

During the winter of 1822–1823 Catlin worked at oil portraits on canvas instead of miniatures. His first attempt was a remarkable self-portrait. In the spring of 1823 he submitted only one miniature on ivory to the Academy for display. A year later, in February 1824, the artists of the Academy, including Thomas Sully, John Neagle, Charles Willson Peale, and his sons Raphael, Rembrandt, and Titian Peale, revived the accolade of "Pennsylvania Academician." For the work that was in progress in his studio, George Catlin was the first to be elected. His fellow painters considered him one of the outstanding painters of the day. In the studio he was working out his own special style, a technique to do rapid work in oil, to enable him to create life-size portraits fast, large-scale landscapes, character studies of men in groups. He had already decided on the technique he would need.

The American Athens housed a most unusual institution: Peale's Philadelphia Museum. Charles Willson Peale had painted the commanders and events of the Revolution,

12

In 1826 The New York Common Council voted Catlin $600 for a portrait of Governor DeWitt Clinton. The governor sponsored Catlin's election to The American Academy of Fine Arts.

the statesmen and citizens of the new Republic, and had displayed them in his own museum—a gallery of instruction available by paying a small entrance fee. Besides portraits, the museum displayed models of steam engines, looms, and sewing machines; birds, fish, and mammals of North America; ores, crystals, and minerals; displays for botanists; skeletons for paleontologists; and Indian crafts, weapons, and tools. There were examples of artifacts gathered by the Lewis and Clark expedition to the Pacific in 1804–1806. There were sketches and specimens, in geology and entomology, collected by Titian Peale when he had accompanied the expedition of Major Stephen H. Long up the Platte to the Rockies in 1819–1820. George Catlin was a frequent visitor to Peale's Museum.

Catlin's reputation in miniatures was bringing him a flood of commissions, but he said he was "continually reaching for some branch or enterprise of the art on which to devote a whole life-time of enthusiasm." During the winter of 1822–1823 a delegation of Indians, on their way to visit the Great White Father's Washington, stopped to visit Peale's Museum "arrayed and equipped in all their classic beauty, with shield and helmet, with tunic and manteau, tinted and tasselled off, exactly for the painter's palette!

"Nothing short of the loss of my life," said Catlin, "shall prevent me from visiting their country, and of becoming their historian."

He was determined, he said, to reach ultimately every tribe of Indians on the continent of North America; to bring home faithful portraits of their principal personages,

13

Miss Clara Gregory of Albany loved to listen to his plans.
They were married in May 1828.

both men and women; views of their villages and games; and "full notes on their character and history." He also planned "to secure their costumes, and a complete collection of their manufactures and weapons, and to perpetuate them in a *Gallery unique,* for the use and instruction of future ages."

He wrote his father because he had heard his father's friend, Colonel Timothy Pickering, planned an expedition to treaty with Red Jacket, the famous Seneca orator. George Catlin said he needed details for an historic painting he planned. Colonel Pickering met with Red Jacket, but replied, through Putnam Catlin, that he didn't see there was much to paint.

Then George Catlin ran into Colonel William Stone, publisher of the New York *Commercial Advertiser,* who was more sympathetic. (Stone was later to write a biography of Red Jacket.) He became Catlin's patron. He got him commissions, introduced him to the powerful men of the new Republic, published his drawings, and would be the publisher of Catlin's *Letters and Notes* from the West.

Colonel Stone, and his newspaper, were the advocates and publicists of New York's Republican Party—the allies of the Virginia hegemony of Jefferson, Madison, and Monroe. Until 1812 the leader of the party in New York was DeWitt Clinton. In 1812 an antiwar faction of the Republican Party, supported by the disintegrating Federalist Party, nominated

14

Red Jacket's baleful glare was too realistic, and Catlin's portrait offended popular taste.

He painted Niagara Falls, but the landscapes in his mind's eye were already in the Far West.

Clinton for the Presidency. He carried every state north of the Potomac, except Vermont and Pennsylvania. Madison carried the South and the new states of the West: Ohio, Kentucky, Tennessee, and Louisiana. Madison was reelected.

But DeWitt Clinton served two terms as governor of New York after 1817. He was also the founder and first president of the Literary and Philosophical Society of New York, and an important figure in the American Academy of Fine Arts. In his first term as governor he started the Erie Canal, one of the many schemes of national improvements begun after the War of 1812. The canal became one of the great gateways west, and would make New York into the principal commercial, shipping, and financial city of America.

Governor Clinton was indebted to Colonel Stone and his *Commercial Advertiser* for support at the polls and support of the canal. In turn, Stone commissioned George Catlin to

16

Cu-sick, civilized son of a Tuscarora chief, wore the frock coat of a Baptist preacher.

make drawings of the construction work of the canal, and published them in an official souvenir book when the canal was opened in 1825.

The October opening of the canal was a carnival of publicity, sideshows, ceremonies, and delegations. Catlin prepared two pictures for the occasion: an elaborate view of Buffalo Harbor with boats ready to begin the trip down to New York, and a section of the canal with a full-length figure of Governor Clinton in the foreground in the costume of a Roman hero. For his part in the ceremonies Catlin was awarded a special medal. The next spring he was elected an Academician of the National Academy of Fine Arts.

By 1826 he was getting $40 or $50 for portraits, which was good money then. For a canvas of Governor DeWitt Clinton, the New York Common Council voted Catlin $600. The money and the connections, Catlin plainly thought, were going to be important for his

17

trips west. And in 1826, in Buffalo, he finally painted Red Jacket.

It was a stunning portrait, a testament that the boy who had fetched the kettle of gold, who carried the scar of the tomahawk on his left cheek, had honed his skills as an artist. But the portrait offended the popular taste. It was too realistic. Catlin did not see Red Jacket as Uncas. He painted an old man, dissipated by liquor, still proud, with one eyelid drooping over an even gaze of hate. Brutal. Ugly. Exact. It was not well received.

He went on with his conventional society paintings, saving money for his expedition. In Governor Clinton's Albany house he met the daughter of Benjamin Gregory, a rich Albany accountant: Miss Clarissa Gregory.

Catlin courted Miss Gregory. He was a dashing fellow, handsome, full of dreams. He was not rich, but he seemed to be succeeding. He was a friend of the governor. He was "the famous painter, Mr. Catlin." He loved to talk of his plans and projects, how he would create his *Gallery unique* of Indians, of the continent to the west spreading out for the American imagination. Clara loved to listen to him. They were married May 28, 1828, in Albany by the Reverend Mr. Lacey.

In Albany Catlin worked on a huge canvas of Niagara Falls; Red Jacket would appear in the foreground. He copied a Clinton portrait for the Franklin Institute of Rochester. He visited and sketched the Seneca, Oneida, and Tuscarora reservations. He sketched Ottawas and Mohegans. He painted Chief Bread and Chief Cusick, who had become a Baptist minister and wore a black frock coat. A dozen of Catlin's works were exhibited by the American Academy of Fine Arts.

By the fall of 1829 both George and Clara Catlin were in bad health. Diagnosis was not exact then—something about an "ague" for Clara and a cough for George. To avoid the harsh upstate New York winter, they went South. In Richmond, Virginia, Catlin was commissioned to paint the 115 delegates assembled to draw a new Virginia Constitution. He worked much of the winter on a watercolor "sketch," a composite of 101 miniature portraits of members of the convention, including Presidents Madison and Monroe, Justice Marshall, and John Randolph of Roanoke. The "sketch" was to serve as a model for a huge oil canvas.

Clara's "ague" continued. While George worked, Dolley Madison frequently came to tend Clara. In gratitude Catlin did a miniature on ivory of Dolley.

But Clara would need a long convalescence, and so in the spring of 1830 George Catlin took his wife to her father's house in Albany. He would rejoin her when ice closed the western rivers. Then, with Clara urging him on, he set off for Washington to get the letters and introductions he would need in the West. He said he would have to hurry before the West was gone.

New states were being created one after another: Indiana in 1816, Mississippi in 1817, Illinois in 1818, Alabama in 1819. Florida had been won from Spain in 1819, Maine became a state in 1820, and Missouri was accepted as a state in 1821—Missouri, and its city of St. Louis at the junction of the Mississippi and Missouri rivers.

Steamboats were toting immigrants to St. Louis from New Orleans. The National Road was being built from Cumberland to Wheeling, out across Ohio, across Indiana to Vandalia, Illinois. And railroads were being started. In 1828 the last surviving signer of the

Declaration of Independence, Charles Carroll, turned the first spadeful to start the Baltimore and Ohio Railroad tracking West.

Preposterous: The wobbly little Republic for which Putnam Catlin had fought, that union which Daniel Webster later described as having its origin "in the necessities of disordered finance, prostrate commerce, and ruined credit," had built ships and cities, had chopped wheat fields out of the forest, and was an empire before it was a nation. The empire already had a fleet stationed in the Mediterranean. It had been sending missionaries to China for thirty years to convert those ignorant heathen to democracy. The empire was one of Manifest Destiny.

In the continental West the spirit of Manifest Destiny would encounter difficulties. In the history of the empire, dividing the West would be one cause of civil war. Perhaps politics failed to achieve its compromises because the geography of the West was so difficult to understand. It was unmapped and unknown. It would continue to astonish men accustomed to the seaboard, or to the Appalachians. Settlers from "backwoods and mountain streams" would need more than one hundred years, perhaps even longer, to adjust to a desert in which the woods started at 8000 feet and the streams were either dry gulches or roaring floodplains.

Never mind. "A virgin continent awaited the plow." That much was manifest. The final tranquility of the Mediterranean for U.S. Navy ships and the conversion of China might take a little longer, but the West would be populated now.

From the time Catlin was graduated by Reeve and Gould in Litchfield in 1821 to the time he set off for Washington in 1830, the population of the wobbly little nation had been marching west. Michigan had almost quadrupled—to 31,639. Illinois had tripled—to 157,445. Ohio, that wilderness from which scouts brought back tall tales to entertain George Catlin, the boy of Wilkes-Barre—Ohio had nearly one million citizens!

Catlin knew if he would realize his dream, if he would preserve for future generations the character of *independent* Indian nations, he would have to hurry. He would have to get out ahead of a frontier that was advancing almost as fast as a man could walk. By traveling down the Ohio River, Catlin finally arrived in St. Louis in the summer of 1830. He was thirty-four.

From St. Louis, gateway to the West, the steamboat *Yellowstone* would provision the beaver trade and assure the continental Manifest Destiny at The Company forts upstream.

III

St. Louis to 1830

The cowards never started and the weak died on the road,
And all across the continent the endless campfires glowed.
We'd taken land and settled—but a traveler passed by—
And we're going West tomorrow—Lordy, never ask us why!

—Stephen Vincent Benét, "Western Wagons"

IN 1830 St. Louis was a frontier town, epicenter of an advancing geopolitical boundary between civilized history and something else: the geography, customs, manners, and traditions of the peoples of the retreating great blank space, the mysterious inheritance, the shadowless mists of apparently indifferent evolution.

In 1830 along the levees of St. Louis, steamboats docked bow upstream. Sternwheelers, side-wheelers, flush deckers, and two-story New Orleans packets—Big Medicine Canoes every one of them, tended off the wharves by spring lines against about three knots of downstream Mississippi mud. They docked on the west bank, the frontier's edge, hard by the warehouses where draymen stacked bales of stinking, greasy beaver pelt. The bales would be going downriver to New York and Paris, London and Berlin, Canton, China, and Saint Petersburg, Russia.

Beaver: cargo of fashion, of fortune and style; trapped in icy mountains streams, a harvest of stinking treasure; traded, the capital of empire. Beaver would soon be succeeded in fashion's warm appraisal by the lowly silkworm from another continent, but not before the beaver flats on the west bank had been transformed—by the alchemy of commerce—into mountains of gold that would have stunned even Cortez. Beaver came downstream.

Coronado reported his passage left no sign in the tall buffalo grass. It rose behind them, the wind combed it, and the plains were empty again. He was wrong. He had left the horse.

Trade: in the warehouses for upstream, the draymen stacked bags of glass from Venice and Florence, glass for beads, an Italian medium of exchange to be ciphered by Indian bankers; three quarters of a pound per string of beads at about thirty-seven cents per pound in St. Louis, higher upriver; Mackinaw blankets, one point, three point, and three and a half point, in blue, green, scarlet, and white; spun on steam looms in the English Midlands, wheel upon wheel turning at magic speeds, manufactured to satisfy Indian squaws, the spinning wheels tended by young English girls praying for the opportunity to meet a lord, or emigrate.

Upstream: axe heads, iron pots, tongs, crowbars, scalping knives stamped "Toronto"; hammered and turned, fired and doused in the angry forges of Vulcan's sons, the civilized peoples.

Trade: tobacco, coffee, sugar, cotton picked by slaves, sundries and stores—misses' white stockings, mirrors, and steel needles. "Let me tell you, once a squaw used a steel needle she'd never go back to a bone awl. She'd harry her man 'til she had steel."

There were rifle balls, flints, smoothbore muskets with short stocks. A short stock,

"Creasing" a wild horse.

like a short bow, was easier for a man to handle riding horseback. The rifles on the west bank were manufactured especially for the upriver trade. And there were barrels of whiskey.

On the streets of St. Louis dozens of languages could be heard: English, sure; also Spanish, French, Crow, several Sioux dialects, Cheyenne, Pawnee, the cadences of Virginia gentlemen, Scots Highlanders, and Black Irish. There were squat bayou flatboat polers, Yankees fashioned like axe handles, riffraff from the Kentucky woods, confidence men, high-born ladies and steamy whores, polecats, sneak thieves, ne'er-do-wells, a few Army men, some of the new nabob merchants, and an iron-fisted aristocracy—Chouteaus, Lisas, Ashley's men, and Astor's. The citizens of St. Louis, population about 7000, claimed it would be the new Rome.

Maybe. The Red Men from the mysterious lands upstream came to gawk at what had already come to pass. Amazed, they were fated to be the first victims of three developing civilized systems: agricultural, industrial, corporate. The subsequent victims have been red, yellow, black, and white, including a number of modified shades between.

23

Catlin called the Wichita "Pawnee Picts," and painted Thighs, a woman of the tribe. It was the Wichita who guided Coronado home from the land of Quivera—down the Santa Fe trail.

The intricate designs of those systems are better understood now. In 1830 geography determined how the systems would develop. From the ridges of the Appalachians to the Rocky Mountain divide, from the Great Lakes to the Gulf of Mexico, the Mississippi River basin spreads as one geographic unit. With New Orleans at the roots, there is but one tree, and its branches—the Mississippi, Missouri, and Ohio river valleys—are inseparable as a working unit.

By understanding geography, Napoleon Bonaparte calculated that if he controlled New Orleans he would control the destiny of the American continent. Failing that, if he sold the Louisiana Territory to Thomas Jefferson, he would give "England a maritime rival who sooner or later would humble her pride."

The same geography lay beneath the issues that would split the United States politically but join them historically—issues that were compromised for a while, then led inevitably to civil war and then to union. It was Missouri that had to be compromised, Kansas that would be "bloody," and Vicksburg that would be crucial. When Lincoln argued the

24

He-Who-Kills-the-Osages, chief of the Missouri—a dwindling tribe on the Platte in 1831. But chiefs of the Missouri had wintered in Paris nearly one hundred years before Lewis and Clark.

Union was indivisible, he showed a map, traced a line west, and could find no boundary along which separation would be feasible.

The geography of the great river valley system was unique. Not only was the heartland immense—so immense its scale and distances escaped understanding—but it was the world's only such river valley system entirely in a temperate zone, a valley whose rivers drained *south* to warm-water ports. A continental system.

It was named the "Mississippi" system by an accident of historical order, because the frontier knew the Mississippi first, and returned with its name. It is the Missouri that curves about 4000 miles to St. Louis from its headwaters west of Yellowstone down through the Gallatin Gateway, north over Great Falls, east through Montana and the Dakotas, then south toward the sea. It does not matter much, but the label given the Missouri as the contributing stream perhaps could have been identified as the continued trunk. Perhaps New Orleans was actually "at the mouth of the Missouri River."

Instructed by Jefferson to explore the upper Missouri as possibly "the most

25

practicable water communication across this continent, for the purposes of commerce," Captains Meriwether Lewis and William Clark returned in September 1806 to report the Missouri was not the legendary "Golden River of the West" because the "Big Stony Mountains" were virtually an impossible barrier.

Lewis and Clark could not find a "northwest passage." Nevertheless, they had mapped the river. There was a wiggly red line that could be drawn through the blank space on the maps of The West. They also reported the country they had traveled was rich in furs, which Indian, French, and English fur traders already knew perfectly well.

Though unmapped, the great blank space had a long history already, some of it tall tale, some of it mythology, some of it with gaping holes—missing the details of reality, all of it romantic. An arbitrary beginning of its history would start in 1541 with the conquistador Francisco de Coronado.

He came up from Spanish Mexico searching for The Seven Cities of Cibola, in the land of Quivera, where, it had been reported, even the common people supped from golden jugs and bowls, the lords of the land were soothed asleep by the tinkling of golden bells, where a stream six miles wide bore the people in great canoes with golden eagles at their prows.

Coronado marched across New Mexico, crossed the Canadian River into the panhandle of Texas, north across Arkansas. "The land is in the shape of a ball," his diarist recorded, "wherever a man stands he is surrounded by the sky at the distance of a cross-bow shot." His diarist was apparently the first to note "the land of the big sky."

He also noted how the land swallowed them up: Coronado's line of five thousand sheep, five hundred beef cattle, a thousand horses, and fifteen hundred men left no sign in the tall buffalo grass. He reported it rose behind them, the wind combed it, and the plains were empty again. He said they left no sign of their passage.

That turned out to be a misunderstanding. Coronado got about as far as Salina, Kansas, where he had his Indian guide strangled for treachery, because there were no Seven Cities of Cibola. Coronado's column was then guided toward home by scouts of the Wichita tribe, sometimes called the Pawnee Picts. They led him over the ancient Indian trade route, later called the Santa Fe trail.

Curiously, if he had marched about another hundred miles east of Salina, Coronado would have found that big river—the Missouri, and with big canoes on it too. The eagles at their prows would have been golden eagles, but they would have been living golden eagles, and tamed.

Coronado found no big river, no Cibola, no gold, but he left behind some horses. The lightning of evolution had struck; as usual, it was all a misunderstanding. Coronado thought he had left no sign of his passage. The people of the plains called the horses "big dogs," because Coronado's "big dogs" could pull a travois farther than their customary "little dogs."

The early French came to the plains without "big dogs." They came in canoes, haphazardly at first, from the St. Lawrence River system, through the Great Lakes, westering the lacework of streams and portages of the flat, glacially scoured subarctic. In June 1673, on a foray south, the canoes of Jolliet and Marquette passed the mouth of the Missouri. The river was in spring flood, and perhaps a river of such size and force, said the astonished Father Marquette, would be the means "to make the discovery of the Vermillion Sea or California." Perhaps it would be.

Imperial systems of French canoes and Spanish horses were contesting for control of the plains as early as 1717. When Spain went to war with France over the seizure of Sicily and Sardinia on one continent, agents of their kings groped toward each other across the blank space on another.

In New Mexico the governor fortified his posts, then sent an expedition north from Santa Fe. He had heard the French were already in Colorado, building up a stock of munitions and, according to the Indian news services who were his only sources, living there in luxury with their beautiful white women. No one was too sure exactly where Colorado was, but it was reported by informed Indian sources that the French were training the Pawnees in the use of guns. The Apache applied for training to their governor. To defeat their ancient enemies the Pawnees, they said, they would need guns, many guns.

The Spanish governor sent Señor Villasur marching north with an expedition of forty-five soldiers, some settlers and traders to see to the business of occupation, seventy Apache allies, a priest, and a French interpreter. Villasur reached the forks of the Platte in August 1720; there he was ambushed by the Pawnee, and his expedition wiped out. According to one of the few survivors, perhaps there were French among the Pawnee, indeed there must have been, they must have had French guns.

Meanwhile, similar Indian news services were reporting to the French about a Spanish march on Illinois. According to similar reliable sources, there were two hundred of them, and a large number of the fearful Comanche, a very large number. The Indian allies of the French would need guns, many guns.

From Paris, the king ordered Etienne de Bourgmont to meet the threat. He was the very model of a French *coureur de bois.* As a young ensign he had commanded Detroit. He had fought in the Fox wars. He had lived for five years among the Missouri Nation, and in the performance of his diplomacy had escorted the Missouri chief to Paris. He was a blood brother of the Missouri and the Osage, and those tribes were middlemen for the trade to tribes beyond.

In November 1723 he built a fort at the mouth of the Grand River among his adopted Missouris. Then in June 1724 he pushed dugouts loaded with trade goods and presents up the Missouri to the mouth of the Kansas River. From there, with Kansas allies, he marched across the plains to the Comanche villages, near the Wichita Mountains, in the land of Quivera, where Coronado had met the Pawnee Picts. The Comanche counciled, traded, agreed to be allies of France forever. Etienne de Bourgmont, his mission a success, went home to Paris and a title.

The fort he built halfway across Missouri was abandoned in 1728, but trade slowly increased. By 1739 the Mallet brothers succeeded in opening trade from New Orleans up the Arkansas, over the trail to Santa Fe.

By 1763 another Frenchman, Pierre Laclede, had won a charter for a new company. He came upriver from New Orleans to select a site for a new post and chose the

conjunction of the Mississippi and Missouri rivers. He named it St. Louis, in honor of his French king, and settled on the west side of the river because he had heard the Treaty of Paris gave the east bank to Great Britain. That was a misunderstanding. By the Treaty of Paris he was on Spanish soil, and in due time—only seven years—Spanish officials came to visit.

By then, however, there were more spectacular misunderstandings operating in The West. For example, the Spanish starting out to look for gold. The plains had little, or none. Spanish missions, in their effort to collect souls, won California, where there was plenty of gold, but by then the Spanish were too busy with their souls.

The first French explorers were Jesuits, who had started looking for souls. Their successors, the *coureurs de bois,* arrived on the plains in ones and twos from bases in Montreal and New Orleans. They set their traps and collected beaver worth more than gold.

And the lightning of evolution still played unnoticed across the plains. If French trappers were too far away to return to their bases, they stayed and married. They became brothers in the tribe, and inevitably, fathers, fathers-in-law, grandfathers, great-grandfathers.

Good sense and custom of the Indian societies held that upon marriage the man joined his wife's lodge. In most cases a Shoshone married to a Mandan woman became a

28

A Sioux caravan might include six hundred lodges, towed on travois across the plains by both dogs and horses. The horse gave the Nations range to follow the buffalo and surplus to trade.

Since his wife, Sand Bar, was Sioux, François Chardon, fur trader and captain at Mr. Astor's forts, had to count himself a Sioux. After all, his children were obviously Sioux.

Mandan, depending upon whether the woman was taken in war or contracted for, and other complications. But a *coureur de bois* married to a Shoshone woman was obviously a Shoshone; not only was the baby, when it was born, clearly a gift of a Shoshone mother, but what other tribe could the father be associated with?

In 1743 Verendrye, one of the great exploring *coureurs,* traded his way south from the lakes of Ontario and Manitoba to the villages of the Mandan peoples on the Upper Missouri. The Mandans controlled the trade to the west and south, certainly as far south as the Missouri Nation. Verendrye reported some Mandans as having blue eyes, and some blond hair. He reported no other white men ever having been in the area. There would have been no way for him to know that chiefs of the Missouri had spent the winter in Paris nearly a half century earlier.

Similarly, when Lewis and Clark arrived at the Mandan villages they were told by the chiefs they were the first white men the Mandan people had ever seen. In the villages in which the welcome hand was being extended, there were French trappers to greet Lewis and Clark. But no white men. Only husbands of Mandan or Shoshone women.

Typical. The silent business of marriage was the first key to the developing West.

29

When Pierre Laclede founded St. Louis in 1763, he had with him a boy of thirteen, Auguste Chouteau. The boy was destined to become "the founder" of the St. Louis aristocracy—lords of the fur empire, which was working its way up the Missouri, one tributary after another secured by a fort, each post celebrating a marriage between Indian princess and St. Louis potentate. By intermarriage in St. Louis, they soon became a law unto themselves.

They married and merged. Brothers, cousins, nephews, and in-laws pushed the chain of forts and posts toward Oregon. Eventually they would defeat the English there, but to do so they would need something more than marriage. They would need to form corporations and trusts, create systems of monopoly trade backed by huge aggregations of capital.

The fur traders and their Indian wives would be the forerunners of western immigration; they would be its scouts and guides. They would construct the geographic system by which the pioneers might go west, but they would also have to adopt the system of trusts and combinations, of economic war created in the East, which, when its time came, would entail them all—Indian, trader, pioneer, settler.

At first the St. Louis aristocracy only had to compete with the Hudson's Bay Company. The Treaty of Paris awarded Canada to Great Britain, and the Hudson's Bay Company became the sovereign government of the wilderness, without boundaries, empowered to make war or peace among the tribes as necessary.

The Company's policy had always been consistent: trade with the Indians for fur, but let them trap their own streams themselves. It was an ecologically sound system because the Indian never trapped more than he needed and had no interest in accumulating surplus capital; hence he always left something for next year in every canyon.

But French trappers, once combined with Scots merchants in Montreal, or Yankees in St. Louis, used a different system. They found it more profitable to set their own traps, to bring their own beaver flats downstream in their own canoes, amass capital this year.

When the Indian trapped only what he needed, he was an unreliable source. The efficient use of capital required a guaranteed source of raw material, the more the better, and if one valley was trapped out, the trapper went on to the next.

In 1783 the new system in Montreal incorporated itself as the North West Company. It soon had London bankers to satisfy. It extended its operations to the Upper Missouri and then into the Rocky Mountains. The Hudson's Bay Company and the North West Company declared war on each other, put up rival posts, burned each other's forts to the ground, killed each other's trappers. The war spread all the way south to the Platte.

The Fur War on the Platte was too close to St. Louis. The traders there, nominally Spanish, formed a "Company of Explorers of the Upper Missouri" to push the English companies out. The Upper Missouri Company proposed a string of forts strategically placed along the river among the tribes, to be extended "gradually until it reaches the South Seas." It would cost only ten thousand pesos annually, they told the government of Spain, to maintain one hundred militiamen and "not only drive the English from the Missouri, but keep them away." Unfortunately for the scheme, Spain was too far away, too weak, and in 1800 the successors of the conquistadors signed Louisiana over to Napoleon.

If Napoleon thought he was a clever geopolitician in selling Louisiana to the United States—and denying it to England—President Jefferson had shrewdly anticipated him. In 1783 Jefferson had attempted to get George Rogers Clark, hero of the Indian wars in the Ohio wilderness, to explore west of the Mississippi. But Clark was involved in the Spanish conspiracies with General James Wilkinson—as was half of St. Louis—and the project had to be tabled. Ten years later Jefferson tried again, commissioning Andrew Michaux, a French botanist, to go west. The American Philosophical Society solicited a fund for the expedition. By April 1800 they had collected a total of $128.25; George Washington had contributed $25, Jefferson and Hamilton $12.50 each. Unfortunately, it turned out that Andrew Michaux was a French spy in the pay of Citizen Genêt. Anyway, he only got as far as Lexington, Kentucky.

Even before Jefferson had sent Robert R. Livingston to Paris to purchase the port of New Orleans, he had sent a secret message to Congress on January 18, 1803, to finance a "scientific expedition" for Lewis and Clark. He had decided that if he were unable to buy Louisiana, the exploding American population would soon fill it up anyway. When Napoleon sold Louisiana for about four cents an acre, Americans paid for what they were already determined to have at any cost.

The Lewis and Clark expedition turned out to be one of the greatest scientific expeditions. It was also a warning to the English, who had encouraged continuous war along the old Northwest frontier. The English still hoped to create an Indian satellite nation north of the Ohio, and if not there, in the upper Mississippi Valley, and if not there, then along the Upper Missouri. There was no boundary west of Lake of the Woods to the Pacific Ocean, nor would there be for another forty-five years. On the maps the Louisiana Territory was still a great blank space.

After 1803, however, the blank space was being traversed by Americans. In 1807 Manuel Lisa of St. Louis employed John Colter of the Lewis and Clark party as a guide and built a fort at the mouth of the Big Horn River in the Crow country—the first post of the Rocky Mountain fur trade. Two years later Lisa formed the Missouri Fur Company; among his partners were William Clark and Pierre Chouteau. In 1811 John Jacob Astor sent two parties to Oregon, one by sea, the other overland. At the mouth of the Columbia, Astoria was founded in territory "jointly" held by Britain and the United States, since they could not agree whose it was. In 1812 Robert Stuart, an "Astorian," went east overland through South Pass, traveling what would become the Oregon Trail.

From 1813 to 1832 the various fur companies battled for the beaver harvests. At first it was a battle between men in the wilderness, then a battle between companies for capital, finally a battle between trusts for control.

Profits were more surely controlled when every element was managed against the risks of chance, or competition. The alliances between men and companies, the combinations of subsidiaries and competitors, constantly shifted and changed, but always tended toward the same end: one remaining corporation to manage all the geography of trade.

In 1813 Astoria had to be surrendered to the British North West Company. By

In the Great American Desert, Indian and trapper both lived on buffalo until *The Yellowstone* took the first load of hides downstream. The new specie of trade doomed all together. See Plate I, following page 270.

1821, after a civil war in the wilderness, Parliament ordered the merger of the North West Company and the Hudson's Bay Company. In 1822 General William H. Ashley formed a partnership with Andrew Henry, and they built a post at the mouth of the Yellowstone. Successor Ashley ventures were incorporated as The Rocky Mountain Fur Company. It was called "The Opposition"; that is, the opposition to The American Fur Company, usually referred to as "The Company."

By 1830 both "The Opposition" and "The Company" had spaced fur posts along the Missouri and into the Rockies. It was said their trappers, the legendary "mountain men," knew every stream, ford, and canyon along the way. But beyond the Missouri's banks in 1830, up on the high plains, the map still showed a blank space as large as European Russia, labeled by one expedition as "The Great American Desert."

The fur traders were the advance parties of the frontier that was to follow. "The Company" was the property of John Jacob Astor, who would abandon the fur trade in 1834 for investment in New York City real estate. Until then, his western operations were directed from St. Louis by Pierre Chouteau, Jr.

"The Company's" field director was Kenneth McKenzie, "The King of the Missouri," a former British North West Company man who had been "bought over." He was

Catlin understood instantly: buffalo and Indian would perish because the demand for trade goods was irreversible. It would make the free men of the plains dependent upon St. Louis.

laird of all he could survey from his post at Fort Union at the mouth of the Yellowstone.

The country of the Yellowstone, of the Shoshone River, of the Tetons, Jackson's Hole, Pierre's Hole, the deserts and mountains, the creeks and alpine meadows, had been explored, trapped, and consigned to the men of the fur trade by 1830. The Indians, their allies against the meanness of nature, played white man against white man, stole and traded, still warred and married as they always had.

Together, mountain men and Indian lived in an immanent nature, without disputing any titles to God's land. If the mountain men took beaver away, they brought guns, cottons and wools, iron and steel, which made survival easier. If the squaws of mountain men sewed with steel needles, so did the squaws of their Indian brothers. For both, the need for goods meant they were dependent on the steamboats at the levees at St. Louis. They were still both "free," that's what they told themselves, but St. Louis was dependent upon New York.

In 1830, before the frontier had advanced even a mile west of the Mississippi, before the first white church tower rose above the grassy plain, before the first buffalo ever saw a wire fence, before a single real estate developer had drawn up his first prospectus, all the main streets of all the pioneer towns still unimagined pointed east.

In 1830, William Clark, partner of Lewis on the great adventure, was sixty—and ruled the West.

IV

Catlin in St. Louis, 1830

Of such rudeness and wilds, Nature has nowhere presented more beautiful and lovely scenes, than those of the vast prairies of the West; and of man and beast, no nobler specimens than those who inhabit them—the Indian and the buffalo—joint and original tenants of the soil, and fugitives together from the approach of civilised man; they have fled to the great plains of the West, and there, under an equal doom, they have taken their last abode, where their race will expire, and their bones bleach together.

—George Catlin, *Letters and Notes on the North American Indians*

WHEN GEORGE Catlin finally arrived in St. Louis in the summer of 1830, General William Clark, partner of Meriwether Lewis on the great exploration, had served since 1813 as Governor of the Missouri Territory, Indian Agent of the Territory of the Upper Louisiana, and as Superintendent of Indian Affairs in the West. Clark was sixty years old, his red hair now white. He knew every trader and tribe in the territory. No expeditions could be mounted, no company formed, no treaty with any tribe effected without his consent. He was friend of the chiefs and their advisor. He was commander of the United States troops. He was partner in the fur trade companies. He ruled the West. He became George Catlin's patron.

Catlin had prepared carefully to meet the great Clark. He brought with him letters of introduction from New York, Philadelphia, and Washington. He brought portraits and sketches done on the reservations in upstate New York. He explained to Clark that he wanted to paint every chief and every tribe; he wanted to gather Indian arts and tools into a *Gallery unique;* and he would do a portrait of the general in oil.

In turn, the general saw to it that Catlin was present when Indian delegations called in St. Louis. While Indian orators presented their cases to the general, Catlin listened and worked from life at Clark's side.

The general got Catlin commissions to paint the citizens of St. Louis so Catlin could support himself. He taught Catlin the lore and the manners of dealing with Indian chiefs. He took Catlin with him in July to Prairie du Chien on the upper Mississippi to attend the treaty councils with Missouri, Iowas, Sioux, Omahas, and Sauk and Fox. It was at Prairie du Chien that Catlin first met Kee-o-kuk and Black Hawk.

Clark arranged for Catlin to go to Cantonment Leavenworth, where Catlin sketched and painted Iowa, Potawatomie, Shawnee, and Kickapoo. He painted No Heart, chief of the Iowa; painted He Who Goes Up the River, chief of the Shawnee; and Tensqua-ta-way, The Open Door, called The Prophet, brother of Tecumseh.

In the fall Clark took Catlin to the villages of the Konza, where he painted The Wolf, head chief, and No Fool, The Man of Good Sense, and The Little White Bear. Clark and Catlin returned to St. Louis together. Before the rivers froze, Catlin went back East to join Clara, but he had begun.

In the spring of 1831 Catlin was back in St. Louis, staying at the house of Benjamin O'Fallon, son of Dr. James O'Fallon, one of the conspirators with James Wilkinson in the Spanish affair. Dr. O'Fallon was the husband of Frances Clark, sister of George Rogers Clark.

Dr. O'Fallon's son, Major Benjamin O'Fallon, was Indian Agent and fur trader, the inspector of Fort Atkinson. His brother, John O'Fallon, also an Indian trader, had been sutler at Fort Atkinson and had grown rich from it. In 1823 John O'Fallon was succeeded at the post by James Kennerly, his former partner. Kennerly was a cousin of General Clark's first wife and a brother of the general's second wife, and thereby an uncle to the O'Fallons. The Clarks, Kennerlys, O'Fallons, and their cousins and in-laws controlled the whiskey trade upriver, which meant, in effect, control of all trade on the Missouri.

Another cousin, Major "Honest John" Dougherty, had been subagent for Manuel Lisa, founder of the Missouri Fur Company, the partners of which, oddly enough, included

Pierre Chouteau, Sr., and William Clark. Now Major Dougherty was subagent for the O'Fallons. Dougherty ran the Agency at Bellevue, at the mouth of the Platte, and had earned something of a reputation for having attempted to halt the Pawnee practice of human sacrifice. In one case he personally attempted to rescue a Cheyenne woman from the hostile Pawnee village. He was unsuccessful. He had to watch her being torn to pieces, the frenzied Pawnees smearing themselves with her blood and whirling her head and severed limbs above their heads in ecstasy.

In the spring of 1831 George Catlin rode out from Bellevue with Major Dougherty, up the Platte route into the territory of the Oto, and then on to the Pawnee villages. He painted He Who Strikes Two at Once, an Oto warrior; The Big Elk, principal chief of the Omaha; and Horse Chief, Grand Pawnee head chief.

Before winter closed in, Catlin was back in St. Louis, painting a party of Knisteneaux and Assiniboin en route from the upper Missouri to Washington. Their guide was Major John F. A. Sanford, Agent to the Mandans and agent of "The Company," who the following spring would marry the daughter of Pierre Chouteau, Jr., director of "The Company." Coincidentally, Sanford owned a black slave, who would one day run away, with the celebrated name of Dred Scott.

With Major Sanford, on his way to Washington, was the son of the Assiniboin chief, Wi-jun-jon, The Light, or Pigeon's Egg Head. Catlin painted him in 1831 and again in 1832 upon his return from Washington. In his *Letters and Notes* he recorded the story of the young chief's tragic death.

Before Catlin left for a second winter trip back East, he arranged with Pierre Chouteau, Jr., for passage the next spring on a new steamboat, the *Yellowstone,* which would attempt a passage all the way up the Missouri to the mouth of the Yellowstone and "The Company's" post at Fort Union. The trip would be a major event in the history of The West. If Fort Union could be supplied by steamboat, perhaps Oregon, that "joint territory" extending west from the Rocky Mountain passes, might be won from the English, and held.

Although still unmapped, by 1831 the essential geography of "the blank space" was well enough understood. To get across the Great Plains and through the Rocky Mountain barrier, traders had to follow three main routes: the Santa Fe Trail, the Platte Trail, or the Missouri. The southern route started at St. Louis, followed the Missouri as far as Independence, and was guarded at that strategic bend in the river by Fort Leavenworth. The route then turned west across Kansas to the big bend in the Arkansas River, where it picked up the ghost of Coronado's trail to Fort Bent, then turned south through Raton Pass to Santa Fe. The southern route was the Santa Fe Trail.

Lieutenant Zebulon Pike led the first American expedition across the southern route in 1806 and 1807. On the way he named Pike's Peak, landed in jail in Santa Fe, Spanish Territory, but was released partly because his father-in-law was United States Senator John Brown, accused in the Spanish Conspiracy, and because he had with him James Biddle Wilkinson, the conspirator's son. The Spanish could not be sure he was not an ambassador.

The middle route also started up the Missouri past Fort Leavenworth, to the Indian Agency at Bellevue that was just north of the mouth of the Platte and was protected by Fort

Catlin rode out with Major Dougherty, up the Platte, into the territory of the Pawnee, who had only recently given up human sacrifice. He painted The Buffalo Bull, Pawnee warrior.

Lay-law-she-kaw, He-Who-Goes-Up-the-River, Shawnee chief. His tribe was removed in 1831 from their lands east of the Mississippi to lands promised in perpetuity in present Kansas.

Atkinson. Then the trail turned west along the Platte (passing the site of what would be Fort Kearney in 1848—built to protect the immigrant trail); followed the north fork of the Platte up to the Sweetwater (passing the site of what would be Fort Laramie in 1849); then up the long slope, twisting and turning with the ridges to South Pass on the southern shoulder of the Wind River Range.

South Pass led into the Green River country—the site of "The Opposition's" rendezvous, The Rocky Mountain Fur Company's annual beaver trade fair. The Green River Country was a strategic plateau at the Continental Divide, from which rivers ran south to the Colorado (called the Green where it starts off) and Gulf of California; north and west to the Snake, Columbia, and Oregon; north and east to the Big Horn, Yellowstone, and Missouri. A circle inscribed 75 miles around South Pass included all three great river systems—the Colorado, Columbia, and Missouri. Southeast from South Pass, and visible on the horizon from a Green River country butte, was the Wasatch range; southwest, the trail continued to Salt Lake, only 240 miles away. This middle route along the Platte was the immigrant wagon route, The Oregon Trail.

In 1819–1820 Major Stephen H. Long headed a government expedition from the

39

site of Fort Atkinson up the Platte as far as the Rockies, then turned south to the Arkansas River where it comes out of the Rockies at Pueblo, then returned east along the Santa Fe Trail. It was his maps that labeled the plains "The Great American Desert."

With Major Long were Titian Peale, whose sketches and artifacts George Catlin studied at Peale's Museum, and Samuel Seymour, an artist and engraver from Philadelphia. Seymour was reported to have painted some 150 pictures on the expedition, but only thirteen are known to exist. Some of them were later on display in Peale's Museum. The few examples remaining show the Rockies as generalized mountains seen at a considerable distance, with deer resembling unicorns, and buffalo having humps like camels.

The northern route, the Missouri River route, was the strategic one. It protected the northern flank of the projected United States against English trade and influence and against the threat of British satellite Indian nations. It was the one route along which alliances with Indian tribes might be maintained all the way to Oregon. The goods carried by

Flank of empire, at the Yellowstone: Fort Union, 2000 miles above St. Louis on the Missouri.

◄

Belle Vue, Indian Agency of Major Dougherty, 870 miles above St. Louis, north of the Platte.

steamboat from St. Louis into Oregon Territory via the Missouri could compete in price with British goods brought by canoe and portage from Hudson's Bay, or through the chain of lakes from Montreal.

The strategic route began by passing Fort Atkinson at the mouth of the Platte, about 700 miles above St. Louis. Then the river turned north to Fort Pierre, at the mouth of the Bad River, about 1300 miles above St. Louis and halfway to the Gallatin Gateway.

The Missouri was the route of Lewis and Clark. They had to pole and drag their boats upstream. In 1804 they counciled with the Teton Sioux at the site of Fort Pierre to win their allegiance from Britain. On this site there had been bastioned Indian fortresses in the fourteenth and fifteenth centuries, its river bottomland cultivated continuously since that time; it was also a crossroads, an ancient Indian capital and meeting ground. Indian trade from the lakes and forests of the East met with trade from the Southwest and West. In 1743 the *coureur* Verendrye, working south from the lakes of Canada, buried a plate there to mark his

41

passage. In 1831 Pierre Chouteau's new steamboat *Yellowstone* got as far as Fort Pierre before returning downstream with the first commercial cargo of buffalo hides for St. Louis. With a steamboat on the Missouri, buffalo became a practical export of the plains. In 1832 the fort was named Pierre in honor of Chouteau.

North of Fort Pierre the Missouri twisted and turned to the site of the Mandan villages—Fort Clark, 1600 miles above St. Louis, near the mouth of the Knife River. Lewis and Clark wintered there before pushing upriver to find the passes in 1805. The Mandan villages were another ancient and strategic trade route site for both Indians and the advancing whites. Just 150 miles north was the eventual border with Canada, along the 49th parallel. More important, by short portages from the Mandan villages, traders could make their way to the arc of the Souris River, which drains *north* across the border. From there they could proceed to Lake Manitoba, Lake Winnipeg, Lake of the Woods, and on to Lake Superior—the east-west route of the Montreal-based British North West Company.

From the Mandan villages to Fort Union was about another 230 miles upstream, almost 2000 miles above St. Louis, the river turning northwest, then west, paralleling the eventual border, the flank of the Canada of Manitoba and of Saskatchewan, the river controlling the trade of the tribes of Alberta as far west as the Rockies. At Fort Union tributaries of the Missouri—the Yellowstone and then the Big Horn—led back southwest to South Pass and the Green River country.

At Fort Union, Kenneth McKenzie, "King of the Missouri," partner of Pierre Chouteau, Jr., and field director of Mr. Astor's "The Company," was engaged in a war for trade on two fronts. Along the Platte Route to South Pass he was in a battle with The Rocky Mountain Fur Company: "The Opposition," his only remaining competitor south of the Missouri's arc into the Rockies. North of that arc McKenzie directed "The Company's" war against his old employers, The British North West Company. Victory on the southern front would secure a rich monopoly; victory on the northern front would gain Oregon, from the Rockies West to the Pacific, perhaps as far North as 54°40′.

To win the Rocky Mountain battles against "The Opposition," and to win unmapped Oregon from the British trade, McKenzie needed steamboat transportation to overcome the power of the downstream Missouri currents. Consequently, the proposed 1832 voyage of the *Yellowstone* was discussed not only in St. Louis, but in the banking houses of New York and London. The *Yellowstone* would make trade goods at Fort Union cheaper than those hauled by wagons into the Rockies, or those portaged by canoe across Canada's lakes. If the *Yellowstone* could trade at Fort Union, Mr. Astor could trade the Rockies and Oregon unopposed. Fort Union's only street would lead east, to New York.

In addition to steamboat transport, and capital from New York, McKenzie needed whiskey. Fur was paid for in specie, in trade goods including Italian glass beads, but especially with whiskey.

Unfortunately, in 1832 Washington put severe restrictions on the shipment of liquor to the Indians, restrictions that were supposed to be enforced by the Superintendent of Indian Affairs in The West, General William Clark, and his partners and relations, the Indian traders and agents of his family.

42

Everyone agreed the Indians had no tolerance of whiskey. Everyone agreed that even after the traders had watered it, an ounce of whiskey strong enough to barely warm a white man would drive an Indian crazy, addict him, and ruin him. Everyone agreed the concern of Congress for their charges west of the Mississippi was most honorable. On the other hand, if the ban on whiskey was really to be enforced as Congress had decreed, control of the river might be impossible, and Oregon lost.

At first General Clark pretended he had received no official notice of the acts banning the shipment of whiskey. Then McKenzie worked out an alternative. Instead of shipping barrels of whiskey, the *Yellowstone* would bring a still upriver—for a friend of McKenzie's over on Canada's Red River, McKenzie said. He would just experiment awhile with the new still before he delivered it; try it out with the fruits native to the country, he said. At Fort Union he had corn planted for his experiments.

By permission of General Clark, the last 250 gallons of legal alcohol started upriver from St. Louis on March 26, 1832, aboard the *Yellowstone*. For the historic trip, Pierre Chouteau, Jr., himself was on board. So was Major John F. A. Sanford, escorting Wi-jun-jon, The Light, or Pigeon's Egg Head, returning from Washington to his people, the Assiniboin.

George Catlin was aboard to paint the tribes. On his way upriver he sketched landscapes, Indian villages, scenes of Indian life, and one portrait after another. At Fort Pierre he sketched Sioux, a visiting Cheyenne and his wife, and two Nez Percé ambassadors dressed in Sioux costumes. When the *Yellowstone* reached Fort Union, he painted the Nations who had come to trade with McKenzie: Blackfeet, Plains Cree, and Plains Ojibway. He painted a visiting Crow warrior from the Snake River country. Catlin's reports to Colonel Stone's New York *Commercial Advertiser* begin with a *Fort Union, mouth of the Yellowstone* dateline. So did his *Letters and Notes on the Manners, Customs, and Condition of the North American Indians.*

From Fort Union Catlin paddled back downriver in a canoe, with two trappers from "The Company" as guides: Jean Baptiste and Abraham Bogard, seasoned men of the trade. They made a long stop at the Mandan villages, so that Catlin could report on that mysterious tribe. Then the pleurisy and cough that had crippled him in Albany in 1829 returned. With Baptiste and Bogard he started for St. Louis on August 16, recovering in the canoe on the way. When he finally arrived back in St. Louis, he learned that Black Hawk, the famous Sauk and Fox War Chief, was being held prisoner at nearby Jefferson Barracks along with The Prophet, Black Hawk's sons, and eleven other hostages of the tribe. They had begun a frenzied war in Illinois against the encroachments of white settlers, but too late. The frontier had long since passed over Illinois. Black Hawk was being held in irons.

In 1832, Black Hawk and his Sauk and Fox followers posed at Jefferson Barracks in chains.

V

How a Frontier Advances

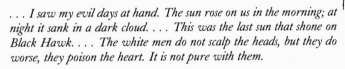

. . . I saw my evil days at hand. The sun rose on us in the morning; at night it sank in a dark cloud. . . . This was the last sun that shone on Black Hawk. . . . The white men do not scalp the heads, but they do worse, they poison the heart. It is not pure with them.

—Black Hawk at Jefferson Barracks, 1832

IN HIS *Letters and Notes* George Catlin described "The Medicine" of the rain dance: It always rained in response to the dances of the chiefs, perhaps, he pointed out, because they kept dancing until it rained. When the chiefs "danced" the buffalo to assure food for the tribe, the buffalo always came, perhaps because the dance could not begin until the chiefs estimated the buffalo were likely to be near. But "The Medicine" of the dances almost always worked. However, when the frontier passed westward over the land, the intrinsic "Medicine" of the land was changed. The rains began to fall of their own accord; the buffalo and the Indian were doomed together—dancing would not make any difference.

It has always been assumed that the first contacts beyond the frontier were beneficial to the Indian. Europeans brought horses, guns, steel needles with which to sew. Without Spanish and French, without English and American traders, the last great moment of each tribe would not have been possible. Surely, the first contacts were beneficial.

But the frontier itself—the advancing boundary between the cultures—was always the zone of disease, despair, and desperation, precisely because it was a tumultuous zone between two Medicines, two conceptions of time and earth and reason, two systems of imagination and faith. It is impossible to differentiate just what was most noxious to the

45

Black Hawk, fought by militiaman Abraham Lincoln; captured by
Lieutenant Jefferson Davis. See Plate III, following page 270.

Indian: the horse, the needle, the smallpox, cholera, whiskey, the long rifle, the steamboat, the
United States Cavalry, or the exhortations of Congregational ministers. Whatever: One faith
cracked, the other advanced. One people dwindled, the other swelled.

The main business of the people of the United States from 1790 to 1890 was to
advance the frontier from the Appalachians to the Pacific. No folk movement in history,
except perhaps the barbarian invasions of Rome, compared in mass, density, or velocity with
the sweep of Manifest Destiny. As the frontier advanced, the differences between the white
man's faith and Indian Medicine were central elements of the ensuing disaster.

The Indian believed that he was part of Nature, as were his brothers the deer, the

White Cloud, called The Prophet, adviser to Black Hawk. He preached return to the old ways. See Plate II, following page 270.

bear, the wolf, and the turtle. He believed that Medicine—what the white man called God—was accomplished by ceremonies in reverence of the sun, the rain, the animation of the land. He believed that The Great Spirit—Medicine—was immanent, in the inherency of things themselves.

The white man believed that God was transcendent, up there somewhere looking down, and that from God the Father he had inherited the earth. The deer, the bear, the wolf, and the turtle were for man's increase, for his use. By fervent prayer the white man might convince God to send the rain down or the sun up, but a summer storm might do just as well. And in any case, dancing would not send the rain in or bring the sun out.

The white man, with his well-developed sense of property, smiled at the Indian's faith in the land itself as magic, or Medicine. For the Indian's superstition, the white man substituted the more reasonable dances of lessor and lessee, riparian and preemptive rights, title guarantees by a company incorporated under State law. If a white man's claim to a hunting ground was disputed, he would not dance revenge with the rattle of a snake. Not at all. He would engage counsel and dance an appeal at the district court.

The mysteries of district courts led to some confusion among the Indian nations. They could not understand that when they transferred God's title to the land, for cash or tithes, it was irrevocable. They imagined they might repeatedly sell the green acres to the foolish white man who, they thought, bought what was free; sometimes they even sold a section several times in a single day—why not?

The Indian needed trade goods for his squaw. He would have no peace until he had procured them. He needed guns to defend himself against his traditional enemies. He would have no security until he had bought them. If his purchases were bought on credit at the company store, if he was required to settle his account by alienating an acre or two, he could move on. He had always been free to move on.

Free: the chiefs gave the signal, the lodgepoles were struck by the women, the goods of camp packed on the travois, and the long file of the tribe, with its dogs barking, stretched out toward the endless horizon of God's own land. Why not sell? They were always free to move. Catlin saw what was happening and proposed a National Park "to preserve some corner of The West against the advancement of civilization," but there would be no corners which were free.

Beyond the frontier Indians waged war on Indians in their ancient ways. *Along* the frontier each system was dependent upon the other, although it was only the Indian's faith in Indian Medicine that was plainly doomed. *Behind* the frontier, under the regime of white man's faith, was a zone of frenzied war, which was to result in the extermination of the Indian way of life.

Beyond the frontier Indian histories were tales of alliances, confederacies, unsteady peaces, and almost constant war between tribes. One reason was that the white man, as he advanced, stirred shock waves beyond the frontier, pushing ahead of him new configurations, new powers, new tribes into ascendancy or despair.

But there were significant differences between simple Indian war and the complex war waged by advancing civilization. Although most Indian societies had refined the function of warrior, the mythical braves of James Fenimore Cooper were paradigms of Alfred, Lord Tennyson's romantic Knights of The Round Table. Both were anachronisms.

Indian war was war waged for trade routes, for women, or for food; but it was especially waged for glory, for revenge, for honor—to count *coups*. The loser in an Indian war might regret the loss of his teepee, might regret his women, his children, his scalp, or his life. But if he fought gallantly, he would still have his honor. If his enemy's shaft dispatched him to the Happy Hunting Grounds, he could, from that vantage point, surely expect to be remembered. After all, his victors would have won nothing if they had not defeated a brave and dangerous enemy. Indian victors danced the spirits of Indian vanquished.

48

Civilized war is organized differently and has different purposes. It spans continents. It rewards not so much bravery as persistence. It maintains long lines of supply. It is concerned with logistics, not raids. The loser in a white war is a system, and the individual may keep his women, his children, and often his life, provided he is willing to give up his system, his honor, his traditions, his "medicine," his faith; that is, in civilized war the loser may reacquire all the comforts of life, provided he trades at the victor's company store. Civilized victors never dance the spirits of the vanquished.

The history of the wars between Indian and white, therefore, was consistently a history of war fought after the frontier had passed, after the Indian faith had been shattered, after the Indian discovered the significance of having alienated his land. They were wars of romance, but they were wars of frenzy. Invariably an Indian nation whose faith was near extinction would hear the word of a prophet urging them to return to the old ways. Maddened by what they had lost, war parties were sent out to redeem the Nation's honor.

The first such wars were fought along the eastern coastline, then moved west with Manifest Destiny. Virginia, for example, began in peaceful coexistence. Powhatan went to London to be crowned with a copper crown. From Powhatan's tribe, the Virginia colonists bought corn at an inch square of copper for one bushel. It was not long before many English came, settled, cleared the land, and farmed. Then they sold back to the Indians four hundred bushels of corn for ". . . a mortgage on their whole countries."

Powhatan asked: "Why should you take by force from us that which you can obtain by love? Why should you destroy us who have provided you with food?"

Well, the English population in Virginia was only about 350 in 1618; by 1622 it had grown to 1200 spread around in little villages, growing surplus corn. More English were on the way. They would need land.

Too many English: In the spring of 1622 the Powhatans killed 350 Virginians in an intense campaign. The Virginians countered by sending three expeditions each year for fourteen successive years, destroying villages, burning crops, killing men, women, and children. A matter of logistics and persistence. By 1641 the Powhatan confederacy was gone from the Virginia colony—wiped out.

Further north, Tammany, chief of the Delaware confederacy, counseled wisdom, virtue, charity, and hospitality to the English and Dutch settlers. His tribal relatives, the Wappingers and Mohegans, sold Manhattan for what they believed to be a reasonable sum, and traded with the white men.

Then in 1643 Wappinger refugees from raiding Mohawks were slaughtered by order of the Dutch governor of New Amsterdam. Their severed heads were kicked through the streets. A wall was built—Wall Street lay behind it—to keep at bay Indians bent on revenge. The Dutch West India Company received a request from the governor to wage war until the Indians were ". . . utterly destroyed and exterminated." They were.

Farther north, the story was the same. When the Puritan colonists landed at Plymouth Rock, Tisquantum was there to greet them. Within a year his Wampanoags and the Puritans sat down to Thanksgiving dinner together. Soon the Great Seal of the Massachusetts Bay Joint Stock Company showed an Indian saying: "Come Over and Help Us."

By 1830 most tribes east of the Mississippi were on reservations. John W. Quinney, called The Dish, a Mohegan, became a missionary preacher. When faith cracked, frenzy soon followed.

By June 1637 some 15,000 settlers had come over to help. The Indians began scattered attacks on New England farms, and for the next forty years a dreadful war was fought across Massachusetts—ending as King Philip's War. Its style was set in the beginning by the burning of a Pequot town and all its inhabitants. At the event the Plymouth governor, good minister of the new faith, wrote: "It was a fearful sight to see them frying in the fire. . . . But victory seemed sweet . . . and praise thereof to God."

The coastline cleared and settled, the white man turned to the woodlands. There, the Five Nations of the League of the Iroquois—Mohawk, Cayuga, Onondaga, Oneida, and Seneca—conquered their fellow Iroquois tribe, the Hurons, allies of the French fur traders in Montreal. Then they obliterated their neighbors, the Erie, thus establishing a hegemony from Maine to the Mississippi, from the Great Lakes to Tennessee. In 1712 when the Tuscarora were driven out of the piedmont of North Carolina, they marched north to become the sixth nation of the Iroquois confederacy—The Great League. For 150 years The League

50

The Ottawa under Pontiac, with the help of a prophet, ravaged the old Northwest. Lord Jeffrey Amherst scattered Pontiac's revolt. By 1830, Big Sail, a chief, was a bitter remnant.

was the dominant force of the woodland frontier and beyond.

In the 1740s the Iroquois granted control of the upper Ohio to a Virginia real estate company. "The land is our Mother," went the Iroquois tradition. "How can we sell our Mother?" The Ohio company bought the rights to the land for about 10,000 pounds; George Washington, Esq., was the surveyor.

Threatened by English control of the forks of the Ohio, the French fought for the territory. The French and their Indian allies defeated General Braddock and young George Washington at Fort Duquesne—Pittsburgh. The French and Indian Wars, begun in Ohio, spread to global war waged from 1754 to 1763, ending in the Treaty of Paris which deeded Canada to the English and transferred the Louisiana Territory to Spain.

After the global war was over, Pontiac, Ottawa chief, unaware of the strategic significance of the treaties made in Paris by his ally France, headed an Indian alliance in a hopeless campaign against the English settlers. His objective was to throw the English out of

The Open Door, Shawnee, known as The Prophet, brother of Tecumseh, promised the tribes they would be immune to the White Man's Medicine if they would only return to the old ways.

Ben Perryman, The Great King, a chief of the Creek Nation, one of the civilized tribes that were driven west from their lands in the south despite the decisions of the Supreme Court.

the old Northwest Territories they already inhabited. Thousands of settlers, from Niagara to Virginia, died by scalping, burning, torture, and impalement. Illinois was cleared of whites. Every fort fell except Detroit and Pittsburgh. The great conspiracy included Chippewas, what was left of the Hurons, Illinois, Kickapoos, Menominees, Miamis, Ottawas, and Potawatomies. Pontiac was aided by a Delaware shaman known as The Prophet, who argued that if the Indians were to survive they would have to go back to the old ways, to the old ceremonies and Medicine; they would have to give up iron, guns, calicoes, brass kettles, alcohol, and trade of any kind with the white man. But it was too late; they could not go back. Lord Jeffrey Amherst conquered all of Pontiac's Indians.

The Mohawk War Chief Joseph Brant made a mistake similar to Pontiac's. He sided with the English in the American Revolution. The Iroquois were as much mercenaries of King George as the Hessians. Unfortunately, King George lost his war. The Great League was divided, its ancient diplomacy ruined, and the advantages of their former neutrality lost. Its power was ended.

Chaos followed inevitably. Mohawks and their allies raided and massacred Yankee settlements on the alienated land. Hideous battles were fought at Oriskany and Cherry Valley, New York, and in the Wyoming Valley of Pennsylvania—where Polly Sutton and her mother, the mother and grandmother of George Catlin, were carried away captive. In Chief Brant's war, Sagoyewatha, the Seneca orator, received a scarlet coat from the British and wore it into battle, from which he earned the title Red Jacket.

The Yankee response to Chief Brant was to send General John Sullivan with four thousand men to end the Iroquois menace forever. Sullivan's men rescued the Yankee captives, wasted the Indian cornfields, burned their villages. The defeated Iroquois had to take refuge under British protection in Fort Niagara, then be moved to Ontario.

Chief Joseph Brant took up translating the Scriptures into Mohawk, traveled to London, and became the intimate friend of the Prince of Wales. Although Brant enjoyed his celebrity as he rode to Epsom Downs to sit in the prince's box at the races, his Medicine was extinct.

The story was always the same dismal one: The frontier continually advanced, the land was sold, the Indians despaired and rebelled, the settlers took revenge, and then the Indians were exterminated.

Tecumseh, Shawnee chief in the Ohio Valley, repeated the pattern. He insisted the land was held by all tribes in common and no one tribe could sell its particular tract: "Sell a country! Why not sell the air, the clouds, and the great sea? . . . Did not the Great Spirit make them all for the use of his children?"

Yes indeed, the settlers could agree to that. By 1810 the citizens of Ohio numbered 230,760; of Kentucky, 406,511; of Indiana, still only 24,520—but 14,000 were coming each year. Tecumseh, The Warrior, and Ten-squa-ta-way, The Prophet—twin brothers—undertook to save the Great Spirit's land.

Besides, Tecumseh had assurances from London that if he drove the white settlers back behind the Ohio again, perhaps Britain's ministers might win his tribes a satellite state at the peace table.

The Prophet spoke to the peoples, and again they listened. They said he had Great Medicine. He had foretold of an eclipse of the sun. He told them they would have to return to the old faiths; they would have to give up the advantages of trade; they would have to give up whiskey. If they did, he promised them, they would be immune to the white man's Medicine. Even the white man's long rifles would not harm them.

The Prophet sent runners as far as Florida, runners all the way to the tribes of the Upper Missouri. Against the advice of their chiefs, young warriors from all the tribes promised to come at Tecumseh's call. The chiefs were women, said the braves, if they would not fight for the old ways.

Tecumseh and The Prophet established headquarters at Tippecanoe Creek on the Wabash River in Indiana. They were defeated there November 7, 1811. The Medicine of The Prophet's charms did not work. He was disgraced. The confederacy scattered.

The tribes sold the land, the air, the clouds, and the great sea. It was to such cessations in perpetuity, the treaty councils, that George Catlin went with General Clark to meet the Chippewa, Kickapoo, Iowa, Menominee, Ottawa, Woods Sioux, and Sauk and Fox. In 1832 the only remaining Indian nations still intact were beyond the frontier in the trans-Mississippi West—on the plains in the great blank space. But not for long.

54

On May 28, 1830, President Andrew Jackson signed into law the Indian Removal Bill. All tribes east of the Mississippi were to cede their lands in exchange for territory in the West. The new lands west of the Mississippi were promised to the tribes "forever." If an Indian wished to stay where he was, he had the option, the Bill said, of becoming an American citizen. Those who went west were promised payment for travel expenses, plus the value of the improvements on the property they left behind, to be determined by the local district courts. Some tribes went to court.

The Creeks, Cherokees, Chickasaws, and Choctaws were known as "The Civilized Tribes," the great Indian nations of the South. They claimed to have farmed their land for four thousand years. More than any other Indian nations, they had adopted the ways of the white man. The Cherokee modeled their government on the Constitution of the United States in order to promote their general welfare. They built roads, schools, and churches. They cleared the land for plantations; they owned slaves and grew cotton. They put out a weekly paper. And they had been marrying; their chiefs, more often than not, had fine Scotch Presbyterian names: Alexander McGillivray, William MacIntosh, John Ross.

The State of Georgia was created from Cherokee land; Alabama from Creek and Cherokee lands; Mississippi from Choctaw and Chickasaw lands. Despite solemn treaty agreements, the white folks wanted the Indian lands—they were often the best lands. The states outlawed tribal governments and put the Indian nations under state law, as tenants-at-will. The tribes went to court.

In *Worcester v. Georgia* the Supreme Court held the states to be in error. President Jackson replied: "John Marshall has made his decision. Now let him enforce it."

The Civilized Nations were driven west. Some were persuaded to sell. Some were bribed. Some were terrorized. Some were starved out. Some were sent in chains along the Trail of Tears to the Oklahoma Territory. Ralph Waldo Emerson spoke up for conscience: "Such a dereliction of all faith and virtue, such a denial of justice, and such deafness to screams of mercy were never heard of in time of peace and in the dealing of a nation with its own allies and wards, since the earth was made."

Between 1829 and 1837 some ninety-four Indian treaties were concluded. In October 1832 a commission was created by Congress to supervise the Removal Treaties in the West. The commission, headed by Henry Ellsworth, arrived at Fort Gibson in Indian, later Oklahoma, Territory. The displaced tribes arriving from the East would in turn have to displace plains tribes. Efforts had to be made to bring representatives of the "wild" tribes into Fort Gibson for peace talks. The first of these expeditions was the Leavenworth-Dodge expedition of dragoons in 1834, first permanent cavalry unit in the U.S. Army.

Two thirds of the men in the expedition were felled by disease; some 150 of them died, including General Leavenworth. But the Comanche were met; the Pawnee Pict (or Wichita), the Kiowa and Waco tribes sending delegates to meet the Creek, Cherokee, Choctaw, Chickasaw, and Delaware delegations waiting at Fort Gibson.

George Catlin rode out from Fort Gibson with the expedition into the land of the Quivera, the site of the Seven Cities of Cibola. He survived, but barely. His *Letters and Notes* describe the voyage. His sketches and paintings record the chiefs.

Col-lee, a chief of the Cherokees, who lost their lands in Georgia. President Jackson replied to the Supreme Court: "John Marshall has made his decision. Now let him enforce it."

The same policy of removal west of the Mississippi forced Chief Kee-o-kuk of the Sauk and Fox to sign treaties ceding the hereditary lands of Illinois to the United States. In his *Letters and Notes* Catlin described the purchase contracts and treaties to which he was witness.

In 1831 when Chief Black Hawk of the Sauk and Fox returned home from a fall hunt, he found squatters enclosing his tribal cornfields. They had even plowed up the graves of his ancestors. Frenzy: In 1832 Black Hawk went on the warpath. To assist him there was, as there always was, a Prophet—White Cloud, who preached a return to the old Medicine. The whites must be driven out of Illinois.

But the frontier had long since passed over Illinois, was over the west bank of the Mississippi and flooding toward the Rockies. By 1830 the white citizens of Illinois numbered 157,445 and more settlers were arriving at the rate of 32,000 per year. The Illinois militia turned out to defend their homesteads. They chased Black Hawk into Wisconsin—a young Mr. Abraham Lincoln commanding a company—and captured him. Black Hawk was brought

56

Tuchee, called "Dutch," of the Cherokee. They put out a paper, built roads, schools, and churches. Many were Presbyterians, and they modeled their government on the U.S. Constitution.

as a prisoner to Jefferson Barracks, St. Louis, in the charge of a young lieutenant, Jefferson Davis. Catlin, upon his return from Fort Union in 1832, painted and described the defeated chief.

East of the Mississippi, one tribe refused to remove. In Florida, the Seminoles resisted the enactments of Congress. From the protection of the Everglades, a Seminole War Chief, Os-ce-o-la, waged a hideous guerrilla war for survival. Seminole women killed their own children to free themselves to fight beside their men. The U.S. Army, charged with pursuing and destroying the enemies of the United States, could not win a victory.

One shameful day Os-ce-o-la came to parlay at the invitation of General T. S. Jesup. Despite a white flag of truce, the conference ground was surrounded and Os-ce-o-la was clapped in chains. Catlin's *Letters and Notes* ends with his account of the Seminole War, and his portrait of Os-ce-o-la, in January 1837, at Fort Moultrie, South Carolina, five days before that cursing chief died in prison of a broken heart.

Osceola, The Black Drink, war chief of the Seminole, died in prison of a broken heart.

VI

Catlin After 1837

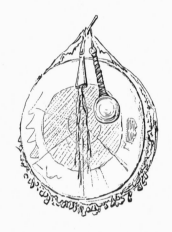

When people want to slaughter cattle they drive them along until they get them to a corral, and then they slaughter them. So it was with us. . . .

—Standing Bear of the Ponca

WEST OF the Mississippi the frontier moved quickly across the treeless plains. There was nothing to stop it. In 1832 the blank spaces on the map were still inhabited by free and independent tribes, but by 1836 the wagons of the first ministers and their wives were already through South Pass into Oregon Territory.

In 1837 smallpox swept away many of the tribes, decimated others, and made the survivors dependent forever on the new Medicine. After the frontier had passed, after their faith had been shattered, then once again Indian heroes made frenzied efforts to redeem their future. The Indian wars of the plains, those dramas of the American romance, especially after 1857, provide another roster of chiefs for whom the bell tolls: Black Kettle, Spotted Tail, Sitting Bull, Gall, Geronimo, Little Big Man, Chief Joseph, Big Foot who was buried at Wounded Knee in 1890, and unnumbered others.

The years 1832 to 1836 provided the last chance for any eyewitness to report on the life, manners, and customs of tribes unvitiated by white man's Medicine. George Catlin's timing was exquisite: He was the reporter who was there.

Curiously, his 1832 trip up the Missouri aboard the *Yellowstone* was coincidentally

59

the high point of the fur trade too. The prescient Mr. Astor sold out of the fur business in 1834, invested in New York City real estate, and became a source of capital for the unfolding systems—the revolutions that were on the heels of the westering frontier. Some say he sold out because he had seen in Paris that fashion had given its preference to silk from China instead of beaver from the Missouri. Perhaps. He may also have understood that owning the company store to which the Indian owed his life was not going to be as profitable as owning the bank to which the settler owed his. Whatever, the fur trade declined.

Fur trappers and Indians depended upon each other and upon nature uncluttered by real estate speculators, ministers, settlers, Army men, or railroad engineers. Fur traders lived off the roaming buffalo, too, and needed to believe that God held title to the land. Fur traders abhorred smallpox not only because it destroyed their best customers but because it took away *their* squaws and children too.

George Catlin also understood how "the state of nature" was fast disappearing. He hurried to stay ahead of the frontier. *Letters and Notes* are diaries of his principal voyages: the Missouri trip aboard the *Yellowstone* in 1832, the return to St. Louis by canoe; the Leavenworth-Dodge expedition to the Comanche Territories in 1834.

In 1835 he worked in the woodland territories of the upper Mississippi: up the falls of St. Anthony, downstream again past Fort Snelling, describing and painting the Ojibway, the woodlands Sioux, the Sauk and Fox again at Chief Kee-o-kuk's village.

The next year he went by steamer from Buffalo through the Great Lakes to Green Bay, Wisconsin. From there he paddled down the Wisconsin to the Mississippi, then up to the pipestone quarry—holy land of all the tribes, source of the magic red stone for the Medicine Pipes of peace and war.

In the winter of 1836–1837 Catlin was back East preparing his Indian gallery—his *Gallery unique*—for the exhibitions he planned. Modeled after Peale's Museum, it would include two complete Crow wigwams, painted robes, helmets and headdresses, examples of medicine bags, men's and women's dresses "fringed with scalp locks," bows and quivers, spears, shields, "Comanchee lances," necklaces, moccasins, belts, pouches, war clubs, tobacco sacks, wampum, whistles, rattles and drums, "twelve calumets and eight ordinary pipes."

It would include his scenes of Indian life, of buffalo hunting, his landscapes of the Missouri, the Mississippi, and the plains. It would include portraits of Indian squaws and children, their chiefs, and "other principal personages."

He took time off to go to the dying captive Os-ce-o-la in Charleston in January 1837, then returned to begin his advocacy of the Indian cause. He urged a National Park, "against the Rockies," to preserve the extraordinary nations against oblivion. He planned to lecture beside his portraits. As each one was set upon an easel, he would explain: this warrior dead from smallpox, this chief in irons, this one alienated from his land, this one now a Baptist minister, this one gone to drink.

Catlin's "Indian Gallery" opened at New York's Clinton Hall on September 25, 1837; admission 50¢. His old patron, Colonel William Stone, gave the full support of the *Commercial Advertiser*. It was the first *Wild West* show. It was a rip-roaring success.

But his lectures troubled many and began to make enemies for him. What he said about Indians ran counter to what many "experts," who had never visited the tribes, held to be true. They doubted the extent of his travels. They doubted his accounts of the O-Kee-Pah, the Mandan torture ceremonies. Catlin argued against the whiskey trade of the fur companies, against the Government "treaties" displacing Indians from their land. Some of his audiences haggled with him for the truth. The sophisticated argued, for example, that no Indian owned any horse as fine as the one on which Kee-o-kuk sat in Catlin's portrait.

By November 1, 1837, Catlin's gallery had moved to Stuyvesant Hall. Admission was up to $1. Kee-o-kuk himself came, identified his horse, and asked the sophisticates: "Why Kee-o-kuk not ride as good a horse as any white man?"

In the spring Catlin took his gallery to Washington, opening April 9, 1838, at the Old Theatre. His advocacy of the Indian cause began to take effect. In the 1837–1838 session of the United States House of Representatives, a resolution was introduced to purchase "the Catlin collection of Indian Portraits & Curiosities." The resolution was referred to committee and was not reported out before the end of the session.

Catlin took his show on to Baltimore and Philadelphia, then to Faneuil Hall in Boston in late October. As Catlin had hoped, his gallery had become a symbol for the Indian reforms he thought were needed. Senator Daniel Webster lobbied for its immediate purchase by Congress, because Webster too wanted Indian reform.

Catlin reopened in New York in 1839. He advertised it as the last time it would be shown in America. He was threatening to take it abroad, where perhaps it might be better appreciated.

The House of Representatives passed a resolution directing the Commissioner of Indian Affairs to inquire of Catlin the terms on which he would part with his gallery. The Commissioner did not write. Catlin wrote the Secretary of War. The Secretary did not answer. Catlin wrote again, begging for action. He would cancel his trip if only the United States would give some sign of interest. On November 25, 1839, Catlin sailed on the packet *Roscius* for Liverpool with eight tons of materials, paintings, his manuscripts and diaries, and two caged grizzly bears that had been added to the show.

On December 30, 1839, he signed a lease for three years at 550 pounds per year for space in Egyptian Hall in London—the great exhibition hall. His show opened February 1, 1840, and once again it was a huge popular success. Moreover, Catlin was an instant celebrity. He could tell of the wild Indians. He could improve with facts and eyewitness reports the genteel romances of the Leatherstocking Tales: Ah, Wilderness! Oh, Noble Savages!

In England James Fenimore Cooper was more popular than even Sir Walter Scott. With George Catlin at the dinner table London could imagine they had a friend of Natty Bumppo, of Uncas, of Magua, of *The Last of the Mohicans*. Mr. George Catlin dined with dukes and duchesses, bishops, earls, lords, barons, and simple knights. He lectured Oxford dons. He was presented to Queen Victoria. He brought Clara over, and they took a lease at Rose Cottage, Waltham Green, with their two daughters, a nursemaid, and a cook. Oh, Vanity Fair!

Catlin's "Gallery Unique" opened in New York, September 1837. It included not only his paintings, but "a Crow lodge of 25 buffalo skins, pipes, tomahawks, drums and scalps."

With a letter of introduction from Washington Irving, he presented his *Letters and Notes on the Manners, Customs, and Condition of the North American Indians, Written During Eight Years' Travel Amongst the Wildest Tribes of Indians in North America, in Two Volumes* to John Murray, the famous English publisher. Although the cost of the accompanying engravings would be cheaper in England than in America, John Murray backed off. Instead, with the help of Sir Charles Murray, Master of the Household for Queen Victoria, Catlin published the book himself "at Egyptian Hall," October 1841. It was to be sold by subscription, for it was high-priced. It won rave reviews.

Letters and Notes sold steadily, but the printer's bills for each new edition had to be met by the proceeds from the sale of the last. With his book, his lecture fees, and attendance receipts from Egyptian Hall, Catlin took in about $10,000, a handsome sum for the years 1840–1843. Yet the expenses of his adventure equaled his income.

Kee-o-kuk on horseback. He asked, "Why cannot Kee-o-kuk ride as good a horse as any white man?"

To boost receipts he took his show on tour: Liverpool, Manchester, Stratford on Avon, Edinburgh, Glasgow, Belfast, and, by June 1843, Dublin. He prepared *Catlin's North American Indian Portfolio,* "25 Plates on Full Royal Sheets, in Printed Tints, Five Guineas"; and a deluxe edition, "Printed Tints, and Coloured, Eight Guineas." It was published in 1844. Some subsequent editions were advertised to contain additional prints, making a total of thirty-one. Some were offered as colored by Catlin himself. There were now four children at Rose cottage—three daughters and a son, George Catlin, Jr. The father needed to find additional income.

Attendance at his shows was beginning to dwindle. He pepped up the lectures with what he called "Tableaux Vivants"—reenactments of stirring scenes from Indian life. At first he hired Cockney actors to play the parts. Then a certain Arthur Rankin appeared in Liverpool with nine "Ojibbeway" Indians. Rankin and Catlin agreed to split the expenses and

Catlin dined with dukes and duchesses. His Ojibway troupe was presented to Queen Victoria.

the income: The Indians would replace the Cockney actors. Catlin took an additional six months' lease on his space in Egyptian Hall.

As Catlin was about to open the improved show, Mr. Rankin took competing space nearby in the same hall, put on his own show with the "Ojibbeway," and collected the income, leaving Catlin with the expenses.

A certain G. H. C. Melody soon arrived in England with fourteen "Ioways" to tour. Again Catlin agreed to split the expenses and the income with Mr. Melody. Crowds did come, but they were shilling-a-head crowds now. The Lords of the Realm had lost interest. Mr. Disraeli received the Iowas for breakfast, but the queen would not receive them. The reputation of George Catlin, artist, was being sullied by the reputation of George Catlin, Barnum. Catlin took the Iowas on tour. In Edinburgh, Little Caesar, son of the warrior Little Wolf, died. Clara Catlin argued with her husband: He should paint—he was not a showman, they should go home to America.

But Catlin was determined to take his Iowas and his *Gallery unique* on to Paris. King Louis Philippe received them at the Palace of the Tuileries, and the show opened at La Salle Valentine on June 3, 1845. Catlin toured George Sand and Victor Hugo through his exhibition. Then the Iowa, Roman Nose, died of consumption. Next, Little Wolf's wife died. The funeral was held in the gloomy Eglise de la Madeleine. After the funeral the Iowas called a council.

64

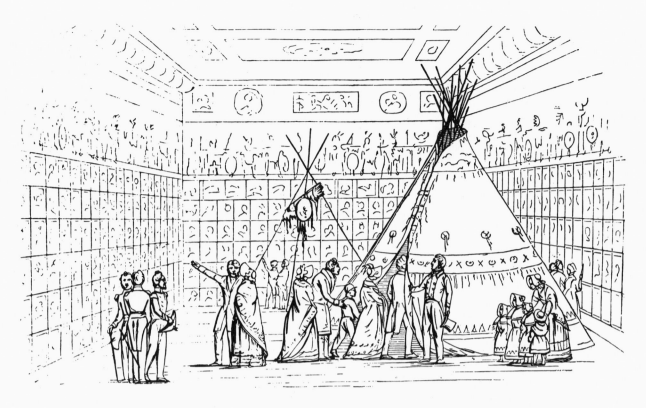

In 1845 he opened his "Gallery Unique" in Paris. He sketched his four children (*on the right*).

The one they called The Doctor spoke: "We should not blame him for being as the Great Spirit created him. He was made to paint with brushes and with words the tribes that have never been, the tribes that will never be. It is for the good of our people a long time from now. To do this he must wall away much truth that he does not dare to see. He cares greatly for us as warriors and dancers; it is joy when we make many cry out and slap their hands. If it is his profit too, only by profit can the white man live. He does not care for us greatly as men. He can not; he does not know our thoughts. I have spoken."

White Cloud, the chief, answered: "If he prisons us it is to keep our sons and our sons' son free. His dream is his friend. His love is deep for his lady and for his little son. Without them he would walk as a lost man, in the forest of too many thoughts. His way is his own. It is not ours."

The Iowas informed Mr. Melody they would sleep six nights more in Paris, no more. Then they would return to their wigwams.

Catlin was almost unaware of their departure, for Clara was shaking with pneumonia. He sat with her day and night. In her delirium she called out for him, cried for the life they had shared in St. Louis and Buffalo and Albany. She wept for home. She died in Paris on July 28, 1845. He sent her home to be buried in the Gregory family plot in Brooklyn.

He would try once more: eleven Ojibway Indians had arrived and Catlin agreed to take them on tour. They went barnstorming to Antwerp, Ghent, and Brussels. They all met the king of Belgium. But in Brussels, the Ojibway came down with smallpox: six went to the hospital, three of those died. Catlin sent the survivors home. He was out $1800 for the expense of the tour, the hospitals, the fares home.

Once back in Paris, things, began to improve. Although the house in which a governess minded his children was shadowed by his grief for his lost Clara, and his savings were still dwindling, King Philippe became his patron. The king ordered fifteen paintings.

Moreover, Catlin learned that on July 24, 1846, the Joint Committee on the Library of the United States Congress had reported ". . . that the Bill for the establishment of the Smithsonian Institute be amended . . . for the purchase of Mr. Catlin's Gallery at the price mentioned by him—namely sixty-five thousand dollars—payable in annual installments of ten thousand dollars."

While he waited for Congress to act, he finished the fifteen copies of Indian Life for King Philippe. His patron then ordered twenty-seven scenes illustrating the expeditions of La Salle. They would take at least a year to do, but Paris was not unpleasant, indeed it was sometimes gay—the elite of Paris thought George Catlin a famous man and asked him to dinners and balls and masques.

Then typhoid came to Paris. One by one the Catlin girls fell sick. And little George, age four, died. His father sent him to New York to be buried beside his mother in Greenwood Cemetery, Brooklyn.

He painted on. The expeditions of La Salle took shape and were finally finished in 1848. Three days after they were completed, the revolution of 1848 deposed King Philippe. Soldiers of the new republic came to search Catlin's apartment because he was known as a friend of the king. They ran their bayonets through the canvases of La Salle. Catlin escaped to London with his three daughters and his famous collection. He was wiped out.

He opened an "Indian Gallery" at 6 Waterloo Place, Pall Mall, a combined studio and living quarters. Few came; no one would pay admission now to see his paintings. He needed money, so he began to paint copies of his own works. He wrote another book, *Notes of Eight Years' Travel and Residence in Europe,* an anecdotal record of the Indians he had toured and introduced to the Courts of England, France, and Belgium. It was the Indians' view of European society, some of it hilarious. But the reviewers didn't think it very amusing.

By 1851 he was so pressed for money he agreed with Sir Thomas Phillipps, the great collector, to paint fifty-five copies of his originals for about $10 each—frames to cost an extra two shillings each. Phillipps had lent 100 pounds to Catlin in 1849 and Catlin had deposited twenty paintings with Phillipps as security. Catlin would later send to Phillipps seventy marvelous watercolors in the hope of borrowing more.

Meanwhile, the House of Representatives had finally passed the bill to buy Catlin's collection for $50,000. In the Senate, Daniel Webster took the floor to argue the Catlin Gallery was more important ". . . than all other drawings and representations on the face of the earth." Senator Jefferson Davis from Kentucky, Catlin's companion on the Leaven-worth-Dodge expedition and Black Hawk's jailor in St. Louis, had seen many of the paintings completed, he said. Catlin was the only artist who had ever recorded really authentic Indians. He said he was reluctant to vote against the bill, but he must, "on principle."

The principle involved was that southern Senators were "anti-Indian," because the South wanted the western Indian lands as slave lands. Senator Davis cast the deciding vote; the bill was defeated by a margin of one. In London, Catlin's creditors closed in.

Among the creditors was Mr. Joseph Harrison, owner of the Harrison Boiler Works in Philadelphia, "largest builders of locomotives in the world." Harrison had just completed building and outfitting the railroad from St. Petersburg to Moscow. He had a ring made with jewels given him by the czar, and $5 million dollars. With $40,000 he stood off Catlin's other creditors in the bankruptcy, then crated and shipped the *Gallery unique* back to Philadelphia, where it was stored on the grounds of the Harrison Boiler Works.

Though Mr. Harrison could save the Gallery, he could not save George Catlin and his daughters from London's bailiffs. They seized everything in the house at 6 Waterloo Place and auctioned it. Clara's family, the Gregorys, insisted on taking charge of Catlin's daughters, and they were sent home to New Jersey. Catlin returned to Paris, to a cheap room in the Hotel des Etrangers on the Rue Tronchet. He was fifty-seven years old. He had his pencil and his talent, and nothing else.

The principal work of his life was complete: his Gallery, his *Letters and Notes,* his work as a great portraitist, his record as an ethnologist, his foresight and courage in advocating the Indian cause "against oblivion." All demanded admiration. What he did next, none but heroes could do.

In 1853 he slipped out of Paris like a fugitive. "I obtained a British passport for Brazil, and an incognito cognomen, as kings and emperors sometimes do," he said. He headed for Venezuela, for he had heard there were ancient gold mines in the Crystal Mountains of northern Brazil, and in any case, he would like to paint the Indians of South America.

Preposterous: He would find the "kettle of gold!" He had with him his paints and bristol board—he figured canvas would stretch and sag in the jungles. In Venezuela he went up the Orinoco, then crossed the Crystals into the valley of the Amazon. He abandoned his search for gold, but he had painted the tribes. He painted up the Amazon and over the Andes to the coast of Peru. There he boarded the *Sally Anne* for San Francisco, after an expedition even the Royal Geographic Society would have found astounding.

Along the way he had picked up a companion, an escaped black slave from Cuba, a giant named Caesar Bolla. With his companions, with a new Colt revolving rifle paid for in paintings, with a fishing pole, Catlin had sketched, painted, and recorded, among others, Angosturo, Chetibo, Cocoma, Iquito, Marahua, Mayoruna, Mura, Omagua, Orejone, Sepibo, Ticuna, Yahua.

From Lima, Peru, he made his way to Panama, then to San Francisco, then to the Aleutians, to the Kamchatka Peninsula, back along the northwest coast to Victoria, painting and sketching Klah-o-quats, Hydas, Nayas, Stone, Dagrib, Athapasca, Aleutians, and the Koriak of Siberia.

From Vancouver he went to Astoria on the Columbia River, up the Columbia to The Dalles: Klatsop, Chinook, Clickatat, Walla Walla, Nez Percé, and Spokan. He followed the valley of the Snake, deep into the Rockies.

Upon arriving in an Indian village it was his practice to spread out some sketches, a

King Louis Philippe received Catlin and his Iowa troupe at the Palace of the Tuileries.

►

Notch-ee-ning-a, son of White Cloud. See Plate IV, following page 270.

portfolio of oils in color, to show the chiefs that he was a peaceful man, and a man of "Medicine." In a valley of the Snake he spread his work in a village of the Crow. They screamed with delight when they recognized a portrait of Bi-eets-e-cure, The Very Sweet Man, whom Catlin had painted at Fort Union more than twenty years before. Runners were sent for The Very Sweet Man, who came down to the village for the reunion, and the two old men smoked.

Down the Columbia again to the coast, and passage to San Diego. From there to the Apache village of LaPaz. Through the Rockies again to Santa Fe pass. He had to skirt Texas to avoid U.S. Cavalry in pursuit of the Apache, went around to the Rio Grande, paddled downstream 800 miles to Matamores, then by ship to Sisal and the Yucatán to investigate those ghostly Indian jungle civilizations. Caesar Bolla deserted him there for a Miss Sally Bool who sold oranges at the head of the quay.

In 1855 Catlin set sail to return to Europe. He felt he needed to talk to Baron Alexander von Humboldt in Berlin. The two grand old wanderers pored over their notes together. The baron convinced Catlin that the study of ocean currents was important to the

history of Indian migrations. Geology, they both agreed, was the key to the secrets of prehistoric migrations. Baron Humboldt gave George Catlin a list of places that should be visited—tropical islands and equatorial mountain ranges. The baron said if he were a younger man he would join Catlin at once. The king and queen of Prussia bought paintings of South American Indians, and George Catlin set off from Le Havre again, alone.

In September 1855 he was exploring the West Indies, then down the coast of Venezuela, southward to Buenos Aires. There he picked up another traveling companion, José Alzar, and together they paddled up the Paraguay River, then overland at Candeloria to the Uruguay River and downstream by canoe, collecting mineral specimens and painting Indians. But age began to collect its wages. Catlin was now nearly deaf. In Uruguay he missed a shot at a jaguar, and the jaguar almost clawed him to death. He recuperated in Buenos Aires, then rode up into the Argentine Pampas to visit the Borroras, who could ride as Catlin thought only the Comanche and Crow could ride. Late in 1856 he sailed around Tierra del Fuego and up the west coast to Panama. He seemed to vanish.

His brother Francis, then in the State Department, grew anxious. For more than a

"The Handsome Dance" in Venezuela. Catlin slipped out of Paris like a fugitive, "as kings and emperors sometimes do." He painted his way up the Amazon, over the Andes to coastal Peru.

year George Catlin was missing. He turned up in England—the statute of limitations had run out for his creditors—and in 1861 published *Life Amongst the Indians—A Book for Youth*. It was a polished collection of anecdotes from his Indian travels, an encyclopedia of Indian life for boys. The reviewers were charmed once again.

He could afford a simple studio in Brussels, and he went to work to copy his own art, to reassemble his great Indian gallery. He worked alone, in the silent world of the deaf, lost in his forest of too many thoughts, just as his Iowas had predicted.

In 1868 he published *Last Rambles Amongst the Indians of the Rocky Mountains and the Andes,* the stories of Pacific coast and South American voyages. In 1870 he began a campaign to get the New-York Historical Society to buy his collection of "cartoons," and perhaps to buy from the Harrison Boiler Works his indentured Gallery. The Historical Society did not answer. He packed his "cartoons" from his "last rambles" and set sail for New York to convince them in person.

He opened one more show in New York, October 24, 1870, at the Sommerville Gallery, Fifth Avenue and 14th Street; admission 50¢, children half-price. "Catlin's Indian Cartoons—North and South American Indian Portraits, six hundred paintings in oil, with

70

In the sierra of the Andes, Catlin shot condor with his colt rifle. He traversed Brazil, paddled the Paraguay, rode the pampas of Argentina, explored the West Indies, always painting.

more than 20,000 full-length figures, illustrating their games, religious ceremonies, and other customs. Mountain and Pampas scenery of the two hemispheres, 27 paintings of La Salle's Discoveries." The show closed the last week of November. New Yorkers were not much interested in George Catlin anymore. But an old friend from his Albany days, Joseph Henry, was the new secretary of the Smithsonian. Henry asked him to bring his "cartoon" collection to Washington, and they were displayed.

Catlin worked on them from a little room in a turret of the Institution. He hoped Congress might still rescue his great collection from the boiler works. He wrote the New-York Historical Society again. But he was sick and getting weaker; he had Bright's disease, which was painful. Sometimes he could not get up unassisted from his cot in the Smithsonian. They took him to his family in Jersey City, where his brother-in-law, Dudley S. Gregory, sheltered him, and his daughters cared for him.

The pain grew worse. He bore it, they said, like an Indian. He said he had dreamt of the Kettle of Gold in the Wyoming Valley in Wilkes-Barre. He said: "Oh, if I was down in the valley of the Amazon I could walk off this weakness." He worried: "What will become of my gallery?" He died at 5:30 in the morning of December 23, 1872. He was seventy-six.

71

Four Bears, of the Mandan: ". . . I have never called a White Man a Dog, but today, I do pronounce them to be a set of Black hearted Dogs. . . ."

VII

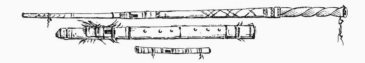

What Happened in
The West After 1837

Shift and turn the combinations of the statement as we may, the problem of the future of America is in certain respects as dark as it is vast. Pride, competition, segregation, vicious wilfulness, and license beyond example brood already upon us. Unwieldy and immense, who shall hold in behemoth? who bridle Leviathan? . . .

—Walt Whitman, *Democratic Vistas*, 1873

IN OCTOBER 1831 four Indians arrived in St. Louis to call upon General William Clark, father to the tribes of The West. The Indian ambassadors wished to obtain instruction for their tribes in the white man's Medicine, of which they had heard so much—the power by which the white man exercised his control over nature. They had correctly understood that the sources for guns and needles, for calico and steam-powered wool looms, were to be found in The Book of Job, in Saint Paul, Saint Augustine, and Saint Thomas Aquinas. The ambassadorial group included a Flathead whose name was Man of the Morning, a Nez Percé chief named Black Eagle, and two young men of his tribe named No Horns on His Head and Rabbit Skin Leggings. They were from the mountain basins west of the divide in Oregon Territory.

The lowlands of St. Louis, that new home of seven thousand citizens, were dangerous with disease. Black Eagle, who died within the month, October 31, was baptized by a Father Saulnier in the faith the chief had sought, and was buried in the Catholic cemetery. Man of the Morning died soon afterward, and he too was given the burial of a convert. The two remaining warriors, having explained to General Clark the need of their Nations for instruction in the mysteries, went back upriver aboard the *Yellowstone* in 1832.

At Fort Pierre the Sioux gave a feast for them, as distinguished visitors from the powerful tribes farther west. They dressed in Sioux costumes, and George Catlin painted them. They went on with him aboard the *Yellowstone* to Fort Union, where disease felled No Horns on His Head. He was buried near the mouth of the Yellowstone River, but probably not as a Christian.

Rabbit Skin Leggings traveled on alone to join a band of his Nez Percé people he discovered hunting east of the mountains. Their band was surprised by Blackfoot, and Rabbit Skin Leggings was killed before the first big snows of 1832.

Nevertheless, word of the tribes' need had reached the Mission Board of the Methodist Church. In 1833 they appointed the Reverend Jason Lee. He followed the fur trade routes, and by 1835 was clearing land for the mission farm in the Willamette Valley. He was nowhere near either Flathead or Nez Percé tribes; but never mind, he was among the docile Chinooks. "Send us families," he wrote the Mission Board, "send us farmers, mechanics, workmen, send us machinery and plows: This is the richest land in the world."

The American Board of Commissioners for Foreign Missions, a joint Congregational-Presbyterian enterprise, had also learned of the great need of the noble savages. The board's agents, the Reverend Samuel Parker and the Reverend Dr. Marcus Whitman, were guided by Lucien Fontanelle, an Astor "Company" man, up the Platte, past Chimney Rock, and through South Pass in 1834.

At the Green River Fur rendezvous they saw with their own eyes Kit Carson killing a man in a duel. The Reverend Dr. Parker was shocked at such godless scenes. He saw fur traders sell playing cards to the Indians with which they would gamble. The two divines reported to their board that a mission was feasible, and certainly necessary.

On July 4, 1836, Dr. Whitman and his wife Narcissa, and the Reverend Henry H. Spaulding and his wife Eliza, camped beside their wagons in the ceaseless wind at South Pass. They planned to meet the Reverend Dr. Parker at Walla Walla.

Dr. Whitman established his mission at Waiilatpu, near Walla Walla, which was in Cayuse country. He and Narcissa died there in 1847. The Cayuse apparently shot them first, then hacked them up with axes in a frenzy. By then the population of Oregon numbered thirteen thousand. It was the Reverend Henry H. Spaulding who bore witness at a mission to the Nez Percé, the answer to Rabbit Skin Legging's final prayers.

Although the Indian Intercourse Act of 1834 forbade all whites without government licenses to trespass on Indian lands, sermons from every pulpit in the East called for action: There were souls to be brought to God, and noble savages to be taught Redemption, Transfiguration, Resurrection, magnanimity, the meaning of transcendentalism. The great migrations began partly because there was a good cause—God's cause. And with the aid of President Jackson's Bank Panic of 1837, immigrants headed west for Oregon, the promised land, the richest land on earth.

*. . . I have never called a White Man a Dog, but today, I do pro-
nounce them to be a set of Black hearted Dogs . . . I have been in
Many Battles, and often Wounded, but the Wounds of My Enemies
I exhalt in. . . . I do not fear Death, my friends. You know it, but to
die with my face rotten, that even Wolves will shrink with horror at
seeing Me. . . . Listen well what I have to say, as it will be the last
time you will hear Me. Think of your Wives, Children, Brothers,
Sisters, Friends, and in fact all that you hold dear, are all Dead, or
Dying, with their faces all rotten, caused by those dogs the whites,
think of all that My friends, and rise all together and Not leave one
of them alive. The 4 Bears will act his part.*

—The speech of The Four Bears, dying of smallpox, quoted by
Francis A. Chardon, at the Mandan Post, August 1837

On June 20, 1837, "The Company's" new steamboat, the *St. Peter's*, finished
unloading at the Mandan Post, Fort Clark, then continued upriver for Fort Union. On July 4
the post's men drank a toast to "Old Hickory," although Martin Van Buren had replaced
Andrew Jackson as President. On July 14 Francis A. Chardon, the post's commander, noted:
"A young Mandan died today of the Smallpox—several others have caught it."

Chardon would later claim he was unable to keep the Indians in his charge away
from the *St. Peter's* when she unloaded, though he had tried, and one of them had stolen a
blanket from an infected member of the steamboat's crew. He had offered a reward for the
return of the blanket, but it could not be gotten back.

Whatever: The Mandans were wiped out. Chardon's son, Andrew Jackson Char-
don, died too. Their neighbors, the Minataree and the Arikara, were slow to catch it, but they
did. Upstream at Fort Union, the post's new commander, Jacob Halsey, caught it himself and
survived, but his Indian wife gave birth to a child and then died from the disease.

At Fort Union they tried inoculation from living cases to the uninfected. They
attempted to quarantine the infected in a small locked room. "There was such a stench in the
fort that it could be smelt at the distance of 300 yards." Some of the quarantined went mad;
others, though living, "were half eaten up by maggots."

Five Assiniboin warriors scaled the pickets of the stockade to run off two horses.
Four members of the post's garrison pursued them, talked them out of the stolen horses, and
brought them back. But one of the posse was an infected man, and the Assiniboin now carried
it. Eight hundred of them died. They infected the Cree, and it was said seven thousand Cree
died.

In the fall a company trader, Culbertson, rode out into Blackfoot country. Approaching their village at Three Forks, he smelled the stench. "Hundreds of decaying forms of human beings, horses, and dogs lay scattered everywhere among the lodges." He found two old women alive, raving, crawling along the corpses.

The Commissioner of Indian Affairs reported the epidemic had first appeared among the Chickasaws, who infected their neighbors the Choctaws. Then it spread "to the northwest." In the six Missouri tribes—Mandan, Arikara, Minataree, Sioux, Assiniboin, and Blackfoot—at least seventeen thousand died. Some experts said the total for all the plains was as high as one hundred and fifty thousand dead. But who could say for sure? There was no census for Indians.

After 1837 the frontier swept across the plains unopposed. Depopulated by disease, the surviving tribes were dependent upon the white man's Medicine—for better or for worse, in sickness and in health.

'Twas a dark night in sixty-six
When we was layin' steel

We seen a flyin' engin come
Without no wing or wheel

It came a roarin' in the sky
With lights along the side . . .
And scales like serpents' hide.

—Song of the 1860s

The American Fur Company posts at Fort Pierre and Fort Union were outposts not only for the advancing frontier but of industrial, then corporate, capitalism. After 1837 those revolutionary systems determined the social structure of the manners and customs behind the frontier.

The Erie Canal that George Catlin painted in 1825 had opened up Ohio, Indiana, Illinois. Three hundred lake vessels arrived at the Port of Chicago in 1833, although the permanent population of that metropolis was said to be only three hundred and fifty. Michigan became a state in 1837, Wisconsin in 1848. By then Polk had won Mexico, and an Oregon Treaty line. Gold was discovered in California. The Mormons chose Utah.

In the 1840s railroad mileage tripled. The first locomotives were brought from England, but by the 1850s the Americans—including Mr. Harrison's boiler works, which stored Catlin's *Gallery unique*—were the builders for the world. By the 1850s the Hudson River Railway connected the New York Central to Buffalo. The Pennsylvania went through to Pittsburgh. The locomotive may have been no more than a technological contraption, but on the neurological receptors of frontier societies the ganglia of railroad tracks, and the influence of railroad corporations, had a stupendous impact. All the railroad tracks led East.

Moreover, the tracks led to urban centers. During the 1840s the population of the United States increased 36 percent, but the urban population increased 90 percent. The developing systems were urban.

In the 1840s when Congress was debating the value of Catlin's Indian Gallery, it quickly appropriated $30,000 for Samuel F. B. Morse, another artist, to establish a telegraph line between Baltimore and Washington. As every schoolboy knows, Morse telegraphed Baltimore in May 1844: "What hath God wrought!" The citation was from Numbers 23:23, of course, but the question was an interesting one.

In 1834 Cyrus H. McCormick patented a reaping machine. By 1851 he was building one thousand reapers a year at his Chicago plant. The prairie wheat farmer was replacing the plantation cotton grower as the king of American agriculture and politics. To haul the produce manufactured by reapers, the railroads finished their tracks all the way to "The Vermillion Sea," and cities of gold sprung up in Quivera.

By 1850 the population of California was 92,597. Gold had brought some, but new horizons brought many more. By 1850 the population of Texas was 212,592. Sam Houston and President Polk defeated Mexico, but farmers and cattlemen won the state.

By the time George Catlin died in 1873, Grant was about to start his second term despite the scandals, and New York to San Francisco was six days by rail for $75. The United States had filled out the map to nearly its present boundaries, had a population of some forty million citizens, and was within reach of being the most powerful industrial system in the world. The frontier had not been "closed" yet, but it was sweeping past. The Indian societies were no longer free, because their Medicine was impotent.

VIII

Catlin's Lifework Saved; and Notes on the Editing of his Reports

The only good Indians I ever saw were dead.

—General Philip Sheridan

IN MAY 1879 Mrs. Joseph Harrison, widow of Catlin's creditor, turned over the *Gallery unique* to The Smithsonian, as an heirloom for the nation. During the thirty years it was stored on the grounds of the Harrison Boiler Works, there had been a number of fires. In each fire it had been smoked, or doused by the fire companies trying to save it. The costumes, robes, teepees, and other things vulnerable to such care were ruined. Yet 80 percent of the 507 paintings listed in Catlin's catalogue for his opening in London in 1840 were saved; in addition, thirty-three of the one hundred works he did between 1840 and 1848 were turned over to The Smithsonian. Ironically, The Smithsonian itself suffered a terrible fire in 1865, so the Harrison locomotive shops may well have been the safer vault.

In addition to The Smithsonian acquisition, Catlin oils, watercolors, sketches, notebooks, and editions of his various works have been faithfully preserved by archivists, librarians, and museums. Some few works are held by private collectors. A portrait of General Leavenworth has turned up at Fort Leavenworth. A Catlin scene of his dinner of dog with The Four Bears has appeared in Bismarck, North Dakota. Scholarship on Catlin and critical appreciation of his work is growing.

◄

Rabbit Skin Leggings, the Nez Percé ambassador: After he died, the ministers came.

Since our modest introduction of Catlin's life and circumstance is intended only as a "stage setting" for his edited *Letters and Notes,* we cannot pause to make a thorough appraisal of Catlin's art as art. Yet a few simple notions should be remarked.

In Catlin's art there were several qualities, some poor, some extraordinary. After going bankrupt he painted from memory copies of his own works stored in the boiler works. He painted in despair and for cash, and fast. Many of these works he called "cartoons." Many were surrounded by an oval of black or dark paint—as if he were using a cheap method of "framing" in place of wood.

The term "cartoon" was often used by artists to mean an oil done as a study for a future work. In that sense Catlin used "cartoon" to cover the paintings he did for quick cash; he also used "cartoon" to describe oils he did as examples of what might be published in books as lithographs.

Many of his South American Indians were displayed with the "cartoon" oval; most of his *copies* of his *Gallery unique* North American Indians used the "cartoon" oval. He reworked scenes he had done as woodcuts for his books as oil "cartoons." The original of Sioux Dog Feast in The Smithsonian collection, for example, is framed square; his copy, now in Bismarck, North Dakota, is framed as a "cartoon."

The "cartoons" were done in the 1850s and after, during the great age of the American lithographers. Curiously, when Catlin painted landscapes during those years he called them part of his "cartoon" collection, but generally framed them square; when he painted portraits they are most often surrounded by the "cartoon" oval.

Some of his later work, especially from South America, is magic: The landscapes are full of an immense and dominating nature, a brooding nature. His portraits of the men in that overwhelming nature are, well—insignificant. He said as much in his notes.

Sometimes his later works seem static and dull compared to his portraits on the plains—as if they were quick studies, even sales promotion jobs for linecuts, or lithograph commissions. Perhaps, if he had found a publisher, they would have been reworked. It is these Catlin "cartoons" that are most often seen, and are best known, and for which he is often judged as an artist.

He always did plan to duplicate the success of his 1844 *North American Indian Portfolio*—the lithographs he had supervised, and in some cases hand colored. The 1844 set of lithographs is superior throughout in energy, detail, and composition to almost all of his "cartoons."

His watercolors, also done as sketches for his oils or sometimes as copies of his own indentured oils, were used to borrow money, or as sales promotion materials for proposed publications. They are invariably superb.

What might be called his "field oils" are amazing for several reasons. In his Philadelphia studio he studied and developed special techniques to match the task he had set for himself—the tools a classically trained artist would need in the field as a reporter. He knew he would often average 20 miles a day on horse or by canoe. He would have to hunt his food or fish for it. He would have to transport his canvas, his boards, his paints and sketch books, his field notes, and his portfolios to show his anxious subjects—and all this through thousands of

miles of unmapped wilderness. He traveled from Fort Union to St. Louis in a canoe—2000 miles—with two trappers and their outfits on the swift and cranky Missouri, doing one hundred oils on the way.

He considered himself pressed for time—and he was. In the opinion of some experts he must have finished some oils in a matter of minutes, and in some villages he painted half a dozen portraits in a single day.

Catlin has often been compared to Carl Bodmer, who traveled the upper Missouri as "the artist" with the scientific survey of Maximilian, Prince zu Wied. An academically trained Swiss, Bodmer was an accomplished draughtsman. He did sketches, watercolors, and oils in the Upper Missouri country in 1833 and 1834. Bodmer, with his patron Maximilian, wintered in the same Mandan villages as Catlin. Bodmer had the advantage of having studied Catlin's work in the home of Major Benjamin O'Fallon in St. Louis. Generally, Bodmer avoided the subjects Catlin had painted, but in a few instances they portrayed the same subjects. Bodmer's painstaking academic portrait of The Four Bears is breathtaking. Bodmer's scenes of the Mandan dances are composed according to the rules of European romantic composition. Bodmer was exact and skilled; he took days, or months, according to his need, to prepare each canvas.

Catlin worked in a hurry not so much for the Gallery but for the record. Yet, without detracting one bit from Bodmer, there exists in Catlin's work a sense of his urgency, his enthusiasm and sympathy, and a tone of melancholy that the precise Swiss missed. Comparing the two artists is to compare two different styles, two different purposes, and to engage two different tastes. It might be possible to conclude that Bodmer was painting real paintings, Catlin real Indians.

At the age of seventy-five Catlin made his own modest assessment. He hoped, he said, posterity would "find enough of historical interest excited by faithful resemblance to the physiognomy and customs of these people to compensate for what may be deficient in them as works of art." He was too modest.

I love the people who have always made me welcome to the best they had.

I love a people who are honest without laws, who have no jails and no poorhouses.

I love a people who keep the commandments without ever having read them or heard them preached from the pulpit.

I love a people who never swear, who never take the name of God in vain.

I love a people "who love their neighbors as they loved themselves."

I love a people who worship God without a Bible, for I believe that God loves them also.

I love the people whose religion is all the same, and who are free from religious animosities.

I love the people who have never raised a hand against me, or stolen my property, where there was no law to punish either.

I love the people who have never fought a battle with white men, except on their own ground.

I love and don't fear mankind where God has made and left them, for there they are children.

I love a people who live and keep what is their own without locks and keys.

I love all people who do the best they can. And oh, how I love a people who don't live for the love of money

—George Catlin's "Creed"

The edited *Letters and Notes* that follow begin at Fort Union, at the mouth of the Yellowstone, because Catlin's first letters published in the *Commercial Advertiser* began there. Thereafter, their order, the sequence of the chapters, and the relation of the chapters to Catlin's actual itineraries is, at best, only approximate. What I have done is to use a *geographic* order rather than a chronological one, to suit the general reader but not the scholar, who can easily consult the original edition if he pleases.

Moreover, I had to condense. I have taken liberties that might cause some scholars to faint. The original editions run to some eight hundred pages in two volumes. No one could afford to publish them today at that length. So I have done my best to retain the most significant of Catlin's descriptions, the best of his anecdotes; almost all of his account of Wi-jun-jon's tragic return from Washington, the horror of the Leavenworth-Dodge expedition, the mystery of the pipestone quarries.

But I have taken whatever liberties I pleased. For example, I took material from Catlin's original appendix—his theory that the Mandans were originally Welsh—and combined it with his paragraphs on the same matter at the Mandan villages. I melded Catlin's unedited version of the O-kee-pah, published in London in 1867, with the tamer version published in the original 1841 *Letters and Notes.*

Although I have retained as much of the Mandan material as possible, I ruthlessly cut material on the dances of other tribes, and all of Catlin's theories that the Indians might be the ten lost tribes of Israel. In addition, I have rearranged sentences, modified verbs, changed their tenses, repunctuated when I wished, omitted ellipses when they should have been included, junked all the rules about footnoting according to custom, or annotating. Finally, it must be said that Catlin's spellings were eclectic, that the names of many of the tribes have changed, that in any case, all Indians had many names. In addition, my own spelling sometimes had to be creative to balance between Catlin's version and later histories. Under these rules errors will pile up. I take responsibility for all, because I wanted to get Catlin's advocacy to the general reader once again.

Just as Catlin's paintings were intended to serve a cause, so also, he thought, his *Letters and Notes* were meant to be a vigorous collection of anecdote, of story, and of parable. His advocacy was not made for scholarly extractions, nor for the syntheses of historians. He believed his readers would delight in vivid descriptions, stirring incidents, in pathos and in absurdity. Sometimes his Indians act foolishly, sometimes they speak shrewdly; they are always real Indians, their histories real stories. Their lives are ours.

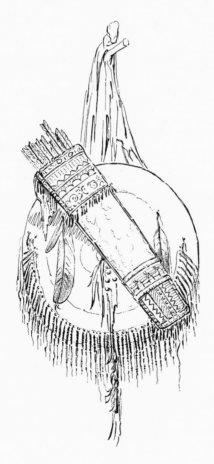

LETTERS AND NOTES ON THE MANNERS, CUSTOMS, AND CONDITION OF THE NORTH AMERICAN INDIANS

BY GEORGE CATLIN

Edited to One Volume

Stu-mick-o-sucks, The Buffalo Bull's Back Fat, head chief, Blood tribe of the Blackfeet.

I

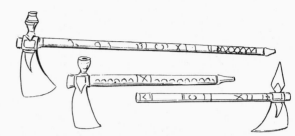

Mouth of the Yellow Stone, *Upper Missouri,* 1832

I ARRIVED at this place yesterday in the steamer "Yellow Stone," after a voyage of nearly three months from St. Louis, a distance of two thousand miles, the greater part of which has never before been navigated by steam. The difficulties which continually oppose the *voyageur* on this turbid stream have been overcome by the indefatigable zeal of Mr. Pierre Chouteau, proprietor of the boat. To the politeness of this gentleman I am indebted for my passage from St. Louis to this place, and I had also the pleasure of his company, with that of Major Sanford, the government agent for the Missouri Indians.

The American Fur Company have erected here a very substantial Fort, three hundred feet square, with bastions armed with ordnance. Our approach to it, amid the continued roar of cannon for half an hour, and the shrill yells of the half-affrighted Indians who lined the shores, presented a scene of the most thrilling and picturesque appearance.

If I am here losing the benefit of the fleeting fashions of the day, and neglecting that elegant polish, which the world says an artist should draw from a continual intercourse with the polite world, yet have I this consolation: in this country, I am entirely divested of those allurements which beset an artist in fashionable life; and have little to steal my thoughts away

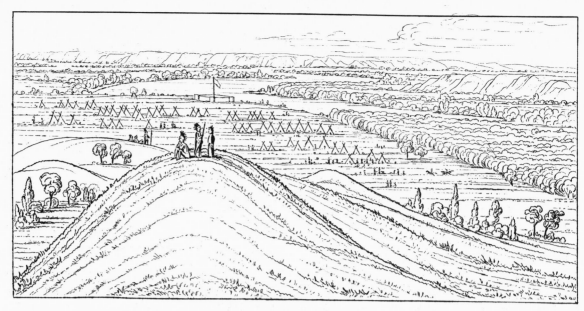

Fort Union.

from the contemplation of the beautiful models that are about me. If I have not here that feeling of emulation, which is the life and spur to the arts, where artists are associates together, yet I feel that I am drawing knowledge from the true source.

The following pages have been compiled from a series of Letters and Notes written by myself during several years' residence and travel among a number of the wildest and most remote tribes of the North American Indians. Amid the multiplicity of books which are, in this enlightened age, flooding the world, I feel it my duty to beg pardon for making a book at all; then proceed to say that I was born in Wyoming, Pennsylvania, in North America, of parents who entered that beautiful and famed valley soon after the close of the revolutionary war, and the disastrous event of the "Indian massacre."

The early part of my life was whiled away with books reluctantly held in one hand, and a rifle or fishing-pole firmly and affectionately grasped in the other.

At the urgent request of my father, who was a practicing lawyer, I commenced reading the law under the direction of Reeve and Gould, of Connecticut. I attended the lectures of these learned judges for two years—was admitted to the bar—and practiced the law, as a sort of *Nimrodical* lawyer, for the term of two or three years when I very deliberately sold my law library and all (save my rifle and fishing-tackle) and converting the proceeds into brushes and paint-pots, I commenced the art of painting in Philadelphia.

For several years my mind was continually reaching for some branch or enterprise of the art on which to devote a whole life-time of enthusiasm when a delegation of some ten or fifteen noble and dignified-looking Indians, from the wilds of the "Far West," suddenly arrived in the city, arrayed and equipped in all their classic beauty—with shield and helmet —with tunic and manteau—tinted and tasselled off, exactly for the painter's palette!

In silent and stoic dignity, these lords strutted about the city for a few days, wrapped in their pictured robes, with their brows plumed with the quills of the war-eagle, attracting the admiration of all who beheld them. After this, they took their leave for

88

Washington City, and I was left to reflect and regret, which I did long and deeply, until I came to the following conclusions.

Black and blue cloth and civilization are destined, not only to veil, but to obliterate the grace and beauty of Nature. Man, in the simplicity and loftiness of his nature, unrestrained and unfettered by the disguises of art, is surely the most beautiful model for the painter—and the country from which he hails is unquestionably the best study or school of the arts in the world. The history and customs of such a people are themes worthy the life-time of one man, and nothing short of the loss of my life shall prevent me from visiting their country, and of becoming their historian.

There was something inexpressibly delightful in my resolve. Armed, equipped, and supplied, I started out and penetrated the vast and pathless wilds which are the great "Far West," to devote myself to describing the living manners, customs, and character of a people who were rapidly passing away from the face of the earth—a dying nation who had no historians or biographers of their own.

I set out with the determination of reaching, ultimately, every tribe of Indians on the Continent of North America, and of bringing home faithful portraits of their principal personages, both men and women: views of their villages, games, and full notes on their character and history. I designed, also, to procure their costumes, and a complete collection of their manufactures and weapons, and to perpetuate them in a *Gallery unique,* for the use and instruction of future ages.

The Indians of the forests and prairies of North America are a subject of great interest and some importance to the civilized world. They are a numerous nation of human beings, whose origin is beyond the reach of human investigation; whose early history is lost; whose term of national existence is nearly expired; three-fourths of whose country has fallen into the possession of civilized man within the short space of two hundred and fifty years; twelve millions of whose bodies have fattened the soil in the meantime; who have fallen victims to whisky, the small-pox, and the bayonet; leaving at this time but a meagre proportion to live a short time longer, in certain apprehension of soon sharing a similar fate.

The Indians of North America are copper-colored, with long black hair, black eyes, and tall, straight, and classic forms. They are now less than two million in number, but they were originally the undisputed owners of the soil, and got title to their lands from the Great Spirit who created them on it. They were once a happy and flourishing people, enjoying all the comforts and luxuries of life. They were then sixteen million in numbers, and sent that number of daily prayers to the Almighty, thanking Him for his goodness and protection. Their country was entered by white men, and thirty million of these are now scuffling for the goods and luxuries of life, over the bones and ashes of twelve million of red men, six million of whom have fallen victims to the small-pox and the remainder to the sword, the bayonet, and whisky—all of which means of their death and destruction have been introduced and visited upon them by acquisitive white men; and by white men, also, whose forefathers were welcomed and embraced in the land where the poor Indian met and fed them with "ears of green corn and with pemican."

Of the two million remaining alive at this time, about one million four hundred thousand are already the miserable living victims and dupes of the white man's cupidity, degraded, discouraged, and lost in the bewildering maze that is produced by the use of whisky and its concomitant vices; and the remaining number are yet unroused and unenticed from their wild haunts or their primitive modes by the dread or love of the white man and his allurements.

The reader, then, to understand me rightly, and draw from these Letters the information which they are intended to give, must follow me a vast way from the civilized world; he must wend his way from the city of New York, over the Alleghany, and far beyond the mighty Missouri, and even to the base and summit of the Rocky Mountains, some two or three thousand miles from the Atlantic coast. He should forget many theories he has read in the books, of Indian barbarities, of wanton butcheries and murders; and divest himself, as far as possible, of the deadly prejudices which he has carried from his childhood, against this most unfortunate and most abused part of the race of his fellow-man.

He should consider that if he has seen the Indians of North America without making such a tour, he has fixed his eyes upon and drawn his conclusions (in all probability) only from those who inhabit the frontier; whose habits have been changed; whose pride has been cut down; whose country has been ransacked; whose wives and daughters have been shamefully abused; whose lands have been wrested from them; whose limbs have become enervated and naked by the excessive use of whisky; whose friends and relations have been prematurely thrown into their graves; whose native pride and dignity have at last given way to the unnatural vices which civilized cupidity has engrafted upon them to be silently nurtured and magnified by a burning sense of injury and injustice, and ready for that cruel vengeance which often falls from the hand that is palsied by refined abuses, and yet unrestrained by the glorious influences of refined and moral cultivation. If the reader has laid up what he considers well-founded knowledge of these people, from books which he has read, and from newspapers only, he should pause at least and withhold his sentence before he passes upon the character of a people who are dying at the hands of their enemies, without the means of recording their own annals—struggling in their nakedness with simple weapons against guns and gunpowder, against whisky and steel, against disease.

Among the numerous historians of these strange people, there have been some friends who have done them justice; yet, justice, whenever it is meted to the poor Indian invariably comes too late, or is administered at an ineffectual distance; or when his enemies are continually about him, and applying the means of his destruction.

Some writers, I have been grieved to see, have written down the character of the North American Indian as dark, relentless, cruel and murderous, in the last degree; with scarce a quality to stamp their existence of a higher order than that of the brutes. Others have given them a high rank, as I feel myself authorized to do, as honorable and highly intellectual beings.

From what I have seen of these people there is nothing very strange or unaccountable in their character. It is a simple one, and easy to be learned and understood if the right means be taken to familiarize ourselves with it. Although it has its dark spots, yet there is

90

much in it to be applauded, and much to recommend it to the admiration of the enlightened world. And I trust that the reader will be disposed to join me in the conclusion that the North American Indian, in his native state, is honest, hospitable, faithful, brave, warlike, cruel, revengeful, relentless—yet an honorable, contemplative, and religious being.

I am fully convinced, from a long familiarity with these people, that the Indians' misfortune has consisted chiefly in our ignorance of their true native character and disposition, which has always held us at a distrustful distance from them; inducing us to look upon them in no other light than that of a hostile foe, and worthy only of that system of continued warfare and abuse that has been forever waged against them.

I have roamed about visiting and associating with some three or four hundred thousand of these people, under an almost infinite variety of circumstances. From their very many and decidedly voluntary acts of hospitality and kindness, I feel bound to pronounce them, by nature, a kind and hospitable people. I have been welcomed in their country, and treated to the best that they could give me, without any charges made for my board. They have often escorted me through their enemies' country at some hazard to their own lives, and aided me in passing mountains and rivers with my awkward baggage. Under all of these circumstances of exposure, no Indian ever betrayed me, struck me a blow, or stole from me a shilling's worth of my property.

And thus in these little communities, strange as it may seem, in the absence of all systems of jurisprudence, I have often beheld peace and happiness, and quiet, reigning supreme, for which even kings and emperors might envy them. I have seen rights and virtue protected, and wrongs redressed. I have seen conjugal, filial, and paternal affection in the simplicity and contentedness of nature. I have, unavoidably, formed warm and enduring attachments to some of these men, which I do not wish to forget—men who have brought me near to their hearts, and in our final separation have embraced me in their arms, and commended me and my affairs to the keeping of the Great Spirit.

If I should live to accomplish my design, the result of my labors will doubtless be interesting to future ages, who will have little else left from which to judge of the original inhabitants of this simple race of beings. They require but a few years more of the march of civilization and death to deprive them of all their native customs and character. I have been kindly supplied by the Commander-in-Chief of the Army and the Secretary of War with letters to the commander of every military post and every Indian agent on the Western Frontier, with instructions to render me all the facilities in their power. The opportunity afforded me, by familiarity with so many tribes of human beings in the simplicity of nature, of drawing fair conclusions on their manners and customs, rites and ceremonies, and the opportunity of examining the geology and mineralogy of this western and yet unexplored country, will enable me occasionally to entertain you.

Before I let you into the amusements and customs of this delightful country, however, I must hastily travel with you two thousand miles from St. Louis to this place over which one is obliged to pass, before he can reach this wild and lovely spot.

The Missouri is, perhaps, different in appearance and character from all other rivers in the world; there is a terror in its manner which is sensibly felt the moment we enter its muddy waters from the Mississippi. The Missouri, with its boiling, turbid waters, sweeps in one unceasing current. In the whole distance there is scarcely an eddy or resting-place for a canoe. Owing to the continual falling in of its rich alluvial banks, its water is always turbid and opaque; having, at all seasons of the year, the color of a cup of chocolate or coffee, with sugar and cream stirred into it.

For the distance of one thousand miles above St. Louis, the shores of this river (and, in many places, the whole bed of the stream) are filled with snags and rafts formed of trees of the largest size, which have been undermined by the falling banks and cast into the stream. Their roots become fastened in the bottom of the river, with their tops floating on the surface of the water, and pointing down the stream, forming the most discouraging prospect for the voyageur. Almost every island and sand-bar is covered with huge piles of these floating trees, and when the river is flooded, its surface is almost literally covered with floating rafts of drift-wood which defy keel-boats and steamers on their way up the river.

With what propriety this "Hell of waters" might be denominated the "River Styx," I will not undertake to decide; but nothing could be more appropriate or innocent than to call it the River *of Sticks.*

The scene is not, however, all so dreary; there is a redeeming beauty in the green and carpeted shores. Much of the way forests of stately cotton-wood stand and frown in horrid dark and coolness over the filthy abyss below into which they are ready to plunge headlong, when the mud and soil in which they were germed and reared are washed out from underneath them, and mixed with the rolling current on their way to the ocean.

The greater part of the shores of this river, however, is without timber. The eye wanders delightfully over beautiful prairies gracefully sloping down to the water's edge, carpeted with the deepest green and, in distance, softening into velvet of the richest hues, entirely beyond the reach of the artist's pencil. Such is the character of the upper part of the river. As one advances towards its source, and through its upper half, it becomes more pleasing to the eye, for snags and raft are no longer to be seen; yet the current holds its stiff and onward turbid character.

One thousand miles or more of the upper part of the river was, to my eye, like fairy-land. During that part of our voyage I was most of the time rivetted to the deck of the boat, indulging my eyes in the boundless pleasure of roaming over the thousand hills and bluffs and dales and ravines where astonished herds of buffaloes, elks, antelopes, sneaking wolves, and mountain-goats were to be seen bounding up and down and over the green fields. Each one and each tribe, band, and gang took their own way and used their own means to the greatest advantage possible, to leave the sight and sound of the puffing of our boat.

From St. Louis to the falls of the Missouri, a distance of two thousand six hundred miles, is one continued prairie, with the exception of a few of the bottoms formed along the bank of the river, and the streams falling into it, which are covered with the most luxuriant growth of timber.

The summit level of the great prairies stretching off to the west and the east from the river, to an almost boundless extent, is from two to three hundred feet above the level of the river, which has formed a bed or valley for its course, varying in width from two to twenty

For 1000 miles above St. Louis a river of sticks.

miles. This valley has been produced by the force of the current, which has gradually excavated, in its floods and gorges, an immense space, and sent its debris into the ocean. By the continual overflowing of the river, its valley has been left with a horizontal surface through which the river winds its serpentine course, alternately running from one bluff to the other, which present themselves to its shores in all the most picturesque and beautiful shapes and colors imaginable—some with their green sides gracefully slope down in the most lovely groups to the water's edge while others, divested of their verdure, present themselves in immense masses of clay of different colors.

These strange and picturesque appearances have been produced by the rains and frosts which are continually changing the dimensions, and varying the thousand shapes of these denuded hills, by washing down their sides and carrying them into the river.

Among these groups may be seen thousands of different forms and figures, of the sublime and the picturesque. In many places as the boat glides along there is an appearance of some ancient and boundless city in ruins—ramparts, terraces, domes, towers, citadels, and castles may be seen—cupolas, and magnificent porticoes, and here and there a solitary column and crumbling pedestal, and even spires of clay which stand alone. Glistening in the distance, the sun's rays are refracted back by the thousand crystals of gypsum imbedded in the clay of which they are formed. Over and through these groups of domes and battlements (as one is compelled to imagine them) the sun sends his long and gilding rays, at morn or in the evening, giving life and light, by aid of shadows cast, to the different glowing colors of these clay-built ruins and shedding a glory over the solitude of this wild and pictured country.

The grizzly bear also has chosen these places for his abode. He sullenly sneaks through the gulphs and chasms and ravines, and frowns away the lurking Indian; whilst the

93

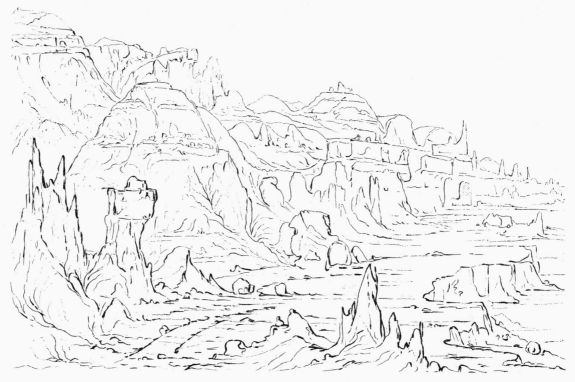

Then the river twists in a land of castled domes.

mountain-sheep and antelope are bounding over and around the hill-tops, safe and free from harm of man and beast.

Such is a hasty sketch of the river scenes and scenery for two thousand miles, over which we tugged and puffed and blowed and toiled for three months before we reached the mouth of the Yellow Stone. Since we arrived, the steamer has returned and left me here to explore the country and visit the tribes in this vicinity. If anything did ever literally and completely astonish and astound the natives, it was the appearance of our steamer, puffing and blowing and paddling and rushing by their villages, which were on the banks of the river.

These people had never before seen or heard of a steamboat, and in some places they seemed at a loss to know what to do, or how to act. They had no name for it—so it was, like everything else with them which is mysterious and unaccountable, called *medicine* (mystery).

We had on board one twelve-pound cannon and three or four eight-pound swivels, which we were taking up to arm the Fur Company's Fort at the mouth of Yellow Stone. At the approach to every village they were all discharged several times in rapid succession, which threw the inhabitants into utter confusion and amazement. Some of them laid their faces to the ground and cried to the Great Spirit. Some shot their horses and dogs, and sacrificed them to appease the Great Spirit, whom they conceived was offended. Some deserted their villages and ran to the tops of the bluffs some miles distant. Others, in some places, as the boat landed in front of their villages, came with great caution, and peeped over the bank of the river to see the fate of their chiefs, whose duty it was (from the nature of their office) to approach us, whether friends or foes, and to go on board. Sometimes, in this plight, they were instantly

94

thrown "neck and heels" over each other's heads and shoulders—men, women and children, and dogs—sage, sachem, old and young—all in a mass, at the frightful discharge of the steam from the escape-pipe, which the captain of the boat let loose upon them for his own fun and amusement.

There were many curious conjectures among their wise men with regard to the nature and powers of the steamboat. Some called it the "big thunder canoe," for in the distance below the village they "saw the lightning flash from its sides, and heard the thunder come from it." Others called it the "big medicine canoe with eyes"; it was *medicine* (mystery) because they could not understand it; and it must have eyes, for said they, "it sees its own way, and takes the deep water in the middle of the channel." They had no idea of the boat being steered by the man at the wheel, and well they might have been astonished at its taking the deepest water.

The Fort in which I am residing was built by Mr. McKenzie, who now occupies it. It is the largest and best-built establishment of the kind on the river, being the great or principal headquarters and depot of the Fur Company's business in this region. A vast stock of goods is kept on hand at this place. At certain times of the year the numerous out-posts concentrate here with the returns of their season's trade, and refit out with a fresh supply of goods to trade with the Indians.

The site for the Fort is well selected, being a beautiful prairie on the bank near the junction of the Missouri with the Yellow Stone rivers. Its inmates and its stores are well protected from Indian assaults.

Mr. McKenzie is a kind-hearted and high-minded Scotchman who seems to have charge of all the Fur Companies' business in this region, from here to the Rocky Mountains. He lives in good and comfortable style inside the Fort, which contains some eight or ten log-houses and stores, and he generally has forty or fifty men and one hundred and fifty horses about him. He has, with the same spirit of liberality and politeness with which Mr. Pierre Chouteau treated me on my passage up the river, pronounced me welcome at his table, which groans under the luxuries of the country; with buffalo meat and tongues, with beavers' tails and marrow-fat; but *sans* coffee, *sans* bread and butter. Good cheer and good living we get at it, however, and good wine also; for a bottle of Madeira and one of excellent Port are set in a pail of ice every day, and exhausted at dinner.

At the hospitable board of Mr. McKenzie I found also another, who is the happy companion of my host; and whose intellectual and polished society has added to my pleasure and amusement since I arrived here. He is an Englishman by the name of Hamilton, of the most pleasing and entertaining conversation, who seems to be a complete store-house of ancient and modern literature and art. We three *bons vivants* form the group about the dinner-table and crack our jokes over bottles of Port and Madeira.

This post is the general rendezvous of a great number of Indian tribes in these regions. They continually concentrate here for the purpose of trade; sometimes coming, the whole tribe together, in a mass. There are now here, and encamped about the Fort, a great many, and I am continually at work with my brush. We have around us at this time the Knisteneaux, Crows, Assiniboin, and Blackfeet, and in a few days are to have large accessions.

Buffalo chase, near Fort Union.

II

Mouth of the Yellow Stone

THE SEVERAL tribes of Indians inhabiting the regions of the Upper Missouri are undoubtedly the finest-looking, best-equipped, and most beautifully costumed of any on the Continent. They live in a country well-stocked with buffaloes and wild horses, which furnish them an excellent and easy living. Their atmosphere is pure, which produces good health and long life. They are the most independent and the happiest races of Indians I have met with. They are all entirely in a state of primitive wildness, and consequently are picturesque and handsome almost beyond description. Nothing in the world, of its kind, can possibly surpass in beauty and grace some of their games and amusements—their gambols and parades.

As far as my travels have yet led me into the Indian country, I have more than realized my former predictions that those Indians who could be found most entirely in a state of nature, with the least knowledge of civilized society, would be found to be the most cleanly in their persons, elegant in their dress and manners, and enjoying life to the greatest perfection. Of such tribes, perhaps the Crows and Blackfeet stand first. No one would be able to appreciate the richness and elegance (and even taste too) with which some of these people dress, without seeing them in their own country. I will do all I can, however, to make their looks as well as customs known to the world. I will paint with my brush and scribble with my pen, and bring their plumes and plumage, dresses, weapons, and everything but the Indian himself. Every one of these red sons of the prairie is a knight and lord—his squaws are his slaves. The only thing which he deems worthy of his exertions are to mount his snorting steed. with his bow and quiver slung, his arrow-shield upon his arm, and his long lance glistening in the war-parade. Or, divested of all his plumes and trappings, armed with a simple bow and quiver, to plunge his steed among the flying herds of buffaloes, and with his sinewy bow, which he seldom bends in vain, to drive deep the whizzing arrow.

The buffalo herds which graze in almost countless numbers on these beautiful prairies afford an abundance of meat. So much is it preferred to all other, that the deer, the elk, and the antelope sport upon the prairies in the greatest security. The Indians seldom kill them, unless they want their skins for a dress.

The buffalo is a noble animal that roams over the vast prairies, from the borders of Mexico on the south to Hudson's Bay on the north. Their size is somewhat above that of our common bullock, and their flesh of a delicious flavor, resembling and equalling that of fat beef. Their flesh, which is easily procured, furnishes the Indian the means of a wholesome and good subsistence, and they live almost exclusively upon it—converting the skins, horns, hoofs, and bones to the construction of dresses, shields, bows, &c. The buffalo bull is one of the most formidable and frightful-looking animals in the world when excited to resistance; his long shaggy mane hangs in great profusion over his neck and shoulders, and often extends quite down to the ground. The cow is less in stature and less ferocious, though not much less wild and frightful in her appearance.

The mode in which the Indians kill the buffalo is spirited and thrilling in the extreme. They are all (or nearly so) killed with arrows and the lance, while at full speed. The reader may easily imagine that these scenes afford the most spirited and picturesque views of the sporting kind that can possibly be seen.

Mr. McKenzie has within his Fort a spacious ice-house in which he preserves his meat fresh for any length of time required. Sometimes, when his larder runs low, he starts out, rallying some five or six of his best hunters (not to hunt, but to "go for meat"). He leads the party, mounted on his favorite buffalo horse (the horse among his whole group which is best trained to run the buffalo) trailing a light and short gun in his hand, the one he can most easily reload while his horse is at full speed.

Such was the condition of the ice-house yesterday morning, which caused these self-catering gentlemen to cast their eyes with a wishful look over the prairies. Our host took the lead, and I, and then Messrs. Chardon, and Baptiste, Défonde and Tullock (who is a trader among the Crows, and is here at this time with a large party of that tribe) and several others followed.

We mounted and all crossed the river, and galloped away a couple of miles or so, where we mounted the bluff. And to be sure, there was a fine herd of some four or five hundred buffaloes, perfectly at rest, and in their own estimation (probably) perfectly secure. Some were grazing and others were lying down and sleeping. We advanced within a mile or so

98

of them in full view, and came to a halt. Mr. Chardon "tossed the feather" (a custom always observed, to try the course of the wind), and we commenced "stripping" as it is termed. Every man strips himself and his horse of every extraneous and unnecessary appendage of dress that might be an incumbrance in running: hats are laid off, and coats—and bullet-pouches; sleeves are rolled up, a handkerchief tied tightly around the head, and another around the waist. Cartridges are prepared and placed in the waist-coat pocket, or a half dozen bullets "throwed into the mouth." All of this takes up some ten or fifteen minutes, and is not, in appearance or in effect, unlike a council of war.

Our leader lays the whole plan of the chase and, preliminaries all fixed, guns charged and ramrods in our hands, we mount and start. The horses are all trained for this business and seem to enter into it with as much enthusiasm, and with as restless a spirit, as the riders themselves. While "stripping" and mounting, they exhibit the most restless impatience. When "approaching" (which is all of us abreast, upon a slow walk, and in a straight line towards the herd until they discover us and run), the horses all seem to catch entirely the spirit of the chase, for the laziest nag among them prances with an elasticity in his step—champing his bit—his ears erect—his eyes strained out of his head and fixed upon the game before him, while he trembles under the saddle of his rider.

In this way we carefully and silently marched until within some two hundred yards. Then the herd, discovering us, wheeled and started to run in a mass. At this instant we started (and all *must* start, for no one could check the fury of those steeds at that moment of excitement) and away we all sailed. Over the prairie we flew in a cloud of dust raised by the trampling hoofs. McKenzie was foremost in the throng and soon dashed off amid the dust and was out of sight—he was after the fattest and the fastest.

I had discovered a huge bull whose shoulders towered above the whole band, and I picked my way through the crowd to get alongside him. I went not for "meat" but for a *trophy;* I wanted his head and horns. I dashed along through the thundering mass as they swept away over the plain, scarcely able to tell whether I was on a buffalo's back or my horse—hit, and hooked, and jostled about, till at length I found myself alongside my game. I gave him a shot as I passed him. I saw guns flash in several directions about me, but I heard them not. Amid the trampling throng, Mr. Chardon had wounded a stately bull, and at this moment was passing him again with his piece levelled for another shot. They were both at full speed and I also, within the reach of the muzzle of my gun, when the bull instantly turned, goring Chardon's horse upon his horns. Poor Chardon made a frog's leap of some twenty feet or more over the bull's back and almost under my horse's heels. I wheeled my horse as soon as possible and rode back where lay poor Chardon, gasping to start his breath again. Within a few paces of him was his huge victim, with his heels high in the air and the horse lying across him. I dismounted instantly, but Chardon was raising himself on his hands, with his eyes and mouth full of dirt, and feeling for his gun, which lay about thirty feet in advance of him.

"Are you hurt, Chardon?"

"Hi-hic-hic-hic-hic-hic-no, -hic-no-no, I believe not. Oh! this is not much, Mr. Cataline—this is nothing new—but this is a hard piece of ground here—hic—oh! Hic!"

At this the poor fellow fainted, but in a few moments arose, picked up his gun, and

Mr. Chardon tossed.

took his horse by the bit, which then opened *its* eyes, and with a *hic* and a *ugh*—UGHK!—sprang upon its feet—shook off the dirt—and here we were, all upon our legs again, save the bull.

I turned my eyes in the direction where the herd had gone with our companions in pursuit, but nothing could be seen of them except the cloud of dust they left behind. At a little distance on the right, however, I beheld my huge victim endeavoring to make as much head-way as he possibly could, from this dangerous ground, upon three legs. I galloped off to him, and at my approach he wheeled around—and bristled up for battle. He seemed to know perfectly well that he could not escape from me, and resolved to meet his enemy and death as bravely as possible.

I found that my shot had entered him a little too far forward, breaking one of his shoulders and lodging in his breast. From his very great weight it was impossible for him to make much advance upon me. As I rode up within a few paces of him, he would bristle up with fury enough in his *looks* alone almost to annihilate me, and making one lunge at me, would fall upon his neck and nose, so that I found the sagacity of my horse alone enough to keep me out of reach of danger. I drew from my pocket my sketch-book, laid my gun across my lap, and commenced taking his likeness. He stood stiffened up, and swelling with awful vengeance, which was sublime for a picture, but which he could not vent upon me. I rode around him and sketched him in numerous attitudes. Sometimes he would lie down, and I would then sketch

Wounded buffalo bull.

him, then throw my cap at him and, rousing him on his legs, rally a new expression and sketch him again. In this way I added to my sketch-book some invaluable sketches of this grim-visaged monster, who knew not that he was standing for his likeness.

No man on earth can imagine what is the look and expression of such a subject. I defy the world to produce another animal that can look so frightful as a huge buffalo bull wounded as he was, turned around for battle and swelling with rage—his eyes blood-shot and his long shaggy mane hanging to the ground, his mouth open, and his horrid rage hissing in streams of smoke and blood from his mouth and through his nostrils, as he is bending forward to spring upon his assailant.

After I had taken the requisite time for using my pencil, McKenzie and his companions came walking their exhausted horses back from the chase, and at our rear came four or five carts to carry home the meat. The party met from all quarters around me and my buffalo bull, whom I then shot in the head and finished. And being seated together for a few minutes, each one took a smoke of the pipe and recited his exploits, and his "coups" or deaths. When all parties had a hearty laugh at me, as a novice, for having aimed at an old bull whose flesh is not suitable for food, the carts were escorted on the trail to bring away the meat.

I rode back with Mr. McKenzie, who pointed out five cows which he had killed, and all of them selected as the fattest and sleekest of the herd. This astonishing feat was all

101

performed within the distance of one mile—all were killed at a full gallop, and every one shot through the heart. In the short space of time required for a horse under "full whip" to run the distance of one mile, he had discharged his gun five times and loaded it four times—selected his animals, and killed at every shot! * There were six or eight others killed at the same time, which altogether furnished, as will be seen, an abundance of freight for the carts. These as well as several packhorses, were loaded with the choicest parts which were cut from the animals, and the remainder of the carcasses were left for the wolves.

Such is the mode by which white men live in this country—such the way in which they get their food: at the hazard of every bone in one's body, to feel the fine and thrilling exhilaration of the chase for a moment, and then as often to upbraid and blame himself for his folly and imprudence.

From this scene we commenced leisurely wending our way back. Dismounting at the place we had stripped, each man dressed himself again, or slung his extra articles of dress across his saddle. We rode back to the Fort, reciting as we rode, and for twenty-four hours afterwards, deeds of chivalry and chase and hair's-breadth escapes that each and either had fought and run on former occasions. McKenzie, with all the true character and dignity of a leader, was silent on these subjects, but smiled while those in his train recited for him the astonishing and almost incredible deeds of his sinewy arms that they had witnessed. From them I learned (as well as from my own observations) that he was reputed (and actually *was)* the most distinguished of all the white men who have flourished in these regions, in the pursuit of the buffalo.

* Keep in mind these were muzzle-loaders.—Ed.

102

On our return to the Fort, a bottle of wine was set upon the table, and around it a half dozen parched throats were soon moistened, and good cheer ensued. Baptiste, Défonde, Chardon, and the rest retired to their quarters, enlarging smoothly upon the events of our morning's work to their wives and sweet-hearts. About this time the gate of the Fort was thrown open, and the procession of carts and packhorses laden with buffalo meat made its entrée, gladdening the hearts of a hundred women and children, and tickling the noses of as many hungry dogs and puppies, who were stealing in and smelling at the tail of the procession. The door of the ice-house was thrown open and the meat discharged into it. I, being fatigued, went asleep.

Wun-nes-tow, Blackfoot Medicine Man, performing his mysteries over the dying chief. See Plate V, following page 270.

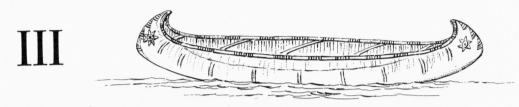

III

Mouth of the Yellow Stone,
Upper Missouri

ENCAMPED ABOUT the Fort is a host of wild, incongruous spirits: chiefs and sachems, warriors, braves, and women and children of different tribes—of Crows and Blackfeet, Ojibways, Assiniboins, and Crees or Knisteneaux. In the midst of them am I, with my paint-pots and canvas, snugly ensconced in one of the bastions of the Fort, which I occupy as a painting-room. My easel stands before me, and the cool breech of a twelve-pounder makes a comfortable seat—her muzzle looking out at one of the port-holes. The operations of my brush are *mysteries* of the highest order to these red sons of the prairie, and they all meet here to be amused and pay me signal honors, but I am sitting in the midst of inflammable and combustible materials, brought together, unarmed, for the first time in their lives.

While in the Fort, their weapons are placed within the arsenal. They are peaceably and calmly recounting the deeds of their lives, and smoking their pipes upon it; yet they gaze upon each other, sending sidelong glances of deep-rooted hatred and revenge around the group. Death and grim destruction will visit back those looks upon each other when these wild spirits again are free to act upon the plains, where the war-cry will be raised, and their deadly bows will again be drawn on each other.

I have this day been painting a portrait of the head chief of the Blackfoot nation. His name is Stu-mick-o-sucks (The Buffalo's Back Fat), that is, the "hump" or "fleece," the most delicious part of the buffalo's flesh. He is a good-looking and dignified Indian, about fifty years of age and superbly dressed. While sitting for his picture he has been surrounded by his own braves and warriors, and also gazed at by his enemies, the Crows and the Knisteneaux, Assiniboins and Ojibways. Distinguished personages of each of these tribes have laid all day around the sides of my room reciting to each other the battles they have fought, and pointing to the scalp-locks, worn as proofs of their victories and attached to the seams of their shirts and leggings.

The dress of Stu-mick-o-sucks consists of a shirt or tunic, made of two deer skins finely dressed and placed together with the necks of the skins downward. The skins of the hind legs are stitched together, the seams running down on each arm, from the neck to the knuckles of the hand. This seam is covered with a band two inches in width of very beautiful embroidery of porcupine quills. Suspended from the under edge of this, from the shoulders to the hands, is a fringe of black hair, which he has taken from the heads of victims slain by his own hand in battle.

The leggings are made of the same material; and down the outer side of the leg, from the hip to the feet, extends a similar band or belt of the same width, wrought in the same manner, with porcupine quills, and fringed with scalp-locks. The scalp, which is worn as a trophy, is procured by cutting out a piece of the skin of the head, the size of the palm of the hand or less, containing the very center or crown of the head, the place where the hair radiates from a point, and exactly over what the phrenologists call "self-esteem." This patch then is kept and dried with great care, as proof positive of the death of an enemy, and evidence of a man's claims as a warrior.

After having been formally "danced" (*i.e.,* after it has been stuck up upon a pole or held up by an "old woman," and the warriors have danced around it for two or three weeks at intervals, the scalp is fastened to the handle of a lance or the end of a war-club, or it is divided into a great many small locks and used to fringe and ornament the victor's dress. When these dresses are seen bearing such trophies, it is of course a difficult matter to purchase them of the Indian, for he often holds them above all price.

The wife (or squaw) of The Buffalo's Back Fat is Eeh-nis-kin (The Crystal Stone). Her countenance is rather pleasing, which is an uncommon thing among the Blackfeet. Her dress is also made of skins. She is the youngest of a bevy of six or eight wives, and the last one taken under his guardianship. He smiles upon her with great satisfaction, and exempts her from the drudgeries of the camp, keeping her continually in the halo of his own person as the apple of his eye.

The grandson of this sachem, a boy of six years of age, too young as yet to have acquired a name, stood like a tried warrior with his bow and quiver slung, and his robe of raccoon skin. His father is dead, and in case of the death of the chief, the boy becomes hereditary chief of the tribe. He has twice been stolen away by the Crows through ingenious stratagems, and twice recaptured by the Blackfeet, at considerable sacrifice to life. At present he is lodged with Mr. McKenzie for safe keeping and protection, until he shall arrive at the

106

Eeh-nis-kin, The Crystal Stone, wife of The Buffalo Bull's Back Fat.

proper age to take the office to which he is to succeed and be able to protect himself.

In the chief's dress, his moccasins are also made of buckskin, and ornamented. Over all is worn his robe, made of the skin of a young buffalo bull, with the hair remaining. On the inner or flesh side, beautifully garnished with porcupine quills, the battles of his life are ingeniously portrayed in pictorial representations.

In his hand he holds a very beautiful pipe, the stem of which is four or five feet long and two inches wide, curiously wound with braids of porcupine quills of various colors. The bowl of the pipe is ingeniously carved from a piece of red steatite of an interesting character, which they all tell me is procured somewhere between this place and the Falls of St. Anthony, on the head waters of the Mississippi.

This curious stone has many peculiar qualities, and has undoubtedly but one origin in this country, and perhaps in the world. It is found only in the hands of the Indian, and every tribe and nearly every individual in the tribe has his pipe made of it. I consider this stone a subject of great interest and curiosity, and I shall most assuredly make it a point, during my Indian rambles, to visit the place from whence it is brought. It seems, from all I can learn, that all the tribes in these regions, and also in the regions of the Mississippi and the Lakes, have been in the habit of going to that place, and meeting their enemies there, whom they are obliged to treat as friends, under an injunction of the Great Spirit.

There is an appearance purely classic in the stance and equipment of these warriors

107

The Eagle Ribs, his lance decorated with eight scalps taken from trappers and traders.

and "knights of the lance." They are almost always on their horses' backs, and they wield their weapons with desperate effect upon the open plains. They kill their game while at full speed, and contend in like manner in battles with their enemies. The plains afford them an abundance of wild and fleet horses, which are easily procured; and on their backs at full speed they can come alongside any animal and easily destroy it.

The bow with which they are armed is small, and apparently an insignificant weapon, though one of great and almost incredible power in the hands of its owner, whose sinews have been habituated to its use and service from childhood. The length of these bows is generally about three feet, and sometimes not more than two and a half. They have, no doubt, studied to get the requisite power in the smallest compass possible, as it is more easily and handily used on horseback than one of greater length. The greater number of these bows are made of ash, or of *bois d'arc* as the French call it, and lined on the back with layers of buffalo or deer's sinews, which give them great elasticity.

Among the Blackfeet and Crows many bows are made of bone, and others of the horns of the mountain-sheep. Those made of bones are decidedly the most valuable, and cannot be procured for less than the price of one or two horses. About these there is a mystery yet to be solved. I have procured several very fine specimens, and when purchasing them have inquired of the Indians what bone they were made of. In every instance the answer was, "That's medicine," meaning that it was a mystery to them, or that they did not wish to be questioned about them.

The bone is certainly not the bone of any animal now grazing on the prairies, or in the mountains between this place and the Pacific Ocean. Some of these bows are made of a solid piece of bone three feet in length, and as close-grained—as hard, as white, and as highly polished—as any ivory. It cannot be made from the elk's horn (as some have supposed), which is of a dark color and porous. Nor can it come from the buffalo. It is my opinion, therefore, that the Indians on the Pacific coast procure the bone from the jaw of the sperm whale, which is often stranded on that coast, and bring the bone into the mountains, trading it to the Blackfeet and Crows, who manufacture it into these bows without knowing any more than we do from what source it has been procured.

One of these little bows in the hands of an Indian is a most effective and powerful weapon in the open plains. No one can easily credit the force with which the arrows are thrown, and the effects produced by their wounds, until he has seen a party of Indians chasing a herd of buffaloes, and witnessed the grace with which their supple arms have drawn the bow, and seen the huge animals tumbling down, gushing out their hearts' blood from their mouths and nostrils.

Their arrows are headed with flints or with bones, of their own construction, or with steel now furnished by the fur traders. The quiver, which is uniformly carried on the back, is made of panther or otter skins. It is a magazine of these deadly weapons, and generally contains two varieties. The one to be drawn upon an enemy is generally poisoned, with long flukes or barbs. They are designed to hang the blade in the wound after the shaft is withdrawn. The other is used for their game, with the blade firmly fastened to the shaft and the flukes inverted so that it may easily be drawn from the wound and used on a future occasion.

Wun-nes-tow, The White Buffalo, Medicine Man, prophet, magician, soothsayer, and oracle.

Their horses are trained to approach the animals on the *right* side, enabling its rider to throw his arrows to the left. The horse runs and approaches without the use of a halter, which hangs loose upon its neck. The horse brings the rider within three or four paces of the animal, when the arrow is shot with great certainty to the heart. Instances sometimes occur where the arrow passes entirely through the animal's body.

An Indian, therefore, mounted on a fleet and well-trained horse, with his bow in his hand, and his quiver containing an hundred arrows slung on his back, of which he can throw fifteen or twenty in a minute, is a formidable and dangerous enemy. Many of them also ride with a lance of twelve to fourteen feet in length, with a blade of polished steel. All of them (as a protection for their vital parts) have a shield or arrow-fender made of the skin of the buffalo's neck, which has been smoked and hardened with glue extracted from the hoofs. These shields are arrow-proof, and will even glance off a rifle shot with perfect effect by being turned obliquely, which they do with great skill.

This shield or arrow-fender is, in my opinion, made of similar materials, and used in the same way and for the same purpose as was the clypcus or small shield in the Roman and Grecian cavalry. They were used in those days as a means of defense on horseback only—made small and light, of bull's hides—sometimes single, sometimes double and tripled. Such was Hector's shield, and of most of the Homeric heroes of the Greek and Trojan wars. In those days also darts or javelins and lances were used; the same were also used by the Ancient Britons; and such exactly are now used by the Arabs and the North American Indians.

"Medicine" is a great word in this country, and it is very necessary that one should know the meaning of it whilst he is scanning and estimating the Indian character, which is made up, in a great degree, of mysteries and superstitions. The word medicine, in its common acceptation here, means *mystery,* and nothing else.

The fur traders in this country are nearly all French. In their language, a doctor or physician is called *"Medicin."* The Indian country is full of doctors. They are all magicians, and skilled, or professed to be skilled, in many mysteries. The word "medicin" has become habitually applied to everything mysterious or unaccountable. The English and Americans, who also trade and pass through this country, have easily and familiarly adopted the same word, with a slight alteration, to convey the same meaning: "Medicine-men" means something more than merely a doctor or physician. Medicine-men are supposed to deal in mysteries and charms, which are aids and handmaids in their practice. Yet is was necessary to give the word or phrase a still more comprehensive meaning, as there were many personages among them, and also among the white men who visit the country, who could deal in mysteries, though not skilled in the application of drugs and medicines. All such men who deal in mysteries are included under the comprehensive and accommodating phrase of "medicine-men." For instance, I am a "medicine-man" of the highest order among these people, on account of the art which I practice, which is a strange and unaccountable thing to them, and of course called the greatest of "medicine." My gun and pistols, which have percussion-locks, are great medicine. No Indian can be prevailed on to fire them off, for they say they will have nothing to do with white man's medicine.

The Iron Horn, his medicine bag in his right hand.

The Woman Who Strikes Many, her dress of mountain goat's skin, her robe of buffalo.

The Indians do not use the word medicine, however. In each tribe they have a word of their own construction, synonymous with mystery or mystery-man.

The "medicine-bag," then, is a mystery-bag. Its meaning and importance must be understood, as it may be said to be the key to Indian life and Indian character. These bags are constructed of the skins of animals, of birds, or of reptiles, and ornamented and preserved in a thousand different ways, as suits the taste or freak of the person who constructs them. These skins are generally attached to some part of the clothing of the Indian, or carried in his hand. They are oftentimes decorated to be exceedingly ornamental to his person, and always are stuffed with grass, or moss, or something of the kind. Generally there are no drugs or medicines within them, as they are religiously closed and sealed, and seldom, if ever, to be opened. I find that every Indian in his primitive state carries his medicine-bag in some form or other, to which he pays the greatest homage, and to which he looks for safety and protection through life. Feasts are often made, and dogs and horses sacrificed, to a man's medicine. Days

112

and even weeks of fasting and penance of various kinds are often suffered to appease his medicine, which he imagines he has in some way offended.

This curious custom has principally been done away with along the frontier, where white men laugh at the Indian for the observance of so ridiculous and useless a form. But in this country, beyond the frontier, "medicine" is in full force, and every male in the tribe carries his supernatural charm or guardian, to which he looks for the preservation of his life, in battle or in other danger: It would be considered ominous bad luck and ill fate to be without it.

A boy, at the age of fourteen or fifteen years, is said to be "making or forming his medicine" when he wanders away from his father's lodge and absents himself for the space of two or three, and sometimes even four or five days. He lies on the ground in some remote or secluded spot, crying to the Great Spirit, and fasting the whole time. When he falls asleep during this period of peril and abstinence, the first animal, bird, or reptile of which he dreams (or pretends to have dreamed, perhaps) he considers having been designated by the Great Spirit as his mysterious protector through life. He then returns home to his father's lodge, and relates his success. After allaying his thirst and satiating his appetite, he sallies forth with weapons or traps until he can procure the animal or bird, the skin of which he preserves entire and ornaments according to his own fancy. He carries it with him through life for "good luck," as he calls it. It is his strength in battle—and in death his guardian *Spirit*. It is buried with him, and is to conduct him safe to the beautiful hunting grounds, which he contemplates in the world to come.

The value of the medicine-bag to the Indian is beyond all price. To sell it, or give it away, would subject him to such signal disgrace in his tribe that he could never rise above it. Again, his superstition would stand in the way of any such disposition of it, for he considers it the gift of the Great Spirit. An Indian carries his medicine-bag into battle, and trusts to it for his protection. If he loses it, he suffers a disgrace scarcely less than that which occurs in case he sells or gives it away. His enemy carries it off and displays it to his own people as a trophy, while the loser is cut short of the respect that is due young men of his tribe and forever subjected to the degrading epithet of "a man without medicine" or "he who has lost his medicine," until he can replace it again. This can only be done by rushing into battle and plundering one from an enemy whom he slays with his own hand. This done, his medicine is restored. He is then reinstated in the estimation of his tribe, and even higher than before, for such is called the best of medicine, or *"medicine honorable."*

It is a singular fact that a man can institute his mystery or medicine but once in his life—equally singular that he can reinstate himself by the adoption of the medicine of his enemy. Both of these regulations are strong and violent inducements for him to fight bravely in battle. The first, that he may protect and preserve his medicine; and the second, in case he has been so unlucky as to lose it, that he may restore it, and his reputation also, while he is desperately contending for the protection of his community.

During my travels thus far I have been unable to buy a medicine-bag of an Indian, although I have offered them extravagant prices. Even on the frontier, where they have been induced to abandon the practice, though a white man may induce an Indian to relinquish his medicine, yet he cannot *buy* it from him. The Indian in such cases will bury it to please a white man, but save it from his sacrilegious touch. He will linger around the spot and at regular times visit it and pay it his devotions, as long as he lives.

These curious appendages to the persons or wardrobe of an Indian are sometimes made of the skin of an otter, a beaver, a musk-rat, a weazel, a raccoon, a polecat, a snake, a frog, a toad, a bat, a mouse, a mole, a hawk, an eagle, a magpie, or a sparrow; sometimes of the skin of an animal so large as a wolf; and at others, of the skins of the lesser animals, so small that they are hidden under the dress, and very difficult to find even if searched for. Such then is the medicine-bag—such its meaning and importance. When its owner dies, it is placed in his grave and decays with his body.

Not many weeks ago, a party of Knisteneaux came here from the north, to make their summer's trade with the Fur Company. At the same time, a party of Blackfeet, their natural enemies, came from the west, also to trade. These two belligerent tribes encamped on different sides of the Fort, and spent some weeks here in the Fort and about it, in apparently good feeling and fellowship, unable in fact to act otherwise, for, according to a regulation of the Fort, their arms and weapons were all locked up by McKenzie in his "arsenal," for the purpose of preserving the peace among these fighting-cocks.

The Knisteneaux completed their trade but loitered about the premises until all, both Indians and white men, were tired of their company, wishing them quietly off. When they were ready to start, with their goods packed upon their backs, their arms were given them, and they started, bidding everybody, both friends and foes, a hearty farewell. They went out of the Fort, and though the party gradually moved off, one of them loitered about the Fort undiscovered until he got an opportunity to poke the muzzle of his gun through the piquets. Then he fired it at one of the chiefs of the Blackfeet, who stood within a few paces talking with Mr. McKenzie. The Blackfoot fell, and rolled about upon the ground in the agonies of death. The Blackfeet who were in the Fort seized their weapons and ran in a mass out of the Fort in pursuit of the Knisteneaux, who were rapidly retreating to the bluffs. The Frenchmen in the Fort, at so flagrant and cowardly an insult, seized their guns and ran out, joining the Blackfeet in the pursuit. I, at that moment, ran to my painting-room in one of the bastions overlooking the plain, where I had a fair view of the affair. Many shots were exchanged back and forth, and a skirmish ensued which lasted half an hour. The parties, however, were so far apart that little effect was produced. The Knisteneaux were driven off over the bluffs, having lost one man, with several others wounded.

The Blackfeet and Frenchmen returned to the Fort, and then I saw a "medicine-man" performing his mysteries over the dying chief. The man who had been shot was still living, though two bullets had passed through the center of his body about two inches apart from each other and no one could indulge the slightest hope of his recovery. Yet the medicine-man must be called, and the hocus-pocus applied to the dying man as the last resort, when all drugs and all specifics were useless, and after all possibility of recovery was extinct.

Medicine (or mystery) men are regularly called and paid as physicians to prescribe for the sick. Many of them acquire great skill in the medicinal world and gain much celebrity

114

in their nation. Their first prescriptions are roots and herbs, of which they have a great variety. When these have all failed, their last resort is to "medicine" or mystery. For this purpose, each one of them has a strange dress, conjured up and constructed during a life-time of practice, in the wildest fancy imaginable, in which he arrays himself, and makes his last visit to his dying patient—dancing over him, shaking his frightful rattles, and singing songs of incantation, in hopes of curing him by a charm. There are some instances, of course, where the exhausted patient unaccountably recovers under the application of these absurd forms. In such cases this ingenious son of Esculapius will be seen for several days after on the top of a wigwam, with his right hand extended and waving over the gaping multitude, to whom he is vaunting forth, without modesty, the surprising skill he has acquired in his art, and the undoubted efficacy of his medicine or mystery. But if, on the contrary, the patient dies, he soon changes his dress and joins in doleful lamentations with the mourners. With his craft and the ignorance and superstition of his people, he easily protects his reputation and maintains his influence by assuring them that it was the will of the Great Spirit that his patient should die.

Such was the case in the instance I am now relating. Several hundred spectators, including Indians and traders, were assembled around the dying man, when it was announced that the "medicine-man" was coming. We were required to "form a ring," leaving a space of some thirty or forty feet in diameter in which the doctor could perform his wonderful operations. A space was also opened to allow him ample room to pass through the crowd without touching anyone. This being done, his arrival was announced in a few moments by a death-like "hush——sh——" through the crowd. Nothing was to be heard save the light and casual tinkling of the rattles upon his dress, which was scarcely perceptible to the ear, as he cautiously and slowly moved through the avenue left for him, which at length brought him into the ring, in view of the pitiable object over whom his mysteries were to be performed.

His entrance and his garb were somewhat thus: He approached the ring with his body in a crouching position, with a slow and tilting step. His body and head were entirely covered with the skin of a yellow bear, the head of which (his own head being inside of it) served as a mask. The huge claws of the bear dangled on his wrists and ankles. In one hand he shook a frightful rattle, and in the other brandished his medicine-spear or magic wand. To the rattling din and discord of this, he added the wild and startling jumps and yelps of the Indian, and the horrid and appalling grunts and snarls and growls of the grizzly bear. With ejaculatory and guttural incantations to the Good and Bad Spirits in behalf of his patient, who was rolling and groaning in the agonies of death, he danced around him, jumping and pawing him about, and rolling him in every direction.

This strange operation proceeded for half an hour, to the surprise of a numerous and deathly silent audience, until the man died. The medicine-man danced off to his quarters, and packed up, tied, and secured from sight his mystery dress and equipments.

IV

Mouth of the Yellow Stone, *Upper Missouri*

I AM seated on the cool breech of a twelve-pounder and have before me my easel, and Crows, and Blackfeet, and Assiniboins whom I am tracing upon the canvas. My painting-room has become so great a lounge, and I so great a "medicine-man," that all other amusements are left, and all other topics of conversation and gossip are postponed for future consideration. The chiefs have had to place "soldiers" (as they are called) at my door, with spears in hand to protect me from the throng, who otherwise would press upon me. None but worthies are allowed to come into my medicine apartments, and none are to be painted except such as are decided by the chiefs to be worthy of so high an honor.

The Crows and Blackfeet who are here together are enemies of the most deadly kind while out on the plains; yet here they sit and smoke quietly together, with a studied and dignified reserve.

The Blackfeet are, perhaps, one of the most (if not entirely the most) numerous and warlike tribes on the Continent. They occupy the whole of the country about the sources of the Missouri, from Fort Union to the Rocky Mountains. Their numbers, from the best computations, are something like forty or fifty thousand. Like all other tribes whose numbers

117

◄
Crow: The Very Sweet Man.

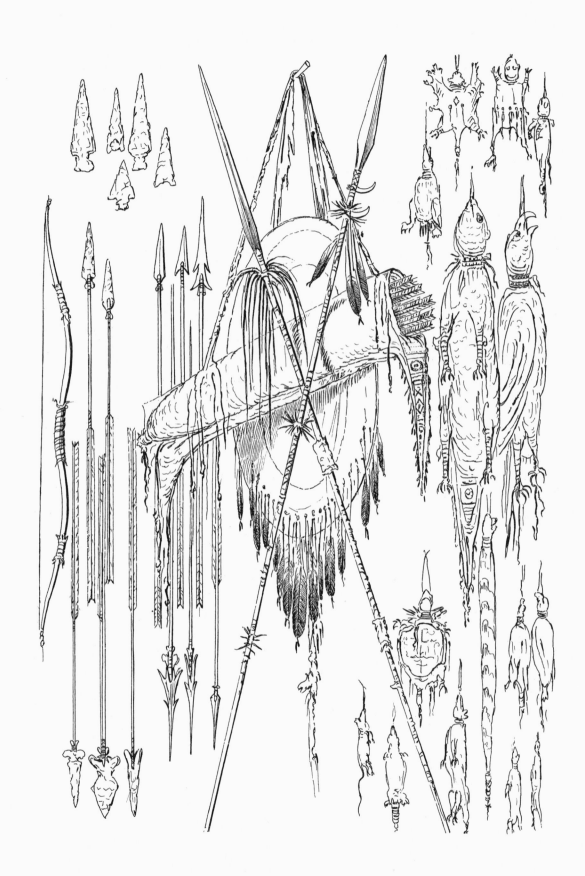

are sufficiently large to give them boldness, the Blackfeet are warlike and ferocious, *i.e.,* they are predatory, roaming fearlessly about the country and carrying war among their enemies, who are, of course, every tribe who inhabit the country about them.

The Crows who live on the head waters of Yellow Stone, and extend from this neighborhood also to the base of the Rocky Mountains, are similar to the Blackfeet: They roam about a great part of the year, seeking their enemies wherever they can find them. They are a much smaller tribe than the Blackfeet, with whom they are always at war and from whose great numbers they suffer prodigiously in battle, and in a few years probably will be entirely destroyed by them.

The Crows have not, perhaps, more than seven thousand in their nation, and probably not more than eight hundred warriors or fighting men. Among the more powerful tribes, like the Sioux and Blackfeet, who have been enabled to preserve their warriors, it is a fair calculation to count one in five as warriors. But among the Crows and Minatarees and Puncahs, and several other small but warlike tribes, this proportion cannot exist. In some of these I have found two or three women to a man in the nation in consequence of the continual losses sustained among their men in war.

The Blackfeet and the Crows, like the Sioux and Assiniboins, have nearly the same mode of constructing their wigwam or lodge. It is made of buffalo skins sewed together after being dressed, and made into the form of a tent; it is supported within by some twenty or thirty pine poles of twenty-five feet in height, with an apex or aperture at the top through which the smoke escapes and the light is admitted. These lodges, or tents, can be taken down in a few minutes by the squaws, when they wish to change their location, and are easily transported to any part of the country where they wish to encamp.

They generally move some six or eight times in the course of the summer, following the immense herds of buffaloes as they range over these vast plains, from east to west and north to south. The objects for which they do this are two-fold: to procure and dress their skins, which in the fall and winter are brought in and sold to the Fur Company for white men's luxury; and also to kill and dry buffalo meat, which they bring in from their hunts in great quantities, packed on horses' backs. They make pemican, and preserve the marrow-fat for their winter quarters.

Winter quarters are generally taken up in some heavy-timbered bottom, on the banks of some stream, deep imbedded within the surrounding bluffs, which break off the winds and make their long and tedious winter tolerable and supportable. They then sometimes erect their skin lodges among the timber and dwell in them during the winter months, but more frequently cut logs and make a miserable and rude sort of log cabin, in which they can live much warmer, and better protected from the assaults of their enemies. A log cabin is a tolerable fort against Indian weapons.

The Crows, of all the tribes of this region, or on the Continent, make the most beautiful lodges. They construct them as the Sioux do, and make them of the same material, yet they oftentimes dress the skins of which they are composed almost as white as linen and beautifully garnish them with porcupine quills, painting and ornamenting them in such a variety of ways as renders them exceedingly picturesque. Highly ornamented and fringed with scalp-locks, one of these lodges is sufficiently large for forty men to dine under. The poles that support it are about thirty in number, made of pine that is cut in the Rocky Mountains, and having been in use some hundred years, perhaps. When erected, the tent is about twenty-five feet high and has a very pleasing effect, with the Great or Good Spirit painted on one side, and the Evil Spirit on the other.

The manner in which Indians strike their tents and transport them is a novel and unexpected sight. I saw an encampment of Sioux, consisting of six hundred of these lodges, struck, and all things packed and on the move in a few minutes. The chief sends his runners or criers (for such work all chiefs keep criers in their employment) through the village, a few hours before they are to start, announcing his determination to move, and the hour fixed upon. At the time announced, the lodge of the chief is seen flapping in the wind, a part of the poles having been taken out from under it. This is the signal, and in one minute, six hundred tents, which have been strained tight and fixed, are seen waving and flapping in the wind. In one minute more all are flat upon the ground. Their horses and dogs, of which they have a vast number, have all been secured upon the spot, in readiness. Each one is speedily loaded with the burden allotted to it, ready to fall into the grand procession.

For this strange cavalcade, preparation is made in the following manner: The poles of a lodge are divided into two bunches, the little ends of each bunch fastened upon the shoulders or withers of a horse, leaving the butt ends to drag behind on the ground on either side. Just behind the horse, a brace or pole is tied across, which keeps the poles in their respective places. Then upon that the tent is placed, rolled up, as well as the other household and domestic furniture. On top of everything sit two, three, sometimes even four women with their children.

Each one of the horses has a conductress, with a tremendous pack upon her own back, who sometimes walks before and leads the horse, and at other times sits astride its back, with a child, perhaps at her breast and another behind her, clinging to her waist with one arm while affectionately embracing a sneaking dog-pup in the other.

In this way five or six hundred wigwams, with all their furniture, may be seen drawn out for miles, creeping over the grass-covered plains of this country. Three times that number of men, on good horses, stroll along in front or on the flank. In some tribes, at the rear of this heterogeneous caravan, at least five times that number of dogs falls into the rank, following in the train and company of the women. Every cur who is large enough, and not too cunning to be enslaved, is encumbered with a sled on which he patiently drags his load—a part of the household goods and furniture of the lodge to which he belongs. Two poles, about fifteen feet long, are placed upon the dog's shoulder, in the same manner as the lodge poles are attached to the horses, leaving the larger ends to drag upon the ground behind him. A bundle is allotted to him to carry, and with it he trots off amid the throng of dogs and squaws, faithfully and cheerfully dragging his load till night, and occasionally loitering by the way,

Catching at little bits of fun and glee,
That's played on dogs enslaved by dog that's free.

120

The Crows, like the Blackfeet, are beautifully costumed, and perhaps with somewhat more taste and elegance insasmuch as the skins of which their dresses are made are more delicately and whitely dressed. The art of dressing skins belongs to Indians of all countries, but the Crows surpass the civilized world in their skin-dressing.

The art of tanning is unknown to them. The usual mode of dressing the buffalo, and other skins, is by immersing them for a few days in a lye made from ashes and water, until the hair can be removed. Then they are strained upon a frame or upon the ground, with stakes or pins driven through the edges into the earth. They remain for several days, with the brains of buffalo or elk spread upon and over them. Lastly, it is finished by "graining," as it is termed. The squaws, who use a sharpened bone,—the shoulder-blade or other large bone of the animal, sharpened at the edge, somewhat like an adze—scrape the fleshy side of the skin, bearing on it with the weight of their bodies and thereby drying and softening the skin.

The greater part of these skins go through still another operation afterwards, which gives them a greater value and renders them much more serviceable—that is, the process of smoking. For this, a small hole is dug in the ground, and a fire is built in it with rotten wood, which will produce a great quantity of smoke without much blaze. Several small poles of the proper length are stuck in the ground around it and are drawn and fastened together at the top, around which a skin is wrapped in the form of a tent, and generally sewed together at the edges to secure the smoke within in. The skins to be smoked are placed within the tent to stand a day or so enclosed in the heated smoke. By some chemical process or other, which I do not understand, the skins thus acquire a quality which enables them, being ever so many times wet, always to dry soft and pliant. It is a secret I have never yet seen practiced in my own country; and for the lack of which, all of our dressed skins when once wet are, I think, chiefly ruined.

An Indian's dress of deer skins, which is wet a hundred times upon his back, dries soft. His lodge also, which stands in the rains and even through the severity of winter, is taken down as soft and as clean as when it was first put up.

A Crow is known wherever he is met by his tall and elegant figure—the greater part of the men being six feet high. The Blackfeet, on the other hand, are more of the Herculean make—about middling stature, with broad shoulders and great expansion of chest. The skins of their dresses are chiefly black or of a dark brown color. They have black leggings or moccasins, from which comes the name Blackfeet.

These people, to be sure, have in some instances plundered and robbed trappers and travellers in their country; and for that I have sometimes heard them called rascals and thieves, and rogues of the first order. Yet they do not consider themselves such. Thieving in their estimation is a high crime, and considered the most disgraceful act that a man can possibly do. They call this *capturing*, where they sometimes run off traders' horses, and make their boast of it, considering it a kind of retaliation or summary justice, which they think it right and honorable that they should administer. And why not? For unlicensed trespass is committed through their country from one end to the other, by mercenary white men who are destroying the game and taking all the beaver and other rich and valuable furs out of their country, without paying them an equivalent or, in fact, anything at all for it. And this too,

when they have been warned time and again of the danger they would be in if they longer persisted in the practice.

Mr. McKenzie has repeatedly told me, within the four last weeks while in conversation relative to the Crows, that they were friendly and honorable in their dealings with the whites, and that he considered them the finest Indians of his acquaintance.

I recollect hearing while in St. Louis that the Crows were a rascally and thieving set of vagabonds, highway robbers, etc. I have been told since that this story arose because they made some depredations upon the camp of Messrs. Crooks and Hunt of the Fur Company when they were passing through the Crow country on their way to Astoria, driving off a number of their horses. This was no doubt true. Equally true, they had good and sufficient reason for it.

Crooks and Hunt were crossing the Crow country with a large stock of goods, of guns and ammunition, of knives and spears and arrow-heads, etc. They stopped for some time and encamped in the midst of the Crow country, wintering there. The Crows assembled in large numbers about them, and treated them in a kind and friendly manner; at the same time the Crows proposed to trade with them for guns and ammunition, of which they were in great want, and for which they brought a great many horses, and offered them repeatedly in trade. The Fur Company men refused, persisting in their determination of carrying their goods to Oregon, thereby disappointing the Indians by denying them the arms and weapons which were in their possession. The Fur Company men were living upon them, and exhausting the game and food of their country. No doubt these gentlemen told the Crows these goods were going to Astoria, of which place the Crows knew nothing. Of course, it was enough for the Crows that the Fur Company men were going to take them farther west, which the Crows would at once suppose was to the Blackfeet, their principal enemy, having eight or ten warriors to one of the Crows. The Crows supposed the white men could get a greater price for their weapons, and arm their enemies in such a way as would enable them to turn upon the

Woman Who Lives in a Bear's Den,
her hair cut off in mourning.

Crows and cut them to pieces without mercy. Under these circumstances, the Crows rode off, and to show their indignation, drove off some of the Company's horses, for which they have ever since been denominated a band of thieves and highway robbers.

I observed the other day that many Crows have cultivated their natural hair to such an almost incredible length that it sweeps the ground as they walk. In some cases, a foot or more of it will drag on the grass as they walk, giving exceeding grace and beauty to their movements. They usually oil their hair with a profusion of bear's grease every morning, which no doubt is one cause of the unusual length to which their hair extends; though it cannot be the sole cause of it, for the other tribes throughout the country use bear's grease in equal profusion without producing the same results.

This extraordinary length of hair among the Crows is confined to the men alone. The women, though all of them have glossy and beautiful hair, and a great profusion of it, are unable to cultivate it to so great a length. Or else they are not allowed to compete with their lords in a fashion so ornamental (and on which the men so highly pride themselves), and are obliged in many cases to cut it short.

The fashion of long hair among the men prevails throughout all the Western and North Western tribes, except for the Sacs, the Foxes, and the Pawnees of the Platte, who, with only two or three other tribes, shave nearly the whole head.

The present chief of the Crows, called "Long-hair," received his name as well as his office from having the longest hair of any man in the nation. Messrs. Sublette and Campbell measured his hair by a correct means and found it to be ten feet and seven inches in length, closely inspecting every part of it at the same time, and satisfying themselves that it was the natural growth.

On ordinary occasions his hair is wound with a broad leather strap, from his head to its extreme end, then folded up into a budget or block of some ten or twelve inches in length, and of some pounds weight, which when he walks is carried under his arm or placed in his

123

Crow: The Four Wolves.

bosom within the folds of his robe. But on any great parade or similar occasion, his pride is to unfold it, oil it with bear's grease, and let it drag behind him, some three or four feet of it spread out upon the grass, and black and shining like a raven's wing.

It is a common custom among most of these upper tribes to splice or add on several lengths of hair by fastening them with glue, probably for the purpose of imitating the Crows, upon whom alone Nature has bestowed this conspicuous and signal ornament.

Among the Crows of distinction now at this place is Chah-ee-chopes (The Four Wolves), a fine-looking fellow, six feet in stature, whose natural hair sweeps the grass as he walks. He is beautifully clad, and carries himself with the most graceful and manly mien—he is in mourning for a brother. According to their custom, he has cut off a number of locks of his long hair, which is as much as a man can well spare of so valued an ornament he has been cultivating for the greater part of his life. A woman who mourns for a husband or child is obliged to crop her hair short to her head, and so remain till it grows out again, ceasing gradually to mourn as her hair approaches its former length.

The Crow women (and Blackfeet also) are not handsome, and I shall at present say but little of them. They are like all other Indian women, the slaves of their husbands, being obliged to perform all the domestic duties and drudgeries of the tribe, and not allowed to join in their religious rites or ceremonies, nor in the dance or other amusements.

The women in all these upper and western tribes are decently dressed, and many of them with great beauty and taste. Their dresses are all of deer or goat skins, extending from their chins quite down to the feet. The dresses are in many instances trimmed with ermine and ornamented with porcupine quills and beads used with exceeding ingenuity.

The Crow and Blackfeet women, like all others I ever saw in any Indian tribe, divide the hair on the forehead, and paint the separation or crease with vermilion or red earth. For what purpose this universal custom is observed, I never have been able to learn.

The men among the Blackfeet tribe have a fashion equally simple, and probably of as little meaning, which seems to be strictly adhered to by every man in the tribe. They

124

separate the hair in two places on the forehead, leaving a lock between the two an inch or two in width, which is carefully straightened down onto the bridge of the nose, and there cut square off. It is more than probable that this is done for the purpose of distinction; that they may thereby be free from the epithet of effeminacy, which might otherwise attach to them.

The Blackfeet are perhaps the most powerful tribe of Indians on the Continent. Being sensible of their strength, they have stubbornly resisted the traders in their country, who have been gradually forming an acquaintance with them and endeavoring to establish a permanent and profitable system of trade. Their country abounds in beaver and buffalo, and most of the fur-bearing animals of North America. The American Fur Company, with an unconquerable spirit of trade and enterprize, has pushed its establishments into their country. Numerous parties of trappers are tracing up their streams and rivers, rapidly destroying the beavers which dwell in them. The Blackfeet have repeatedly informed the traders of the Company that if their men persist in trapping beavers in Blackfeet country, the Blackfeet should kill them whenever they meet. They have executed their threats in many instances, and the Company loses some fifteen to twenty men annually at the hands of the Blackfeet in defense of what they deem their property and their rights. Trinkets and whisky, however, will soon spread their charms among these, as they have among other tribes; and white man's voracity will sweep the prairies and the streams of their wealth, to the Rocky Mountains and the Pacific Ocean, leaving the Indians to inhabit, and at last to starve upon, the dreary and solitary waste.

Besides the Blackfeet and Crows assembled at Fort Union, there are also the Knisteneaux (or Crees, as they are commonly called), a very pretty and pleasing tribe of Indians of about three thousand in number, living north of here; also there are the Assiniboins and Ojibways, both of which tribes also inhabit the country to the north and north-east of the mouth of the Yellow Stone.

The Knisteneaux are of small stature, but well-built for strength and activity combined. They are a people of wonderful prowess for their numbers, and have waged an unceasing warfare with the Blackfeet, who are their neighbors and enemies on the west. Because of the disparity in numbers, the Knisteneaux are rapidly thinning the ranks of their warriors, who bravely sacrifice their lives in contentions with their powerful neighbors. This tribe occupies the country from the mouth of the Yellow Stone, in a north-western direction, far into the British territory, and trades principally at the British N. W. Company's Posts.

The Assiniboins of seven thousand, and the Objibways of six thousand, occupy a vast extent of country in a north-eastern direction from this, extending also into the British possessions as far north as Lake Winnepeg and trading principally with the British Company. These three tribes are in a state of nature, living as neighbors, and are also on terms of friendship with each other. This friendship, however, is probably but a temporary arrangement brought about by the traders among them, which, like most Indian peace establishments, will be of short duration.

The Objibways are undoubtedly a part of the tribe of Chippewas with whom we are more familiarly acquainted, who inhabit the south-west shore of Lake Superior. Their language is the same, though they are separated by several hundred miles from any of them, and seem to have no knowledge of them, or traditions of the manner in which, or of the time when, they became severed from each other.

The Assiniboins are undoubtedly a part of the Dahcotas, or Sioux, for their personal appearance as well as their language is very similar.

At what time, or in what manner, these two parts of a nation strayed away from each other is a mystery, yet such cases have often occurred. Large parties, straying off in pursuit of game or in the occupation of war, are oftentimes intercepted by their enemy; and, being prevented from returning, are run off to a distant region where they take up their residence and establish themselves as a nation.

There is a very curious custom among the Assiniboins, from which they have taken their name, a name given them by their neighbors, from a singular mode they have of boiling their meat. It is done in the following manner: When they kill meat, a hole is dug in the ground about the size of a common pot, and a piece of the raw hide of the animal, taken from the back is put over the hole, then pressed down with the hands close around the sides, and filled with water. The meat to be boiled is then put in this hole or pot of water. In a fire that is built near by, several large stones are heated to a red heat, then successively dipped and held in the water until the meat is boiled. From this singular and peculiar custom, the Ojibways have given them the appellation of Assiniboins, or stone boilers. This custom is a very awkward and tedious one, used as an ingenious means of boiling their meat only by a tribe that was too rude and ignorant to construct a kettle or pot.

The traders have recently supplied these people with pots, but long before that, the Mandans had instructed them in the secret of manufacturing very good and serviceable earthen pots, which together have entirely done away with the custom, excepting at public festivals, where they seem, like all others of the human family, to take pleasure in cherishing and perpetuating their ancient customs.

The Assiniboins, or stone boilers, are a fine and noble-looking race of Indians. The men are tall and graceful in their movements, and wear their pictured robes of buffalo hide with great skill and pleasing effect. They are good hunters, and tolerably supplied with horses. They live in a country abounding with buffalo, are well supplied with the necessaries of Indian life, and may be said to live well. Their games and amusements are many, of which the most valued one is the ball-play. In addition, they have the game of the moccasin, horse-racing, and dancing, some one of which they seem to be almost continually practicing.

The Assiniboins, somewhat like the Crows, cultivate their hair to a very great length, in many instances reaching nearly to the ground. But in most instances of this kind, I find the great length is produced by splicing or adding on several lengths, which are fastened very ingeniously by means of glue. The joints are obscured by a sort of paste of red earth and glue with which the hair, at intervals of every two or three inches, is filled, then divided into locks and slabs of an inch or so in breadth falling straight down over the back to the heels.

I have painted the portrait of a very distinguished young man, son of the chief of the Assiniboins, Wi-jun-jon (The Pigeon's Egg Head), about whom is told an amazing but melancholy story.

Wi-jun-jon, The Pigeon's Egg Head, going to and returning from Washington. See Plate VI, following page 270.

Wi-jun-jon was a brave and a warrior of the Assiniboins—young—proud—handsome—valiant—graceful. He had fought many a battle and won many a laurel. The numerous scalps from his enemies' heads adorned his dress, and his claims were fair and just for the highest honors that his country could bestow upon him, for his father was chief of the nation.

This young Assiniboin was selected by Major Sanford, the Indian agent, to represent his tribe in a delegation which visited Washington City in the winter of 1831. The Pigeon's Egg Head, together with representatives from several other North Western tribes, descended the Missouri River, several thousand miles, with Major Sanford on their way to Washington.

While descending the river in a Mackinaw boat from the mouth of Yellow Stone, Wi-jun-jon and another of his tribe who was with him, at the first approach of the civilized settlements, commenced a register of the white men's houses (or cabins), by cutting a notch for each on the side of a pipe-stem, in order to be able to show when they got home how many white men's houses they saw on their journey. At first the cabins were scarce, but as they advanced down the river, more and more rapidly increased in numbers. They soon found their pipe-stem filled with marks. They determined to put the rest of them on the handle of a war-club, which they soon marked all over likewise. At length, while the boat was moored at the shore for the purpose of cooking the dinner of the party, Wi-jun-jon and his companion stepped into the bushes and cut a long stick, from which they peeled the bark. When the boat was again underway, they sat down and, with much labor, copied the notches onto it from the pipe-stem and club; and also kept adding a notch for every house they passed. This stick was soon filled, and in a day or two several others. They seemed much at a loss to know what to do with their troublesome records, until they came in sight of St. Louis, which is a town of seven thousand inhabitants. After consulting a little, they pitched their sticks overboard into the river.

I was in St. Louis at the time of their arrival and painted their portraits. Wi-jun-jon was the first who reluctantly yielded to the solicitations of the Indian agent and myself. He appeared as sullen as death in my painting-room, with eyes fixed like those of a statue. In his nature's uncowering pride he stood a perfect model; but superstition had hung a lingering curve upon his lip, and pride had stiffened it into contempt. He had been urged into a measure against which his fears had pleaded. Yet he stood unmoved and unflinching amid the mysteries that were hovering about him, foreboding ills of every kind, and misfortunes that were to happen to him in consequence of his travels.

He returned from Washington City, still with Major Sanford, in 1832. His return to his own people, in the dress and with the airs of a civilized beau, was one of no ordinary occurrence, and produced a sensation among his tribe, the Assiniboin.

I saw him step ashore (on a beautiful prairie, where several thousand of his people were encamped) in a full suit of regimentals, "en militaire!" It was, perhaps, presented to him in Washington City by the President. It was a colonel's uniform of the finest blue broadcloth trimmed with gold lace. On his shoulders were mounted two immense epaulets. His neck was strangled with a shining black stock and his feet were pinioned in a pair of water-proof boots with high heels, which made him "step like a yoked hog."

128

On his head was a high-crowned beaver hat with a broad silver lace band surmounted by a huge red feather some two feet high. His coat collar, stiff with lace, came higher up than his ears, and over it flowed, down towards his haunches, his long Indian locks, stuck up in rolls and plaits with red paint.

A large silver medal was suspended from his neck by a blue ribbon. And across his right shoulder passed a wide belt, supporting by his side a broad sword. On his hands he had drawn a pair of white gloves, and he held a blue umbrella in one and a large fan in the other. In this fashion was poor Wi-jun-jon metamorphosed on his return from Washington. He had a keg of whisky with him.

According to Major Sanford, Wi-jun-jon, on his extraordinary voyage, had been the foremost on all occasions: The first to enter the levee, the first to shake President Jackson's hand and make his speech to him, the last to extend the hand on leaving the company of the curious white man but the first to catch the smiles and admiration of the gentler sex. He travelled the giddy maze, and beheld amid the buzzing din of civil life their tricks of art, their handiworks, and their finery. He visited their principal cities. He saw their forts, their ships, great guns, their steamboats and balloons. In the spring he was returned to St. Louis, and from there the two thousand miles to the mouth of Yellow Stone and his people.

In his blue colonel's uniform, with his umbrella and his fan, and with the keg of whisky under his arm, he took up a position on the bank among his friends—his wife and other relations. Not one of them exhibited the least symptoms of recognition, although they knew well who was before them.

He also gazed upon them—upon his wife and parents, and little children, who were about, as if they were foreign to him, and as if he had not a feeling or thought to interchange with them. Thus the mutual gazings upon and from this would-be stranger lasted for full half an hour. Then a gradual, but cold and exceedingly formal, recognition began to take place, and an acquaintance ensued, which ultimately and smoothly resolved itself, without the least apparent emotion. The mutual kindred intercourse seemed to flow on exactly where it had been broken off, as if it had been but for a moment and nothing had transpired in the interim to check or change its character or expression.

This man created a wonderful sensation among his tribe, who daily and nightly gathered in gaping and listless crowds around him while he lectured upon what he had seen in the fashionable world, which to them was unintelligible and beyond their comprehension. They began to set him down as a liar and impostor.

"He has been," they said, "among the whites, who are great liars, and all he has learned is to come home and tell lies."

He sank rapidly into disgrace in his tribe, and his high claims to political eminence all vanished. He was reputed worthless—the greatest liar of his nation—and the chiefs shunned him and passed him by as one of the tribe who was lost. Yet the ears of the gossiping portion of the tribe were open, and the camp-fire circle and the wigwam fireside gave silent audience to the whispered narratives of the "travelled Indian."

The day after he arrived among his friends, the superfluous part of his coat (which was a laced frock) was converted into a pair of leggings for his wife. His hat-band of silver lace

The Fire Bug That Creeps,
wife of Wi-jun-jon.

furnished her a magnificent pair of garters. The remainder of the coat, curtailed of its original length, was seen buttoned upon the shoulders of his brother, over and above a pair of leggings of buckskin. Wi-jun-jon paraded about among his gaping friends with a bow and quiver slung over his shoulders, exhibiting a fine linen shirt with studs and sleeve buttons. His broad-sword kept its place, but about noon, his boots gave way to a pair of garnished moccasins. He gossiped away the day among his friends, while his heart spoke so freely and so effectually from the bung-hole of a little keg of whisky that he had brought the whole way (as one of the choicest presents made him at Washington) that his tongue became silent.

One of his little fair enamoratas, or "catch crumbs," such as live in the halo of all great men, fixed her eyes and her affections upon his beautiful silk braces, and the next day, while the keg was yet dealing out its kindnesses, he was seen paying visits to the lodges of his old acquaintances, swaggering about with his keg under his arm, whistling "Yankee Doodle" and "Washington's Grand March." His white shirt, or that part of it that had been flapping in the wind, had been shockingly tithed. His pantaloons of blue, laced with gold, were razed into a pair of comfortable leggings. His bow and quiver were slung, and his broad-sword which trailed on the ground had taken a position between his legs and, dragging behind him, served as a rudder to steer him over the earth's troubled surface.

Two days' revel of this kind had drawn from his keg all its charms. In the mellowness of his heart, all his finery had vanished, and all of its appendages, except his umbrella, to which his heart's strongest affections still clung, and with it, and under it, in rude dress of buckskin, he was afterwards to be seen acting the fop and the beau, as well as he could with his limited means.

In this dress, with his umbrella always in his hand (as the only remaining evidence of his *quondam* greatness), he began in his sober moments to entertain and instruct his people, by honest and simple narratives of things and scenes he had beheld during his tour of the East; but which (unfortunately for him) were to them too marvellous and improbable to be believed.

He told the gaping multitude constantly gathered about him of the distance he had

130

travelled—of the astonishing number of houses he had seen—of the towns and cities, with all their wealth and splendour—of travelling on steamboats, in stages, and on railroads. He described our forts, and seventy-four-gun ships, which he had visited—their big guns—our great bridges—our great council-house in Washington, and its doings—the curious and wonderful machines in the patent office (which he pronounced the *greatest medicine place* he had seen). He described the great war parade, which he saw in the city of New York—the ascent of the balloon from Castle Garden—numbers of white people, the beauty of the white squaws—their red cheeks; and many thousands of other things, all of which were so much beyond their comprehension that they "could not be true" and he must be "the greatest liar in the whole world." Most unfortunately for this poor fellow, the other man of his tribe who had travelled with him and could have borne testimony to the truth of his statements, died of the quinsy on his way home.

But Wi-jun-jon was beginning to acquire a reputation of a different kind. He was denominated a *medicine-man,* and one, too, of the most extraordinary character. They deemed him far above the ordinary sort of human beings because his mind could invent and conjure up for their amusement such ingenious fabrication of novelty and wonder. He had an exhaustless theme to descant upon through the remainder of his life; and he seemed satisfied to lecture all his life, for the pleasure which it gave him.

So great was his medicine, however, that they began to look upon him as a most extraordinary being, and the customary honors and forms began to be applied to him, and respect be shown him, which belongs to all men in Indian country who are distinguished for their medicine or mysteries. In short, when all became familiar with the astonishing representations that he made and with the wonderful alacrity with which "he created them," he was denominated the very greatest of medicine; and not only that, but the "lying medicine."

His medicine became so alarmingly great they were unwilling he should live. They were disposed to kill him for a wizard. One of the young men of the tribe took the duty upon himself, and after much perplexity, hit upon the following plan: He had fully resolved, in conjunction with others who were in the conspiracy, that the medicine of Wi-jun-jon was too great for the ordinary mode, and that he was so great a liar that a rifle bullet would not kill him. While the young man was in this distressing dilemma, which lasted for some weeks, he had a dream one night, which solved all difficulties. He loitered about the store in the Fort, at the mouth of the Yellow Stone, until he could procure, *by stealth* (according to the injunction of his dream) the handle of an iron pot, which he supposed to possess the requisite virtue. Taking it into the woods, he there spent a whole day in straightening and filing it to fit into the barrel of his gun; after which, he made his appearance again in the Fort, with his gun under his robe, charged with the pot handle. Getting behind poor Wi-jun-jon while he was talking with the Trader, he placed the muzzle behind Wi-jun-jon's head and blew out his brains!

Thus ended the days, and the greatness, and all the pride and hopes of Wi-jun-jon, The Pigeon's Egg Head—a warrior and a brave of the valiant Assiniboins, who travelled eight thousand miles to see the President, and all the great cities of the civilized world. And who, for telling the truth, and nothing but the truth, was disgraced and killed as a wizard.

"The Brick Kilns," clay bluffs, 1900 miles above St. Louis.

V
Upper Missouri

SOON AFTER the writing of my last Letter, which was dated at the Mouth of Yellow Stone, I embarked on the river with Jean Baptiste and Abraham Bogard as travelling companions. When Baptiste and Bogard had taken their last spree, and fought their last battles, and forgotten them in the final and affectionate embrace and farewell, all of which are habitual with these game-fellows, when settling up long-standing accounts with their fellow-trappers of the mountain streams; and after Mr. McKenzie had procured for me a canoe to waft us down the mighty torrent, we launched off one fine morning, taking our leave of Fort Union.

Our canoe, which was made of green timber, was heavy and awkward, but our course being with the current promised us a fair and successful voyage. Ammunition was laid in, a good stock of dried buffalo tongues, a dozen or two of beavers' tails, and a good supply of pemican. Bogard and Baptiste occupied the middle and bow, with their paddles in their hands. I took my seat in the stern of the boat, at the steering oar.

Besides ourselves, our little craft carried several packs of Indian dresses and other articles, which I had purchased of the Indians. Also my canvas and easel, and our culinary

articles, which were few and simple, consisting of three tin cups, a coffee-pot, one plate, a frying pan, and a tin kettle.

Thus fitted out and embarked, we swept off at a rapid rate under the shouts of the savages and the cheers of our friends, who lined the banks as we gradually lost sight of them, and turned our eyes towards St. Louis, which was two thousand miles below us, with nought intervening save the wide-spread and wild regions inhabited by the roaming Indians.

We rapidly made our way down the river—the rate of the current being four or five miles per hour—through one continued series of picturesque grass-covered bluffs and knolls, which everywhere had the appearance of an old and highly cultivated country, with houses and fences removed.

Much of the way, a bold and abrupt precipice three or four hundred feet high slopes down from the level of the prairies above, which sweep off from the brink of the precipice, almost level, to an unknown distance. It is along the rugged fronts of these cliffs, whose sides are formed of hard clay, that the mountain-sheep dwell in great numbers. Their habits are much like those of the goat, which they resemble except in the horns, which resemble those of the ram, sometimes making two entire circles in their coil. At the roots, each horn is from five to six inches in breadth.

On the second day of our voyage we discovered a number of these animals skipping along the sides of the precipice, always keeping about equidistant between the top and bottom of the ledge. We landed our canoe and endeavored to shoot one. After he had led us a long and fruitless chase through the cliffs, we thought we had fairly entrapped him, when he suddenly bounded from his narrow foothold on the ledge and tumbled down a distance of more than a hundred feet, among the fragments of rocks and clay, where I thought we must certainly find his carcass without further trouble. Then to my great surprise, I saw him bounding off and out of sight.

Bogard, who was an old hunter and well acquainted with these creatures, shouldered his rifle and said to me: "Now you see the use of those big horns; when they fall by accident, they fall upon their head unharmed, even though they fall on the solid rock."

Part of our labors were vainly spent in the pursuit of a war-eagle. This noble bird is the one the Indians value so highly for their tail feathers, which are the most valued plumes for decorating the heads and dresses of their warriors. It is a beautiful bird and, the Indians tell

134

me, conquers all other varieties of eagles in the country. It has often been called the calumet eagle and war-eagle from the fact that the Indians almost invariably ornament the calumets or pipes of peace with its quills.

Our day's loitering brought us through many a wild scene. We crossed the tracks of a grizzly bear and saw a band of buffaloes "which got wind of us," leaving us to return to our canoe at night, with a mere speck of good luck. Just before we reached the river, I heard the crack of a rifle, and in a few moments Bogard came in sight and threw down from his shoulders a fine antelope which added to our larder. We were ready to proceed.

We embarked and travelled until nightfall, when we encamped on a beautiful little prairie at the base of a series of grass-covered bluffs. The next morning we cooked our breakfast and ate it, then rowed on until late in the afternoon, when we stopped at the base of some huge clay bluffs forming one of the most curious and romantic scenes imaginable. At this spot the river expands itself into the appearance somewhat of a beautiful lake. In the midst of it, and on and about its sand-bars, floated and stood hundreds and thousands of white swans and pelicans.

The whole country behind us seemed to have been dug and thrown up into huge piles, as if some giant mason had been there mixing his mortar and paints and throwing together his rude models for some sublime structure of a colossal city; with its walls, its domes, its ramparts, its huge porticoes and galleries, its castles, its fosses and ditches. In the midst of his progress, he had abandoned his works to the destroying hand of time, which had already done much to tumble them down and deface their noble structure by jostling them together, with all their vivid colors, into an unsystematic and unintelligible mass of sublime ruins. To this group of clay bluffs, which line the river for many miles, the voyageurs have very appropriately given the name of "the Brick-kilns."

During the day that I loitered about this strange scene, I left my men stretched upon the grass by the canoe. Taking my rifle and sketch-book in my hand, I wandered and clambered through the rugged defiles between the bluffs.

Most of that time, Bogard and Baptiste laid enjoying the pleasure of a "mountaineer's nap." We met together, took our coffee and dried buffalo tongues, spread our buffalo robes upon the grass, and enjoyed during the night the sleep that belongs to the tired voyageur in these realms of pure air and dead silence.

In the morning, and before sunrise, as usual, Bogard (who was a Yankee, and a "wide-awake-fellow," just retiring from a ten years' siege of hunting and trapping in the Rocky Mountains) thrust his head out from under the robe, rubbed his eyes open, and exclaimed as he grabbed for his gun: "By darn, look at old Cale! will you!" Baptiste, who was more fond of his dreams, snored away, muttering something that I could not understand. Bogard seized him with a grip that instantly shook off his iron slumbers. I rose at the same time, and all eyes were turned at once upon *Caleb* (as the grizzly bear is called by the trappers in the Rocky Mountains—or more often "Cale," for brevity's sake), who was sitting up in the dignity and fury of her sex a few yards away, gazing upon us with her two little cubs at her side.

I turned my eyes to the canoe fastened at the shore a few paces from us. Everything had been pawed out of it, and all eatables had been devoured. My packages of dresses and Indian curiosities had been drawn out upon the bank and deliberately opened and inspected. Everything had been scraped and pawed out from the bottom of the boat; even the rawhide thong, with which it was tied to a stake, had been chewed. There was no trace of it remaining. Nor was this peep into our luggage enough for her insatiable curiosity—we saw by the prints of her huge paws that she had been perambulating our humble mattresses, smelling at our toes and our noses, without choosing to molest us; verifying a trite saying of the country: "Man lying down is *medicine* to the grizzly bear"; though it is well-known that man and beast, upon their feet, are sure to be attacked.

I proposed a mode of attack. But Bogard and Baptiste both remonstrated vehemently, saying that the standing rule in the mountains was "never to fight Caleb, except in self-defense."

Baptiste suddenly thrust his arm over my shoulder and, pointing in another direction, exclaimed in an emphatic tone, "Voilà! voilà un corps de reserve—Monsr. Catline—voilà son mari! allons—allons! déscendons la riviére, toute de suite! toute de suite! Monsr.," to which Bogard added, "These darned animals are too much for us, and we had better be off." At which my courage cooled.

We packed up and re-embarked as fast as possible, firing our rifles as we drifted off in the current, which brought the she-monster, in all her rage and fury, to the spot where we, a few moments before, had passed our most prudent resolve.

During the rest of this day we passed on rapidly, gazing upon and admiring the beautiful shores, which were continually changing, from the high and ragged cliffs to the graceful and green slopes of the prairie bluffs, and then to the wide expanded meadows with their long waving grass enamelled with myriads of wild flowers.

The scene was one of enchantment the whole way; our chief conversation was about grizzly bears and hair's-breadth escapes; of the histories of which my companions had volumes in store.

Baptiste explained he was in the employment of the American Fur Company as a free trapper: "I am enlist for tree year in de Fur Comp in St. Louis—for a bounty, vous comprenez, ha?—eighty dollars.

"I ave come up de Missouri, et I am trap beavare putty much for six years, for wages you see, until I am learn very much. Den you see, Monsr. McKenzie is give me tree horse: one pour ride et two pour pack. He is not sell them to me, he is lend them. And he is lend me twelve traps.

"Then I ave make start into de Rocky Montaigne, et I am live all alone on de leetle rivares to trap les beavares—for sometimes six months, sometimes five months each year, and I come back to Yellow Stone, et Monsr. McKenzie is give me one dollare pour one beavare. One dollare per skin.

"If it not pour de dam Riccaree, et de dam Pieds noirs, de Blackfoot Injun, I am make very much money. But I am rob—rob—rob too much, I suppose five time. I am been free trappare seven year, et I am rob five time. Take all de horse. Take my gun. Take all my clothes. Take all de beavare, et I come back on foot.

"Whisky in de fort is sixteen dollares pour gallon. Some clothes is cost putty much money. And I owe Monsr. McKenzie pour de horse and de traps; so you see I am owe de Fur Comp six hundred dollare, by Gar! That is what is call being a free trapper, n'est-ce pas?"

We plied the paddles and proceeded several miles farther, eventually dragging our canoe to the shore in the dark in a wild spot. Then spreading our robes for our slumbers, we slept away from our fires, because they might lead a war-party upon us.

On the morning of the next day, not long after we had stopped and taken our breakfast, and while our canoe was swiftly gliding along under the shore of a beautiful prairie, I saw in the grass, on the bank above me, what I supposed to be the back of a fine elk, busy at his grazing. I left our craft float silently by for a little distance and slyly ran in to the shore. I pricked the priming of my fire-lock, and taking a bullet or two in my mouth, stepped ashore, and trailing my rifle in my hand, went back under the bank, carefully crawling up in a little ravine, quite sure of my game. Then to my utter surprise, I found the elk to be no more nor less than an Indian pony, getting his breakfast! A little beyond him, a number of others were grazing. Near me, on the left, a war-party was reclining around a little fire. And within twenty paces of the muzzle of my gun, the naked shoulders of a brawny Indian, who seemed busily engaged in cleaning his gun.

From this critical dilemma, I vanished with all the secrecy possible, bending my course towards my canoe. Bogard and Baptiste correctly construing the expression of my face, and the agitation of my hurried retreat, prematurely unmoored from the shore. The force of the current carried them around a huge pile of drift wood, leaving me to my own resources.

They finally got in, near the shore, and I into the boat. We plied our sinews in silence till we were wafted far from the ground which we deemed dangerous to our lives. We had been daily in dread of meeting a war-party of the revengeful Riccarees, which we had been told was on the river in search of the Mandans. After this exciting occurrence, the entries in my journal for the rest of the voyage to the village of the Mandans were as follows:

Saturday, fifth day of our voyage from the mouth of Yellow Stone, at eleven o'clock. Landed our canoe in the Grand Détour (or Big Bend) as it is called, at the base of a stately clay mound, and ascended, all hands, to the summit level, to take a glance at the magnificent works of Nature that were about us. Spent the remainder of the day in painting a view of this grand scene, for which purpose Baptiste and Bogard carried my easel and canvas to the top of a huge mound, where they left me at my work. I painted my picture while they amused themselves with their rifles, decoying a flock of antelopes, of which they killed several, and abundantly adding to the stock of our provisions.

The mode by which Bogard and Baptiste had been entrapping the timid antelopes was one which is frequently and successfully practiced in this country. This little animal seems to be endowed, like many other gentle and sweet-breathing creatures, with an undue share of curiosity, which often leads them to destruction. The hunter who wishes to entrap them saves himself the trouble of travelling after them. He has only to elevate above the top of the grass a red or yellow handkerchief on the end of his gun-rod, which he sticks in the ground, and to which they are sure to advance, though with great coyness and caution, while he lies close with rifle in hand. Then it is quite an easy matter to make sure of two or three at a shot.

On Sunday, we departed from our encampment in the Grand Détour, and having passed for many miles through a series of winding and ever-varying bluffs and fancied ruins, like those already described, we arrived before "the Grand Dome." Our canoe was here hauled ashore, and a day whiled away again among these clay-built ruins.

We clambered to their summits and enjoyed the distant view of the Missouri for many miles below, wending its way through the countless groups of clay- and grass-covered hills. We wandered back on the plains in an unsuccessful pursuit of a herd of buffaloes. Though we were disappointed, we were repaid in amusements, which we found in paying a visit to an extensive village of prairie dogs.

The prairie dog of the American prairies is undoubtedly a variety of the marmot, probably not unlike those which inhabit the vast steppes of Asia. It bears no resemblance to any variety of dog, except in the sound of its voice, which when excited by the approach of danger, is something like that of a very small dog, and still much more resembling the barking of a gray squirrel.

The size of these curious little animals is not far from that of a very large rat, and they are not unlike in their appearance. Their burrows are uniformly built in a lonely desert, away from the proximity of both timber and water. Each individual, or each family, digs its hole in the prairie to the depth of eight or ten feet, throwing up the dirt from each excavation in a little pile, in the form of a cone, which forms the only elevation for them to ascend. There they sit, to bark and chatter when an enemy is approaching their village. These villages are sometimes several miles in extent, containing myriads of their excavations and little dirt hillocks. To the ears of visitors, the din of their barkings is too confused and too peculiar to be described.

We made many endeavors to shoot them, but found our efforts to be in vain. As we were approaching them, each one seemed to be perched up on his hind feet on his appropriate domicile, with a significant jerk of his tail at every bark, positively disputing our right of

138

Prairie dog village.

approach. I made several attempts to get near enough to "draw a bead" upon one of them. Just before I was ready to fire (and as if they knew the utmost limits of their safety), they sprang down into their holes, and instantly turning their bodies, showed their ears and the ends of their noses as they peeped out at me. They would hold that position until the shortness of the distance subjected their scalps to danger again. Then from the aim of my rifle they instantly disappeared from sight, and all was silence thereafter about their premises as I passed over them. When I had advanced by them, their ears were again discovered, and at length themselves, at full length, perched on the tops of their little hillocks and threatening as before, thus gradually sinking and rising like a wave before and behind me.

Their food is simply the grass in the immediate vicinity of their burrows, which is cut close to the ground by their flat, shovel teeth. As they sometimes live twenty miles from any water, it is supposed they get moisture enough from the dew on the grass, on which they feed chiefly at night. Or, they sink wells from their under-ground habitations, by which they descend low enough to get their supply. In the winter, they are for several months invisible; existing, undoubtedly, in a torpid state, as they certainly lay by no food for that season, nor can they procure any. These curious little animals belong to almost every latitude in the vast plains of prairie in North America, and their villages compel a party to ride several miles out of its way to get by them, for their burrows are generally within a few feet of each other, and dangerous to the feet and limbs of horses.

On Monday, the seventh day from the mouth of the Yellow Stone River, we floated away from the prairie village. But at every bend and turn in the stream we were introduced to other scenes—and others—and yet others, almost as strange and curious. Just before night, we landed our little boat in front of the Mandan village. Among the hundreds and thousands who flocked towards the river to meet and to greet us was Mr. James Kipp, the agent of the American Fur Company, who has charge of the Fort at this place. He kindly ordered my canoe to be taken care of, and my things to be carried to his quarters.

Bird's-eye view of the Mandan Village.

VI

Mandan Village,
Upper Missouri

THE MANDANS (or See-pohs-kah-nu-mah-kah-kee, "People of the Pheasants," as they call themselves) are perhaps one of the most curious tribes of Indians in our country. Their origin, like that of all the other tribes, is, from necessity, involved in mystery and obscurity. They take great pride in relating their traditions, especially with regard to their origin, contending that they were the *first* people created on earth. Their existence in these regions has not been from a very ancient period. From what I could learn of their traditions, they have, at a former period, been a very numerous and powerful nation, but the continual wars which have existed between them and their neighbors have reduced them to their present numbers.

They formerly lived fifteen or twenty miles farther down the river, in ten contiguous villages, the marks or ruins of which are yet plainly to be seen. At that period their numbers were much greater than at the present day.

Now they are located on the west bank of the Missouri, about eighteen hundred miles above St. Louis and two hundred below the Mouth of Yellow Stone River. They have two villages, which are about two miles distant from each other; and number in all about two thousand souls. Their present villages are judiciously located for defense against the assaults of their enemies.

The site of the lower (or principal) town is in the midst of an extensive valley, embraced within a thousand graceful swells and parapets or mounds of interminable green, changing to blue as they vanish in distance. On an extensive plain without tree or bush to be seen, rising from the ground and towards the heavens, are domes of dirt—and the thousand spears and scalp-poles of the semi-subterraneous village of the hospitable Mandans.

The ground on which the Mandan village is built sits on a bank forty or fifty feet above the bed of the river. The greater part of this bank is nearly perpendicular, and of solid rock. The river, suddenly changing its course to a right-angle, protects two sides of the village, which is built upon this promontory or angle. They have therefore but one side to protect, which is effectually done by a strong piquet, and a ditch inside it of three or four feet in depth. The piquet is composed of timbers a foot or more in diameter and eighteen feet high, set firmly in the ground at sufficient distances from each other to permit guns and other missiles to be fired between them. The ditch (unlike that of civilized modes of fortification) is inside the piquet so that the warriors can screen their bodies from the view and weapons of their enemies while they are reloading and discharging their weapons through the piquets. The Mandans are undoubtedly secure from attack in their villages and have nothing to fear except when they meet their enemy on the prairie.

Their lodges are closely grouped together, leaving just room enough for walking and riding between them. They appear to be built entirely of dirt, but one is surprised when entering them to see the neatness, comfort, and spacious dimensions of these earth-covered dwellings. All the lodges have a circular form, and are from forty to sixty feet in diameter. Their foundations are prepared by digging some two feet in the ground, and forming the floor of earth, by levelling the requisite size for the lodge. These floors or foundations are all perfectly circular, and vary in size in proportion to the number of inmates, or of the quality or standing of the families which are to occupy them. The superstructure is then produced by arranging, inside of this circular excavation, a barrier or wall of timbers, some eight or nine inches in diameter, of equal height (about six feet), placed on end and resting against each other, supported by a formidable embankment of earth raised against them outside.

Then, resting upon the tops of these timbers or piles, are others of equal size and numbers, of twenty or twenty-five feet in length, sending their upper or smaller ends towards the center and top of the lodge. These poles rise at an angle of forty-five degrees to the apex or sky-light, which is about three or four feet in diameter, answering as a chimney and a sky-light at the same time. The roof of the lodge thus formed is supported by beams passing around the inner part of the lodge about the middle of these poles or timbers, and themselves upheld by four or five large posts passing down to the floor of the lodge.

On top of the poles forming the roof is a complete mat of willow-boughs, of half a foot or more in thickness, which protects the timbers from the dampness of the earth. The lodge is covered with these from bottom to top, to the depth of two or three feet, and then

with a hard or tough clay which is impervious to water, and which with long use becomes quite hard. The hardened roof becomes a lounging place for the whole family in pleasant weather —for sage, for wooing lovers, for dogs and all; an airing place—a look-out—a place for gossip and mirth—a seat for the solitary gaze and meditations of the stern warrior, who sits and contemplates the peaceful mirth and happiness that is breathed beneath him, fruits of his hard-fought battles.

The floors of these dwellings are of earth, but so hardened by use, and swept so clean, tracked by bare and moccasined feet, that they have almost a polish, and would scarcely soil the whitest linen. In the center, immediately under the sky-light, is the fire-place—a hole of four or five feet in diameter, of a circular form, sunk a foot or more below the surface, and curbed around with stone. Over the fire-place, and suspended from the apex of diverging props or poles, is the pot or kettle, filled with buffalo meat. Around it are the family, reclining in all the most picturesque attitudes and groups, resting on their buffalo-robes and beautiful mats of rushes. These cabins are so spacious that they hold from twenty to forty persons—a family and all their connections.

They all sleep on bedsteads similar in form to ours, but generally not quite so high; made of round poles lashed together with thongs. A buffalo skin, fresh stripped from the animal, is stretched across the bottom poles, and about two feet from the floor. When it dries, it becomes much contracted and forms a perfect sacking-bottom. The fur side of this skin is placed uppermost, on which they lie with great comfort, with a buffalo-robe folded up for a pillow, and others drawn over them instead of blankets.

These beds are uniformly screened with a covering of buffalo or elk skins, often-times beautifully dressed and placed over the upright poles or frame, like a suit of curtains; leaving a hole in front, sufficient for the occupant to pass in and out, to and from his or her bed. Some of these coverings or curtains are exceedingly beautiful, being cut tastefully into fringe, and handsomely ornamented with porcupine's quills and picture writing or hiero-glyphics. From the great number of inmates in these lodges, they are necessarily very spacious, and the number of beds considerable. It is no uncommon thing to see these lodges fifty feet in diameter inside (which is an immense room), with a row of these curtained beds extending quite around their sides, being some ten or twelve of them, placed four or five feet apart.

The space between them is occupied by a large post, fixed quite firm in the ground, six or seven feet high, with large wooden pegs or bolts in it, on which are hung and grouped, with a wild taste, the arms and armor of the respective proprietor: his whitened shield, embossed and emblazoned with the figure of his protecting *medicine* (or mystery), his bow and quiver, his war-club or battle-axe, his dart or javelin, his tobacco pouch and pipe, his medicine-bag, and his eagle, ermine, or raven head-dress.

Over all, and on the top of the post (as if placed by some conjuror or Indian magician, to guard and protect the spell of wildness that reigns in this strange place), is hung the head and horns of a buffalo, which is, by a village regulation, owned and possessed by every man in the nation, and hung at the head of his bed, which he uses as a mask when called upon by the chiefs to join in the buffalo-dance.

This arrangement of beds and of arms combines the most vivid display and arrangement of colors, of furs, of trinkets, of barbed and glistening points and steel, of mysteries and hocus-pocus, together with the sombre and smoked color of the roof and sides of the lodge. The graceful occupants—conversational, garrulous, story-telling and happy—smoke their pipes, woo their sweethearts, and embrace their little ones about their peaceful fire-sides. There is no error more common, nor more easily refuted, than the one that "the Indian is a sour, morose, reserved, and taciturn man." They are a far more talkative and conversational race than can be seen in the civilized world. This assertion will somewhat startle folks in the East, yet it is true. Small-talk, gossip, garrulity, and story-telling are the leading passions with them as they while away their lives in innocent and endless amusement, mirth and enjoyment.

They live in communities where it is not customary to look forward into the future with concern, for they live without incurring the expenses of life, which are absolutely necessary and unavoidable in the enlightened world; and of course, their faculties are solely directed to the enjoyment of the present day, without sober reflections on the past or apprehensions of the future.

With minds uninfluenced by the thousand passions and ambitions of civilized life, it is easy to concentrate their conversation upon the little and trifling occurrences of their lives. They are fond of fun and good cheer, and can laugh heartily at a slight joke, examples of which their life furnishes them from an inexhaustible fund, enabling them to cheer their little circle about the fire-side with endless laughter and garrulity.

Washington City is not the proper place to study the Indian character; yet it is the place where the sycophant and the scribbler go to gaze and frown upon him—to learn his character and write his history. And because he does not speak, and because he quaffs the delicious beverage which he receives from white men's hands, "he's a speechless brute and drunkard." An Indian is a beggar in Washington City, and a white man is almost equally so in the Mandan village. An Indian in Washington is mute, is dumb and embarrassed; and so is a white man (and for the very same reasons) in this place—he has nobody to talk to.

I have this morning perched myself upon the top of one of the earth-covered lodges, which I have before described, and having the whole village beneath and about me, shall be able, I hope, to give some sketches more to the life than mere recollection.

In the center of the village is an open space, or public area, of one hundred and fifty feet in diameter, and circular in form, which is used for all public games and festivals, shows and exhibitions. The lodges around this open space front in, with their doors towards the center. In the middle of this circle stands an object of great religious veneration, as I am told, on account of the importance it has in the conduct of the annual religious rites. This object is in the form of a large hogshead, some eight or ten feet high, made of planks and hoops, and containing within it some of their choicest medicines or mysteries, and religiously preserved unhacked or unscratched, as a symbol of the "Big Canoe," as they call it.

One of the lodges fronting on this circular area, and facing this strange object of their superstition, is called the "Medicine Lodge," or council house. It is in this sacred building that these wonderful ceremonies, in commemoration of "The Flood," take place. I am told by the traders that these scenes are frightful and abhorrent in the extreme; and this huge wigwam, which is now closed, has been built exclusively for this grand celebration. I am every day reminded of the near approach of the season for this strange affair.

On the roofs of the lodges, besides the groups of living, are buffaloes' skulls, skin canoes, pots and pottery, sleds and sledges. Suspended on poles, erected some twenty feet above the doors of their wigwams, are displayed the scalps of warriors, preserved as trophies—exposed as evidence of their warlike deeds. On other poles are the warriors' whitened shields and quivers, with medicine-bags attached. Here and there is a red cloth, or other costly stuff, offered up to the Great Spirit, over the door of some benign chief, in humble gratitude for the blessings which he is enjoying. Such is a part of the strange medley that is before and around me. Amid the blue streams of smoke rising from these hundred "coal-pits" can be seen in the distance the green, treeless, bushless prairie. On it, and contiguous to the piquet which encloses the village, are a hundred scaffolds, on which their dead "live," as they term it.

These people never bury the dead, but place the bodies on slight scaffolds just above the reach of human hands, and out of the way of wolves and dogs. They are left there to moulder and decay. This cemetery, or place of deposit for the dead, is just back of the village, on a level prairie.

Whenever a person dies in the Mandan village, the customary honors and condolences are paid to his remains. The body is dressed in its best attire; painted, oiled, feasted, and supplied with bow and quiver, shield, pipe and tobacco; knife, flint and steel, and provisions enough to last him a few days on the journey which he is to perform. A fresh buffalo's skin, just taken from the animal's back, is wrapped around the body and tightly bound and wound with thongs of raw hide from head to foot. Then other robes are soaked in water till they are quite soft and elastic, and are also bandaged around the body, then tied fast with thongs, which are wound with great care so as to exclude the action of the air from all parts of the body.

Then a scaffold is erected, constructed of four upright posts, a little higher than human hands can reach. On the tops of these are small poles passing around from one post to the others, across which are a number of willow-rods, just strong enough to support the body, which is laid upon them on its back, with its feet carefully presented towards the rising sun. Hundreds of these bodies may be seen reposing in this manner in this curious place, which the Indians call "the village of the dead."

146

There is not a day in the year in which one many not see in this place that which will bring tears to his eyes and kindle in his bosom a spark of respect and sympathy for the Indian. Fathers, mothers, wives, and children may be seen lying under these scaffolds, prostrate upon the ground, with their faces in the dirt, howling forth incessantly the most heart-broken lamentations for the misfortunes of their kindred; tearing their hair, cutting their flesh with knives, and doing other penance to appease the spirits of the dead, whose misfortunes they attribute to some sin or omission of their own, and for which they sometimes inflict the most excruciating self-torture.

When the scaffolds on which the bodies rest decay and fall to the ground, the nearest relations bury the rest of the bones, take the skulls, which are perfectly bleached and purified, and place them in circles of an hundred or more on the prairie. The skulls are placed some eight or nine inches from each other with the faces all looking to the center. There they are religiously protected and preserved in their precise positions from year to year, as objects of religious and affectionate veneration.

There are several of these "Golgothas" or circles of twenty or thirty feet in diameter, and in the center of each ring or circle is a little mound about three feet high, on which rest two buffalo skulls (a male and female). In the center of the little mound is a "medicine pole," about twenty feet high, supporting many curious articles of mystery and superstition to guard and protect this sacred arrangement. The people come to these circles of skulls—not in groans and lamentations, however, for several years have cured the anguish, but fond affections and endearments are here renewed, and conversations are held and cherished with the dead.

Each one of these skulls is placed upon a bunch of wild sage, which has been pulled and placed under it. The wife knows (by some mark or resemblance) the skull of her husband or her child. A day seldom passes that she does not visit it, with a dish of the best cooked food that her wigwam affords. She sets it before the skull at night, and returns in the morning. As soon as the sage on which the skull rests begins to decay, the woman cuts a fresh bunch and places the skull carefully upon it.

Independent of the duties which draw the women to this spot, they visit it from inclination, and linger upon it to converse with the dead. There is scarcely an hour on a pleasant day when some of these women may not be seen sitting or laying by the skull of their child or husband—talking to it in the most pleasant and endearing language they can use and seemingly getting an answer back. It is not unfrequently the case that the woman brings her needle-work with her, spending the greater part of the day sitting by the side of the skull of her child, chatting incessantly with it, while she is embroidering or garnishing a pair of moccasins. Then, perhaps, overcome with fatigue, she falls asleep, with her arms encircled around it, forgetting herself for hours. Afterward she gathers up her things and returns to the village. There is something exceedingly impressive in these scenes: In one they pour forth the frantic anguish of their souls; and afterwards pay their visits to the other, to jest and gossip with the dead.

Ha-na-tah-nu-mauh (The Wolf Chief) is head-chief of the nation, and familiarly known by the name of "Chef de Loup," as the French Traders call him. He is a haughty, austere, and overbearing man, respected and feared by his people rather than loved. The tenure by which this man holds his office is that of inheritance. The office of chief belongs to the eldest son of a chief, provided he shows himself by his conduct to be as worthy of it as any other in the nation—making it hereditary on a very proper condition, in default of which the office is elective.

The next and second chief of the tribe is Mah-to-toh-pa (The Four Bears). This extraordinary man, though second in office, is undoubtedly the most popular man in the nation. Free, generous, elegant, and gentlemanly in his deportment—handsome, brave, and valiant; wearing a robe on his back with the history of his battles emblazoned on it which would fill a book of themselves, if properly translated.

After him, there are Mah-tahp-ta-ha (He Who Rushes Through the Middle); Seehk-hee-da (The Mouse-Colored Feather); San-ja-ka-ko-kah (The Deceiving Wolf); Mah-to-he-ha (The Old Bear), and others, distinguished as chiefs and warriors. And there are belles also, such as Mi-neek-e-sunk-te-ca (The Mink) and the little gray-haired Sha-ko-ka-mint, and fifty others who are famous for their conquests not with the bow or the javelin, but with their small black eyes, which shoot out from under their unfledged brows and pierce the boldest, fiercest chieftain to the heart.

The Mandans are not a warlike people. They seldom, if ever, carry war into their enemies' country, but when invaded, show their valor and courage to be equal to that of any people on earth. Being a small tribe, and unable to contend on the wide prairies with the Sioux and other roaming tribes, who are ten times more numerous, they have very judiciously located themselves in a permanent village, which is strongly fortified. By this means they have advanced further in the arts of manufacture; have supplied their lodges more abundantly with the comforts, and even luxuries, of life than any Indian nation I know of.

A stranger in the Mandan village is first struck with the different shades of complexion, and various colors of hair, which he sees in a crowd about him and is at once disposed to exclaim that "these are not Indians." There are a great many of these people whose complexions appear light. Among the women, particularly, there are many whose skins are almost white; with hazel, gray, and blue eyes.

Why this diversity of complexion I cannot tell, nor can they themselves account for it. Their traditions, so far as I have yet learned them, afford us no information of their having had any knowledge of white men before the visit of Lewis and Clark made to their village thirty-three years ago. Since that time there have been very few visits by white men, and surely not enough to have changed the complexions and customs of a nation. And I recollect that Governor Clark told me that I would find the Mandans a strange people and half white.

The diversity in the color of hair is also as great as that in the complexion. There may be seen every shade and color of hair that can be seen in our own country, with the exception of red or auburn. There are very many of both sexes and of every age, from infancy to manhood and old age, with hair of a bright silvery gray, and in some instances almost perfectly white. This eccentric appearance is much oftener seen among the women than it is with the men. Many men who have it seem ashamed of it, and artfully conceal it by filling their hair with glue and black and red earth. The women, on the other hand, seem proud of it, and

The Mouse-Colored Feather, also called The White Eyebrows, Mandan brave with yellow hair.

display it often in an almost incredible profusion, which spreads over their shoulders and falls as low as the knee.

About one in ten or twelve of the whole tribe are grayhairs. This unaccountable phenomenon is not the result of disease, but unquestionably a hereditary character which runs in families. And by passing this hair through my hands, as I often have, I have found it uniformly to be as coarse and harsh as a horse's mane, differing materially from the hair of other colors, which, among the Mandans, is generally as fine and as soft as silk. All other primitive tribes known in America are dark copper-colored, with jet black hair.

From these few facts alone, the reader will see that I am among a strange and interesting people, and will pardon me if I lead him through a maze of novelty and mysteries of a strange yet kind and hospitable people, whose fate, like that of all their race, is sealed; whose doom is fixed, to live just long enough to be imperfectly known, and then to fall before the disease or sword of civilizing devastation.

The Mandans are pleasingly erect and graceful, both in their walk and their attitudes. The hair of the men, which generally spreads over their backs, falling down to the hams, and sometimes to the ground, is divided into plaits or slabs two inches in width, and filled with a profusion of glue and red earth or vermilion, at intervals of an inch or two, which becoming very hard, remains unchanged from year to year.

This mode of dressing the hair gives the Mandans the most singular appearance. The hair of the men is uniformly all laid over from the forehead backwards, carefully kept

149

The Wolf Chief, head chief of the Mandans.

above and resting on the ear, and thence falling down over the back, in these flattened bunches, and painted red, extending sometimes as far as the calf of the leg, and sometimes in such profusion as almost to conceal the whole figure from the person walking behind them.

The hair of the women is also worn as long as they can possibly cultivate it, oiled very often, which preserves on it a beautiful gloss and shows its natural color. They often braid it in two large plaits, one falling down just back of the ear, on each side of the head. On any occasion which requires them to "put on their best looks," they pass their fingers through it, drawing it out of braid and spreading it over their shoulders. The Mandan women observe strictly the same custom which I observed among the Crows and Blackfeet (and, in fact, all other tribes I have seen, without a single exception) of parting the hair on the forehead and always keeping the crease or separation filled with vermilion or other red paint. In mourning, like the Crows and other tribes, the women are obliged to crop their hair all off. The usual term of condolence is until the hair has grown again to its former length.

When a man mourns for the death of a near relation the case is quite different. His long, valued tresses are of much greater importance, and only a lock or two can be spared. Just enough to tell his grief to his friends, without destroying his most valued ornament, is sufficient reverence and respect to the dead.

At the distance of half a mile or so above the village is the place where the women and girls go every morning in the summer months to bathe in the river. Every morning at sunrise on a beautiful beach, hundreds can be seen running and glistening in the sun, playing their innocent gambols and leaping into the stream. They all learn to swim well, and the poorest swimmer among them will dash fearlessly into the boiling and eddying current of the Missouri, and cross it with perfect ease. At the distance of a quarter of a mile back from the river, a terrace or elevated prairie, running north from the village, forms a kind of semicircle around this bathing-place. On this terrace, which is some twenty or thirty feet higher than the meadow between it and the river, several sentinels are stationed every morning with their bows and arrows in hand, to guard and protect from the approach of boys or men from any directions.

Below the village is the place where the men and boys go to bathe and learn to swim. After their morning ablution, they return to their village, wipe their limbs dry, and use a profusion of bear's grease through their hair and over their bodies.

The art of swimming is known to all the American Indians. Perhaps no people on earth have taken more pains to learn it, nor any who turn it to better account. Many tribes spend their lives on the shores of vast lakes and rivers, paddling about from their childhood in their fragile bark canoes, which are liable to continual accidents and which often throw the Indian upon his natural resources for the preservation of his life.

There are also many times when out upon their long marches in the prosecution of their almost continued warfare that it becomes necessary to swim across the wildest streams and rivers. Swimming is learned at an early age by both sexes. The squaws can take their child upon their back and successfully swim any river that lies in their way.

Swimming among the Mandans, as well as among most of the other tribes, is quite different from that practiced in the civilized world. The Indian, instead of parting his hands simultaneously under the chin, and making the stroke outward, in a horizontal direction, throws his body alternately upon the left and right side, raising one arm entirely above the water and reaching as far forward as he can, to dip it, and like a paddle propel him along. While this arm is making a half circle in the water behind him, the opposite arm is describing a similar arch in the air over his head, to be dipped in the water as far as he can reach before him. He turns his hand under, forming a sort of bucket to act as it passes in its turn underneath him. By this powerful mode of swimming, a man will preserve his strength and his breath much longer in this alternate and rolling motion than he can in the usual mode of swimming in the polished world.

The Mandans have another mode of bathing which is a much greater luxury, and often resorted to by the sick. Each village has several steam baths, which seem to be a kind of public property—accessible to all and resorted to by all, male and female, old and young, sick and well.

In every Mandan lodge is a crib or basket, much in the shape of a bathing-tub, curiously woven with willow boughs, and sufficiently large to receive any person of the family in a reclining or recumbent posture. When any one is to take a bath the crib is carried by the squaw to the steam bath for the purpose, and brought back to the lodge again after it has been used.

These steam baths are always near the village on the bank of the river. They are generally built of skins in the form of a Crow or Sioux lodge, which I have before described. They are covered with buffalo skins sewed tight together, with a kind of furnace in the center. In other words, in the center of the lodge are two walls of stone about six feet long and two and a half apart, and about three feet high. Across and over this space, between the two walls, are laid a number of round sticks, on which the bathing crib is placed.

Contiguous to the lodge, and outside of it, is a little furnace in the side of the bank, where the woman kindles a hot fire, and heats to a red heat a number of large stones, which are kept at these places for this particular purpose. Having them all in readiness, she goes home or sends word to inform her husband that all is ready. He makes his appearance entirely naked, though with a large buffalo robe wrapped around him. He then enters the lodge and places himself in the crib or basket, either on his back or in a sitting posture (the latter of which is generally preferred), with his back towards the door of the lodge. The squaw brings in a large stone red hot, between two sticks (lashed together somewhat in the form of a pair of tongs) and, placing it under him, throws cold water upon it, which raises a profusion of steam about him.

He is enveloped in a cloud of steam, and a woman or child will sit at a little distance and continue to dash water upon the stone while the matron of the lodge is out preparing to make her appearance with another heated stone. He will sit and dip from a wooden bowl, with a ladle made of the mountain-sheep's horn, and throw upon the heated stones, with his own hands, the water which he is drawing through his lungs and pores. The steam distills through a mat of wild sage and other medicinal and aromatic herbs, which he has strewed over the bottom of his basket, and on which he reclines.

During all this time the lodge is shut perfectly tight. He quaffs this renovating

Steam bath of the Mandans.

draught to his lungs with deep-drawn sighs and extended nostrils, until he is drenched in the most profuse degree of perspiration. Then he makes a kind of strangled signal, at which the lodge is opened, and he darts forth with the speed of a frightened deer and plunges headlong into the river.

He instantly escapes from the river, wraps his robe around him, and runs as fast as possible for home. Here his limbs are wiped dry and wrapped close and tight within the fur of the buffalo robes. He takes his nap with his feet to the fire, then oils his limbs and hair with bear's grease, dresses and plumes himself for a visit, a feast, a parade or a council. Or he slicks down his long hair and rubs his oiled limbs to a polish with a piece of soft buckskin, prepared to join in games of ball or Tchung-kee.

Such is the steam bath of the Mandans. It is reported as an everyday luxury and is also used by the sick as a remedy for nearly all the diseases they know. Fevers are very rare among these people, but in the few cases of fever which have been known, this treatment has been applied, and without the fatal consequences which we would naturally predict. The greater part of their diseases are inflammatory rheumatisms and other chronic diseases. For these, this mode of treatment does admirably well. This custom is similar among nearly all of these Missouri Indians, and among the Pawnees, Omahas, Puncahs, and other tribes.

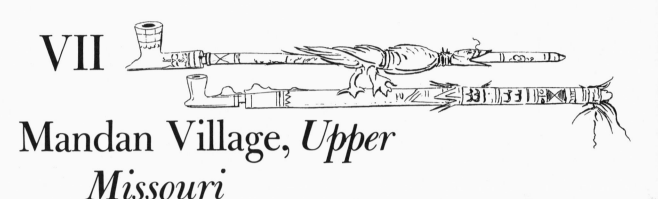

VII

Mandan Village, *Upper Missouri*

THERE IS evidently much preparation for the Mandan religious ceremony. From what I can learn, no one in the nation save the medicine-men have any knowledge of the exact day on which it is to commence. I am informed by the chiefs that it takes place as soon as the willow-tree is in full leaf. They say, "The twig which the bird brought in was a willow bough, and had full-grown leaves on it." So it seems that this celebration has some relation to the Flood.

In the meantime, these people are astonished by the operations of my brush. The art of portrait-painting was a subject entirely new to them, and of course unthought of. My appearance here has commenced a new era in medicine or mystery. Soon after arriving here, I commenced and finished the portraits of the two principal chiefs. This was done without having awakened the curiosity of the villagers, as they had heard nothing of what was going on, and even the chiefs themselves seemed to be ignorant of my designs, until the pictures were completed. No one else was admitted into my lodge during the operation. When finished, it was amusing to see them mutually recognizing each other's likeness, and assuring each other of the striking resemblance which they bore to the originals. Both of these pressed

◄
Mah-to-he-ha, The Old Bear, Mandan Medicine Man.

their hand over their mouths awhile in dead silence (a custom among most tribes when anything surprises them very much), looking attentively upon the portraits and myself, and upon the palette and colors with which these unaccountable effects had been produced.

They then walked up to me in the most gentle manner, taking me in turn by the hand with a firm grip. With head and eyes inclined downwards, and in a tone a little above a whisper, they pronounced the words "Te-ho-pe-nee Wash-ee!" and walked off.

At that moment I was christened with a new name, one by which I am now familiarly hailed and talked of in this village. I was recognized in that short sentence as a "great medicine white man." And since that time I have been regularly installed medicine or mystery, which is the most honorable degree that could be conferred upon me there. I now hold a place among the most eminent and envied personages, the doctor and conjurati of this titled community.

Te-ho-pe-nee Wash-ee (or Medicine White Man) will prove to me, no doubt, of more value than gold, for I have been called upon and feasted by the doctors, who are all mystery-men; it has been an easy and successful passport already to many strange and mysterious places. It has put me in possession of curious and interesting information, which I am sure I never should have otherwise learned. I am daily growing in the estimation of the medicine-men and the chiefs. By assuming all the gravity and circumspection due from so high a dignitary (and even considerably more), and endeavoring to perform now and then some art or trick that is unfathomable, I am in hopes of supporting my standing until the great annual ceremony commences. Then perhaps I may be allowed a seat in the medicine-lodge by the doctors to witness this great source and fountain of all priest-craft and conjuration in this country.

After I had finished the portraits of the two chiefs, they returned to their lodges. They seated themselves by their respective fire-sides and silently smoked a pipe or two. Then they gradually began to tell what had taken place. Crowds of gaping listeners thronged their lodges. A throng of women and girls gathered about my house. Through every crack and crevice I could see their glistening eyes piercing my hut in a hundred places.

An hour or more passed. The soft throng continually increased until some hundreds of them were clinging about my wigwam like a swarm of bees hanging on the sides of their hive.

During this time, not a man made his appearance about the premises. After awhile, however, they could be seen folded in their robes, gradually siding up towards the lodge with a silly look upon their faces, which confessed at once that curiosity was leading them reluctantly where their pride forbade them to go. The rush soon became general, and the chiefs and medicine-men took possession of my room, placing soldiers (braves with spears in their hands) at the door, admitting no one but such as were allowed by the chiefs to come in.

Mr. Kipp (the agent of the Fur Company) took a seat with the chiefs. He explained to them the objects for which I was painting these portraits. He explained to them the manner in which the paintings were made—at which they all seemed to be very much pleased. The necessity of exposing the portraits to the view of the crowds who were assembled around the house became imperative, and they were held up together over the door. The whole village

156

had a chance to see their chiefs. The likenesses were instantly recognized, and many of the gaping multitude commenced yelping. Some were stamping off in jarring dance. Others were singing, and others again were crying. Hundreds covered their mouths with their hands and were mute. Others, indignant, drove their spears frightfully into the ground. Some shot a reddened arrow at the sun, and went home to their lodges.

The next curiosity was to see the man who made such pictures, and I was called. I stepped forth and was instantly hemmed in by the throng. Women were gaping and gazing. Warriors and braves were offering me their hands. Little boys and girls, by dozens, were struggling through the crowd to touch me with the ends of their fingers. I was engaged, from the waist upwards, in fending off the throng and shaking hands. My legs were assailed by children, who were creeping between the legs of the bystanders for the curiosity or honor of touching me with the end of their finger. The eager curiosity and expression of astonishment with which they gazed upon me plainly showed they looked upon me as some strange and unaccountable being. They pronounced me the greatest medicine-man in the world. They said I had made living beings. They said they could see their chiefs alive, in two places—those that I had made were a *little* alive—they could see their eyes move—could see them smile and laugh, and that if they could laugh they could certainly speak, if they should try, and they must therefore have *some life* in them.

The squaws generally agreed they had discovered life enough in my pictures to render my medicine too great for the Mandans. They said such an operation could not be performed without taking away from the original something of his existence.

This curtailing of the primary existence, for the purpose of instilling life into the secondary one, they decided to be a useless and destructive operation, and one which was calculated to do great mischief in their happy community. They commenced a mournful and doleful chant against me, crying and weeping bitterly through the village, proclaiming me a most dangerous man, one who could make living persons by looking at them, and at the same time could, as a matter of course, destroy life in the same way, if I chose. They said my medicine was dangerous to their lives, and I must leave the village immediately: Bad luck would happen to those whom I painted—that I was to take a part of the existence of those whom I painted and carry it home with me among the white people, and that when they died they would never sleep quiet in their graves.

In this way the women and some old quack medicine-men together succeeded in raising an opposition against me. The reasons they assigned were so plausible and so exactly suited for their superstitious feelings that they completely succeeded in exciting a general panic in the minds of a number of chiefs who had agreed to sit for their portraits, and my operations were, of course, for several days completely at a standstill.

A grave council was held on the subject. There seemed great difficulty in deciding what was to be done with me and the dangerous art which I was practicing, which had far exceeded their original expectations. I finally got admittance to their sacred conclave and assured them that I was but a man like themselves—that my art had no medicine or mystery about it but could be learned by any of them if they would practice it as long as I had—that my intentions towards them were of the most friendly kind, and that in the country where I lived, brave men never allowed their squaws to frighten them with their foolish whims and stories.

They all immediately arose, shook me by the hand, and dressed themselves for their pictures. After this, there was no further difficulty about sitting. All were ready to be painted. The squaws were silent, and my painting-room a continual resort for the chiefs and braves and medicine-men, where they waited with impatience for the completion of each one's picture. They could decide as to the likeness as it came from under the brush. They would laugh, and yell, and sing a new song, and smoke a fresh pipe to the health and success of him who had just been safely delivered from the hands and the mystic operation of the "white medicine."

In each of these operations, as they successively took place, I observed that a pipe or two were well filled. As soon as I commenced painting, the chiefs and braves, who sat around the sides of the lodge, commenced smoking for the success of the picture, and probably as much or more so for the safe deliverance of the sitter from harm while under the operation. They continued to pass the pipe around until the portrait was completed.

In this way I proceeded with my portraits, stopping occasionally very suddenly as if something were wrong, then taking a tremendous puff or two at the pipe, and streaming the smoke through my nostrils, exhibiting in my looks and actions an evident relief, enabling me to proceed with more facility and success. By flattering and complimenting each one on his good looks after I had got done, and taking them according to rank or standing (making it a matter of honor with them), I pleased them exceedingly, and won for myself and my art the stamp of respectability.

I was then taken by the arm by the chiefs and led to their lodges, where feasts were prepared for me in elegant style.

I was waited upon in due form and ceremony by the medicine-men, who received me upon the old adage, "Similis simili gaudet." I was invited to a feast, and they presented me a doctor's rattle and a magical wand, or doctor's staff, strung with claws of the grizzly bear, with hoofs of the antelope, with ermine, with wild sage, and bat's wings, perfumed with the choice and savoury odor of the pole-cat. A dog was sacrificed and hung by the legs over my wigwam, and I was thereby initiated into the arcana of medicine or mystery, and considered a Fellow of the Extraordinary Society of *Conjurati*.

Since this signal success and good fortune in my operations, things have gone on very pleasantly. Some altercation has taken place, however, among the chiefs and braves with regard to standing or rank, of which they are exceedingly jealous. They must sit (if at all) in regular order, according to that rank. The trouble is all settled at last, however, and I have had no want of subjects, though a great many have again become alarmed and are unwilling to sit, for fear they will die prematurely if painted. Others say that if they are painted the picture will live after they are dead, and they cannot sleep quiet in their graves.

There have been three or four instances where aspiring young men have been in my lodge, and after gazing at the portraits of the head chiefs across the room (which sits looking them in the eyes), have raised their hands before their faces and walked around to the side of the lodge, on the right or left, to take a long side-look at the chief, instead of staring him full in the face, which is a most unpardonable offense in all Indian tribes. After having got in that position, and cast their eyes again upon the portrait which was yet looking them full in the face, they threw their robes over their heads and bolted out of the lodge, filled with indignation and averring they "saw the eyes move." As they walked around the room "the eyes of the portrait followed them." Repeated efforts have been made by the traders, and also by the chiefs and doctors, who understand the illusion, to convince them of their error by explaining the mystery, but they will not hear of any explanation whatever, saying: "What they see with their eyes is always evidence enough for them"; that they always "believe their own eyes sooner than a hundred tongues." All efforts to get them a second time to my room, or into my company in any place, have proved entirely unsuccessful.

I had trouble brewing also the other day from another source. One of the "medicines" commenced howling and haranguing around my domicile, and among the throng outside, proclaiming that all who were inside and being painted were fools and would soon die; and very materially affecting thereby my popularity.

I called him in the next morning and told him that I had my eye upon him for several days, and had been so well pleased with his looks that I had taken great pains to find out his history, which had been explained as one of a most extraordinary kind, and his character and standing in his tribe as worthy of my particular notice. I told him that I had since resolved that as soon as I had practiced my hand long enough upon the others, to get the stiffness out of it (after paddling my canoe so far as I had), I would begin on his portrait. I was now prepared to commence, and now felt I could do him justice. He shook me by the hand, giving me the "doctor's grip," and beckoned me to sit down, which I did, and we smoked a pipe together. After this was over, he told me that although he had been telling the chiefs that they were all fools, and all would die who had their portraits painted, that although he had set the old women and children all crying, and even made some of the young warriors tremble, yet he had no unfriendly feelings towards me, nor any fear or dread of my art. "I know you are a good man; I know you will do no harm to any one, your medicine is great and you are a great 'medicine-man.' I would like to see myself very well—and so would all of the chiefs; but they have all been many days in this medicine-house, and they all know me well, and they have not asked me to come in and be *made alive* with paints. My friend, I am glad that my people have told you who I am—my heart is glad—I will go to my wigwam and eat, and in a little while I will come, and you may go to work."

Another pipe was lit and smoked, and he got up and went off. I prepared my canvas and palette, and whistled away the time until twelve o'clock, before he made his appearance. He used the whole of the fore-part of the day at his toilette, arranging his dress and ornamenting his body for his picture. Instead of preaching against me, he is now one of my strongest and most enthusiastic friends in the village.

Indian beaus or dandies may be seen on every pleasant day, strutting and parading around the village in the most beautiful and unsoiled dresses, without the honorable trophies, however, of scalp-locks and claws of the grizzly bear attached to their costume, for with those things they deal not.

They are not peculiarly anxious to hazard their lives in equal and honorable combat with the one, or disposed to cross the path of the other, but generally remain about the village to take care of the women, and attire themselves in the skins of such animal as they can easily kill, without seeking the rugged cliffs for the war-eagle, or visiting the haunts of the grizzly bear. They plume themselves with swan's-down and quills of ducks, with braids and plaits of sweet-scented grass, and other harmless ornaments, which have no other merits than they themselves have—that of looking pretty and ornamental.

These elegant gentlemen, a few in each tribe, are held in low estimation by the chiefs and braves because they have an aversion to arms. They are called "faint hearts" or "old women" by the whole tribe, and are little respected. They seem to be tolerably well content, however. They acquire celebrity among the women and children for the beauty and elegance of their personal appearance; and most of them seem to take and enjoy their share of the world's pleasures, although they are looked upon as drones in society.

These gay bucks may be seen astride of their pied or dappled ponies, with a fan in the right hand, made of a turkey's tail, with whip and a fly-brush attached to the wrist of the same hand, and underneath them a white, beautiful, and soft pleasure-saddle, ornamented with porcupine quills and ermine. They parade through the village for an hour or so, then bend their course to the suburbs of the town. They will sit or recline upon their horses for an hour or two, watching the games of the braves and the young men. When they are fatigued with this severe effort, they wend their way back again, lift off their fine white saddle of doe's skin, which is wadded with buffalo hair, turn out their pony, take a little refreshment, smoke a pipe, fan themselves to sleep, and doze away the rest of the day.

While I have been painting, two or three of these fops have been strutting their attitudes in front of my door, decked out in all their finery. The chiefs, I observed, passed them by without notice, and of course without inviting them in. The fops stand about my door from day to day in their best dresses and best attitudes, as if in hopes I will select them as models.

It was natural I should do so, for their costume and personal appearance was more beautiful than anything else to be seen in the village. One day when I had got through with all of the head-men who were willing to be painted, I stepped to the door and tapped one of these fellows on the shoulder, who stepped in, delighted with the honorable notice I had at length taken of him and his beautiful dress. Gratitude beamed forth in his face, and his heart beat with pride at the idea of my selecting him to be immortal, alongside of the chiefs and worthies whose portraits he saw arranged around the room.

I placed him before me, and a canvas on my easel, and chalked him out at full length. He was truly a beautiful subject. His dress from head to foot was of the skins of the mountain-goat, as soft and as white as Canton crape—around the bottom and the sides it was trimmed with ermine, and porcupine quills of beautiful dyes garnished it in a hundred parts. His hair spread over his back and shoulders, extending nearly to the ground, and was all combed back and parted on his forehead like that of a woman. He was a tall and fine figure, with ease and grace in his movements that were well worthy a man of better caste. In his left hand he held a beautiful pipe. In his right hand he plied his fan. On his wrist was still attached his whip of elk's horn and his fly-brush made of the buffalo's tail.

Then the three chiefs, who had been seated around the lodge, and whose portraits I had painted before, arose suddenly, and wrapping themselves tightly in their robes, crossed

160

The Four Bears, second chief of the Mandan.

my room with a quick and heavy step and took leave of my cabin. In a few moments the interpreter came into my room, addressing me furiously: "My God, this never will do. You have given great offense to the chiefs. They tell me this is a worthless fellow—a man of no account in the nation, and if you paint his picture you must instantly destroy theirs. You have no alternative, and the quicker this chap is out of your lodge the better."

The matter was explained by the interpreter to my sitter, who picked up his robe, wrapped himself in it, plied his fan nimbly about his face, and walked out of the lodge in silence, taking his old position in front of the door for a while, after which he drew himself quietly off without further exhibition. So highly do Mandan braves and worthies value the honor of being painted; and so little do they value a man, however lavishly Nature may have bestowed her master touches upon him, who has not the pride and noble bearing of a warrior.

Mah-to-toh-pa (The Four Bears), the second chief of the nation and the most popular man of the Mandans, a high-minded and gallant warrior, stepped into my painting-room about twelve o'clock one day, in full and splendid dress, and passing his arm through mine, pointed the way, and led me in the most gentlemanly manner through the village and into his own lodge, where a feast was prepared waiting our arrival.

161

The lodge in which he dwelt was a room of immense size, some forty or fifty feet in diameter, in a circular form, and about twenty feet high—with a sunken curb of stone in the center of five or six feet in diameter and one foot deep, which contained the fire over which the pot was boiling. I was led near the edge of this curb and seated on a very handsome robe, most ingeniously garnished and painted with hieroglyphics. He seated himself gracefully on another one at a little distance from me. The feast, prepared in several dishes and resting on a beautiful rush mat, was placed between us.

The simple feast which was spread before us consisted of three dishes only, two of which were served in wooden bowls, and the third in an earthen vessel, somewhat in the shape of a bread-tray in our own country. It contained a quantity of pemican and marrow-fat. One of the wooden bowls held a fine brace of buffalo ribs, delightfully roasted. The other was filled with a kind of paste or pudding made of the flour of the "pomme blanche," as the French call it, a delicious turnip of the prairie, finely flavored with the buffalo berries, and used in cooking, as we in civilized countries use dried currants.

A handsome pipe and a tobacco-pouch made of the otter skin, filled with k'nick-k'neck (Indian tobacco), was laid by the side of the feast. When we were seated, my host took up his pipe and filled it. He drew a few strong whiffs through it, then presented the stem of it to my mouth, through which I drew a whiff or two while he held the stem in his hands. This done, he laid down the pipe, and drawing his knife from his belt, cut off a very small piece of the meat from the ribs, and pronouncing the words "Ho-pe-ne-chee wa-pa-shee" (meaning a medicine sacrifice), threw it into the fire.

He then requested me to eat, and I commenced, after drawing out from my belt my knife, which every man in this country carries. I sat and ate my dinner *alone,* for such is the custom in this strange land. A chief never eats with his guests, but while they eat, he sits by, at their service and ready to wait upon them, charging and lighting the pipe which is to be passed around after the feast is over.

While I was eating, Mah-to-toh-pa sat cross-legged before me, cleaning his pipe and preparing it for a smoke when I had finished my meal. After he had taken enough of the k'nick-k'neck, or bark of the red willow, from his pouch, he rolled out of it also a piece of the "castor" to give it a flavor. My appetite satiated, I straightened up, and with a whiff the pipe was lit, and we enjoyed together for a quarter of an hour the most delightful exchange of good feelings, amid clouds of smoke.

While sitting at this feast the lodge was as silent as death, although we were not alone in it. This chief, like most others, had a plurality of wives, and all of them (some six or seven) were seated around the sides of the lodge, upon robes or mats placed upon the ground, and not allowed to speak, though they were in readiness to obey his orders or commands, which were uniformly given by manual signs, and executed in the neatest and most silent manner.

When I arose to return, the pipe through which we had smoked was presented to me. He gracefully raised the robe on which I had sat by the corners and tendered it to me, explaining that the paintings which were on it were representations of the battles of his life,

162

Dinner with The Four Bears.

where he had fought and killed with his own hand fourteen of his enemies. He had been two weeks in painting it for me, and he had invited me here on this occasion to present it to me. I took the robe upon my shoulder, and he took me by the arm and led me back to my painting-room.

The chiefs of the Mandans frequently have a plurality of wives. Such is the custom among all of the tribes. It is no uncommon thing to find a chief with six, eight, or ten, and some with twelve or fourteen wives in his lodge. Women are always held in a rank inferior to that of the men. They serve as menials and slaves. They are the "hewers of wood and drawers of water." It becomes a matter of necessity for a chief (who must be liberal, keep open doors, and entertain for the support of his popularity) to have in his wigwam a sufficient number of such handmaids to perform the numerous duties and drudgeries of so large and expensive an establishment.

There are two other reasons for this custom which operate with equal force. In the first place, these people have still more or less the same passion for the accumulation of wealth, for the luxuries of life, as the civilized world. A chief with a wish to furnish his lodge with something more than ordinary for the entertainment of his own people, as well as

The Mint, Mandan girl with gray hair.

strangers who fall upon his hospitality, marries a number of wives, who are kept at hard labor during most of the year. The results of their labor enable him to procure those luxuries, and give to his lodge the appearance of respectability.

The women are kept dressing buffalo robes and other skins for the market. The brave or chief with the greatest number of wives is considered the most affluent and envied man in the tribe. His table is most bountifully supplied. His lodge is the most abundantly furnished with the luxuries of manufacture.

Manual labor among Indians is all done by the women. There are no daily laborers or persons who will "hire out" to labor for another, and it becomes necessary for him who requires more than the labor or services of one, to add to the number by legalizing and compromising by the ceremony of marriage his stock of laborers. They can thus, and thus alone, be easily enslaved, and the results of their labor turned to good account.

There is another inducement, which probably is more effective: the natural inclination which belongs to a man who stands high in the estimation of his people and wields the

The Mink.

sceptre of power—surrounded by temptations which he considers it would be unnatural to resist, where no law or regulation of society stands in the way of his enjoyment. His accumulation of a household, instead of quadrupling his expenses (as would be the case in the civilized world), actually increases his wealth, as the result of his wives' labor.

Besides, all nations of Indians are unceasingly at war with the tribes that are about them, for the adjustment of ancient and never-ending feuds, as well as from a love of glory, to which in Indian life the battle-field is almost the only road. Their warriors are killed off to the extent that in many instances two and sometimes three women to a man are found in a tribe. The custom of polygamy has kindly helped the community to a relief from a cruel and prodigious calamity.

Polygamy is generally confined to the chiefs and medicine-men, though there is no regulation prohibiting a poor or obscure individual from marrying several wives, other than the personal difficulties which lie between him and the hand which he wishes in vain to get, for want of sufficient celebrity in society, or from a still more frequent objection, that of his

165

inability (from want of worldly goods) to deal in the customary way with the fathers of the girls whom he would appropriate to his own household.

There are very few instances where a poor or ordinary citizen has more than one wife. But among the chiefs and braves of great reputation, and doctors, it is common to see some six or eight living under one roof, and all apparently quiet and contented.

Wives are mostly bargained for with the father. In all instances they are bought and sold. In many cases the bargain is made with the father alone, without every consulting the inclinations of the girl, and seems to be conducted on his part as a mercenary contract entirely, where he stands out for the highest price he can possibly command for her. There are other instances, to be sure, where the parties approach each other, and from the expression of a mutual fondness make their own arrangements and pass their own mutual vows, which are quite as sacred and inviolable as similar assurances when made in the civilized world. Yet even in such cases, the marriage is never consummated without the necessary form of making presents to the father of the girl.

It becomes a matter of absolute necessity for the white men who are traders in these regions to connect themselves by marriage to one or more of the most influential families in the tribe. Marriage identifies their interest with that of the nation, and enables them, with the influence of their new family connections, to carry on successfully their business transactions. Young women of the best families aspire to such an elevation. Most of them are exceedingly ambitious for such a connection inasmuch as they are certain of a delightful exemption from the slavish duties that devolve upon them when married under other circumstances. They expect to lead a life of ease and idleness, covered with mantles of blue and scarlet cloth, with beads and trinkets and ribbons, in which they flounce and flirt about, the envied and tinselled belles of every tribe.

These connections are generally entered into purely as a mercenary or business transaction, in which they are very expert and shrewd at exacting an adequate price from the purchaser they deem able to pay liberally for so delightful a commodity.

Almost every trader who commences in the business of this country speedily enters into such an arrangement. It is done with as little ceremony as he would bargain for a horse, and just as unceremoniously do they annul and abolish the connection when they wish to leave the country, or change their positions from one tribe to another. At that time the woman becomes a fair and proper candidate for matrimony or speculation, when another applicant comes along, and her father equally desirous for another horse or gun, which he can easily command at her second espousal.

From the enslaved and degraded condition in which the women are held in the Indian country, the world would naturally think that theirs must be a community destitute of the fine, reciprocal feelings and attachments which flow from the domestic relations in the civilized world. Yet it would be untrue, and doing injustice to the Indians, to say that they were in the least behind us in conjugal, in filial, and in paternal affection. There is no trait in the human character which is more universal than the attachments which flow from these relations.

The Mandan women are beautiful and modest. Among the respectable families,

166

virtue is as highly cherished and as inviolate as in any society whatever. Yet at the same time a chief may marry a dozen wives if he pleases, and so may a white man. And if either wishes to marry the most beautiful and modest girl in the tribe, she is valued only equal, perhaps, to two horses, a gun with powder and ball for a year, five or six pounds of beads, a couple of gallons of whisky, and a handful of awls.

The girls of this tribe, like those of most of these North Western tribes, marry at the age of twelve to fourteen, and some at the age of eleven years. Their beauty soon vanishes, from the slavish life they lead. Their occupations are almost continual, and they seem to go industriously at them, either from choice or inclination, without a murmur.

The principal occupations of the women consist of procuring wood and water, of cooking, dressing robes and other skins, of drying meat and wild fruit, and of raising corn (maize).

The Mandans are agriculturists. They raise a great deal of corn and some pumpkins and squashes. This is all done by the women, who make their hoes from the shoulder-blade of the buffalo or the elk, and dig the ground over instead of ploughing it.

They raise a small sort of corn, with ears which are no longer than a man's thumb. The variety is well adapted to their climate, as it ripens sooner than other varieties, which would not mature in so cold a latitude. The green corn season is one of great festivity, and one of much importance. The greater part of their crop is eaten during these festivals, and the remainder is gathered and dried on the cob, before it has ripened, and packed away in "caches" (as the French call them), holes dug in the ground, some six or seven feet deep, the insides of which are somewhat in the form of a jug, and tightly closed at the top. The corn, and even dried meat and pemican, are placed in these *caches,* being packed tight around the sides with prairie grass, and effectually preserved through the severest winters.

Corn and dried meat are generally stored in the fall, in sufficient quantities to support them through the winter. In addition, they often store great quantities of dried squashes and dried "pommes blanches," a kind of turnip which grows in great abundance in these regions. These are dried in great quantities and pounded into a sort of meal to be cooked with the dried meat and corn. Great quantities also of wild fruit of different kinds are dried and laid away in store for the winter season, such as buffalo berries, service berries, strawberries, and wild plums.

The buffalo meat, however, is the great staple and "staff of life" in this country. There are, from a fair computation, something like two hundred and fifty thousand Indians in these western regions, who live almost exclusively on the flesh of the buffalo. During the summer and fall months they use the meat fresh, and cook it in a great variety of ways— roasting, broiling, boiling, stewing, smoking, and boiling the ribs and joints with the marrow in them to make a delicious soup.

The pot is always boiling over the fire, and anyone who is hungry (either of the household or from any other part of the village) has a right to order it taken off, and to fall to eating as he pleases. I very much doubt whether the civilized world have in their institutions any system which can properly be called more humane and charitable. Every man, woman, or child in Indian communities is allowed to enter anyone's lodge, and even that of the chief of the nation, and eat when they are hungry, provided misfortune or necessity has driven them to it. Even the poorest and most worthless drone of the nation, if he is too lazy to hunt or to supply himself, can walk into any lodge and everyone will share with him as long as there is anything to eat. He, however, who thus begs when he is able to hunt, pays dear for his meat, for he is stigmatized with the disgraceful epithet of a poltroon and a beggar.

The Mandans, like all other tribes, sit at their meals cross-legged, or rather with their ankles crossed in front of them and both feet drawn close under their bodies. Or they take their meals in a reclining posture, with the legs thrown out and the body resting on one elbow and fore-arm. The dishes are invariably on the ground or floor of the lodge, and the diners rest on buffalo robes or mats.

The position in which the women sit, at their meals and on other occasions, is different from that of the men. They squat, but they can rise with great ease and grace by merely bending the knees both together, inclining the body back and the head and shoulders quite forward, without using their hands in any way to assist them.

The women are not allowed to sit with the men at meals. I never have seen an Indian woman eating with her husband. Men form the first group at the banquet, and women and children and dogs all come together at the next; and these gormandize and glut themselves to an enormous extent, though the men very seldom do.

I venture to say there are no persons on earth who practice greater prudence and self-denial than Indian men do. They are constantly at war or on the chase, or in their athletic sports and exercises. They are excited by the highest ideas of pride and honor, and every kind of excess is studiously avoided. For a great part of their lives they enforce the most painful abstinence upon themselves to prepare their bodies and their limbs for these extravagant exertions.

Many a man who has spent a few weeks along the frontier among the drunken, naked, and beggared part of the Indian race, and run home and written a book on Indians, has, no doubt, often seen them eat to beastly excess. He has seen them guzzle whisky and perhaps has *sold* it to them. He has seen them glutted and besotted, without will or energy to move. Where white people have made beggars of them, they have nothing to do but lie under a fence and beg a whole week to get meat and whisky enough for one feast and one carouse. But among the wild Indians in this country there are no beggars—no drunkards—and every man, from a beautiful natural precept, studies to keep his body and mind in such a healthy shape and condition as will at all times enable him to use his weapons, or struggle for the prize in their games.

These men generally eat only twice a day, and many times not more than once. Meals are light and simple compared with the meals swallowed in the civilized world. There are, however, many seasons and occasions in the year when all Indians fast for several days in succession; and other occasions when they can get nothing to eat. And after such times they may commence with an enormous meal. This habit aside, I am fully convinced that the North American Indians eat less than any civilized population.

Their mode of curing and preserving the buffalo meat is almost incredible: It is all cured or dried in the sun, without the aid of salt or smoke! The method of doing this is the same among all the tribes, and is as follows: The choicest parts of the flesh from the buffalo are cut out by the squaws, carried home on their backs or on horses, and there cut "across the grain," so as to alternate layers of lean and fat. Having prepared it in strips about half an inch in thickness, it is hung up by hundreds and thousands of poles resting on crotches, out of the reach of dogs or wolves, and exposed to the rays of the sun for several days. It becomes so dried it can be carried to any part of the world without damage.

I presume it will be new to most of the world that meat can be cured in the sun without the aid of smoke or salt. It is a fact equally true and equally surprising that none of these tribes use salt in any way, although their country abounds in salt springs. In many places the prairie is covered with an incrustation of salt as white as the drifted snow. Yet I have been unable to prevail on them to use salt in any quantity whatever.

But everywhere along our frontier, where the game of the country has long since been destroyed, and the Indians have become semi-civilized, raising and eating, as we do, a variety of vegetable food, they use (and no doubt require) a great deal of salt; and in many instances they use it even to destructive excess.

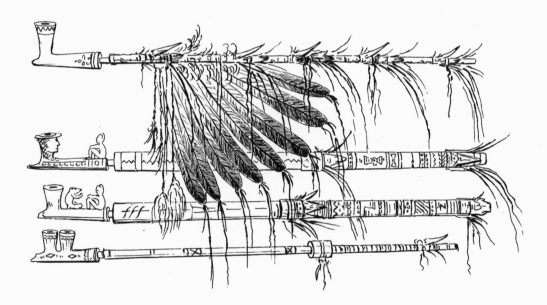

Wak-a-dah-ha-hee, The White Buffalo's Hair, took his turn at rain-making with double success.

VIII

Mandan Village, *Upper Missouri*

THE MANDANS lead lives of idleness and leisure, and devote a great deal of time to their sports and amusements, of which they have a great variety. Of these, dancing is one of the principal, and may be seen in a variety of forms, such as the buffalo dance, the boasting dance, the begging dance, the scalp dance, and a dozen other kinds, all of which have their peculiar characters and meanings or objects.

These exercises are exceedingly grotesque in their appearance. To the eye of a traveller who knows not their meaning, they are an uncouth and frightful display of starts and jumps and yelps and jarring gutturals, which are sometimes truly terrifying. But when one gives them a little attention, and has been lucky enough to be initiated into their mysterious meaning, they become a subject of the most intense and exciting interest.

Every dance has its peculiar step, and every step has its meaning. Every dance has its peculiar song, so intricate and mysterious sometimes that not one in ten of the young men who are dancing and singing it know the meaning of the song they are chanting. None but the medicine-men are allowed to understand them. Even they are generally only initiated into these secret arcana, which require much application and study, upon payment of a liberal

Making the buffalo come.

stipend for their tuition. There is evidently a set song and sentiment for every dance. The songs are perfectly measured and sung in exact time with the beat of the drum, always with a uniform and invariable set of sounds that are expressed by the voice and clearly indicate certain sentiments, although sometimes not given in any known language whatever.

They have other dances and songs which are not so mystifying but are sung and understood by every person in the tribe, with much poetry in them and perfectly metered, but without rhyme. For several days I have been engrossed and my senses almost confounded with the stamping, grunting, and bellowing of the buffalo dance, which closed a few days ago at sunrise and which I will describe to you.

Buffaloes are roaming creatures, congregating occasionally in huge masses, and strolling about the country from east to west or from north to south, just where their whims or strange fancies may lead them. As a result, the Mandans are sometimes left without anything to eat. Being a small tribe, and unwilling to risk their lives by going far from home in the face of their more powerful enemies, they are sometimes left almost in a state of starvation. In this emergency, every man musters and brings out of his lodge his mask (the skin of a buffalo's head with the horns on), which he is obliged to keep in readiness for such an occasion. Then the buffalo dance commences, held for the purpose of making "buffalo come." They dance to induce the buffalo herds to change the direction of their wanderings, to bend their course

172

towards the Mandan village, to graze about on the beautiful hills and bluffs in its vicinity, where the Mandans can shoot them down and cook them as they want them for food.

By riding out a mile or two from the village, for most of the year, the young warriors and hunters can kill meat in abundance. But when the young men range the country as far as they are willing to risk their lives, on account of their enemies, without finding meat, the chiefs and doctors sit in solemn council and consult on the measures to be taken, until they decide upon the old and only expedient which "never has failed."

The chief issues his orders to his runners or criers, who proclaim them through the village, and in a few minutes the dance begins in the public area in the center of the village, before the great medicine or mystery lodge. About ten or fifteen Mandans at a time join in the dance, each one with the skin of the buffalo's head (or mask), with the horns on, placed over his head, and in his hand his favorite bow or lance.

The dance always has the desired effect. It never fails. Nor can it, for it cannot be stopped, going incessantly day and night until "buffalo come." Drums beat and rattles shake, songs and yells are shouted, and lookers-on stand ready with masks on their heads and weapons in hand to take the place of each dancer as he becomes fatigued.

During this time of general excitement, spies or "lookers" are kept on the hills in the neighborhood of the village. When they sight buffaloes, they give the signal by "throwing their robes," which is instantly seen in the village and understood by the whole tribe. At this joyful intelligence there is a shout of thanks to the Great Spirit, and more especially to the mystery-man, and the dancers, who *have been the immediate cause of their success!*

These dances sometimes continue two or three weeks without stopping an instant, until the joyful moment when buffaloes make their appearance. So they *never fail;* and they believe the dance has been the means of bringing the buffalo.

The mask worn by these dancers is put over the head, and generally has a strip of the skin hanging to it, of the whole length of the animal, with the tail attached to it. The skin passes down over the back of the dancer, dragging on the ground. When one dancer becomes fatigued, he bends foward, sinking his body towards the ground. Another draws a bow upon him and hits him with a blunt arrow. The exhausted dancer falls like a buffalo, is seized by the bystanders, and dragged out of the ring by the heels. The bystanders brandish their knives about him, and go through the motions of skinning and cutting him up. Then they let him off, and his place is at once supplied by another, who dances into the ring with his mask on. By this taking of places the scene is easily kept up night and day until "the buffalo come."

The day before yesterday commenced in joy and thanksgiving to the Great Spirit for the signal success of several days of dancing and supplication. But it ended in a calamity which threw the village of the Mandans into mourning and tears. When the signal was given to the village from the top of a distant bluff that a band of buffaloes were in sight, every heart beat with joy, and every eye watered and glistened with gladness.

The dance had lasted some three or four days. Then the stamping of horses was heard as they were led and galloped through the village. Young men threw off their robes and their shirts, snatched a handful of arrows from their quivers, strung their sinewy bows, glanced their eyes and their smiles at their sweethearts, and mounted their ponies.

There had been a few minutes of bustle and boasting, bows were twanging and spears were being polished by running their blades into the ground. Every face and every eye was filled with joy and gladness. Horses pawed and snuffed in fury. Then Louison Frénié, an interpreter of the Fur Company, galloped through the village with his rifle in his hand and his powder-horn at his side. His head and waist were bandaged with handkerchiefs and his shirt sleeves rolled up to his shoulders. The hunter's yell issued from his lips and was repeated through the village. He flew to the bluffs, and behind him and over the graceful swells of the prairie galloped the Mandan youths, hearts beating quick for the hunt.

In the village, where hunger had reigned, all was instantly joy and gladness. For some days the chiefs and doctors had been dealing out minimum rations to the community from the public crib. Now they spread before their subjects the contents of their own private *caches,* and the last of everything that could be mustered, that they might eat a thanksgiving to the Great Spirit for his goodness in sending them a supply of buffalo meat. A general banqueting ensued, which occupied the greater part of the day. Their hidden stores saved for an emergency were consumed, bones were half picked, and dishes half emptied and then handed to the dogs. After the dogs had licked the dishes, the usual games and amusements ensued—and there was hilarity and mirth in every nook and corner of the village. Suddenly screams and shrieks echoed everywhere. Women and children scrambled to the tops of their lodges with their eyes and their hands stretched in agonizing earnestness to the prairie. Blackened warriors ran furiously through every winding maze of the village, issuing their gutturals of vengeance. They snatched their weapons from their lodges.

Two hunters were bending their course down the sides of the bluff towards the village. Another suddenly broke out of a deep ravine. Yet another was dashing down the green hill. All were goading their horses at full speed! Then came another, and another, and all entered the village amid the shouts and groans of the villagers who crowded around them.

The story was told in their looks. One was bleeding, and the blood had crimsoned his milk-white steed as it had dripped over him. Another grasped in his left hand a scalp reeking in blood. Another grasped nothing save the reins in one hand and the mane of the horse in the other, having thrown his bow and his arrows away and trusted to the fleetness of his horse for his safety.

The fatal tragedy was recited in irregular and almost suffocating ejaculations. The names of the dead were in turns pronounced, and screams and shrieks burst forth at their recital. Murmurs and groans ran through the village.

Their band of hunters had been surrounded by their enemy, the Sioux, and eight of them killed. The Sioux, who had probably reconnoitered their village during the night and ascertained that they were dancing for buffaloes, laid a strategem to entrap them.

Some six or eight Sioux appeared the next morning but under the skins of buffaloes, imitating the movements of those animals while grazing. The Mandan look-outs signalled the news of buffalo to the village, which brought out the Mandan hunters. The masked buffaloes were seen grazing on the top of a high bluff, and when the hunters had approached within half a mile or so of them, they suddenly disappeared over the hill. Louison Frénié, who was leading the little band of hunters, became at that moment suspicious of so strange a movement, and came to a halt.

"Look!" said a Mandan, pointing to a little ravine to the right. From the foot of the hill broke some forty or fifty furious Sioux on fleet horses. The Mandan hunters wheeled, but in front of them, came another band, more furious, from the other side of the hill. The Mandans started for home, straining every nerve, but the Sioux were too fleet for them, and every now and then the whizzing arrow and the lance were heard to rip the flesh of their naked backs, and with a grunt and a groan, they tumbled from their horses. Several miles were run in this desperate race. Frénié got home along with several Mandans, though eight of them were killed and scalped by the way.

So ended that day, and the hunt. *This* day, though, has been one of a more joyful kind, for the Great Spirit, who was indignant at so flagrant an injustice, has sent the Mandans an abundance of buffaloes. All hearts have joined in a general thanksgiving to Him for his goodness and justice.

The sham-fight and sham scalp-dance of the Mandan boys is a part of their regular exercise and constitutes a material branch of their education. During the pleasant mornings of the summer, the little boys between the age of seven and fifteen are called out, to the number of several hundred, and divided into two companies, each of which is headed by some experienced warrior, who leads them, in the character of a teacher.

They are led out into the prairie at sunrise. Their bodies are naked, and each one has a little bow in his left hand, and a number of arrows made of large spears of grass, which are harmless in their effects. Each one also has a little belt or girdle around his waist, in which he carries a knife made of a piece of wood and equally harmless. On the tops of their heads are slightly attached small tufts of grass, which answer as scalps, and in these costumes they follow the dictates of their experienced leaders, who lead them through the judicious evolutions of Indian warfare—of feints—of retreats—of attacks—and at last to a general fight. Many maneuvers are gone through, and eventually they are brought up face to face, within fifteen or twenty feet of each other, with their leaders at their head stimulating them on. Their bows are bent upon each other and their missiles flying while they dodge and fend them off.

If anyone is struck with an arrow on any vital part of his body, he is obliged to fall, and his adversary rushes up to him, places his foot upon him, and snatching from his belt his wooden knife, grasps hold of his victom's scalp-lock of grass, and making a feint at it with his wooden knife, twitches it off and puts it into his belt, then enters again into the ranks of battle.

This training generally lasts an hour or more in the morning, is performed on an empty stomach, and affords them a rigid and wholesome exercise while they are instructed in the important science of war. Some five or six miles of ground are run over during these evolutions, giving suppleness to their limbs and strength to their muscles.

After this exciting exhibition is ended, they all return to their village, where the chiefs and braves pay profound attention to their vaunting, and applaud them for their artifice and valor. Those who have taken scalps then step forward, brandishing them and making their boasts as they enter into the *scalp-dance* (in which they are also instructed by their leaders or

Sham war for Mandan boys.

teachers), jumping and yelling, brandishing their scalps, and reciting their sanguinary deeds to the great astonishment of their tender-aged sweethearts, who are gazing with wonder upon them.

The games and amusements of these people are in most respects like those of other tribes, consisting of ball plays, game of the moccasin, the platter, feats of archery, and horse-racing. The Mandans have yet another, which may be said to be their favorite amusement, and unknown to the other tribes about them. It is the game of Tchung-kee, a beautiful athletic exercise, which they seem to practice unceasingly while the weather is fair.

Tchung-kee is decidedly their favorite amusement. It is played near the village on a pavement of clay, which has been used until it has become as smooth and hard as a floor. Two champions form their respective parties, alternately choosing players until the requisite numbers are made up. Then their bets are made, and the stakes are held by some of the chiefs present.

Play commences with two (one from each party), who start off upon a trot, abreast of each other. One of them rolls on the pavement ahead of them a little ring of two or three inches in diameter, cut out of a stone. They each follow it up with their "Tchung-kee," a stick of six feet in length, with little bits of leather an inch or more in length projecting from its sides. Each throws the Tchung-kee before him as he runs, sliding it along upon the ground after the ring, endeavoring to place it in such a position that when it stops, the ring may fall on

The game of Tchung-kee.

one of the little projections of leather, which counts for game, one, or two, or four, according to the position of the leather on which the ring is lodged.

The last winner always rolls the ring. Both start and throw the Tchung-kee together. If either fails to catch the ring, he forfeits the amount of the number he is nearest to, and he loses his throw; another steps into his place. This game is a very difficult one to describe and to give an exact idea of unless one can see it played. It is a game of great beauty and fine bodily exercise, and these people become excessively fascinated with it, often gambling away everything they possess, and sometimes, when everything else is gone, staking their liberty upon the issue of these games, offering themselves as slaves to their opponents in case they get beaten.

Feasting and fasting are important customs observed by the Mandans, as well as by most other tribes, at stated times and for particular purposes. These observances are strictly religious and rigidly observed.

Sacrificing is also a religious custom with these people, and is performed in many different modes, and on numerous occasions. Human sacrifices have never been made by the Mandans, nor by any of the North Western tribes (so far as I can learn) excepting the Pawnees of the Platte. They practiced it, though they have relinquished it of late.

The Mandans sacrifice their fingers to the Great Spirit, and of their worldly goods, the best and the most costly. If a horse or a dog, it must be the favorite one. If it is an arrow from their quiver, they will select the most perfect one as the most effective gift. If it is meat, it is the choicest piece from the buffalo or other animal. If it is anything from the stores of the traders, it is the most costly—it is blue or scarlet cloth, which costs them an enormous price, and is chiefly used to cover the scaffolds where the bones of their departed relations rest.

Of these kinds of sacrifices there are three of an interesting nature, erected over the great medicine-lodge in the center of the village. They consist of ten or fifteen yards of blue and black cloth, each purchased from the Fur Company at fifteen or twenty dollars per yard, which are folded up to resemble human figures, with quills in their heads and masks on their faces. These singular-looking figures, like "scare crows," are erected on poles about thirty feet high, over the door of the mystery-lodge, and are left there to decay. Now, by the side of them, hangs another, which was added a few days ago: the skin of a white buffalo.

A few weeks ago a party of Mandans returned from the Mouth of the Yellow Stone, two hundred miles up river, with information that a party of Blackfeet were visiting Fort Union on business with the American Fur Company. They had with them a white buffalo robe for sale. This was looked upon as a subject of great importance by the chiefs, and one worthy of public consideration. A white buffalo robe is a great curiosity, even in the country of buffaloes, and will always command an almost incredible price from its extreme scarcity. Because it is the most costly article of traffic in these regions, it is usually converted into a sacrifice, being offered to the Great Spirit as the most acceptable gift that can be procured. Among the vast herds of buffaloes which graze on these boundless prairies, there is not one in an hundred thousand, perhaps, that is white. When one is obtained, it is considered great medicine or mystery.

On learning of the white robe, the chiefs convened in council. At the close of their deliberations, eight men were fitted out on eight of their best horses. They took from the Fur Company's store, on the credit of the chiefs, goods exceeding even the value of their eight horses. They started for the Mouth of the Yellow Stone, where they arrived in due time and made the purchase by leaving the eight horses and all the goods which they carried. They returned on foot to their own village, bringing home with them the white robe. This wonderful anomaly lay several days in the chief's lodge, until public curiosity was gratified. Then it was taken by the high-priests, and with a great deal of form and mystery, consecrated and raised on the top of a long pole over the medicine-lodge. It now stands as an offering to the Great Spirit, until it decays and falls to the ground.

Now I introduce to you a new character—not a doctor or a high-priest, yet a medicine-man, and one of the highest and most respectable order, a "rain maker!"

The Mandans raise a great deal of corn, but sometimes a drought visits the land, destructive to their promised harvest. Such was the case when I arrived at the Mandan village. Rain had not fallen for many a day. The dear little girls and the ugly old squaws (all of whom had fields of corn) were groaning and crying to their lords, and imploring them to intercede for rain. Their little patches were now turning pale and yellow, withered, and they would be deprived of the pleasure of their customary annual festivity, and the joyful occasion of the "roasting ears" and the "green corn dance."

The chiefs and doctors sympathized with the distress of the women, and recommended patience. Great deliberation, they said, was necessary in these cases. Though they resolved on making the attempt to produce rain for the benefit of the corn, they were wisely resolved that to being too soon might ensure their entire defeat in the endeavor. The longer they put it off, the more certain they would be of ultimate success.

After a few days of further delay, when the importunities of the women had become clamorous, and even mournful, and almost insupportable, the medicine-men assembled in the council-house with all their mystery apparatus about them: an abundance of wild sage and other aromatic herbs, with a fire prepared to burn them and send forth their savory odors to the Great Spirit. The lodge was closed to all the villagers except some ten or fifteen young men who were willing to hazard the dreadful alternative of either making it rain or suffering the everlasting disgrace of having made a fruitless attempt.

Only they were allowed as witnesses to the hocus-pocus and conjuration devised by the doctors inside the medicine-lodge. They were called up by lot, each one in his turn, to spend a day upon the top of the lodge, to test the potency of his medicine. In other words, to see how far his voice might be heard and obeyed among the clouds of the heavens. Meanwhile, the doctors would burn incense in the lodge below, and with their songs and prayers to the Great Spirit, send forth grateful fumes and odors to Him "who lives in the sun and commands the thunders of Heaven."

Wah-kee (The Shield) was the first who ascended the lodge at sunrise. He stood all day and looked foolish as he counted over and over his string of mystery-beads. The whole village assembled around him and prayed for his success. Not a cloud appeared. The day was calm and hot. At the setting of the sun, he descended from the lodge and went home—"his medicine was not good," nor could he ever be a medicine-man.

Om-pah (The Elk) was next. He ascended the lodge at sunrise the next morning. His body was entirely naked, being covered with yellow clay. On his left arm he carried a beautiful shield, and a long lance in his right. On his head was the skin of a raven, the bird that soars amid the clouds and above the lightning's glare. He flourished his shield and brandished his lance and raised his voice, but in vain. At sunset the ground was dry and the sky was clear. The squaws were crying, and their corn was withering at its roots.

War-rah-pah (The Beaver) was next. He also spent his breath in vain upon the empty air, and came down at night.

Wak-a-dah-ha-hee (The White Buffalo's Hair) took the stand the next morning. He was a small but beautifully proportioned young man. He was dressed in a tunic and leggings of the skins of the mountain-sheep, splendidly garnished with quills of the porcupine, and fringed with locks of hair taken by his own hand from the heads of his enemies. On his arm he carried a shield made of the buffalo's hide. Its boss was the head of the war-eagle, and its front was ornamented with "red chains of lightning." In his left hand he clenched his sinewy bow and one single arrow. The villagers all gathered about him.

He threw up a feather to decide on the course of the wind, and he commenced: "My friends! People of the pheasants! You see me here a sacrifice. I shall this day relieve you from great distress, and bring joy among you, or I shall descend from this lodge when the sun goes down and live among the dogs and old women all my days. My friends! You saw which way the feather flew, and I hold my shield this day in the direction where the wind comes. The lightning on my shield will draw a great cloud, and this arrow, which is selected from my quiver, and which is feathered with the quill of the white swan, will make a hole in it.

"My friends! This hole in the lodge at my feet shows me the medicine-men, who are seated in the lodge below me and crying to the Great Spirit. Through it comes and passes into my nose delightful odors, which you see rising in the smoke to the Great Spirit above, who rides in clouds and commands the winds! Three days they have sat here, my friends, and nothing has been done to relieve your distress. On the first day was Wah-kee. He could do nothing. He counted his beads and came down. His medicine was not good—his name was bad, and it kept off the rain. The next was Om-pah. On his head the raven was seen, who flies *above* the storm, and he failed. War-rah-pa was the next, my friends; the beaver lives *under* the *water*, and he never wants it to rain.

"My friends! I see you are in great distress, and nothing has yet been done. This shield belonged to my father the White Buffalo. The lightning you see on it is red. It was taken from a black cloud, and that cloud will come over us today. I am the white buffalo's hair—and I am the son of my father."

It happened on this memorable day about noon that the steamboat *Yellow Stone* approached and landed at the Mandan village. A salute of twenty guns of twelve pounds

180

calibre was fired when it first came in sight of the village. The Mandans at first supposed the new sound to be thunder, and the young man upon the lodge turned it to good account, gathering fame in rounds of applause, which were repeated and echoed through the whole village. All eyes were centered upon him. Chiefs envied him—mothers' hearts were beating high. They decorated and led up their fair daughters to offer him in marriage. The medicine-men left the lodge and came out to bestow upon him the envied title of "medicine-man," or "doctor," which he had so deservedly won. Wreaths were prepared to decorate his brows, and eagles' plumes and calumets were in readiness for him. His friends all rejoiced. His enemies wore on their faces a silent gloom and hatred. His old sweethearts, who had formerly cast him off, gazed intensely upon him as they glowed with the burning fever of repentance.

During all this excitement Wak-a-dah-ha-hee kept his position, assuming the most commanding and threatening attitudes, brandishing his shield in the direction of the new thunder, although there was not a cloud to be seen, until he, poor fellow, being elevated above the rest of the village, spied to his inexpressible amazement the steamboat ploughing its way up the windings of the river below, puffing her steam from her pipes and sending forth the thunder from a twelve-pounder on her deck!

The White Buffalo's Hair stood motionless and turned pale. He looked awhile, then turned to the chiefs and to the multitude and addressed them with a trembling lip: "My friends, we will get no rain! There are, you see, no clouds. But my medicine is great. I have brought a *thunder-boat!* Look and see it. The thunder you hear is out of her mouth, and the lightning which you see is on the waters!"

At this, the whole village flew to the tops of their lodges, or to the bank of the river, where the steamer was in full view, ploughing along, to their utter dismay and confusion.

In this promiscuous throng of chiefs, doctors, women, children, and dogs, Wak-a-dah-ha-hee descended from his high place to mingle with the frightened throng.

Dismayed at the approach of such an unaccountable object, the Mandans stood their ground for a few moments. Then, by order of the chiefs, all hands took up their posts within the piquets of their village, and all the warriors armed for a desperate defense. A few moments brought the boat in front of the village. All was still and quiet as death. Not a Mandan was to be seen upon the banks. The steamer was moored, and three or four of the chiefs soon walked boldly down the bank and on to her deck, with a spear in one hand and the calumet or pipe of peace in the other. The moment they stepped on board they met (to their great surprise and joy) their old friend, Major Sanford, their agent, which circumstance put an instant end to all their fears. The villagers were soon apprized of the fact, and the whole race of the beautiful and friendly Mandans was paraded on the bank of the river, in front of the steamer.

The "rain-maker" had secreted himself in some secure place. He was the last to come forward, the last to be convinced that this visitation was a friendly one from the white people, the last to believe that his medicine had not in the least been instrumental in bringing the thunder-boat. The news at length gave him great relief, and quieted his mind as to his danger. Yet in his breast there was a rankling thorn. Though he had escaped the dreaded vengeance which he had thought a few moments before was at hand, he had the mortification and disgrace of having failed in his mysterious rain-making.

During the day he pretended his medicines as the cause of its approach, asserting everywhere and to everybody that he knew of its coming, and that he had by his magic brought the occurrence about. This plea, however, did not get him much audience. In fact, everything else was pretty much swallowed up in the guttural talk, and bustle, and gossip about the mysteries of the "thunder-boat."

So passed the day until evening, when The White Buffalo's Hair (more watchful of such matters on this occasion than most others) observed that a black cloud had been jutting up in the horizon, and was almost directly over the village. In an instant his shield was on his arm and his bow in his hand, and he was again on top of the lodge. Stiffened and braced to the last sinew, he stood with his face and his shield presented to the cloud, and his bow drawn. He drew the eyes of the whole village upon him as he vaunted forth his superhuman powers, and at the same time commanding the cloud to come nearer, that he might draw down its contents upon the heads and the corn-fields of the Mandans.

He stood waving his shield over his head, stamping his foot and frowning as he drew his bow and threatened the heavens, commanding it to rain. His bow was bent, and the arrow sent to the cloud, and he exclaimed, "My friends, it is done! Wak-a-dah-ha-hee's arrow has entered that black cloud, and the Mandans will be wet with the waters of the skies!"

His predictions were true. In a few moments the cloud was over the village, and rain fell in torrents. He stood for some time wielding his weapons and presenting his shield to the sky, while he boasted of his power and the efficacy of his medicine. Those who had been about him were driven to the shelter of their lodges. At length, he finished his vaunts and his threats, and descended from his high place, perfectly drenched, prepared to recieve the honors and the homage that were due to one so potent in his mysteries, and to receive the style and title of "medicine-man."

He had "made it rain," and of course was to receive more than usual honors, as he had done much more than ordinary men could do. All eyes were upon him, and all were ready to admit that he was skilled in the magic art; and he must be so nearly allied to the Great or Evil Spirit that he must needs be a man of great and powerful influence in the nation, and well entitled to the style of doctor or medicine-man.

When the Mandans undertake to make it rain, *they never fail to succeed*, for their ceremonies never stop until rain begins to fall. But, in addition, it is the custom that he who has once "made it rain" never attempts it again. His medicine is undoubted. On future occasions of the kind, he stands aloof, giving an opportunity to other young men who are ambitious to signalize themselves in the same way.

During the night the steamboat remained by the side of the Mandan village. The rain that had commenced falling continued to pour down its torrents until midnight. Black thunder roared, and living lightning flashed until the heavens appeared to be lit up with one unceasing and appalling glare. At this frightful moment a flash of lightning buried itself in one of the earth-covered lodges of the Mandans, and killed a beautiful girl. Here was food and fuel fresh for superstitions. A night of vast tumult and excitement ensued.

The dreams of the new-made medicine-man were troubled, and he had dreadful apprehensions for the coming day. For he knew he was subject to the irrevocable decree of the chiefs and doctors, who canvass every strange and unaccountable event with close and superstitious scrutiny, and let their vengeance fall without mercy upon its immediate cause.

He looked upon his well-earned fame as likely to be withheld from him. He also considered that his life might perhaps be demanded as the forfeit for this girl's death, which would certainly be charged to him. He looked upon himself as culpable, and supposed the accident to have been occasioned by his criminal desertion of his post when the steamboat was approaching the village.

Morning came, and he soon learned from some of his friends the opinions of the wise men, and the nature of the tribunal that was preparing for him. He sent to the prairie for his three horses, which were brought in, and he mounted the medicine-lodge, around which, in a few moments, the villagers were all assembled.

"My friends!" he said. "I see you all around me, and I am before you. My medicine, you see, is great—it is *too great*. I am young, and I was too fast. I knew not when to stop. The wigwam of Mahsish is laid low, and many are the eyes that weep for Ko-ka (The Antelope). Wak-a-dah-ha-hee gives three horses to gladden the hearts of those who weep for Ko-ka. His medicine was great. His arrow pierced the black cloud, and the lightning came, and the thunder-boat also! Who says the medicine of Wak-a-dah-ha-hee is not strong?"

At the end of this sentence a unanimous shout of approbation ran through the crowd, and The White Buffalo's Hair descended among them, where he was greeted by shakes of the hand. He now lives and thrives under the honorable appellation of The Big Double Medicine.

Mah-to-toh-pa (The Four Bears) agreed to stand before me for his portrait. I sat with my palette of colors prepared and waited till twelve o'clock, before he could leave his toilette with feelings of satisfaction as to the propriety of his looks and the arrangement of his equipments. Then it was announced that "Mah-to-toh-pa was coming in full dress!"

There is no man among the Mandans so generally loved, nor any who wear a robe so justly famed and honorable as that of Mah-to-toh-pa. In a skirmish near the Mandan village, when they were set upon by their enemies the Riccarees, the brother of Mah-to-toh-pa was missing for several days. Mah-to-toh-pa found the body shockingly mangled, and a handsome spear left piercing the body through the heart. He brought the spear into the Mandan village, where it was recognized by many as a famous weapon belonging to a noted brave of the Riccarees by the name of Won-ga-tap. This spear was brandished through the Mandan village by Mah-to-toh-pa (with the blood of his brother dried on its blade), crying most piteously, and swearing that he would some day revenge the death of his brother with the same weapon.

He kept this spear in his lodge for four years, when his indignant soul, impatient of further delay, burst forth in the most uncontrollable frenzy and fury. He again brandished it through the village, and said that the blood of his brother's heart on its blade was still fresh, and he called loudly for revenge: "Let every Mandan be silent, and let no one sound the name of Mah-to-toh-pa—let no one ask for him, nor where he has gone, until you hear him sound the war-cry in front of the village, when he will enter it and show you the blood of Won-ga-tap. The blade of this lance shall drink the heart's blood of Won-ga-tap, or Mah-to-toh-pa mingles his shadow with that of his brother."

With this he sallied forth from the village, and over the plains, with the lance in his hand. His direction was towards the Riccaree village, and all eyes were upon him, though none dared to speak till he disappeared over the distant grassy bluffs. He travelled the distance of two hundred miles entirely alone, with a little parched corn in his pouch, making his marches by night and laying secreted by days, until he reached the Riccaree village. Then studying its shapes and its habits, and learning the position of the wigwam of his doomed enemy, he loitered about in disguise, mingling himself in the throng. At last, silently and alone, he observed through the rents of the wigwam the last movements of his victim as he retired to bed with his wife.

He saw him light his last pipe and smoke it "to its end." He saw the last whiff, and saw the last curl of blue smoke that faintly steeped from its bowl. He watched the village awhile in darkness and silence, until the embers that were in the middle of the wigwam had nearly gone out.

Then he walked softly, but not slyly, into the wigwam and seated himself by the fire, over which was hanging a large pot with a quantity of cooked meat remaining in it. By the side of the fire were the pipe and tobacco-pouch which had just been used. Knowing that the twilight of the wigwam was not sufficient to disclose the features of his face to his enemy, he very deliberately turned to the pot and completely satiated his desperate appetite, which he had got in a journey of six or seven days, with little or nothing to eat. Then, just as deliberately, he charged and lighted the pipe, and sent a prayer to the Great Spirit for the consummation of his design. While he was eating and smoking, the wife of his victim, laying in bed, several times inquired of her husband what man it was who was eating in their lodge. To which her husband replied: "It's no matter; let him eat, for he is probably hungry."

Mah-to-toh-pa knew his appearance would cause no other reply than this, for among the Northern Indians, any one who is hungry is allowed to walk into any man's lodge and eat. While smoking his last gentle and tremulous whiffs on the pipe, Mah-to-toh-pa leaned back and turned gradually on his side to get a better view of the position of his enemy, and to see a little more distinctly the shapes of things. He stirred the embers with his toes until he saw his way was clear. Then, with his lance in his hands, he rose and drove it through the body of his enemy, and snatching the scalp from his head, he darted from the lodge.

The village was soon in an uproar, but he was off, and no one knew the enemy who had struck the blow. Mah-to-toh-pa ran all night and lay close during the days, thanking the Great Spirit for strengthening his heart and his arm to this noble revenge. He prayed fervently for a continuance of aid and protection till he should get back to his own village.

His prayers were heard. On the sixth morning, at sunrise, Mah-to-toh-pa descended the bluffs and entered the village amid deafening shouts of applause, while he brandished and showed to his people the blade of his lance, with the blood of his victim dried upon it, over that of his brother; and the scalp of Won-ga-tap suspended from its handle.

At another time, a party of about one hundred and fifty Cheyenne warriors made an

184

assault upon the Mandan village at an early hour one morning, drove off a considerable number of horses, and took one scalp. Mah-to-toh-pa took the lead of a party of fifty warriors, all he could at that time muster, and went in pursuit of the enemy. About noon of the second day they came in sight of the Cheyennes. The Mandans seeing their enemy much more numerous than they had expected, were generally disposed to turn back and return without attacking them.

They started to go back, when Mah-to-toh-pa galloped out in front upon the prairie and plunged his lance into the ground. The blade was driven into the earth to its hilt. He made another circuit around, and in that circuit tore from his breast his reddened sash, which he hung upon his lance's handle as a flag, calling out to the Mandans: "What! Have we come to this? We have dogged our enemy two days, and now when we have found them, are we to turn about and go back like cowards? Mah-to-toh-pa's lance, which is red with the blood of brave men, has led you to the sight of your enemy, and you have followed it. It now stands firm in the ground, where the earth will drink the blood of Mah-to-toh-pa! You may all go back, and Mah-to-toh-pa will fight them alone!"

During this maneuver the Cheyennes, who had discovered the Mandans behind them, had turned about and were gradually approaching, in order to give them battle. The chief of the Cheyenne war-party seeing and understanding the difficulty, and admiring the gallant conduct of Mah-to-toh-pa, galloped his horse forward within hailing distance, in front of the Mandans, and called out to know "who he was who had struck down his lance and defied the whole enemy alone?"

"I am Mah-to-toh-pa, second in command of the brave and valiant Mandans."

"I have heard often of Mah-to-toh-pa. He is a great warrior. Dares Mah-to-toh-pa to come forward and fight this battle with me alone, and our warriors will look on?"

"Is he a chief who speaks to Mah-to-toh-pa?"

"My scalps you see hanging to my horse's bits, and here is my lance with the ermine skins and the war-eagle's tail!"

"You have said enough."

The Cheyenne chief made a circuit or two at full gallop on a beautiful white horse, then struck his lance into the ground, and left it standing by the side of the lance of Mah-to-toh-pa, both of which were waving together their little red flags—tokens of blood and defiance. The two parties then drew nearer, on a beautiful prairie, and the two full-plumed chiefs, at full speed, drove furiously upon each other, both firing their guns at the same moment. They passed each other and wheeled, when Mah-to-toh-pa drew off his powder-horn, and by holding it up, showed his adversary that the bullet had shattered it to pieces and destroyed his ammunition. He then threw it away, and his gun also, drew his bow from his quiver, and an arrow, with his shield upon his left arm. The Cheyenne instantly did the same. His horn was thrown, and his gun was thrown into the air, his shield was balanced on his arm, his bow drawn. Quick as lightning, they were both on the wing for a deadly combat.

Like two soaring eagles in the open air, they made their circuits around, and the twangs of their sinewy bows were heard, and the war-whoop, as they dashed by each other, parrying off the whizzing arrows with their shields. Some lodged in their legs and others in

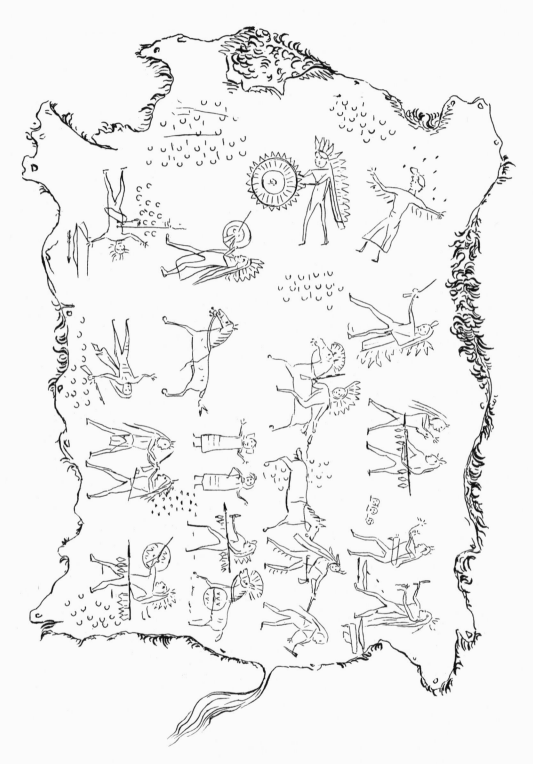

The buffalo robe of Mah-to-toh-pa told the history of his exploits.

their arms, but both protected their bodies with their bucklers of bull's hide. Many were the shafts that fled from their murderous bows.

At length the horse of Mah-to-toh-pa fell to the ground with an arrow in his heart. His rider sprang upon his feet prepared to renew the combat. The Cheyenne, seeing his adversary dismounted, sprang from his horse too, and presenting the face of his shield towards his enemy, invited him to come on. A few more arrows were exchanged, then the Cheyenne, having discharged all his arrows, held up his empty quiver, and dashing it furiously to the ground, with his bow and his shield, drew and brandished his naked knife!

"Yes!" said Mah-to-toh-pa, as he also threw his shield and quiver to the earth and grasped for his knife. But his belt was empty. He had left it at home! His bow was in his hand, with which he parried the Cheyenne's thrust and knocked him to the ground. A desperate struggle now ensued for the knife. The blade was several times drawn through the right hand of Mah-to-toh-pa, inflicting the most frightful wounds, and he was severely wounded in several parts of his body. At length he succeeded in wresting the knife from the Cheyenne's hand, and plunged it into his heart.

Mah-to-toh-pa held up, and claimed in deadly silence, the knife and scalp of the noble Cheyenne chief.

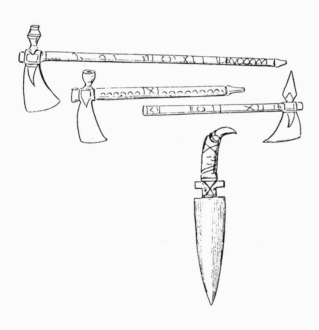

"O-kee-pa": Mandan torture ceremony.

IX

Mandan Village, *Upper Missouri*

THANK GOD, it is over and I have seen it, and am able to tell it to the world.

The annual religious ceremony of four days, which I have so long been wishing to see, has at last been enacted in this village. I have, fortunately, been able to see and to understand it in most of its bearings, which was more than I had reason to expect; for no white man has ever before been admitted to the medicine-lodge during these most remarkable and appalling scenes.

I was lucky enough to have painted the medicine-man, who was high-priest or conductor of the ceremonies, on this grand occasion. He had had me regularly installed doctor or "medicine" and on the morning when these grand refinements in mysteries commenced, he took me by the arm and led me into the medicine-lodge. I took my sketch-book with me and made many drawings of what I saw, and full notes of everything as translated to me by the interpreter. Since the close of that horrid and frightful scene, which was a week ago or more, I have been in an earth-covered wigwam, with a fine sky-light over my head, endeavoring with my palette and brushes to put the whole of what I saw upon canvas. I have made four paintings of these strange scenes, containing several hundred figures, representing the transactions of

189

each day. If I live to get them home, they will be found to be exceedingly curious and interesting.

I shudder even at the thought of these barbarous and cruel scenes, and am almost ready to shrink from the task of reciting them. I entered the medicine-house as I would have entered a church, and expected to see something extraordinary and strange, but yet in the form of worship or devotion. Little did I expect to see the interior of their holy temple turned into a slaughter-house, and its floor strewed with the blood of its fanatic devotees. Little did I think that I was entering a house of God where his blinded worshippers were to pollute its sacred interior with their blood, the tortures surpassing, if possible, the cruelty of the rack or the Inquisition. But such has been the scene, and as such I will endeavor to describe it.

The Mandans believe in the existence of a Great or Good Spirit, and also in the existence of an Evil Spirit, who they say existed long before the Good Spirit, and is far superior in power. They believe in a future state of existence, and a future administration of rewards and punishments. The punishments are not eternal but commensurate with their sins.

Since they live in a climate in which they suffer from cold in the severity of winter, they have very naturally reversed our ideas of Heaven and Hell. They describe Hell as a country very far north, barren and hideous, covered with eternal snows and ice. They describe the torments of this eternally freezing place as most excruciating. Heaven they suppose to be in a warmer and more delightful latitude, where nothing is felt but the keenest enjoyment, and where buffaloes and the other luxuries of life abound.

They believe the Great or Good Spirit dwells in frozen Hell for the purpose of meeting there those who have offended him. By being present himself, administering the penalties due, he can increase the agony of their sufferings. Similarly, they believe the Bad or Evil Spirit resides in sunny Paradise, still tempting the happy.

For those who have gone to the icy regions of punishment, they believe the punishments are proportionate to their transgressions, that they are then to be transferred to the land of the happy, where they are again liable to the temptations of the Evil Spirit, and answerable again at a future period for any new offenses.

In order to appease the Good and Evil Spirits, and to secure their entrance into those "Elysian fields," or beautiful hunting grounds, the young men subject themselves to horrid and sickening cruelties.

There are three distinct objects for which these religious ceremonies are held.

First, they are held annually as a celebration of the event of the subsiding of the Flood, which they call Mee-nee-ro-ka-ha-sha (the sinking down or settling of the waters).

Secondly, for the purpose of dancing what they call Bel-lochk-na-pic (the bull dance); to the strict observance of which they attribute the coming of buffaloes to supply them with food during the season.

Thirdly, for the purpose of conducting the young men of the tribe, as they reach the age of manhood, through an ordeal of privation and torture. It is supposed to harden their muscles and prepare them for extreme endurance. It also enables the chiefs to decide upon their comparative bodily strength and ability to endure the extreme privations and sufferings

190

that often fall to the lots of Indian warriors. The chiefs also decide who is the most hardy and best able to lead a war-party in case of extreme exigency.

In the center of the Mandan village is an open, circular area of one hundred and fifty feet in diameter, always kept clear as a public ground for the display of all their public feasts and parades. Around it the lodges are placed as near to each other as they can stand, their doors facing the center of this public area.

In the middle of this ground, which is a hard pavement, is a frame (somewhat like a large hogshead standing on its end) made of planks (and bound with hoops) some eight or nine feet high, which they religiously preserve and protect from year to year, free from mark or scratch, and which they call the "big canoe." It is undoubtedly a symbolic representation of a part of their traditional history of the Flood. This object of superstition, from its position at the very center of the village, is the rallying point of the whole nation. Devotions are paid to it on occasions of feasts and religious exercises during the year.

The Mandan religious ceremony commences, not on a particular day of the year (for these people keep no record of days or weeks), but in a particular season, which is designated by the full expansion of the willow leaves under the bank of the river. According to their tradition "the twig that the bird brought home was a willow bough, and had full-grown leaves on it." The bird is the mourning or turtle-dove, which is often to be seen feeding on the sides of their earth-covered lodges, and which is a medicine-bird, not to be destroyed or harmed by anyone—even their dogs are instructed not to do it injury.

At sunrise we were suddenly startled by the shrieking and screaming of the women, and the barking and howling of dogs, as if an enemy were actually storming their village. Groups of women and children were gathered on the tops of their earth-covered lodges, and all were screaming. All eyes were directed to the prairies in the west, where, a mile away, a solitary individual was descending a prairie bluff and making his way towards the village.

The whole community joined in the general expression of great alarm, as if they were in danger of instant destruction. Bows were strung and thrummed to test their elasticity. Horses were caught upon the prairie and run into the village. Warriors blackened their faces, dogs were muzzled, and every preparation made as if for combat.

During this deafening confusion, the figure on the prairie continued to approach in a straight line towards the village. All eyes were upon him. At length he made his appearance (without opposition) within the piquets, and proceeded towards the center of the village, where all the chiefs and braves stood ready to receive him, which they did in a cordial manner. They shook hands with him, recognizing him as an old acquaintance, and pronounced his name *Nu-mohk-muck-a-nah* (The First or Only Man). The body of this strange personage was chiefly naked, and was painted with white clay so as to resemble a white man. He wore a robe of four white wolf skins falling back over his shoulders. On his head he had a splendid head-dress made of two ravens' skins, and in his left hand he carried a large pipe, which he guarded as something of great importance. After greeting the chiefs and braves, he approached the medicine or mystery lodge, which he had the means of opening, and which had been religiously closed during the year except for the performance of these religious rites.

Having opened and entered it, he called in four men whom he appointed to clean it out and put it in readiness for the ceremonies. They swept it and strewed a profusion of green willow-boughs over its floor. They gathered wild sage and many other aromatic herbs from the prairies, and scattered them over its floor. They arranged a curious group of buffalo and human skulls over these, and other articles to be used during this strange transaction.

During the remainder of the day, and while these preparations were making in the medicine-lodge, Nu-mohk-muck-a-nah travelled through the village, stopping in front of every man's lodge and crying until the owner of the lodge came out and asked "Who's there?" and "What's the matter?" Nu-mohk-muck-a-nah would reply by relating the sad catastrophe which had happened on the earth's surface by the overflowing of the waters. He would say that he was the only person saved from the universal calamity; that he landed his big canoe on a high mountain in the West, where he now resides; that he had come to open the medicine-lodge; that he must receive a present of some edged tool from the owner of every wigwam so that it may be sacrificed to the water; that if this is not done, there will be another flood, and no one will be saved, as it was with such tools that the big canoe was made.

He visited every lodge in the village during the day and received a present at each, such as a hatchet or a knife. At evening he deposited them in the medicine-lodge, where they were to remain until the afternoon of the last day of the ceremony.

During the first night in the village, no one could tell where this strange character slept. Every person, both old and young, and dogs, and all living things were kept within doors, and dead silence reigned everywhere.

The next morning he made his appearance at sunrise and entered the medicine-lodge. At his heels, in single file, came all the young men who were candidates for the self-tortures. There were about fifty young men who entered the lists, and as they went into the sacred lodge, each one's body was naked but covered with clay of different colors: Some were red, others were yellow, and some were covered with white clay, giving them the appearance of white men. Each one of them carried in his right hand his medicine-bag. On his left arm was his shield of the bull's hide. In his left hand were his bow and arrows, with his quiver slung on his back. When all had entered the lodge, they placed themselves in reclining postures around its sides, and each one suspended over his head his respective weapons and medicine.

Nu-mohk-muck-a-nah was in the midst of them. He lit and smoked his medicine-pipe for their success. He addressed them in a short speech, stimulating and encouraging them to trust to the Great Spirit for His protection during the severe ordeal they were about to pass through. He called into the lodge an old medicine or mystery-man, whose body was painted yellow, and whom he appointed master of ceremonies during this occasion, whom they denominated in their language *O-kee-pah Ka-se-kah* (Keeper or Conductor of the Ceremonies). He was appointed, and the authority passed by the presentation of the medicine-pipe, on which hangs all the power of holding and conducting all these rites.

After this delegated authority had thus passed over to the medicine-man, Nu-

For four days and four nights the young men fast and wait inside the Big Medicine lodge.

mohk-muck-a-nah shook hands with him and bade him good-bye, saying that he was going back to the mountains in the West, from whence he should assuredly return in just a year from that time, to open the lodge again.

He then went out of the lodge, and passing through the village, took formal leave of the chiefs, and soon disappeared over the bluffs from whence he came. No more was seen of this character during the occasion.

The conductor, O-kee-pah, the medicine or mystery-man just appointed, had as his duty to lie by a small fire in the center of the lodge with his medicine-pipe in his hand, crying to the Great Spirit incessantly, watching the young men, and preventing their escape from the lodge, and all communication whatever with people outside, for the space of four days and nights, during which time they were not allowed to eat, or drink, or to sleep, preparatory to the excruciating self-tortures which they were to endure on the fourth day.

193

In addition to the willow-boughs, sage, and herbs in the interior of the medicine-lodge, there was a curious arrangement of buffalo and human skulls placed on the floor. They were divided into two parcels. Between them, and in front of the reclining group of young candidates, was a small and delicate scaffold elevated about five feet from the ground, made of four posts or crotches not larger than a gun-rod and placed some four or five feet apart, supporting four equally delicate rods resting in the crotches and thus forming the frame of the scaffold, which was completed by a number of still smaller and more delicate sticks transversely resting upon them. On the center of this little frame rested some small object, which I could not exactly understand from the distance of twenty or thirty feet which intervened between it and my eye. I started several times from my seat to approach it, but all eyes were instantly upon me, and every mouth in the assembly sent forth a hush—sh—! which brought me back to my seat again. At length I stifled my curiosity as well as I could. So sacred was that object, and so important its secrets or mysteries, that not even the young men who were passing the ordeal, nor any of the village save the conductor of the mysteries, could approach it, or know what it was.

From where I sat, this little mystery-thing, whatever it was, had the appearance of a small tortoise, or frog, lying on its back, with its head and legs quite extended, and tasselled off with exceedingly delicate red and blue and yellow ribbons or tassels, and other bright-colored ornaments. It seemed, from the devotions paid to it, to be the very nucleus of their mysteries—the *sanctissimus sanctorum,* from which seemed to emanate all the sanctity of their proceedings, and to which all seemed to be paying the highest devotional respect.

This strange yet important *essence* of their mysteries I made every enquiry about. But I got no further information than what I could learn by my eyes at the distance at which I saw it, and from the silent respect which I saw paid to it. I tried with the doctors, and all of the fraternity answered me that it was "great-medicine," assuring me that it "could not be told."

Immediately under the little frame or scaffold, on the floor of the lodge, was a knife. By the side of it was a bundle of splints or skewers, which were kept in readiness for the infliction of the cruelties. There were also a number of cords of rawhide hanging down from the top of the lodge and passing through its roof. The young men were to be suspended by the splints passed through their flesh, and drawn up with these by men placed on the top of the lodge.

There were also four sacks of great veneration lying on the floor of the lodge, each containing some three or four gallons of water. They were made with great labor and much ingenuity. Each one was constructed from the skin of the buffalo's neck and most elaborately sewed together in the form of a large tortoise lying on its back, with a bunch of eagle's quills appended to it as a tail. Each of them had a stick, shaped like a drum-stick, lying on them, with which, in a subsequent stage of the ceremonies, they are beaten upon by several mystery-men as a part of the music for their strange dances. By the side of these sacks, which they call *Eeh-teeh-ka,* are two other articles of equal importance, which they call *Eeh-na-dee* (rattles), in the form of a gourd-shell also made of dried skins and also used in the music of their dances.

The four sacks of water have the appearance of very great antiquity. By enquiring of my friend and patron, the medicine-man, after the ceremonies were over, he very gravely told me that "those four tortoises contained the waters from the four quarters of the world—that these waters had been contained therein ever since the settling down of the waters!"

There were many curious ceremonials enacted in the open area in front of the medicine-lodge by members of the community. One of these, which they call *Bel-lochk-na-pic* (the bull dance), is repeated four times during the first day, eight times on the second day, twelve times on the third day, and sixteen times on the fourth day; and always around the frame, or "big canoe."

Eight men, with skins of buffaloes thrown over their backs, with the horns and hoofs and tails remaining on, their bodies in a horizontal position, imitated the actions of the buffalo. The bodies of these men were naked and all painted in the most extraordinary manner: their limbs, bodies, and faces with black, red, or white paint. Each one of these strange characters had a lock of buffalo's hair tied around his ankles. In his right hand was a rattle, and a slender white rod or staff, six feet long, in the other. Each carried on his back a bunch of green willow-boughs about the usual size of a bundle of straw. These eight men, being divided into four pairs, took their positions on the four different sides of the frame, or big canoe, representing thereby the four cardinal points.

Between each pair was another figure with his back turned to the big canoe, engaged in the same dance, keeping step with them, with a similar staff in one hand and a rattle in the other, and (being four in number) answering again to the four cardinal points. These four young men were also naked, with no other dress upon them except a beautiful kelt (or quartz-quaw) around the waist, made of eagles' quills and ermine, and very splendid head-dresses made of the same materials. Two of these figures were painted entirely black with pounded charcoal and grease. They were called the "firmament or night," and the numerous white spots dotted all over their bodies were called "stars." The other two were painted from head to foot as red as vermilion could make them. These represented the day, and the white streaks painted up and down over their bodies were "ghosts which the morning rays were chasing away."

These twelve are the only persons actually engaged in the bull dance, which is repeated each time in the same form, without the slightest variation. There are, however, a great number of characters engaged in giving the whole effect to this strange scene, each one acting well his part.

The dance takes place in the presence of the whole nation, who are gathered around on the tops of the lodges, or otherwise, as spectators. On the first day the bull dance is given *once* to each of the cardinal points, and the medicine-man smokes his pipe in those directions. On the second day, *twice* to each, *three times* to each on the third day, and *four times* to each on the fourth.

As a signal for the dancers to assemble, the old man, master of ceremonies, with the medicine-pipe in hand, dances out of the lodge singing (or rather crying) forth a pitiful lament, until he approaches the big canoe, against which he leans, with the pipe in his hand, and continues to cry. At this instant four very aged and patriarchal-looking men, whose bodies are painted red, and who have been guarding the four sides of the lodge, enter it and bring out

The Bull Dance is repeated for four days and four nights around The Big Canoe.

the four sacks of water, which they place near the big canoe. Then they seat themselves and commence thumping on them with the drumsticks which have been lying on them.

Another brandishes and shakes the *Eeh-na-dees* or rattles. All unite their voices, raised to the highest pitch possible. The music for the bull dance is continued for fifteen minutes or more. When the music and dancing stop, the whole nation raise the huzza!—a deafening shout of approbation. The master of ceremonies dances back to the medicine-lodge. The old men return to their former place. The sacks of water and all rest as before, until they are again called into action.

The other characters who play their parts in this grand spectacle are well worth description. By the side of the big canoe are two men with the skins of grizzly bears thrown over them, using the skins as a mask over their heads. These ravenous animals are continually growling and threatening to devour everything before them, and interfering with the forms of the religious ceremony. To appease them, the women place before them dishes of meat, which are snatched up and carried to the prairie by two men whose bodies are painted black and their

196

heads white, whom they call bald eagles. These are chased upon the plains by a hundred or more small boys who are naked, with their bodies painted yellow and their heads white, whom they call *Cabris,* or antelopes. At length they get the food away from the eagles and devour it.

During the intervals between these dances, all these characters, except those from the medicine-lodge, retire to a lodge close by, which they use on the occasion as a sacred place. It is occupied exclusively by them while they are at rest, and also for the purpose of painting and ornamenting their bodies.

During each of these dances, the old men beat upon the sacks and sing, chanting their supplications to the Great Spirit for the continuation of his influence in sending them buffaloes to supply food during the year. They administer courage and fortitude to the young men in the lodge by telling them that "the Great Spirit has opened his ears in their behalf—that the very atmosphere all about them is peace—that their women and children can hold the mouth of the grizzly bear—that they have invoked from day to day O-ke-hee-de(The Evil Spirit)—that they are still challenging him to come, and yet he has not dared to make his appearance!"

But in the last of these dances, on the fourth day, in the midst of all their mirth and joy, and about noon, and in the height of exultations, a scream bursts from the tops of the lodges. Men, women, dogs, and all seemed actually to howl and shudder with alarm as they fixed their glaring eye-balls upon the prairie bluff, about a mile in the west, down the side of which a man was descending at full speed towards the village!

This character darted about in a zig-zag course on the prairie, like a boy in pursuit of a butterfly, until he approached the piquets of the village. His body was entirely naked and painted as black as a Negro, with pounded charcoal and bear's grease—shining black, except white rings of an inch or more in diameter, marked here and there all over him. Frightful indentures of white around his mouth resembled canine teeth. Adding to his hideous appearance, he gave frightful shrieks and screams as he dashed through the village and entered a terrified group, which was composed (in that quarter) chiefly of females.

A small thong encircled his waist. Attached to it, behind, was a buffalo's tail. In front, under a bunch of buffalo hair covering the pelvis, he had an artificial penis, ingeniously carved in wood, of colossal dimensions, pendulous as he ran, and extending somewhat below his knees. This, like his body, was painted jet-black, with the exception of the glans, which was a glaring red vermilion. He carried in his two hands a wand or staff eight or nine feet in length, with a red ball at the end of it, which he continually slid on the ground ahead of him as he ran. By elevating this wand, there was a corresponding rising of the penis, probably caused by some small, invisible thong connecting the two together.

All eyes in the village were centered upon him, and he made a desperate rush towards the women, who screamed for protection as they endeavored to retreat, falling upon each other as they struggled to get out of his reach. In this moment of general terror there was an instant check. All were as silent as death.

The old master of ceremonies, who had run from his position at the big canoe, met this monster, thrust the medicine-pipe before him, and held him still and immovable under its charm! This check gave the females an opportunity to get out of his reach. When they were free from their danger, though all hearts still beat with excitement, their alarm soon cooled down into the most exorbitant laughter, and shouts of applause at his sudden defeat, and the awkward and ridiculous posture in which he was stopped and held.

The old man stood braced, with his eye-balls glaring, while the medicine-pipe held in its mystic chains his *Satanic* Majesty, annulling all the powers of his magical wand, and also depriving him of the powers of locomotion!

Surely no two human beings ever presented a more striking group than these two individuals did for a few moments, with their eye-balls set in direst mutual hatred upon each other, both struggling for supremacy, relying on the potency of their medicine or mystery. The Evil Spirit frowning vengeance, the other sternly gazing back with a look of exultation and contempt as he held him in check and disarmed him under the charm of his sacred mystery-pipe.

When the superior powers of the medicine-pipe had been fully tested and acknowledged, and the women had had requisite time to withdraw from the reach of this fiendish monster, the pipe was very gradually withdrawn from before him. He seemed delighted to recover the use of his limbs again, and the power of changing his position from the really ridiculous one he had been caught in, and was compelled to maintain, a few moments before.

All joined in rounds of applause for the success of the magic spell placed upon him. All voices were raised in shouts of satisfaction at his defeat. All eyes gazed upon him, chiefs and warriors, matrons, and even their tender-aged and timid daughters, whose education had taught them to receive the *moral* of these scenes without the shock of impropriety which might have startled a more fastidious people.

His locomotion regained, The Evil Spirit joined the buffalo dance, which had begun. He was jostled, apparently by accident, by one of the eight buffalo dancers. He stepped back, and looking at the animal, placed himself in the attitude of a buffalo bull in the rutting season. Then he mounted on one of the dancing buffaloes, elevating his wand, and consequently his penis, which was inserted under the skin of the animal. The man underneath continued to dance, with his body in a horizontal position.

In his endeavor to keep time in the dance to the steps of the animal under him, an indescribable excitement was produced. The women and children of the whole tribe, looking on, were instructed to clap their hands and shout their approbation, as they all wanted buffaloes to supply them with food during the coming year, and which supply they attributed to the performance before their eyes.

In succession, he approached and leaped upon four of the eight dancers, without in the least checking the dance, producing something like a quarter of an hour of the highest excitement and amusement in the crowd. But then he appeared much fatigued and exhausted, which brought the women and children around him, no longer afraid of him. The women danced up to him and back, in lascivious attitudes, tempting him with challenges which, for all his gallantry, he was now apparently unable to accept.

In this awkward predicament he became the laughing-stock and butt for the women. His dilemma soon became a sad one. One of the women stole up behind him with both hands full of yellow dirt, dashed it into his face and eyes and all over him, and since his body was covered with grease, it instantly took a different hue. He seemed heart-broken at this disgrace, and commenced crying most vehemently. Another caught his wand from his hand and broke it across her knee. It was snatched for by others, who broke it into bits and then threw them at him. His power was now gone, his bodily strength was exhausted, and he made a bolt for the prairie. He dashed through the crowd and made his way through the piquets at the back of the village. An hundred or more women and girls escorted him as he ran for half a mile or more, beating him with sticks and stones and dirt, and kicks and cuffs, until he finally escaped their clutches, retreating over the prairie bluffs from which he first appeared. At the moment of this victory, when all eyes lost sight of him as he disappeared over the bluffs, the whole village united their voices in shouts of satisfaction.

The frightful appendage had been wrested from his body and brought by its captor into the village, wrapped in a bunch of wild sage. She carried it triumphantly, in her arms, as she would have carried an infant. She was escorted by two matrons on each side. They lifted her up on the front of the medicine-lodge, directly over its doors. From there she harangued the village for some time, claiming she held the power of creation, and of life and death over them; that she was the ancestor of all buffaloes and that she could make them come or stay away as she pleased.

She demanded the handsomest dress in the Mandan tribe, which the master of ceremonies had in readiness, and presented to her, for which he received from her hands her singular trophy. He appointed her to the envied position of conductress of the *Feast of the Buffaloes,* to be given that night. She then ordered the buffalo dance to be stopped and the "Pohk-hong" (or torturing scenes) to commence in the medicine-lodge.

The master of ceremonies and musicians returned to the medicine-lodge. At the same time a number of young men, who were to be instruments of the cruelties to be inflicted, entered with the chiefs and doctors of the tribe.

The chiefs seated themselves on one side of the lodge, dressed in their robes and splendid head-dresses. The band of music arranged themselves. The old master of ceremonies placed himself in front of a small fire in the center of the lodge, with his "big pipe" in his hands, and commenced smoking to the Great Spirit, with all possible vehemence for the success of the aspirants.

After having removed the *sanctissimus sanctorum,* or little scaffold, of which I spoke before, and having removed the buffalo and human skulls from the floor, and attached them to the posts of the lodge, two men took their positions near the middle of the lodge, for the purpose of inflicting the tortures—one with the scalping-knife and the other with the bunch of splints in his hand.

One at a time the young fellows, emaciated with fasting, thirsting, and being awake for nearly four days and nights, advanced from the side of the lodge to submit to the cruelties. An inch or more of the flesh on each breast was taken up between the thumb and finger by the man who held the knife in his right hand. The knife had been ground sharp on both edges, then hacked and notched with the blade of another to make it produce as much pain as possible. It was forced through the flesh below the fingers, and being withdrawn, was followed

199

with a splint or skewer, from the other, who held a bunch of such in his left hand, and was ready to force them through the wound.

Then two cords were lowered down from the top of the lodge (by men who were placed on the lodge outside, for the purpose), which were fastened to these splints or skewers, and they instantly began to haul the aspirant up. He was raised until his body was suspended above the ground, then the knife and a splint were passed through the flesh in a similar manner on each arm below the shoulder (over the *brachialis externus),* below the elbow (over the *extensor carpi radialis),* on the thighs (over the *vastus externus),* and below the knees (over the *peroneus).*

In some instances they remained in a reclining position on the ground until this painful operation was finished, which was performed, in all instances, exactly on the same parts of the body and limbs. Each time it took some five or six minutes.

Each one was then raised with the cords until the weight of his body was suspended by them, and then, while the blood was streaming down their limbs, the bystanders hung upon the splints each man's appropriate shield, bow, and quiver. In many instances, the skull of a buffalo with the horns on it was attached to each lower arm and each lower leg, for the purpose, probably, of preventing, by their great weight, the struggling, which might otherwise have taken place to their disadvantage while they were hung up.

When these things were all adjusted, each youth was raised higher by the cords, until these weights all swung clear from the ground, leaving his feet, in most cases, some six or eight feet above the ground. They became appalling and frightful to look at. The flesh, to support the weight of their bodies, with the additional weights which were attached to them, were raised six or eight inches by the skewers. Their heads sunk forward on their breasts, or were thrown backwards in a much more frightful condition, according to the way in which they were hung up.

The unflinching fortitude with which every one of them bore this part of the torture surpassed credulity. Each one sustained an unchangeable countenance as the knife was passed through the flesh. Several of them, seeing me make sketches, beckoned me to look at their faces, which I watched through all this horrid operation without being able to detect anything but the pleasantest smiles as they looked me in the eye, while I could hear the knife rip through the flesh, and feel enough of it myself to start uncontrollable tears down my cheeks.

When raised and completely suspended by the cords, new and improved refinements in cruelty were staged. A dozen or more imps and demons gathered around. One of them advanced towards the suspended victim, sneering, and commenced turning him around with a pole. This was done in a gentle manner at first, but gradually increased until the brave fellow, whose proud spirit could control its agony no longer, burst out in the most lamentable and heart-rending cries the human voice is capable of producing, crying forth a prayer to the Great Spirit to support and protect him in this dreadful trial.

He was turned faster and faster. There was no hope of escape, nor chance for the slightest relief, until by fainting, his voice faltered and his struggling ceased, and he hung, apparently a still and lifeless corpse.

While he was gradually brought to faint, which generally took ten or fifteen minutes, a close scrutiny of him was made by his tormentors, who checked and held each other back as long as the least struggling or tremor could be discovered, lest he should be removed before he was (as they term it) "entirely dead."

When his voice and strength gave out, when he hung entirely still, apparently lifeless, when his tongue was distended from his mouth, and his medicine-bag, which he had superstitiously clung to with his left hand dropped to the ground, the signal is given to the men on top of the lodge, by gently striking the cord with the pole below. They gradually and carefully lower him to the ground.

He lies like a corpse in the keeping of the Great Spirit, whom he trusts will protect him and enable him to get up and walk away. As soon as he is lowered to the ground, one of the bystanders advances and pulls out the two splints or pins from the breasts and shoulders, thereby disengaging him from the cords by which he has been hung up, but leaving all the others with their weights hanging to his flesh.

He lies for six or eight minutes, until he gets strength to rise and move himself. No one is allowed to assist him. He is enjoying the most valued privilege of which a Mandan can boast: "trusting his life to the keeping of the Great Spirit."

As soon as he gets enough strength to rise to his hands and feet and drag his body around the lodge, he crawls with the weights still hanging to his body to another Indian sitting with a hatchet in his hand, and a dried buffalo skull before him. In the most earnest manner, he holds up the little finger of his left hand to the Great Spirit and expresses to Him in a speech of a few words his willingness to give it as a sacrifice. Then he lays it on the dried buffalo skull. The other, with a blow of the hatchet, chops it off near the hand.

Nearly all of the young men whom I saw passing this horrid ordeal gave the little finger of the left hand. I saw several who immediately afterwards (and apparently with very little concern or emotion), with a similar speech, extended in the same way the *fore*-finger of the same hand, and that too was struck off, leaving on the hand only the two middle fingers and the thumb, which they deem absolutely essential for holding the bow, the only weapon for the left hand.

I have since examined several of the head chiefs and dignitaries of the tribe, who have also given, in this manner, the little finger of the right hand, which is considered by them to be a much greater sacrifice than both of the others. I have found a number of their most famous men, who furnish me incontestable proof, by five or six corresponding scars on each arm and each breast and each leg, that they had several times in their lives submitted to this almost incredible operation. It seems to be optional with them: The oftener they volunteer to go through it, the more famous they become in the estimation of their tribe.

No bandages are applied to the fingers which have been amputated, nor any arteries taken up. Nor is any attention whatever paid to them or the other wounds. They are left, as they say, "for the Great Spirit to cure, who will surely take good care of them."

I learned from a close inspection of their wounds that the bleeding is very slight and soon ceases, probably from their extreme exhaustion and debility, caused by want of sustenance and sleep, which checks the natural circulation and at the same time prepares them to

201

O-ke-hee-de, The Evil Spirit.

Bull Dancers: Night and Day.

O-kee-pa: hung by rawhide thongs tied to skewers run through their flesh, and then spun.
See Plate VII, following page 270.

meet the severity of these tortures without the same degree of sensibility and pain which, under other circumstances, might result in inflammation and death.

During the whole of the time of this cruel part of these most extraordinary inflictions, the chiefs and dignitaries of the tribe look on to decide who are the hardiest and "stoutest hearted": who can hang the longest by his flesh before he faints; who will be soonest up, after he has been down. They may learn who to appoint to lead a war party, or place at the most honorable and desperate post. The four old men incessantly beat upon the sacks of water and sing the whole time, their voices strained to the highest key, encouraging the young men with the power and efficacy of the medicine-pipe, which has disarmed the monster O-ke-hee-de (or Evil Spirit) and driven him from the village, and will be sure to protect them and watch over them through their present severe trial.

As soon as six or eight had passed the ordeal they were led out of the lodge, with their weights hanging to their flesh and dragging on the ground, to undergo another, and a still more appalling mode of suffering in the center of the village, and in the presence of the whole nation.

The signal for this part of the cruelties was given by the old master of ceremonies, who again ran out as in the buffalo dance and, leaning against the big canoe, with his medicine-pipe in his hand, began to cry. This was done several times in the afternoon, as often as there were six or eight who had passed the ordeal within the lodge. They were then taken out in the open area.

About twenty young men had been selected of equal height and equal age. Their bodies were naked. Beautiful head-dresses of war-eagles' quills were on their heads. A wreath made of willow-boughs was held in their hands, connecting them in a chain or circle in which they ran around the big canoe with all possible speed, raising their voices in screams and yelps to the highest pitch possible.

Then the young men were led forward. They were placed equal distance apart outside the ring. Each one was taken in charge by two athletic young men, fresh and strong, who stepped up to him, one on each side. They wrapped a broad leather strap around his wrists, without tying it, grasped it firm underneath the hand, and stood prepared for what they call Eh-ke-nah-ka-nah-pick (the last race).

The initiates stood, pale and ghastly, until all were prepared and the word was given. Then all started to run around outside the ring. Each poor fellow, his weights dragging on the ground and his furious conductors by his side hurrying him forward by the wrists, struggled in desperate emulation to run longer without "dying" (as they call it). His comrades were fainting around him and sinking down, like himself, but their bodies were dragged with all possible speed, often with their faces in the dirt.

At the beginning of the last race they start at a moderate pace but gradually increase their speed. The pain became so excruciating that their languid and exhausted frames gave out, and they were dragged by their wrists until they were disengaged from the weights attached to their flesh. This was done by such violent force it tore the flesh out with the splint. They claim it can never be pulled out endwise without offending the Great Spirit and defeating the object for which they have thus far suffered.

The splints or skewers which are put through the breast and the shoulders take up a part of the pectoral or trapezius muscle, which is necessary to support the great weight of their bodies, and which are withdrawn as he is lowered down. But all the others, on the legs and arms, seem to be very ingeniously passed through the flesh and integuments without taking up the muscle. To be broken out requires so violent a force that most of the poor fellows faint under the operation.

When they were freed from the last of the buffalo skulls and other weights (which

204

They were dragged by their wrists until the weights tore from their flesh: The Last Race.

was often done by some of the bystanders throwing the weight of their bodies onto them as they were dragging on the ground), they were dropped by the persons who dragged them. Their bodies were left looking like a mangled and loathsome corpse. At this frightful juncture the two men who had dragged them fled through the crowd and away upon the prairie, as if they were guilty of some enormous crime and were fleeing from summary vengeance.

Each poor fellow, having thus patiently and manfully endured the privations and tortures devised for him, and torn himself loose from his tormentors, lies the second time in the "keeping of the Great Spirit," to whom he issues his repeated prayers, and entrusts his life, and in whom he reposes the most implicit confidence for his preservation and recovery.

There is no person, not a relation or a chief of the tribe, who is allowed, or who would dare, to step forward to offer an aiding hand, even to save a life. The pride of the youth who has entrusted his life to the keeping of the Great Spirit would sternly reject such a tender. Their superstition, which is the strongest of all arguments in an Indian community, would alone hold all the tribe in fear and dread of interfering. They consider they have good reason to believe the Great Spirit has undertaken the special care and protection of his devoted worshippers.

In this "last race," the struggle which finally closed their sufferings, each one was dragged until he fainted. Each one lay until he was seen gradually rising, at last reeling and staggering like a drunken man through the crowd to his lodge. There his friends and relatives stood ready to take him into hand and restore him.

In this frightful scene, as in the buffalo dance, the whole nation was assembled as spectators. All raised the most piercing and violent yells and screams they could possibly produce to drown the cries of the suffering ones. Six or eight young men were brought from the medicine-lodge at a time, until the whole number, some forty-five or fifty, had run in the sickening circle.

There was one poor fellow who was dragged around and around the circle, with the skull of an elk hanging to the flesh on one of his legs. Several had jumped upon it, but to no effect, for the splint was under the sinew, which could not be broken. The dragging became more and more furious. Apprehensions for the poor fellow's life grew, apparent by the piteous howl which was set up for him by the multitude around. The medicine-man, with his medicine-pipe in his hand, held them in check. The body dropped, and was left upon the ground, with the skull yet hanging to it.

He was an extremely fine-looking youth. When he recovered his senses and his strength, he looked deliberately at his torn and bleeding limbs, and with the most pleasant smile of defiance, crawled through the crowd to the prairie, and then for a distance of half a mile, to a sequestered spot. He lay three days and three nights, without food, praying to the Great Spirit, until suppuration took place in the wound. As the flesh decayed, the weight was dropped and the splint also, which he dared not extricate in another way. Then he crawled back to the village on his hands and knees, too much emaciated to walk, and begged for something to eat, which was at once given him. He was soon restored to health.

After the young men had run their "last race," the old medicine-man, master of ceremonies, returned, still crying to the Great Spirit, sole tenant of the medicine-lodge, and brought out the "edged tools," which had been collected at the door of every man's lodge to be given as a sacrifice to the water. Leaving the lodge securely fastened, he approached the bank of the river. All the medicine-men attended him, and all the nation were spectators. In their presence he threw the tools from a high bank into very deep water. They were made a sacrifice to the water. This affair took place just exactly at sun-down, and closed the scene, the finale of the Mandan religious ceremony.

That these people should have a tradition of the Flood is by no means surprising. They have a high mountain where they insist the big canoe landed. They hold an annual celebration of the event, and the season is decided by such circumstances as the full leaf of the willow. The medicine-lodge is opened by Nu-mohk-muck-a-nah (who appears to be a white man), and he makes his appearance "from the high mountains in the West." The circumstances are a remarkable thing.

206

Their tradition says that at a very ancient period such a man did actually come from the West; that his body was white; that he wore a robe of four white wolf skins; that his head-dress was made of two raven's skins; and that in his left hand was a huge pipe. He said "he was at one time the only man." He told them of the destruction of everything on the earth's surface by water; that he stopped in his big canoe on a high mountain in the West, where he landed and was saved.

He said the Mandans were bound to make yearly sacrifices of some edged tools to the water, for of such things the big canoe was made. He instructed the Mandans how to build their medicine-lodge, and taught them also the forms of these annual ceremonies. He told them that as long as they made these sacrifices, and performed their rites to the full, they would be the favorite people of the Almighty, and would always have enough to eat and drink. As soon as they should depart in one tittle from these forms, their race would decrease and finally run out, and they might date their nation's calamity.

The Minatarees, and some other of the neighboring tribes, have seasons of abstinence and self-torture somewhat similar, but bearing no other resemblance to the Mandans than a feeble imitation.

It would seem from the Mandan tradition of the willow branch and the dove that these people must have had some proximity to some part of the civilized world. There are other strong and almost decisive proofs in my opinion: the diversity of color in their hair and complexions; their tradition of the "first or only man," whose body was white, and who came from the West, telling them of the destruction of the earth by water. In addition, I will add the following very curious stories, which I had from several of their old and dignified chiefs.

The Mandans (People of the Pheasants) were the first people created in the world, and they originally lived inside the earth. They raised many vines, and one of these vines had grown up through a hole in the earth overhead. One of their young men climbed up it until he came out on the top of the ground, on the bank of the river where the Mandan village stands. He looked around and admired the beautiful country and prairies about him. He saw many buffaloes, killed one with his bow and arrows, and found that its meat was good to eat. He returned and related what he had seen. A number of others went up the vine with him and witnessed the same things.

Among those who went up were two pretty young women. They were favorites of the chiefs because they were virgins. Among those who were trying to get up was a very large and fat woman who had been ordered by the chiefs not to go up, but whose curiosity led her to try it as soon as she got a secret opportunity. When she got part of the way up, the vine broke under the great weight of her body, and she fell down. She was much hurt by the fall but did not die. The Mandans were very sorry about this. She was disgraced for being the cause of a very great calamity, which she had brought upon them, and which could never be averted, because thereafter no more could ascend, nor could those descend who had got up. They built the Mandan village, where it formerly stood, a great way downstream on the river. The remainder of the people live under ground to this day.

The tradition is told with great gravity by their chiefs and doctors or mystery-men.

The latter profess to hear their friends talk through the earth at certain times and places, and even consult them for their opinions and advice on many important occasions.

Another tradition runs that at a very ancient period, O-kee-hee-de (The Evil Spirit) came to the Mandan village with Nu-mohk-muck-a-nah (The First or Only Man) from the West, and sat down by a woman who had but one eye, and was hoeing corn. Her daughter, who was very pretty, came up, and the Evil Spirit desired the daughter to go and bring some water. Before she started, however, she should come to him and eat some buffalo meat. He told her to take a piece out of his side. She did this, and ate it. It proved to be buffalo-fat. She then went for the water, which she brought, and met him in the village where they had walked, and they both drank of it. Nothing more was done.

Soon after, the friends of the girl endeavored to disgrace her by telling her that she was pregnant, which she did not deny. But she declared her innocence at the same time, and boldly defied any man in the village to come forward and accuse her. This raised a great excitement in the village. No one would stand forth to accuse her, because she was looked upon as *great medicine*. She soon after went off secretly to the upper Mandan village where the child was born.

A great search was made for her before she was found. It was presumed the child would also be great medicine or mystery, and of great importance to the existence and welfare of the tribe. They were induced to this belief from the very strange manner of its conception and birth, and were soon confirmed in it from the wonderful things which it did at an early age. They say that when the Mandans were about to starve, he gave them four buffalo bulls, which filled the whole village—leaving as much meat after they had eaten as there was before they had eaten. He told them these four bulls would supply them forever. But Nu-mohk-muck-a-nah was bent on the destruction of the child. After making many fruitless searches, he found it hidden in a dark place, and put it to death by throwing it into the river.

When O-ke-hee-de (The Evil Spirit) heard of the death of this child, he sought Nu-mohk-muck-a-nah with intent to kill him. He traced him a long distance, and at length found him at Heart River, about seventy miles below the village, with the big medicine-pipe in his hand, the charm or mystery of which protects him from all his enemies. They soon agreed, however, to become friends. They smoked the big pipe together, and returned to the Mandan village. The Evil Spirit was satisfied. And Nu-mohk-muck-a-nah told the Mandans never to pass Heart River to live, because it was the center of the world. To live beyond it would be destruction of them; and he named it *Nat-com-pa-sa-hah* (Heart or Center of the World).

I advance these stories not in support of any theory, but merely as I have heard them related by the Indians. When an Indian story is told, it is like all other gifts: "to be taken for what it is worth." Any seeming inconsistency in their traditions is immaterial. Questioning them generally incurs their distrust and ill-will. One of the Mandan doctors told me very gravely a few days ago that the earth was a large tortoise, that it carried the dirt on its back, that a tribe of people who are now dead and whose faces were white used to dig down very deep in this ground to catch badgers, and that one day they struck a knife through the tortoise-shell and it sunk down so that the water ran over its back, and drowned all but one man. And on the next day while I was painting his portrait, he told me there were four tortoises: one in the North, one in the East, one in the South, and one in the West; that each one of these rained ten days, and the water covered over the earth.

These conflicting accounts, both from the same man, give as good a demonstration of Indian traditions as anything I could at present mention. However ridiculous they may seem, they are yet worthy of consideration.

The Mandan chiefs and doctors, in all their feasts where the pipe is lit and about to be passed around, extend the stem of the pipe *upwards* before they smoke it themselves. They offer the stem to the four *cardinal points* in succession, and then drawing a whiff through it, pass it around among the group.

The annual religious ceremony invariably lasts *four* days, seeming to have some allusion to the *four* cardinal points or the "four tortoises." *Four* men are selected by Nu-mohk-muck-a-nah to cleanse out and prepare the medicine-lodge for the occasion—one he calls from the *north* part of the village, one from the *east,* one from the *south,* and one from the *west.* The *four* sacks of water, in the form of large tortoises, rest on the floor of the lodge. *Four* buffalo and *four* human skulls rest on the floor of the same lodge. The *four* couples of dancers in the bull dance, and the *four* intervening dancers in the same dance, seem to signify the same magic.

The bull dance in front of the medicine-lodge, repeated on the *four* days, is danced *four* times on the first day, *eight* times on the second, *twelve* times on the third, and *sixteen* times on the fourth. There are *four* sacrifices of black and blue cloths erected over the door of the medicine-lodge. The visits of O-ke-hee-de (or Evil Spirit) were paid to *four* of the buffaloes in the buffalo dance. In every instance, the young men who underwent the tortures had *four* splints or skewers run through the flesh on their legs, *four* through the arms, and *four* through the body.

I have dwelt longer on the history and customs of these people than I have or shall on any other tribe, in all probability, and that because I have found them a very peculiar people. From the striking peculiarities in their personal appearance, in their customs, traditions, and language, I have been led conclusively to believe that they are a people of a decidedly different origin from that of any other tribe in these regions.

They are a small and feeble tribe, against whom the powerful tribes of Sioux wage a deadly war with the prospect of their extermination. With their limited numbers, the Mandans are not likely to hold out long in their struggle for existence, but no set of men that ever I associated with have better hearts than the Mandans, and none are quicker to embrace and welcome a white man than they. None press him closer to his bosom so that the pulsation of his heart may be felt, than a Mandan; and no man in any country keeps his word and guards his honor more closely.

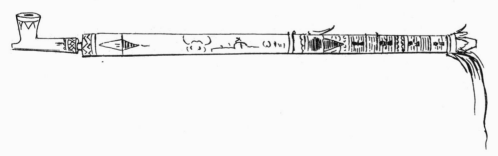

The Minataree village, on the banks of the Knife River, eight miles above the Mandans.

X

Minataree Village, *Upper Missouri*

SOON AFTER witnessing the annual religious ceremonies of the Mandans, I went to the village of the Minatarees, which is also located on the west bank of the Missouri River, eight miles above the Mandans.

The Minatarees (People of the Willows) are a small tribe of about one thousand five hundred souls, residing in three villages of earth-covered lodges on the banks of Knife River, a small stream meandering through an extensive prairie, and uniting its waters with the Missouri.

This small community is undoubtedly a part of the tribe of Crows who live at the base of the Rocky Mountains. At some remote period, either in their war or hunting excursions, the Minatarees were run off by their enemies. Their retreat prevented, they threw themselves upon the hospitality of the Mandans, to whom they have since looked for protection and under whose wing they are now living in a sort of confederacy, ready to intermarry and also to join, as they often have done, in the common defense of their country.

In language and personal appearance, as well as in many of their customs, they are a type of Crow. Yet having lived so long under the system of the Mandans, they are much like

211

them in many respects, and continually assimilating. Among their various traditions they have some disjointed authority for the manner in which they came here, but no account of the time. They say that they came poor, without wigwams or horses, were nearly all women, as their warriors had been killed off in their flight. The Mandans would not take them into their village, nor let them come nearer than where they are now living, but assisted them to build their villages. Their lodges have been constructed exactly in the same manner as those of the Mandans, entirely distinct from any custom to be seen in the Crow tribe.

Notwithstanding the long familiarity in which they have lived with the Mandans, and the complete adoption of most of their customs, there is scarcely a man in the tribe who can speak half a dozen words of the Mandan language. On the other hand, most of the Mandans are able to converse in the Minataree tongue, leaving us to conclude that the Mandan language, being different from any other language in the country, is an exceedingly difficult one to learn.

The chief sachem of this tribe is a very ancient man by the name of Eeh-tohk-pah-shee-pee-shah (The Black Moccasin). He counts more than an hundred snows. For some days I have been an inmate in his hospitable lodge. He sits tottering with age, and silently reigns sole monarch of the little community around him. They continually drop in to cheer his sinking energies and to render him their homage. His voice and sight are nearly gone, but the gestures of his hand are still energetic and youthful, and speak the language of his heart.

I have been treated in the kindest manner by this old chief. I have painted his portrait as he was seated on the floor of his lodge smoking his pipe, and he recounting to me some of the extraordinary feats of his life. He sits with a beautiful Crow robe wrapped around him, his hair wound up in a conical form upon his head, and fastened with a small wooden pin to keep it in its place.

He has many distinct recollections of Lewis and Clark, the first explorers of this country, who crossed the Rocky Mountains thirty years ago. They too were treated with great kindness by Black Moccasin. In consequence, they constituted him chief of the tribe, with the consent of his people. He has remained their chief ever since. He enquired very earnestly for "Red Hair" and "Long Knife."

I told him that "Long Knife" has been many years dead but "Red Hair" was still living in St. Louis, and would be glad to hear of him. He seemed much pleased, and has signified to me that he will make me bearer of some peculiar dispatches to him.

The name by which these people are generally called is Grosventres, a name given them by the French traders. The Minatarees are generally tall and heavily built. There is no tribe better entitled to be called "warlike" than the Minatarees. Unlike the Mandans, they continually carry war into their enemies' country, sometimes drawing the poor Mandans into unnecessary broils, and suffering so much themselves in their desperate wars that I find the proportion of women to men two or three to one.

The son of Black Moccasin, whose name is Ee-a-chin-che-a (The Red Thunder) is reputed one of the most desperate warriors of his tribe. I painted him full-length, in his war-dress, with his bow in his hand, his quiver slung, and his shield upon his arm. In this plight, *sans* head-dress, *sans* robe, and *sans* everything that might be a useless incumbrance—with the body naked, and so profusely bedaubed with red and black paint as to form an almost perfect disguise—the Indian warriors sally forth to war. The chief, however, always plumes himself and leads his band, tendering his enemies a conspicuous mark, with all his ornaments and trophies upon him. His enemies, if they get him, get a prize worth fighting for.

Besides chiefs and warriors, there are many beautiful and voluptuous-looking women. They continually crowd in throngs to gaze upon a stranger. Perhaps they shed more bewitching smiles from necessity, growing out of the great disparity in numbers between them and the rougher sex. From the numerous groups that have constantly pressed upon me, overlooking the operations of my brush, I have been unable to get more than one who would consent to have her portrait painted. They dread what might eventually ensue in consequence.

The one whom I have painted is a descendant of the old chief. Though not the most beautiful, she is yet a fair sample of them, and dressed in a beautiful costume of mountain-sheep skin that is handsomely garnished with porcupine quills and beads. This girl was almost *compelled* to stand for her picture by her relatives who urged her on. She had modestly declined, offering as her excuse that "she was not pretty enough, and that her picture would be laughed at." The beauty of her name, Seet-se-be-a (The Midday Sun), is quite enough to make up for any deficiency, if there were any, in the beauty of her face.

I found these people raising abundant corn or maize. I happened to visit them in the season of their festivities, which take place when the ears of corn are the proper size for eating. The green corn is considered a great luxury by all tribes who cultivate it. It is ready for eating as soon as the ear is of full size and the kernels are expanded to their full growth but are still soft and pulpy. In this green state it is boiled and dealt out in great profusion to the whole tribe, who feast upon it while it lasts. They render thanks to the Great Spirit for the return of this joyful season by making sacrifices, by dancing, and by singing songs of thanksgiving.

The feast lasts for a week or ten days, the term the corn remains tender and palatable. During this time all hunting, all war-excursions, and all other avocations are positively dispensed with. All join in the most excessive gluttony and conviviality that can possibly be conceived. The fields of corn are pretty well stripped, and the poor improvident Indian thanks the Great Spirit for the indulgence he has had, and is satisfied to ripen merely the few ears that are necessary for his next year's planting. He has laid waste his fine field, robbing himself of the golden harvest that might have gladdened his heart and those of his wife and little children through the cold and dreariness of winter.

Women are the proprietors and cultivators of all crops in Indian countries. The men never turn their hands to such degrading occupations. When the corn is supposed to be nearly ready, several old women, owners of fields or patches of corn, are delegated by the medicine-men to look at the corn-fields every morning at sun-rise and bring into the council-house, where the kettle is ready, several ears of corn. The women are not allowed to break open the husks or even to peep through. The women then are from day to day discharged and the doctors left to decide, after repeated examinations, if the corn is ready. Then they dispatch runners or criers, announcing to every part of the village that the Great

The Black Moccasin.

His son: The Red Thunder.

The Midday Sun.

Spirit has been kind to them, and they must all meet on the next day to return thanks for his goodness; that all must empty their stomachs and prepare for the feast that is approaching.

On the day appointed by the doctors, the villagers are all assembled. In the midst of the group a kettle is hung over the fire and filled with green corn, which is to be boiled and given to the Great Spirit as a sacrifice before anyone can indulge the cravings of his appetite.

While this first kettleful is boiling, four medicine-men, each with a stalk of corn in one hand and a rattle (she-she-quoi) in the other, and with their bodies painted with white clay, dance around the kettle, chanting a song of thanksgiving to the Great Spirit to whom the offering is being made. At the same time a number of warriors dance around in a more extended circle, with stalks of the corn in their hands, joining in the song of thanksgiving. During this scene there is an arrangement of wooden bowls laid upon the ground, in which the feast is to be dealt out, each one having in it a spoon made of the buffalo or mountain-sheep's horn.

The dance continues until the doctors decide that the corn is sufficiently boiled.

215

The Green Corn Dance.

Then it stops for a few moments, and resumes in a different form and with a different song. The doctors place the ears on a scaffold of little sticks over the fire, where they are entirely consumed.

The fire is then removed, and with it the ashes, which are buried together in the ground. A new fire is started on the same spot where the old one was, by friction. This is done by desperate exertion by three men seated on the ground facing each other, violently drilling the end of a stick into a hard block of wood by rolling it between the hands, each one catching it in turn from the others without allowing the motion to stop until smoke, and at last a spark of fire, is seen and caught in a piece of punk. Then there is great rejoicing in the crowd. When the fire is kindled and the kettleful of corn boiled for the feast, the chiefs, doctors, and warriors are seated. After this, unlimited license is given to the whole tribe, who indulge in all their excesses until the fields of corn are exhausted.

216

A visiting chief of the Crow.

There are at this present time some distinguished guests in the lodge of The Black Moccasin: two chiefs of a party of Crows, who arrived here a few days ago to visit their ancient friends and relatives. Feasting and carousing have been the "order of the day" here for some time. A distinguished chief of the Minatarees, with several others in company, visited the Crows some months past and returned attended by some remarkably fine-looking fellows, all mounted on fine horses.

No part of the human race could present a more picturesque and thrilling appearance on horseback than a party of Crows rigged out in all their plumes and trappings, galloping about and yelping in what they call a war-parade, a sort of tournament or sham-fight in which they pass rapidly through the evolutions of battle. This is an amusement of which they are excessively fond. Great preparations are made for these occasional shows.

The Crows may be justly said to be the most beautifully clad of all the Indians in these regions. They bring from the base of the Rocky Mountains a fine and spirited breed of wild horses, and they create a great sensation among the Minatarees, who have been paying them all attention and all honors for some days. I have selected one of the most conspicuous, and transferred him and his horse, with arms and trappings, as faithfully as I could to the canvas.

I have painted him as he sat for me, balanced on his leaping wild horse, with his shield and quiver slung on his back, and his long lance decorated with the eagle's quills in his right hand. His shirt and his leggings and his moccasins were of mountain-goat skins, beautifully dressed; their seams everywhere fringed with a profusion of scalp-locks taken from the heads of his enemies slain in battle. His long hair, which reached almost to the ground when he was standing, floated in black waves over the hips of his leaping charger. On his head he wore a magnificent head-dress made of the quills of the war-eagle and ermine skins. On his horse's head was another of equal beauty and precisely the same in pattern and material.

I have just been amused with a formal and grave meeting that was called around me. It was formed by a number of young men, and even chiefs and doctors of the tribe, who have heard that I was *great medicine* and a great chief. They took it upon themselves to suppose that I might be a man of influence among the "pale faces," and capable of rendering them some relief in a case of very great grievance.

They represented that about five or six years ago an unknown, small animal, not differing much in size from a ground squirrel, but with a long, round tail, showed himself about one of the chief's lodges, peeping out from under the pots and kettles. They looked upon it as great medicine. No one dared kill it. Hundreds came to watch and look at it.

On one of these occasions, one of the spectators saw this strange animal catch and devour a small "deer mouse." Their lodges contained many of these little destructive animals. It was at once determined that this had been an act of the Great Spirit, as a means of putting a stop to the spoliations committed by these little sappers, who cut their clothing and other things to pieces in a lamentable manner.

Councils were called and solemn decree issued for protection of this new visitor and its progeny, which soon increased rapidly. It was then learned from one of the fur traders, however, that this new animal, object of their superstition, had landed himself from one of the trader's keel boats. He was Mr. Rat.

For a while, this curtailed the extraordinary respect they had been paying to the visitor, but its continual war upon mice, which it was using for food, continued to command their respect. In spite of the manner in which it had been introduced, the Indians were unwilling to believe that it had come without the agency in some way of the Great Spirit.

Having been thus introduced and nurtured, the number of rats wonderfully increased. Every lodge soon was infested with them. The Indians' *caches*, where they bury their corn and other provisions, were robbed and sacked. The very pavements under their lodges were vaulted and sapped. Mr. Rat had to be looked upon as a disastrous nuisance and a public calamity. The object of the meeting was to call my attention to the situation, evidently in hopes that I might be able to designate some successful mode of relieving them from this misfortune.

I assured them of my deep regret for their situation, which was, to be sure, a very unpleasant one, and told them there was really a great deal of medicine in the thing, and that I should therefore be quite unwilling to have anything to do with it.

Soon after, Baptiste, Bogard, and I started on a visit to the upper town of the Minatarees, which is half a mile or more away and on the other bank of the Knife River. The old chief, having learned we were to cross the river, gave directions to one of the women of his numerous household. She took upon her head a skin-canoe (called a bull-boat), made in the form of a large tub, of a buffalo's skin stretched on a frame of willow-boughs. She carried it to the water's edge, placed it in the water, and made signs for us three to get into it.

When we were in, and seated flat on its bottom, there was scarce room to adjust our legs or our feet. We sat necessarily facing each other. She stepped before the boat and, pulling it along, waded towards the deeper water, with her back towards us. With one hand she attended to her dress, which seemed to be but a light slip. It floated upon the surface until the water was above her waist, then she pulled it over her head and threw it ashore. She plunged forward, swimming and drawing the boat with one hand with apparent ease.

We were conveyed to the middle of the stream, where we were soon surrounded by a dozen or more beautiful girls, from twelve to fifteen and eighteen years of age, who had been bathing on the opposite shore.

They all swam as confidently as otters or beavers. They gathered around us, their long black hair floating on the water, their faces glowing with fun. They were cracking jokes about us which we could not understand.

In the midst of this delightful aquatic group, we three sat in our little skin-bound tub like the "three wise men of Gotham, who went to sea in a bowl," floating along down the current, losing sight of and all thoughts of the shore, which was equi-distant from us on either side. The dear creatures floated about in the clear water, catching their hands onto the sides of our boat, occasionally half out of the water, then sinking again, like so many mermaids.

In the midst of this tantalizing entertainment, in which poor Baptiste and Bogard, as well as myself, were all taking infinite pleasure, and which we supposed was all intended for our amusement, we found ourselves suddenly in the dilemma of floating down the current in the middle of the river. We were being turned round and round to the amusement of the villagers, who were laughing at us from the shore. We had neither an oar nor anything else that we could wield in self-defense, or self-preservation.

We now learned they had peremptorily discharged our conductress, who had undertaken to ferry us safely across the river. They had ingeniously laid their plans, of which we had been ignorant until the moment, to extort from us some little evidences of our liberality. It was impossible to refuse them, after so bewitching an exhibition on their part, and the awkwardness of our situation.

I had some awls in my pockets, which I presented to them, and a few strings of beautiful beads, which I placed over their delicate necks as they raised them out of the water by the side of our boat. After this they all joined in conducting our craft to shore, swimming behind it, pushing it along until the water became so shallow their feet were upon the bottom. Then they waded along with great coyness until their bodies, in a crouching position, could no longer be half concealed under the water. They gave our boat a last push for the shore, and with an exulting laugh, plunged back again into the river. We waded in and soon escaped our little tormentors, and the numerous lookers-on, on our way to the upper village.

There I was very politely treated by The Yellow Moccasin, quite an old man who seemed to be chief of this band. Their little community was thirty or forty lodges, averaging perhaps twenty persons to each. I was feasted in this man's lodge. Afterwards I was invited to accompany him and several others to a prairie a mile or so above the village, where the young men and young women of town had assembled to race their horses.

After I had been watching for some time, I felt some degree of sympathy for a fine-looking young fellow whose horse had been twice beaten on the course and whose losses had been considerable. His sister, a very modest and pretty girl, was most piteously howling and crying. I selected and brought forward an ordinary-looking pony, obviously too fat and sleek to run against the fine-limbed little horse that had disappointed his high hopes. I began to comment extravagantly upon my pony's muscle, until he began to cheer up with the hope of getting me and my pony on to the turf with him. He soon made me a proposition.

Having lauded the limbs of my little nag too much to "back out," I agreed to run a short race with him of half a mile, for three yards of scarlet cloth, a knife, and half a dozen strings of beads, which I was willing to stake against a handsome pair of leggings which he was wearing at the time.

The greatest imaginable excitement was now raised among the crowd by this arrangement: to see a white man preparing to run with an Indian jockey, and that with a scrub of a pony in whose powers of running no Indian had the least confidence. Yet there was no one in the crowd who dared to take up the several other little bets I was willing to tender for their amusement, and for their final exultation. I had ventured on the merits of this little horse, which the tribe had all overlooked, in a bold and confident manner. Perhaps it had some medicine about it.

So far was this panic carried that even my champion was ready to withdraw. But his friends encouraged him, and we galloped our horses off to the other end of the course, where we were to start.

Some considerable delay then took place, from a condition which I had not known before: In all the races of this day, every rider was to run entirely denuded on a naked horse! Here I was completely balked, and having no one by me to interpret a word, I was quite at a loss to decide what was best to do. I found that remonstrance was of little avail. As I had volunteered to gratify and flatter them, I thought it best not to displease them. So I laid off my clothes, and straddled the naked back of my round and glossy little pony by the side of my competitor. He was also mounted and stripped to the skin, panting with restless anxiety for the start. With my trembling little horse underneath me, and the cool atmosphere floating about, we "were off."

Though my little Pegasus seemed to dart through the clouds, and I wafted on the wings of Mercury, yet my red adversary was leaving me too far behind for further competition. I wheeled to the left, making a circuit on the prairie, and came in at the starting point, much to the satisfaction and exultation of the jockeys, but greatly to the murmuring

220

Horse racing: the White Medicine Man lost.

disappointment of the women and children, who had assembled in a dense throng to witness the "coming out" of the "white medicine-man." I clothed myself instantly and acknowledged my defeat, the superior skill of my competitor, and the wonderful muscle of his little charger, which pleased him. His sister's lamentations were soon turned to joy by the receipt of a beautiful scarlet robe and a profusion of vari-colored beads, which were speedily paraded on her copper-colored neck.

     After I had seen enough of these amusements, I succeeded with some difficulty in pulling Baptiste and Bogard from among the women and girls. We trudged back to the little village of earth-covered lodges, hemmed in and almost obscured from the eye by the fields of corn and luxuriant growth of wild sun-flowers. We loitered about this little village awhile, looking into most of its lodges and tracing its winding avenues, after which we recrossed the river and wended our way back again to head-quarters.

XI

Extinction of the Mandans

FOR SEVERAL days I have been suffering somewhat with an influenza, which has induced me to leave my bed on the side of the lodge to sleep on the floor, wrapped in a buffalo robe, with my feet to the fire in the center of the room. A constant and watchful friend has importuned me, night after night, into using his bedaubed and bear-greased body for a pillow.

Unwilling to deny the poor fellow the satisfaction he seemed to be drawing from this singular freak, I took some pains to inquire into his character. I learned that he was a Riccaree brave by the name of Pah-too-ca-ra (He Who Strikes), who is here with several others of his tribe on a friendly visit, though in a hostile village. He lives as they do, unprotected, except by the mercy of their enemies. I think it probable that he is endeavoring to ingratiate himself in my affections, and consequently to insure my guardianship and influence for his protection. Be this as it may, he is rendering me many kind services, and I have in return traced him on my canvas for immortality.

His village is situated on the west bank of the river, two hundred miles below the Mandans. It is built in much the same manner, being constituted of one hundred and fifty earth-covered lodges, in part surrounded by a barrier of piquets set firmly in the ground, of ten or twelve feet in height.

The Riccaree village is built upon an open prairie. Undulating hills rise in the

223

distance behind it, covered with a verdant turf but without a tree or a bush anywhere to be seen. The feelings of these people towards the *pale faces* are hostile and deadly. They harbor the most resentful feelings towards the traders, and any others passing on the river. There is great danger to the lives of any white men who unluckily fall into their hands. They have recently sworn death and destruction to every white man who comes in their way, and there is no doubt they are ready to execute their threats.

When Lewis and Clark first visited these people thirty years ago—it will be found by a reference to their history—the Riccarees received and treated them with great kindness and hospitality. But owing to the system of trade, they have been inflicted with abuses, for which they are harboring the most inveterate feelings towards the whole civilized race.

The Riccarees are unquestionably a part of the tribe of Pawnees living on the Platte River some hundreds of miles below this. Their language is nearly the same. Their personal appearance and customs are as similar as could be reasonably expected among a people so long since separated from their parent tribe and continually subjected to innovations from the neighboring tribes around them.

I shall leave my Riccaree companion and the Mandans in the morning, and then with my canvas, easel, and paint-pots in my canoe, with Baptiste and Bogard to paddle and my own oar to steer, wend my way again on the mighty Missouri. Taking leave will be done with decided feelings of regret. The singular customs of the Mandans have raised an irresistible belief in my mind that they have had a different origin, or are of a different character, from any other tribe that can be in North America. I have been disposed not to advance it as a *theory* but only to enquire whether among the Mandans was to be found the remains of the *Welsh colony*—the followers of Madoc.

According to numerous and accredited authors, ten ships in the fourteenth century, under the command of Prince Madoc, or Madawe, from North Wales, never returned to their country, having landed somewhere on the coast of North or South America. The best authorities (which I will assume everybody has read rather than quote them at this time) have pretty clearly proved that the party of Prince Madoc landed either on the coast of Florida or near the mouth of the Mississippi. Then, according to the history and poetry of Wales, they settled somewhere in the interior of North America. The Mandans might possibly be the remains of this lost colony, amalgamated with a tribe or part of a tribe of natives, which would account for their unusual appearance and also for the changed character and customs of the Welsh colonists, or the remains of the original party.

Long after I had completed this journal of my journeys in the West, when the magic of the prairie skies was but a memory, I had time to reflect on the meaning of the Mandan colonies. I will insert these reflections at this place in the narrative of my journal, and then add the dismal story of the extinction of the Mandans:

Since these notes were written, I have descended the Missouri River from the Mandan village to St. Louis, a distance of eighteen hundred miles, and taken pains to examine its shores. On the banks of that river I saw repeated remains of old Mandan villages. I am fully convinced that I have traced them down nearly to the mouth of the Ohio.

Their ancient fortifications are numerous. Some of them enclose a great many acres. Built on the banks of the river, with walls in some places twenty or thirty feet in height, and covered ways to the water, they evince a knowledge of the science of fortifications not a century behind that of the present day. I submit they were never built by any nation of Indians in America, and present to us incontestable proof of the former existence of a people far advanced in the arts of civilization.

Now I am inclined to believe that the ten ships of Madoc made their way up the Mississippi, and their brave and persevering colonists made their way through the interior to a position on the Ohio River, where they cultivated their fields and established in one of the finest countries on earth, a flourishing colony. At length they were set upon by the Indians, whom perhaps they had provoked to warfare by being trespassers on their hunting-grounds. They were besieged. It was necessary to erect fortifications for their defense. In the end they all perished, except those perhaps who might have formed alliances by marriage with the Indians. Their offspring would have been half-breeds. At length, being despised, as all half-breeds of enemies are, they gathered themselves into a band, moved off, and increased in numbers and strength as they advanced up the Missouri River to the place where they had been known for many years past by the name of the *Mandans*, a corruption, or abbreviation perhaps, of "*Madawgwys,*" the name applied by the Welsh to the followers of Madawe.

If this be a startling theory, be sure to read the following brief reasons which I bring in support of my opinion. If my reasons do not support me, they will at least be worth knowing, and may be the means of eliciting further and more successful enquiry.

The marks of the Mandan villages are excavations of two feet or more in depth, and thirty or forty feet in diameter, of a circular form, made in the ground for the foundations of their lodges. They leave a decided remain for centuries, and one that is easily detected. After leaving the Mandan village, I found the marks of their former residence about sixty miles below where they were then living, and from which they removed (from their own account) about sixty or eighty years since. From the appearance of the number of their lodges, I should think there must have been then three times the number than when I was among them. Near the mouth of the big Cheyenne River, two hundred miles below their last location, I found still more ancient remains, and in as many as six or seven other places between that and the mouth of the Ohio. Each one, as I visited them, appeared more and more ancient. Wherever these people might have come from, they have gradually made their moves up the Missouri.

For most of this distance they have been in the heart of the great Sioux country, and are looked upon by the Sioux as trespassers. They have been continually at war. The Sioux have endeavored to extinguish them. But the Mandans were always fortified by a strong piquet, or stockade, and successfully withstood the assaults of their enemies, thus preserving the remnant of their tribe. Through this gauntlet they have run, passing through the countries of warlike and hostile tribes.

It may be objected that the Riccarees and Minatarees build their lodges in the same way. But the Minatarees are Crows, from the north-west. By their own account they fled to the Mandans for protection, and built their villages next to them, and their lodges in the same manner.

The Riccarees have been a very small tribe, far inferior to the Mandans. By the

Riccaree brave: He Who Strikes.

traditions of the Mandans, as well as from the evidence of the first explorers, Lewis and Clark, and others, the Riccarees have lived, until quite lately, on terms of intimacy with the Mandans, whose villages they have successively occupied as the Mandans have moved and vacated them.

Whether my derivation of the word *Mandan* from *Madawgwys* be correct or not, I will pass it over to the world. I offer the Welsh word *Mandon* (the woodroof, a species of madder used as a red dye) as the name that might possibly have been applied by the Welsh neighbors to these people, on account of their very ingenious mode of giving the beautiful red and other dyes to the porcupine quills with which they garnish their dresses. In their own language they called themselves *See-pohs-ka-nu mah-ka-kee* (The People of the Pheasants), which was probably the name of the primitive stock, before they were mixed with any other people. To have got such a name, it is natural to suppose that they must have come from a country where *pheasants* existed, which cannot be found short of reaching the timbered country at the base of the Rocky Mountains, some six or eight hundred miles west of the Mandans, or the forests of Indiana and Ohio, some hundreds of miles to the south and east of where they last lived.

As evidence in support of my opinion that they came from the banks of the Ohio and have brought with them some of the customs of the civilized people who erected those ancient fortifications, numerous specimens of pottery have been taken from the graves and tumuli about those ancient works. Great numbers of this pottery were in use by the Mandans. There was scarcely a day when the visitor would not see the women at work with their hands and fingers, molding this pottery from black clay into vases, cups, pitchers, and pots, and baking them in their kilns in the sides of the hill, or under the bank of the river.

226

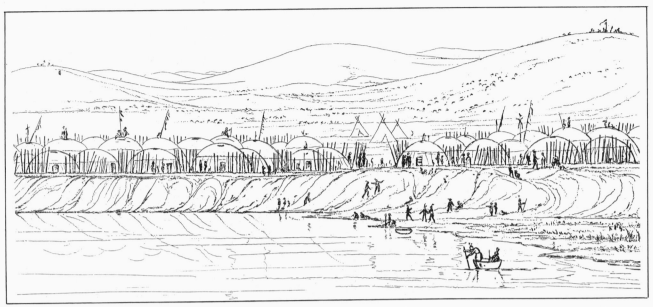

Riccaree village.

In addition to this art, which I am sure belongs to no other tribe on the Continent, these people have as a secret with themselves, the extraordinary art of manufacturing a very beautiful and lasting kind of blue glass beads, which they wear on their necks in great quantities, and decidedly value above all others that are brought to them by the fur traders.

This secret is not only that the traders did not introduce beads to them, but that one cannot learn from them—an art perhaps introduced by some civilized people, as it is as yet unknown to other Indian tribes elsewhere. Of this interesting fact Lewis and Clark gave an account thirty-three years ago.

The Mandan canoes are altogether different from those of all other tribes. They are exactly the Welsh *coracle:* made of raw-hides, the skins of buffaloes, stretched underneath a frame made of willow or other boughs, and shaped nearly round, like a tub. A woman can carry it on her head from her lodge to the water's edge, and having stepped into it, stands in front, and propels it by dipping her paddle *forward,* and *drawing it to her,* instead of paddling by the side.

At the moment I first saw these people, I was so struck with the peculiarity of their appearance. I was convinced they were an amalgam of a native with some civilized race. From what I have seen of them, and of the remains on the Missouri and Ohio rivers, I feel convinced these people emigrated from the Ohio. They and many of their customs have been preserved from the almost total destruction of the bold colonists of Madawe. In adducing the support of this theory, if I have failed to complete it, I have the satisfaction that I have not taken up much of the reader's time, and I can therefore claim his attention a few moments longer while I refer him to a brief vocabulary of the Mandan language, so that he may compare it with that of the Welsh. There is a striking similarity sufficient to excite the mind of the attentive reader.

English	Mandan	Welsh	Pronounced
I	Me	Mi	Me
You	Ne	Chwi	Chwe
He	E	A	A
She	Ea	E	A
It	Ount	Hwynt	Hooynt
We	Noo	Ni	Ne
They	Eonah	Hwna *mas*	Hoona
		Hona *fem*	Hona
Those ones		Yrhai Hyna	
No, or there is not	Megosh	Nagoes	Nagosh
No		Nage	
		Nag	
		Na	
Head	Pan	Pen	Pan
The Great Spirit	Maho peneta	Mawr penaethir*	Maoor panaether
		Ysprid mawr†	Uspryd maoor

For the dismal history of the extinction of the Mandans I am dependent on the accounts brought to New York in the fall of 1838 by Messrs. McKenzie, and others of the Upper Missouri.

It seems that in the summer of 1837 small-pox was introduced among the Mandans by the fur traders. In the course of two months they all perished, except some thirty or forty, who were taken as slaves by the Riccarees, an enemy living two hundred miles downstream, who moved up and took possession of the village soon after the disease had subsided. After living some months in it, they were attacked by a large party of Sioux. While fighting the Sioux, the Mandan prisoners took an active part. But then the Mandans created a plan for their own destruction. Both men and women ran through the piquets onto the prairie, calling out to the Sioux to kill them "because they were Riccaree dogs, their friends were all dead, and they did not wish to live." They wielded their weapons as desperately as they could to excite the fury of their enemy, and they were cut to pieces and destroyed.

The accounts given by white men who were among the Mandans during the ravages of small-pox are appalling and too heart-rending and disgusting to be recorded. The disease was introduced by the Fur Company's steamer from St. Louis, which had two of its crew sick with the disease when it approached the Upper Missouri. It imprudently stopped to trade at the Mandan village. The chiefs and others were allowed to come on board, and the disease returned to shore with them.

I believe the gentlemen in charge of the steamer did not believe it to be the small-pox. If they had known, I cannot conceive of such imprudence to their own interests in the country or to the fate of these poor people.

At that unlucky time, the Mandans were surrounded by several war-parties of the

* To act as a great chief—head or principal—sovereign or supreme.
† The Great Spirit.

powerful Sioux. They could not therefore disperse upon the plains, by which means many of them could have been saved. They were necessarily inclosed within the piquets of their village. So slight were their hopes when they were attacked that nearly half of them destroyed themselves with their knives, with their guns, and by leaping head-foremost from a thirty-foot ledge of rocks in front of their village, dashing their brains out.

The first symptom of the disease was a rapid swelling of the body. So very virulent did it become that many died two or three hours after the attack and, in many cases, without any appearance of the disease upon the skin. Utter dismay seemed to possess all classes and all ages; they gave themselves up in despair as entirely lost. There was continual crying and howling and praying to the Great Spirit for his protection night and day. With only a few living, and those in appalling despair, nobody thought of burying the dead. Their bodies, whole families together, were left in loathsome piles in their own lodges, with a few buffalo robes thrown over them, to decay and be devoured by their own dogs.

That such a proportion of the community should have perished in so short a time seems an unaccountable thing, but this frightful disease is far more fatal among the native population, owing to some extraordinary constitutional susceptibility. Or, the exposed lives they live may lead more directly to fatal consequences. As they did for most of their diseases they imprudently plunged into the coldest water in the highest state of fever, and often died before they could get out of the water.

During the ravages of the Asiatic cholera which swept over the western country and the Indian frontier, I was able to witness its effects. I learned from what I saw, as well as from what I have heard since that time, that it travelled to and fro over the frontiers, carrying dismay and death among those tribes that had adopted the civilized modes of life, with its dissipations, using vegetable food and salt. But wherever it came to the tribes living exclusively on meat, and without the use of salt, its progress was suddenly stopped. I mention this as an important note to science, and therefore one on which I made many careful enquiries.

From the trader who was present at the destruction of the Mandans I learned many incidents of this dreadful scene, but I dread to recite them. Among them, however, there is one that I must briefly describe: the death of that noble gentleman to whom I became so much attached, Mah-to-toh-pa, "The Four Bears." After he had recovered from the disease himself, he sat in his lodge and watched every one of his family die about him, his wives and his little children. Then he walked around the village and wept over the destruction of his tribe: his braves and warriors, whose sinewy arms he must depend on for a continuance of their existence, all laid low. He came back to his lodge, covered his whole family in a pile with a number of robes, and wrapping another around himself, went out upon a hill at a little distance, where he laid several days, despite all the solicitations of the traders, resolved to starve himself to death. He remained there till the sixth day, when he had just strength enough to creep back to the village. He entered the horrid gloom of his own lodge, and laying his body alongside his family, drew his robe over him and died on the ninth day of his fatal abstinence.

So have perished the Mandans. They are extinct.

229

Sioux: The Black Rock, a chief.

XII

Mouth of the Teton River, *Upper Missouri*

SINCE WRITING the above I have descended the Missouri six or seven hundred miles in my little bark, with Baptiste and Bogard as my *"compagnons du voyage."* I am now in the heart of the country belonging to the Sioux or Dahcotas—one of the most numerous tribes in North America, and also one of the most vigorous and warlike. They number some forty or fifty thousand, and are able to muster at least eight or ten thousand warriors, well mounted and well armed.

The name Sioux (pronounced *see-oo)* was given to them by the French traders, the meaning of which I never have learned. In their own language their name is Dah-co-ta. The personal appearance of these people is very prepossessing. They are tall and straight, their movements elastic and graceful. They are considerably taller than the Mandans and Ricca- rees, or Blackfeet, but about as tall as the Crows, Assiniboins, and Minatarees. Half their warriors are six feet or more in height.

I am enjoying the hospitality of a Scotsman by the name of Laidlaw, who is attached to the American Fur Company and who, along with Mr. McKenzie and Lamont, has the agency of the Fur Company's transactions in the regions of the Upper Missouri and the Rocky Mountains.

Fort Pierre.

The Fort here is two or three hundred feet square, enclosing eight or ten factories, houses, and stores. Mr. Laidlaw occupies comfortable apartments, well supplied with the comforts and luxuries of life, and neatly conducted by a fine-looking, modest, and dignified Sioux woman. She is the affectionate mother of his little flock of pretty children.

This Fort is the most important and productive of the American Fur Company's posts. It is in the center of the great Sioux country, drawing from all quarters an almost incredible number of buffalo robes, which are carried to New York and other Eastern markets, and sold at a great profit. This post is thirteen hundred miles above St. Louis, on the west bank of the Missouri, on a beautiful plain near the mouth of the Teton River which empties into the Missouri from the West, and has been named Fort Pierre, in compliment to Monsr. Pierre Chouteau.

The country about is almost entirely prairie, in one of the Missouri's beautiful plains, and hemmed in by a series of gracefully undulating, grass-covered hills, rising like a series of terraces, to the summit level of the prairies, some three or four hundred feet in elevation.

The Sioux occupy a vast tract of country, from the banks of the Mississippi River to the base of the Rocky Mountains. They are a migratory or roaming tribe, divided into forty-two bands or families, each having a head chief. One principal division of this tribe is into what are called the *Mississippi* and *Missouri* Sioux. Those bordering on the banks of the Mississippi, concentrating at Prairie du Chien and Fort Snelling, are called the Mississippi Sioux. These are somewhat advanced towards civilization, and familiar with white people, with whom they have held intercourse for many years, and are consequently excessive whisky drinkers. They are a meagre proportion and imperfect sample of the great mass of the tribe, Sioux who roam the plains between the Missouri and the Rocky Mountains.

There are no finer-looking men than the Sioux. They congregate here in great

232

masses to make their trades with the American Fur Company; six hundred families living in tents covered with buffalo hides. Among these there were twenty or more of the different bands, each one with their chief at their head, over whom was a *superior chief* and leader, a middle-aged man, of middling stature, with a noble countenance, and a figure almost equalling the Apollo, and I painted his portrait. The name of this chief is Ha-won-je-tah (The One Horn) of the Mee-ne-cow-e-gee band, who has risen rapidly to the highest honors in the tribe.

He told me that he took the name of "One Horn" (or shell) from a simple small shell that was hanging on his neck, which descended to him from his father, and which, he said, he valued more than anything he possessed; affording a striking instance of the living affection which these people often cherish for the dead, inasmuch as he chose to carry this name through life in preference to many others and more honorable ones he had a right to have taken, from different battles and exploits of his extraordinary life. He treated me with great kindness and attention, considering himself highly complimented by the honor I had conferred upon him by painting his portrait.

On the long route between Fort Pierre and St. Louis, I passed the Sacs and Ioways, the Konzas, and Omahaws, and the Ottoes (making notes on them all, which are reserved for another place), and landed at the Puncahs, a small tribe residing in one village on the west bank of the river, one thousand miles above St. Louis.

The Puncahs all live in seventy-five or eighty wigwams made of buffalo skins, the frames for which are poles of fifteen or twenty feet in length, with the butt ends standing on the ground and the small ends meeting at the top, forming a cone, which sheds off the rain and wind perfectly. This small remnant of a tribe are not more than four or five hundred in number. I should think at least two-thirds of these are women. Their men suffer when they range the buffalo country for meat. They are now obliged to travel a great way because the buffaloes have dwindled in their country. The extended hunt exposes their lives to the numerous enemies about them.

Their chief is a noble specimen of native dignity and philosophy. He related to me with great coolness the poverty and distress of his nation. He predicted the certain extinction of his tribe, which he had not the power to avert. Like Caius Marius weeping over the ruins of Carthage, he shed tears as he described the poverty of his ill-fated little community. He told me the Puncahs had once been powerful and happy; that the buffaloes which the Great Spirit had given them for food, and which formerly spread all over their green prairies, had all been killed or driven out by the approach of white men, who wanted their skins. Now their country was entirely destitute of game. As his young men were obliged to penetrate the countries of their enemies for buffaloes, they were cut to pieces and destroyed in great numbers. Worse, his people had foolishly become fond of fire-water and had given away everything in their country for it. It had destroyed many of his warriors, and soon would destroy the rest. His tribe was too small and his warriors too few to go to war with the tribes around them. They were met and killed by the Sioux on the north, by the Pawnees on the west, and the Osages and Konzas on the south. He was still more alarmed by the constant advance of the pale faces—their enemies from the east.

233

Puncah: The Smoke.　　　　　　　　　　　　His wife: The Pure Fountain.

The son of this chief, a youth of eighteen years, distinguished himself by taking to himself *four wives in one day!* This extraordinary and unprecedented freak was just the thing to make him the greatest sort of *medicine* in the eyes of his people. He may date much of his success and greatness through life to this bold and original step, which suddenly raised him into importance.

The old chief Shoo-de-ga-cha, considering his son to have arrived at the age of maturity, fitted him out for house-keeping by giving him a handsome wigwam to live in, and nine horses, with many other valuable presents. The boy, whose name is Hongs-kay-de (The Great Chief), soon laid his plans.

Wishing to connect himself with some of the most influential men in the tribe, he held an interview with one of the most distinguished. Being the son of a chief, he easily made an arrangement for the hand of this man's daughter, which he was to receive on a certain day and at a certain hour. For her he was to give two horses, a gun, and several pounds of tobacco.

In like manner he made similar arrangements with three other leading men of the tribe, each of whom had a young and beautiful daughter of marriageable age. To each of the fathers he promised two horses, and other presents similar to those stipulated in the first instance, and all under injunctions of secrecy. The hour approached, and he announced to the whole tribe that he was to be married.

At the time appointed they all assembled. All were in ignorance of the fair hand that

234

The Great Chief: four wives in a day.

was to be placed in his on this occasion. He had got some of his young friends to lead up the eight horses. He took two of them by the halters, and the other presents agreed upon in his other hand, and advancing to the first of the parents, whose daughter was standing by his side, said to him: "You promised me the hand of your daughter on this day, for which I was to give you two horses." The father assented, received the presents, and gave his child.

A great confusion ensued from the simultaneous remonstrances made by the other three parents. They too had brought their daughters forward, and then were shocked at this sudden disappointment. They heard from each other of the similar contracts that each one had secretly entered into with the chief's son.

As soon as they could be pacified, and silence was restored, he exultingly replied: "You have all acknowledged in public your promises with me, which I shall expect you to fulfill. I am here to perform all the engagements which I have made, and I expect you all to do the same."

No more was said. He led up the two horses for each, and delivered the other presents. Then he lead off to his wigwam his four brides—taking two in each hand—and commenced at once upon his new mode of life, keeping only one of his horses for his own daily use.

I visited the wigwam of this young installed medicine-man several times, and saw his four modest little wives seated around the fire. They all seemed to harmonize very well, entering happily on the duties and pleasures of married life. I selected one of them and painted her portrait: Mong-shong-shaw (The Bending Willow), in a pretty dress of deer skins covered with a buffalo robe, handsomely ornamented, and worn with much grace.

These young brides were probably all between twelve and fifteen years—the season of life in which most of the girls in this wild country contract marriage. Women mature in these regions at that early age. There have been some instances where marriage has taken place even at eleven, and the juvenile mother has been blest with her first offspring at the age of twelve. The early maturity among the females may be a natural and constitutional difference, or perhaps because they lead an exposed and active life. Yet there is another general cause of early marriages (and consequently apparent maturity). Most of the marriages are contracted with the parents, hurried on by the impatience of the applicant, and prematurely accepted on the part of the parents, who are often impatient for the presents they are to receive as the price of their daughters. There is also the ease with which the marriage contract may be dissolved, which does away with the most serious difficulties to retard its consummation. In the fashionable world, education and accomplishments require time and a season to flourish and show them off, which is necessarily a great part of a young lady's life. The Indian girl finds herself weaned from the familiar embrace of her parents, her mind and her body maturing, and her thoughts and her passions searching for some theme or some pleasure to cling to. So she easily follows her ardent dictates and prematurely enters that system of life which consists of reciprocal dependence and protection.

In the instance described, the young man was in no way censured by his people, but most loudly applauded. In this country polygamy is allowed, and in this tribe where there are two or three times as many women as there are men, such an arrangement answers a good purpose. The females are provided for and taken care of. And in the instance it was to the great satisfaction of the parties and families concerned when so many fell to the son of a chief, into whose wigwam it was considered an honor to be adopted.

When we were about to leave the village of the Puncahs we found that they too were packing up all their goods. They were starting for the prairies farther west in pursuit of buffaloes for their winter's supplies. They took down their wigwams, and all were flat on the ground and everything packing up ready for the start. My attention was directed to one of the most miserable and helpless-looking objects I have ever seen in my life: a very aged and emaciated man of the tribe, who was to be *exposed.*

The tribe were going where hunger compelled them to go. The old man, who had once been a chief and a man of distinction in the tribe, was now too old to travel. He was reduced to mere skin and bones. He was to be left to starve, or meet with such death as might fall to his lot, and his bones to be picked by the wolves. I lingered around this poor old forsaken patriarch for hours, to indulge the tears of sympathy which flowed for his sake. His worn-out limbs were no longer able to support him. His body and his mind were doomed to linger in the withering agony of decay and gradual solitary death.

I wept, and it was a pleasure to weep for the painful looks and the dreary prospects of this old veteran. His eyes were dimmed. His venerable locks were whitened by an hundred years. His limbs were almost naked. He trembled as he sat by a small fire which his friends had left him, with a few sticks of wood within his reach and a buffalo's skin stretched upon some

236

The Bending Willow: one of his four wives.

crotches over his head. It was to be his only dwelling, and his chances for life were reduced to a few half-picked bones laid within his reach, and a dish of water. He was without weapon of any kind to replenish his supply, or strength to move his body from its fatal locality.

He had unluckily outlived the fates and accidents of wars to die alone at death's leisure. His friends and his children had all left him and were preparing to be on the march. He had told them to leave him: "I am old," he said, "and too feeble to march.

"My children," said he, "our nation is poor, and it is necessary that you should all go to the country where you can get meat. My eyes are dimmed and my strength is no more. My days are nearly all numbered, and I am a burden to my children. I cannot go, and I wish to die. Keep your hearts stout, and think not of me. I am no longer good for anything."

They finished the ceremony of *exposing* him and took their final leave of him. I advanced to the old man, and was undoubtedly the last human being who held converse with him. I sat by his side. Though he could not distinctly see me, he shook me heartily by the hand and smiled, evidently aware that I was a white man, and that I sympathized with his inevitable misfortune. I shook hands again with him, and left him.

This cruel custom of exposing their aged people is followed by all the tribes who roam the prairies. They make severe marches, and when such decrepit persons are totally unable to ride or to walk, they have no means of carrying them. It becomes absolutely necessary that they be left. And they uniformly insist upon it, saying, as this old man did, that they are old and of no further use; that they left their fathers in the same manner; that they wish to die and their children must not mourn for them.

When passing the site of the Puncah village a few months later in my canoe, I went

237

ashore with my men and found the poles and the buffalo skin standing as they were left, over the old man's head. The firebrands were lying nearly as I had left them, and a few yards away I found the skull, and his bones, which had been picked clean by the wolves, which is probably all that any human being can ever know of his melancholy fate.

At Fort Pierre, I painted the portrait of the head-chief of the Sioux (The One Horn). It was finished before any of the tribe knew anything of it. Several of the chiefs and doctors were allowed to see it, and it was talked of through the village. Of course, great numbers at once gathered around me. Nothing short of hanging it out of doors on the side of my wigwam would in any way answer them. I had the satisfaction of beholding, through a small hole I had made in my wigwam, the admiration and respect they all felt for their chief, as well as the great estimation in which they held me as a painter and a magician. They conferred upon me the distinguished appellation of Ee-cha-zoo-kah-ga-wa-kon (The Medicine Painter).

Some years later, when I was already returned to New York, I heard the story of this chief's death. Ha-wan-je-tah (The One Horn) had in some way been the accidental cause of the death of his only son, a very fine youth. So great was the anguish of his mind that he became frantic and insane. In one of these moods he mounted his favorite war-horse with his bow and his arrows in his hand, and dashed off at full speed upon the prairies, repeating the most solemn oath "that he would slay the first living thing that fell in his way, be it man or beast, friend or foe."

No one dared follow him. After he had been absent an hour or two, his horse came back to the village with two arrows in his body, and covered with blood. Fears were now entertained for the fate of the chief, and a party of warriors immediately mounted their horses and retraced the animal's tracks to the place of the tragedy. They found the body of their chief horribly mangled and gored by a buffalo bull, whose carcass was stretched by the side of him.

A close examination of the ground was then made by the Indians. They ascertained by the tracks that their unfortunate chief had met a buffalo bull in the season when they are very stubborn, and unwilling to run from anyone. He had incensed the animal by shooting a number of arrows into him. The chief had then dismounted and turned his horse loose, having given it a couple of arrows from his bow, which sent it home at full speed. He then had thrown away his bow and quiver, encountering the infuriated buffalo with his knife alone. The desperate battle resulted in the death of both. Many of the bones of the chief were broken. He was gored and stamped to death, but his huge antagonist lay by his side, weltering in blood from an hundred wounds made by the chief's long, two-edged knife.

While painting portraits of chiefs and braves of the Sioux, my painting-room was the continual rendezvous of the worthies of the tribe. I was obliged to paint them according to rank, for they looked upon the operation as a great honor. It was fortunate, however, that the honor was not a sufficient inducement for all to overcome the fears which stood in the way of their consenting to be painted. If all had been willing to be painted, I would have had to leave many discontented and, as they would think, neglected. About one in eight was willing to be painted. The rest thought they would be much more sure of "sleeping quiet in their graves" after they were dead if their pictures were not made. By this lucky difficulty I got great relief, and easily got through with those who were willing and worthy of so signal an honor.

238

Sioux: The One Horn, Chief of the Miniconjou.

After I had done with the chiefs and braves, I proposed to paint a few of the women. I at once got myself into a serious perplexity, I was heartily laughed at by the whole tribe, both by men and by women, for my unaccountable condescension in seriously proposing to paint a woman, conferring on her the same honor that I had done the chiefs and braves. Those whom I had honored were laughed at by hundreds of the jealous, who had been decided unworthy of the distinction and were now amusing themselves with the *very enviable honor* which the *great white medicine-man* had conferred, *especially* on *them,* and was now to confer equally upon the *squaws!*

From those whom I had painted I heard that if I was to paint women and children I had better destroy *their* pictures. They said I had represented to them that I wanted their pictures to exhibit to white chiefs, to show who were the most distinguished and worthy of the Sioux. Their women had never taken scalps, nor did anything better than make fires and dress skins.

I was quite awkward in explaining to them that I wanted the portraits of the women to hang *under* those of their husbands, merely to show how their women looked and how they dressed, without saying any more of them. After much deliberation on the subject through the village, I succeeded in getting a number of women's portraits.

The vanity of these men, after they had agreed to be painted, was beyond all description, far surpassing what is often immodest enough in civilized society. The Indian often lays down from morning till night in front of his portrait, admiring his own beautiful face and faithfully guarding it from day to day, to save it from accident or harm. I was for a long time at a loss for the true cause of their devotion. At last I learned they believe there may be life to a certain extent in a picture. If harm or violence be done to it, it may in some mysterious way affect their health, or do them other injury.

It was announced that a grand feast was to be given to the *great white chiefs,* who

239

Sioux: Tobacco, an Oglala chief.

Sioux: The Steep Wind, warrior of the Bad Arrow Points.

were visitors among them. Preparations were made accordingly. Two chiefs brought their two tents together, forming them into a semi-circle enclosing a space sufficiently large to accommodate one hundred and fifty men. We sat down with that number of the principal chiefs and warriors of the Sioux nation, along with Mr. Chouteau, Mr. Sanford, the Indian agent, Mr. McKenzie, and myself. We were placed on elevated seats in the center of the crescent, while the rest of the company all sat upon the ground, and mostly cross-legged.

In the center of the semi-circle was a flag-staff on which was a white flag, and to which was tied the calumet, both expressive of their friendly feelings towards us. Near the foot of the flag-staff, in a row on the ground, were six or eight kettles with iron covers on them, shutting them tight, in which were cooking the viands for our voluptuous feast. Near the kettles, and also on the ground, bottomside upwards, were a number of wooden bowls in which the meat was to be served. And in front were two or three men placed as waiters, to light the pipes for smoking and also to deal out the food.

All sat, with thousands climbing and crowding around, for a peep at the grand

240

A great dinner of dog.

pageant. At length Ha-wan-je-tah (The One Horn), head chief of the nation, rose in front of the Indian agent and addressed him: "My father, I am glad to see you here to-day—my heart is always glad to see my father when he comes—our great father, who sends him here, is very rich, and we are poor. Our friend Mr. McKenzie, who is here, we are also glad to see. We know him well, and we shall be sorry when he is gone. Our friend who is on your right hand we all know is very rich. We have heard that he owns the great medicine-canoe. He is a good man, and a friend to the red man. Our friend the White Medicine, who sits with you, we did not know. He came among us a stranger, and he has made me very well. All the women know it and think it good. He has done many curious things, and we have all been pleased with him. He has made us much amusement and we know he is great medicine.

"My father, I hope you will have pity on us, we are very poor. We offer you to-day not the best that we have got, for we have a plenty of good buffalo hump and marrow, but we give you our hearts in this feast. We have killed our faithful dogs to feed you—and the Great Spirit will seal our friendship. I have no more to say."

After these words he took off his beautiful war-eagle head-dress, his shirt, and leggings, his necklace of grizzly bears' claws, and his moccasins. Tying them together, he laid them gracefully down at the feet of the agent as a present. He put a handsome pipe on top of them. Then he walked around into an adjoining lodge, where he got a buffalo robe to cover his shoulders, and returned to the feast, taking his seat.

Major Sanford then rose and made a short speech in reply, thanking him for the valuable present which he had made him, and for the very polite and impressive manner in which it had been done; and sent for a quantity of tobacco and other presents, which were given in return. After several other chiefs had addressed Major Sanford in a similar manner,

241

and also disrobed themselves and thrown their beautiful costumes at his feet, one of the three men in front lit a handsome pipe and brought it to Ha-wan-je-tah to smoke.

He took it, and after presenting the stem to the North—to the South—to the East—to the West—and then to the Sun that was over his head, he pronounced the words "How—how—how," and drew a whiff or two of smoke through it. Then, holding the bowl in one hand and its stem in the other, he held it to each of our mouths. We successively smoked it. Afterwards it was passed around through the whole group, who smoked through it, or as long as its contents lasted. Another of the three waiters was ready with a second, and at length a third one.

This smoking was conducted with the strictest adherence to exact and established form, and in the most positive silence. After the pipe is charged, and is being lit, until the time that the chief has drawn the smoke through it, it is considered an evil omen for anyone to speak. If anyone break silence, even in a whisper, the pipe is instantly dropped by the chief. They would not dare use it. Another one is called for and used in its stead. After the smoking, the waiters proceed to distribute the meat.

The lids were raised from the kettles, which were all filled with dog's meat. It had been made into a sort of stew and had a savory smell, promising to be palatable food. Each guest had a large wooden bowl placed before him, with a huge quantity of dogs' flesh floating in a profusion of soup, or rich gravy, with a large spoon resting in the dish, made of buffalo's horn.

But we sat in a dilemma, all of us knowing the solemnity in which it was given, and the absolute necessity of falling to and devouring a little of it. We all tasted it a few times, then resigned our dishes. They were quite willingly taken and passed around to every part of the group, who all ate heartily.

We all agreed the meat was well cooked, and seemed to be well-flavored and palatable food, and no doubt it could have been eaten with relish if we had been hungry, and ignorant of the nature of the food we were eating.

The dog meat stew was repeatedly dipped out of the kettles, and soon entirely devoured. Then each one rose as he felt disposed and walked off without uttering a word. In this way the feast ended and all retired silently, and gradually, until the ground was left vacant to the charge of the waiters.

This feast was unquestionably given to us as the most undoubted evidence they could give of their friendship. Knowing the spirit in which it was given, we could not but treat it respectfully, and receive it as anything but a high and marked compliment. The dog feast is a truly religious ceremony. The Indian sees fit to sacrifice his faithful companion to bear testimony to the sacredness of his vows of friendship. He invites his friends to partake of its flesh, to remind him forcibly of the reality of the sacrifice, and the solemnity of his professions.

Among all Indian tribes the dog is more valued than among any part of the civilized world. The Indian has more time to devote to his company, and his untutored mind more nearly assimilates that of his faithful servant. He keeps his dog closer company, and draws him nearer to his heart. They hunt together, and are equal sharers in the chase. Their bed is one. On rocks and on their coats of arms they carve his image as the symbol of fidelity. Yet the

242

Indian will sacrifice his faithful follower, with tears in his eyes. He will offer him as a sacrifice to seal a sacred pledge of friendship he has made. Since a feast of venison or buffalo meat is due anyone who enters an Indian's wigwam, it conveys but passive or neutral evidence of friendship and counts for nothing.

I have seen the master take from the bowl the head of his victim and talk of its former affection and fidelity with tears in his eyes. And I have seen civilized men by my side jesting and sneering at Indian folly and stupidity. I have said in my heart they never deserved a name as honorable as that of the animal whose bones they were picking.

I witnessed another curious scene in the after part of the day on which we were honored with the dog feast. I was called upon to see a man "looking at the sun!"

We found him naked except for his breech-cloth, with splints and skewers run through the flesh on both breasts, leaning back and hanging with the weight of his body to the top of a pole fastened in the ground. He was fastened to the upper end by a cord tied to the splints. In this position he was leaning back, with nearly the whole weight of his body hanging to the pole, the top of which was bent forward, allowing his body to sink about half-way to the ground. His feet were still upon the ground, supporting a small part of his weight. He held in his left hand his favorite bow, and in his right, with a desperate grip, his medicine-bag. Blood was trickling down over his body, which was covered with white and yellow clay. A great crowd were looking on, sympathizing and encouraging him.

He was "looking at the sun" without paying the least attention to anyone about him. In the group reclining around him several mystery-men were beating their drums and shaking their rattles, and singing as loud as they could yell, to encourage him and strengthen his heart to stand and look at the sun, from its rising in the morning until its setting at night. Then, if his heart and his strength have not failed him, he is "cut down." He then receives the liberal donation of presents, which have been thrown into a pile before him during the day. He also earns the name of doctor, or medicine-man, which ensures him respect through life.

It is a sort of worship, or penance, of great cruelty, with only one palliative circumstance about it: It is a voluntary torture of a very rare occurrence. The poor man who undertakes it puts his reputation at stake upon the issue. When he takes his stand, he expects to face the sun and gradually turn his body in listless silence, until he sees the sun go down. If he faints and falls, of which there is imminent danger, he loses his reputation as a brave or mystery-man. He then suffers a signal disgrace in the estimation of the tribe, like all men who have the presumption to set themselves up as mystery-men and fail to sustain the character.

The Sioux seem to have many modes of worshipping the Great or Good Spirit, and many of conciliating the Evil Spirit. They have numerous fasts and feasts, and many modes of sacrificing, but they seem to pay less strict attention to them than the Mandans do, perhaps because of the wandering life they pursue, rendering it difficult to adhere rigidly to the strict form of custom.

Looking at the sun.

XIII

Mouth of the Teton River, *Upper Missouri*

DURING MY stay among the Sioux I received many pipes from them as presents, given as assurances of their friendship. The luxury of smoking is known to all the North American Indians. They are excessive smokers, and many of them would seem to be smoking one-half of their lives. There are many weeds and leaves and barks of trees that are narcotics and of spontaneous growth, which the Indians dry and pulverize and carry in pouches and smoke to great excess—and which in several of the languages is called *k'nick-k'neck*.

They have bestowed much pain and ingenuity to the construction of their pipes. The bowls of these are generally made of red steatite, or "pipe-stone." Many of them are carved with taste and skill, with figures and groups in relief, standing or reclining upon them.

The red stone of which these pipe bowls are made is a great curiosity. I am sure it is a variety of steatite, differing from that in any known European locality, and also from any locality known in America other than the one from which all these pipes come. All are traceable, I have found, to one source. That source is a place of vast importance to the Indians—given to them by the Great Spirit for their pipes, and strictly forbidden for any other use.

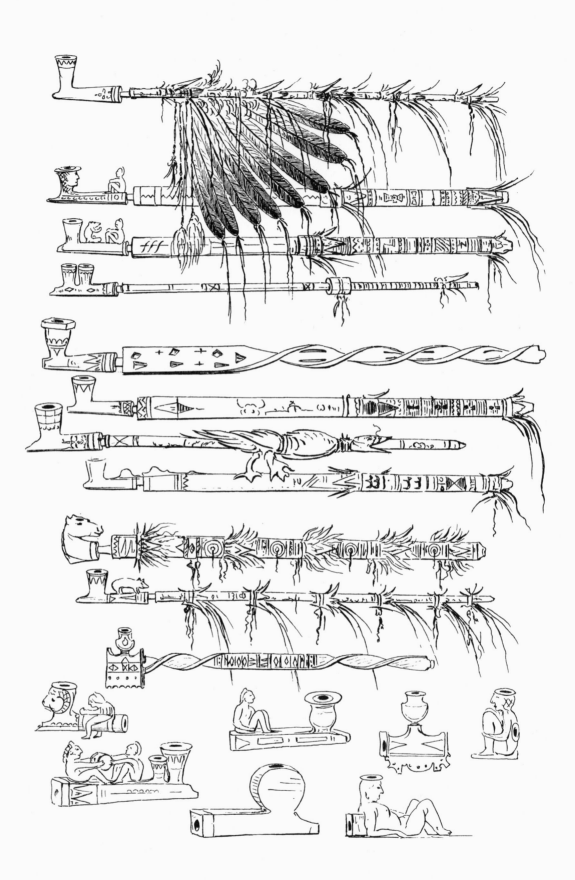

The source is somewhere between this place and the Mississippi River. The Indians all speak of it as a great medicine-place. I shall certainly lay my course to it, if I am able, and give the world some account of its mysteries.

The Indians shape out the bowls of these pipes from solid stone, which is not quite as hard as marble, with nothing but a knife. The stone is cherry red and takes a beautiful polish. The Indian makes the hole in the bowl of the pipe by drilling into it a hard stick with a quantity of sharp sand and water kept constantly in the hole. Drilling requires much patience.

The shafts or stems of these pipes are from two to four feet long, sometimes round but most generally flat. They are an inch or two in breadth, and wound half their length or more with braids of porcupine's quills. They are often ornamented with beaks and tufts from the wood-pecker's head, with ermine skins, and with long red hair dyed from white horse hair or the white buffalo's tail.

The *calumet*, or pipe of peace, ornamented with the war-eagle's quills, is a sacred pipe, and never allowed to be used on any other occasion than that of peace-making. The chief brings it into treaty, and unfolding the many bandages which are carefully kept around it, has it ready to be mutually smoked. After the terms of the treaty are agreed upon, it is the means of solemnizing or signing by an illiterate people who cannot draw up an instrument and sign their names to it, as is done in the civilized world.

The mode of solemnizing is by passing the sacred stem to each chief, who draws only one breath of smoke through it, thereby passing the most inviolable pledge they can possibly give for the keeping of the peace. This sacred pipe is then carefully folded up and stowed away in the chief's lodge until a similar occasion calls it out.

Indian weapons are mostly manufactured by themselves, except the scalping-knives and tomahawks, which are of civilized manufacture, made expressly for Indian use, and are carried into Indian country by thousands and tens of thousands and sold at an enormous price. The scabbards of the knives and handles for the tomahawks the Indians construct themselves, according to their own taste, and often ornament very handsomely.

The Indian works not in metals. He has not been ingenious enough to design or execute anything so *savage* or destructive. In his simplicity he shapes out his rude hatchet from a piece of stone, and heads his arrows and spears with flints. His knife is a sharpened bone, or the edge of a broken silex. But his war-club is a civilized refinement, with a blade of steel eight or ten inches in length set in a club and studded around and ornamented with some hundreds of brass nails.

The scalping-knife is carried under the belt and is the knife most generally used in all parts of the Indian country. It is a common and cheap butcher knife with one edge, manufactured at Sheffield, England, perhaps for sixpence. It is sold to the poor Indian for a horse! If I should live to get home, and should ever cross the Atlantic, a curious enigma would be solved for the English people, should they enquire about the scalping-knife. They will find that nearly every one to be seen in Indian country, from the Rocky Mountains to the Pacific Ocean, bears on its blade the impress of G. R., which they will doubtless understand.

As I have introduced the scalping-knife, it may be well for me to give some further account of the customs of taking the scalp, a custom practiced by all the North American

Scalp dance.

Indians. When an enemy is killed in battle, the victor's left hand grasps the hair on the crown of the victim's head. The knife passes around it through the skin, tearing off a piece of the skin with the hair, as large as the palm of the hand. It is then dried, ornamented, and preserved, and highly valued as a trophy. Scalping is an operation not calculated of itself to take life. It only removes the skin, without injuring the bone of the head. Necessarily, to be a genuine scalp, it must contain and show the crown or center of the head, that part of the skin which lies directly over what the phrenologists call "self-esteem," where the hair divides and radiates.

      Besides taking the scalp, the victor generally cuts off and brings home the rest of the hair, which his wife will divide into a great many small locks, and with them fringe off the seams of his shirt and his leggings, which also are worn as trophies and ornaments to the dress, and then are familiarly called "scalp-locks."

      The scalp, then, is a patch of skin taken from the head of an enemy killed in battle, and preserved as the record of a death produced by the hand of the individual who possesses it. It may be of great service to a man living in a community where there is no historian to enroll the names of the famous. It is a record of heroic deeds of the brave, who have gained their laurels in mortal combat with their enemies. It is as lawful and as glorious, after all, for an

Indian to slay an enemy in battle as it is in Christian communities. But the Indian is bound to keep the record himself, for no one in the tribe will keep it for him.

As the scalp is taken as the evidence of a death, it is obvious the Indian has no inclination to take it from the head of the living. But sometimes a man falls in the heat of battled, stunned with the blow of a weapon or a gunshot, and the Indian, rushing over his body, snatches off his scalp, supposing him dead. Afterwards, the victim rises from the field of battle, and recovers from this superficial wound of the knife, wearing a bald spot on his head during the remainder of his life. There are frequent examples on our Western frontiers.

The scalp must be from the head of an enemy, or it subjects its possessor to disgrace and infamy. There may be instances where an Indian is justified in the estimation of his tribe in taking the life of one of his own people. But their laws are such that no circumstances, however aggravating, will allow him taking the scalp. One of the principal denunciations against the custom of taking the scalp is its alleged cruelty, which it certainly is not. Cruelty would be in the *killing*, not in the act of cutting the skin from a man's head after he is dead. To say the worst of it, it is a disgusting custom. I wish I could be as sure the civilized and Christian world (which kills hundreds where the poor Indian kills one) treated their *enemies dead* in equally as decent a manner as the Indian does by taking the scalp.

And if reading of Indian barbarities—of scalps, and scalping-knives, and scalping—has ossified your heart against these people, and would shut out their advocate, I will annoy you no longer on this subject. I will withdraw, and leave you to cherish the very beautiful, humane, and parental moral that was carried out by the United States and British governments during the Revolutionary Wars, when they mutually employed thousands of their "Red children" to aid in fighting their battles, and paid them, according to contract, so many pounds, shillings, and pence or so many dollars and cents for every "scalp" of a "red" or a "blue coat" they could bring in.

The usual way of preparing and dressing a scalp is to stretch it on a little hoop at the end of a stick two or three feet long, for the purpose of "dancing it" in the *scalp-dance*. Some, which are small and not "dressed" and no longer than a crown piece, are hung to different parts of the dress. In public shows and parades, they are often suspended from the bridle bits or halter. Sometimes they are cut out, into a string, the hair forming a beautiful fringe to line the handle of a war-club. Sometimes they are hung at the end of a club, and at other times, by the order of the chief, are hung over the wigwams, suspended from a pole, which is called the "scalp-pole." This is often done by the chief of a village by his erecting over his wigwam a pole with all the scalps that he has taken arranged upon it. At the sight of this all the chiefs and warriors of the tribe who have taken scalps "follow suit." Every member of the community can stroll about the village on that day and "count scalps," learning thereby the standing of every warrior, which is decided in a great degree by the number of scalps taken in battles with their enemies.

Dancing is one of the most valued amusements of the Indians, and much more frequently practiced by them than by any civilized society. It enters into their forms of worship, and is often their mode of appealing to the Great Spirit, of paying their usual devotions to their medicine, and of honoring and entertaining strangers of distinction.

Instead of the "giddy maze" of the quadrille or the country dance, the cheering smiles and graces of silkened beauty, the Indian performs with jumps and starts and yells, much to the satisfaction of his own exclusive self, and the infinite amusement of the gentler sex, who are always lookers-on but are seldom allowed so great a pleasure, or so signal an honor, as that of joining with their lords in this or any other entertainment.

I saw so many different varieties of dances among the Sioux that I should almost be disposed to denominate them the "dancing Indians." They had dances for everything. There was scarcely an hour, day or night, but that the beat of the drum could not be heard. The dances are almost as various and different in their character as they are numerous. Some of them are exceedingly grotesque and laughable. They can keep bystanders in an irresistible roar of laughter. Others are calculated to excite pity and forcibly appeal to sympathies. Others disgust. Still others terrify and alarm with frightful threats and contortions.

As it is often done in the enlightened world, dancing is also done here to get favors—to buy the world's goods. In both instances it is danced with about equal merit, except that the Indian has surpassed us in honesty by christening it the "beggar's dance." This spirited dance was given not by a set of *beggars* but by the first and most independent young men in the tribe, beautifully dressed, with their lances and pipes and rattles in their hands, and a medicine-man beating the drum and joining the song at the highest key of his voice. In this dance everyone sings as loud as he can halloo, uniting his voice in an appeal to the Great Spirit to open the hearts of the bystanders to give to the poor, and not to themselves, assuring them that the Great Spirit will be kind to those who are kind to the helpless and poor.

The scalp-dance is given as celebration of a victory. Among the Sioux it is danced at night, by the light of their torches, and just before retiring to bed. When a war-party returns from a war excursion, bringing home with them the scalps of their enemies, they generally "dance them" for fifteen nights in succession. They make the most extravagant boasts of their prowess in war, while they brandish their war weapons. A number of young women are selected to aid (though they do not actually join in the dance), by stepping into the center of the ring and holding up the scalps that have been recently taken. The warriors dance around in a circle, brandishing their weapons and barking and yelping in the most frightful manner, all jumping on both feet at a time, with a simultaneous stamp and blow and thrust of their weapons. It would seem as if they were actually cutting and carving each other to pieces. During these frantic leaps and yelps and thrusts, every man distorts his face to the utmost, darting about his glaring eye-balls and snapping his teeth as if he were in the heat (and actually breathing through his inflated nostrils the very hissing death) of battle!

There is no doubt that one great object in these exhibitions is public exultation. Yet there are other essential motives for formally displaying the scalp. Among some tribes it is the custom to bury the scalps after they have gone through this series of public exhibitions, which may be to give them notoriety, or award public credit to the persons who obtained them and now are obliged to part with them. The great respect which seems to be paid to them while they use them, as well as the pitying and mournful song which they howl to the *manes* of their unfortunate victims, and the precise solemnity with which they afterwards bury the scalps, sufficiently convince me they have a superstitious dread of the spirits of their slain enemies,

251

Dance to the Bear Spirit.

and by performing many conciliatory offices, one of which is the dance, ensure their own peace.

I have given some account of the buffaloes, which inhabit these regions in great herds. I must say a little more. These animals are a subject of great importance in this vast wilderness, but they are rapidly wasting away at the approach of civilized man—and like the Indian, in a very few years they will live only in books or on canvas.

The American buffalo is the largest of the ruminating animals now living in America. The buffalo seems to have been spread over the plains by the Great Spirit for the use and subsistence of the red men, who live almost exclusively on its flesh, and clothe themselves with its skin. Its color is a dark brown, but changes as the season varies from warm to cold. Its hair or fur, long in winter and spring, turns quite light from exposure to the weather; then, when the winter coat is shed, the new growth is almost a jet black.

The buffalo bull often grows to two thousand pounds. He shakes a long and shaggy black mane that falls in great profusion over his head and shoulders, and often down quite to the ground. The horns are short but very large, and are a simple arch like those of the common ox.

The female is much smaller than the male, and always distinguishable by the peculiar shape of the horns, which are much smaller and more crooked, turning their points more in towards the center of the forehead.

One of the remarkable characteristics of the buffalo is the peculiar formation and expression of the eye. The ball is very large and white, and the iris jet black. The lids always seem to be strained open, and the ball rolling forward and down. A considerable part of the iris

252

The Beggar's Dance, given by the leading young men of the tribe, for kindness to the poor.

is hidden behind the lower lid, while the pure white of the eye-ball glares out over it in an arch, in the shape of a moon at the end of its first quarter.

These animals are, truly speaking, gregarious, but not migratory. They graze in almost incredible numbers at times, and roam about and over vast tracts of country.

Fort Pierre is at the very heart or nucleus of the buffalo country. The finest animals that graze on the prairies are to be found here. I am sure I could never discover a better source for the history of death and destruction that is being dealt these noble animals, and hurrying their final extinction.

The Sioux are bold horsemen and great hunters. In the heart of their country is the most extensive assortment of goods, of whisky, and other saleable commodities, as well as the most indefatigable men, who constantly demand every robe that can be stripped from these animals' backs.

It is truly melancholy to anticipate the period when the last of these noble animals will fall victim to the improvident rapacity of white and red men, leaving these beautiful green fields a vast and idle waste, unstocked for ages to come, until the bones of the one and the traditions of the other will have vanished and left scarce an intelligible trace behind.

That the reader should not think me visionary in these contemplations, or romancing in making such assertions, I will cite the following item of the extravagances which are practiced in these regions.

When I first arrived at Fort Pierre the chiefs of the Sioux told me that only a few days before, an immense herd of buffaloes had showed themselves on the opposite side of the river, almost blackening the plains for a great distance. A part of five or six hundred Sioux

253

Indians on horseback forded the river about mid-day. They recrossed the river at sun-down and came into the Fort with *fourteen hundred fresh buffalo tongues.* The tongues were thrown down in a mass, and were traded for a few gallons of whisky, which were soon demolished in a harmless carouse.

This was a profligate waste of these useful animals. Not a skin or a pound of the meat (except the tongues) was brought in. And this at a season when their skins were without fur and not worth taking off, and their camp was well stocked with fresh and dried meat. They had no occasion for using the flesh, which is a fair exhibition of the improvident character of the Indian and his recklessness in catering to his appetite, so long as inducements are held out to him for its gratification.

The Indians have no laws or regulations making it a vice or an impropriety to drink to excess. They think it no harm to indulge as long as they are able to buy whisky to drink. They look to white men as wiser than themselves, and able to set them examples. They see none but sellers of whisky, who are constantly tendering it to them, and most of them setting the example by using it themselves. They easily acquire a taste for whisky sold at sixteen dollars per gallon. It soon impoverishes them, and they must soon strip the skin from the last buffalo's back to be dressed by their squaws and vended to the traders for a pint of diluted alcohol.

Nowhere has Nature presented more beautiful scenes than those of the vast prairies of the West. Of man and beast, no nobler specimens than the Indian and the buffalo—joint and original tenants of the soil, and fugitives together from the approach of civilized man. They have fled to the great plains of the West, and there, under an equal doom, they have taken up their *last abode,* where their race will expire, and their bones will bleach together.

It may be that *power* is *right* and *voracity* a *virtue;* that these people and these noble animals are righteously doomed to an issue that will not be averted. It can be easily proved. We have a civilized science that can easily do it, or anything else that may be required to cover the iniquities of civilized man in catering to his unholy appetites. It can be proved that the weak and ignorant have no rights; that there can be no virtue in darkness; that God's gifts have no meaning or merit until they are appropriated by civilized man—converted to his use and luxury. We have a mode of reasoning (I forget what it is called) by which all this can be proved, and even more. The *word* and the *system* are entirely of *civilized* origin. Latitude is given to them in proportion to the increase of civilized wants. These wants often require a judge to overrule the laws of nature. I say that *we* can prove such things; but an *Indian* cannot. It is a mode of reasoning unknown to him, but admirably adapted to serve the interests of the enlightened world, who are always their own judges when dealing with the Indian.

It is not enough in this polished age that we get from the Indian his lands, and the clothes from his back, but the food from their mouths must be stopped, to add a new article to the fashionable world's luxuries. The ranks of the buffalo must be thinned, and the Indians of the great plains left without the means of supporting life, so that white men may spread buffalo robes for their pleasure and elegance over the backs of their sleighs, or trail them ostentatiously amid the busy throng.

254

Sioux women dressing buffalo hides.

It seems odd that we civilized people with all the comforts of the world about us should be drawing from the backs of these animals the skins for our luxury, leaving their carcasses to be devoured by the wolves—that we should draw from that country some two hundred thousand robes annually, the greater part of which are taken from animals killed expressly for the robe, at a season when the meat is not cured and preserved, and for each of which skins the Indian has received but a pint of whisky.

It may be answered, perhaps, that the necessaries of life are given in exchange for these robes. But what, I would ask, are the necessities in Indian life, where they have buffaloes in abundance to live on? The Indian's necessities are entirely artificial—are all created. When the buffaloes have disappeared, who is to supply the Indian with the necessaries of life then?

Thus much I wrote and painted at this place. I am to descend the river still further in a few days. I throw my notebook and canvas and brushes into my canoe. It will be launched tomorrow morning, and on its way towards St. Louis. I will be at the steering-oar, as usual. Baptiste and Bogard will paddle. I beg the reader's pardon for having said nothing of them of late, though they have been my constant companions. Our way is now over the foaming and muddy waters of the Missouri, and amid snags and drift logs. There is a sweeping freshet on her waters.

255

Prairie bluffs burning.

XIV

On the Missouri

MY VOYAGE from the mouth of the Teton River has been the most rugged, yet the most delightful, of my whole tour. Our canoe was generally landed at night on some projecting barren sand-bar. We slept on our buffalo robes, secure from the annoyance of mosquitoes, and out of the walks of Indians and grizzly bears. In addition to the opportunity to visit the tribes of Indians on the river, and fill my portfolio with the beautiful scenery of its shores, the sportsman's fever was roused and satisfied. Swan, ducks, geese, and pelicans, deer, antelope, elk, and buffaloes were "stretched" by our rifles.

I often landed my skiff, mounted the green-carpeted bluffs, whose soft grassy tops invited me to recline, and was at once lost in contemplation. Soul-melting scenery was about me. I mean the prairie, whose enamelled plains lay beneath me, softening into sweetness if the distance like an essence. A thousand thousand velvet-covered hills were tossing and leaping down the river's edge, as if to grace its shores.

At sunset the green hill-tops are turned into gold. Their long shadows of melancholy are thrown over the valleys. All the breathings of day are hushed, and nought but the soft notes of the dove can be heard; or the still softer and more plaintive notes of the wolf, who sneaks through these scenes of enchantment and mournfully howls as if lonesome, lost in the

Floyd's grave.

stillness about him. I mean *this* prairie, where Heaven sheds its purest light and lends its richest tints.

"Floyd's Grave" is the name given to one of the lovely bluffs on the Missouri River, about twelve hundred miles above St. Louis. It is named for Sergeant Floyd, of Lewis and Clark's expedition in 1806, who died on the way. His body was taken to this beautiful hill and buried at its top. A cedar post bears his initials.

I landed my canoe in front of this grass-covered mound, and all hands being fatigued, we encamped a couple of days at its base. I several times ascended it and sat upon his grave, overgrown with grass and delicate wild flowers. I sat and contemplated in solitude and stillness. From its top I could see the windings of the Missouri, its thousand hills and domes of green, vanishing into blue distance. Nothing but the soft-breathing winds was heard to break the stillness of the scene. No chirping bird or sound of cricket, nor soaring eagle's scream, were interposed between God and man. Nothing to check man's whole surrender of his soul to his Creator.

I roamed from hill-top to hill-top, and culled wild flowers, and looked into the valley below me, both up the river and down, and contemplated the thousand hills and dales that are now carpeted with green, streaked as they *will* be with the plough, and yellow with the harvest sheaf, spotted with lowing kine, with houses and fences, and groups of hamlets and villas, and these lovely hill-tops ringing with giddy din or secret earnest whispers of love-sick swains.

A few miles from Floyd's Bluff we landed our canoe and spent a day in the vicinity

Blackbird's grave.

of "Black Bird's Grave." This is a celebrated point on the Missouri, a sort of telegraphic place, which all the travellers in these realms, both white and red, are in the habit of visiting. The bluff is called "Black Bird's Grave" because a famous chief of the Omahaws was buried on its top, at his own peculiar request. A cedar post was erected over his grave by his tribe some thirty years ago. It is still standing.

The Omahaw village was about sixty miles up river. The chief had been on a visit to Washington City, in company with the Indian agent, but died of the small-pox, near this spot, on his return home. As he was dying, he enjoined his warriors to take his body down river to his favorite haunt, on the pinnacle of this towering bluff, and bury him on the back of his favorite war-horse. It was to buried alive under him. Then he could see, as he said, "the Frenchmen passing up and down the river in their boats."

He owned a white horse that was led to the top of the grass-covered hill. With great pomp and ceremony, in presence of the whole nation, and several of the fur traders and the Indian agent, he was placed astride his horse's back, with his bow in his hand, and his shield and quiver slung, with his pipe and his medicine-bag, with his supply of dried meat, and his tobacco-pouch replenished to last him through his journey to the "beautiful hunting grounds of the shades of his fathers."

The scalps he had taken from his enemies' heads could be trophies for nobody else, and were hung to the bridle of his horse. He was in full dress and fully equipped. On his head waved, to the last moment, his beautiful head-dress of war-eagle's plumes. After the last

259

funeral honors were performed by the medicine-men, every warrior of his band painted the palm and fingers of his right hand with vermilion. They stamped their prints on the milk-white sides of his devoted horse.

This done, turfs were brought and placed around the feet and legs of the horse, and gradually laid up its sides, and finally over the back and head of the unsuspecting animal, and even the eagle plumes of its rider. Completely smothered, they remain undisturbed to the present day. The mound is covered with green turf and spotted with wild flowers. The cedar post in its center can easily be seen at a distance of fifteen miles, and forms a useful landmark.

There have been some surprising tales told of Black Bird, whether they be truth or matters of fiction. Of many, the most current is that he gained his authority by the most diabolical series of murders in his own tribe. He administered arsenic (with which he was supplied by the fur traders) to the enemies he wished to get rid of, and even to others in his tribe whom he was willing to sacrifice to establish his superhuman powers. The tribe dreaded him from the certainty with which his victims fell, precisely at the times he would predict their death. It has been said he administered this potent drug, and unknown *medicine,* to many of his friends as well as to foes. By such unparalleled depravity, he succeeded in exercising the most despotic authority until the time of his death.

This story may be true, and it may not. I cannot contradict it, but I cannot believe it. If it be true, it furnishes an instance of Indian depravity that I never have heard of elsewhere in my travels. In any case, it carries the most conclusive proof of the incredible enormity of white man's dealings in this country, who must have introduced the poisonous drug into the country, and taught the poor chief how to use it. They were silent accessories to the murders he was committing.

The story is told by the fur traders. Although I have not always the highest confidence in their justice to the Indian, I cannot believe them to be so depraved and so wicked, nor so weak, as to reveal such iniquities of this chief, which if they were true, would directly implicate themselves as accessories to his willful murders.

We embarked from Black Bird's Hill, and glided through constantly changing scenes of beauty until we landed our canoe at the base of a beautiful series of grass-covered bluffs, which, like thousands and thousands of others on the banks of this river, are designated by no name that I know of.

My canoe was landed at noon at the base of these picturesque hills—and we rested until the next morning. As soon as we were ashore, I scrambled to their summits, took my easel and canvas and brushes to the top of the bluff, and painted two views from the same spot: one looking up, and the other down the river. These two views were taken about five miles above "the Tower," the name given by travellers through the country to a high and remarkable clay bluff rising to the height of some hundreds of feet from the water, and having the castellated appearance of a fortification.

While strolling about on the western bank of the river, I found the ancient site of an Indian village, which, from the character of the marks, I am sure was once the residence of the Mandans. Within the recollection of some of their oldest men, the Mandans lived some sixty or eighty miles down the river from the place of their present residence. They then lived in nine villages. On my way down, I landed my canoe, and examined the ground where the foundation of every lodge can still be distinctly seen. At that time they must have been much more numerous than at present, from the many marks they have left.

The Mandans have a peculiar way of building their lodges by digging down a couple of feet in the earth and then fixing the ends of the poles which form the walls of their houses. There are other marks: their caches, their mode of depositing their dead on scaffolds, their skulls in circles on the prairies. Their peculiar customs can be distinctly recognized in each of these places, as well as in similar remains I have examined on the river between here and the Mandans. The evidence convinces me they formerly occupied the lower parts of the Missouri, and gradually made their way through the heart of the great Sioux country. Having well-fortified locations, as in their present one, they have been able to successfully resist the continual assaults of the Sioux, though that numerous tribe still are endeavoring to effect their destruction.

I have examined at least fifteen of their ancient locations on the banks of this river, and can imagine the differences in the ages of their antiquity. Around them all I have found many bits of their broken pottery, corresponding with that which they are now manufacturing. It is made by no other tribe in these regions.

Almost every mile on the river, I met evidences or marks of Indians in some form or other. They have generally been those of the Sioux, who occupy the greater part of this immense region. In the latter part of my voyage, however, I met the ancient sites of the Omahaw and Otto towns, which are easily detected when they are met. The usual mode of the Omahaws in depositing their dead is in the crotches and on the branches of tress, enveloped in skins, and never without a wooden dish hanging by the head of the corpse, probably to dip up water to quench its thirst on the long and tedious journey they expect to enter on after death. These corpses are so frequent along the banks of the river that in some places a dozen or more may be seen at one time.

In most of these sites of the ancient Mandan towns, however, I have been unable to find about their burial places and their characteristic deposits of skulls. I conclude that whenever they deliberately moved to a different region, they buried the skulls out of respect to the dead. I found, just back of one of these sites of their ancient towns, however, and at least five hundred miles below where they now live, the same arrangement of skulls as I have before described. They had laid so long exposed to the weather they were reduced almost to a powder, except the teeth, which seemed polished and sound as ever. It seemed no human hands had dared to meddle with the dead. Even their enemies had respected them. Every one, and there were at least two hundred in one circle, had mouldered to chalk, in its exact position placed in the circle. In this case, I believe the village must have been besieged by the Sioux and entirely destroyed, or the Mandans were driven off without being able to stop and bury the bones of their dead.

Belle Vue is a lovely scene on the west bank of the river, about nine miles above the mouth of the Platte, and is the agency of Major Dougherty, one of the oldest and most effective agents on our frontiers. This spot is lovely in itself, but doubly so to the eye of the weather-beaten *voyageur* from the Upper Missouri who steers his canoe in to the shore, as I

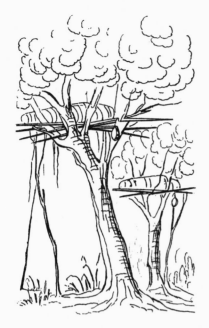

The Omaha put their dead in the crotches of trees.

The Sioux bury on hills.

The Mandan sites are easily distinguished.

did, and soon finds himself a welcome guest at the comfortable board of the Major, with a *table* again to eat from.

At Belle Vue I was in the country of the Pawnees, a numerous tribe whose villages are on the Platte River. Major Dougherty has been for many years the agent for this hostile tribe. By his knowledge of Indian character, and his strict honesty and integrity, he has been able to effect a friendly intercourse with them. But the mouth of the Platte is beautiful, and no doubt will be the site of a large and flourishing town as soon as Indian titles shall have been extinguished to the lands in these regions, which will be done within a few years.

From the mouth of the Platte, I have the great satisfaction of announcing that we escaped *snags* and *sawyers,* and arrived safe at Fort Leavenworth. Baptiste, Bogard, and I are comfortably quartered in the barracks of this frontier military post.

The cantonment, situated on the west bank of the Missouri River, six hundred miles above its mouth, was constructed some years ago by General Leavenworth, from whom it has taken its name. It is the concentration point of a number of hostile tribes in the vicinity, and has its influence in restraining their warlike propensities. There is a regiment of men stationed here to hold the Indians in check and preserve peace among the hostile tribes. There are six or seven companies of infantry, and ten or fifteen officers. Several have their wives and daughters with them, forming a pleasant little community who are almost continually together in social enjoyment of the pleasures of this wild country. Of these they have many, such as riding horseback or riding carriages over the green prairies, picking strawberries and wild plums, deer chasing, grouse shooting, horse-racing, and other amusements, enjoying life to a high degree. I joined several times in the deer hunts, and frequently in grouse shooting.

262

Bogard, Baptiste, and I meet buffalo in the Missouri.

This delicious bird is generally called the prairie hen, and from what I can learn is much like the English grouse in size, color, and habits. They appear in the months of August and September from the higher latitudes, where they go in the early part of the summer to raise their broods. This is the season for them, and the whole garrison, in fact, are almost subsisting on them at this time.

The other day, with one of the officers of the garrison, I brought in seventy-five of these birds in one afternoon. We had a fine pointer, and legitimately followed the sportsman's style for a part of the afternoon. But seeing the prairies on fire several miles ahead of us, and the wind driving the fire gradually towards us, we found these poor birds driven before its long line, which seemed to extend from horizon to horizon. They were flying in swarms or flocks that would at times almost fill the air. They generally flew half a mile or so, then lit down again in the grass, where they would sit until the fire was close, and then rise again. We observed they lit in great numbers in every solitary tree. We placed ourselves near each of these trees in turn, and shot them as they settled in them.

263

The burning prairie is one of the most beautiful scenes. Every acre for hundreds and hundres of miles is grass, which dies and dries, then burns over, leaving the ground a black doleful color.

There are many ways the fire is started either by white men or by Indians by accident, but the fires are often deliberately started to get a fresh crop of grass, for the grazing of horses, or to make easier travelling during the next summer—so there will be no old grass to entangle the feet of man or horse.

Over the elevated prairie bluffs, where the grass is thin and short, the fire slowly creeps with a feeble flame, which one can easily step over. The wild animals often rest in their lairs until the flames almost burn their noses, then reluctantly rise, leap over it, and trot off among the cinders. At night these scenes become indescribably beautiful. The flames are seen many miles, creeping over the sides and tops of the bluffs, sparkling chains of liquid fire hanging suspended in graceful festoons from the skies.

But there is another character of burning prairie, when the grass is seven or eight feet high for many miles on the Missouri bottoms. Then the flames are driven forward by hurricanes which sweep over denuded country. There are many of these meadows on the Missouri, the Platte, and the Arkansas, many miles in breadth, which are perfectly level, with a waving grass so high that we are obliged to stand erect in our stirrups in order to look over its waving tops as we ride through it.

In these, the fire travels at a frightful rate and often destroys parties of Indians on their fleetest horses, if they are so unlucky as to be overtaken by it. It does not travel as fast as a horse at full speed, but the high grass is filled with wild pea-vines and other impediments which render it necessary for the rider to guide his horse in the zig-zag paths of the deers and buffaloes, retarding his progress. Then he may be overtaken by the dense column of smoke sweeping before the fire—alarming the horse, which stops and stands terrified, till the burning grass falls about him, kindling up in a moment a thousand new fires, which move on like a black thunder-cloud rolling over the earth, with its lightning's glare and its thunder rumbling as it goes.

I have been moving about among different tribes in this vicinity. The Indians that may be said to belong to this vicinity, and who constantly visit this post, are the Ioways, Konzas, Pawnees, Omahaws, Ottoes, Missouries, Delawares, Kickapoos, Potawatomies, Weahs, Peorias, Shawanos, Kaskaskias—semi-civilized remnants of tribes that have been removed to this neighborhood by the Government. These tribes are, to a considerable degree, agriculturalists, getting their living principally by ploughing and by raising corn and cattle and horses. They have been left on the frontier, surrounded by civilized neighbors, where they have at length been induced to sell out their lands, or exchange them for a much larger tract of wild lands which the Government has purchased from the wilder tribes.

Of these, the Ioways are most dependent on their corn-fields for subsistence, though their appearance, both in their dwellings and personal looks, dress, modes, is that of the primitive Indian. They are a small tribe, of about fourteen hundred persons, living in a snug little village within a few miles of the eastern bank of the Missouri River, a few miles above Fort Leavenworth.

The present chief is Notch-ee-ning-a (The White Cloud), the son of a very

264

She-Who-Bathes-Her-Knees, wife of a Cheyenne chief, who was visiting at Fort Pierre.

distinguished chief of the same name, who died recently after gaining the love of his tribe and the respect of all the civilized world who knew him. The son of White Cloud, who is now chief, was tastefully dressed with a buffalo robe wrapped around him; with a necklace of grizzly bears' claws on his neck; with shield, bow, and quiver on, and a profusion of wampum strings on his neck.

Wy-ee-yogh (The Man of Sense), another of this tribe, is distinguished for his bravery and early warlike achievements. His head was dressed with a broad silver band passing around it, and decked out with a crest of horse-hair.

Pah-ta-coo-che (The Shooting Cedar), and Was-com-mun (The Busy Man) are also distinguished warriors of the tribe, tastefully dressed and equipped, the one with his war-club on his arm, the other with bow and arrows in his hand. Both wore around their waists beautiful buffalo robes, and both had turbans made of vari-colored cotton shawls, purchased from the

265

fur traders. Around their necks were necklaces of bears' claws, and a profusion of beads and wampum. Their ears were strung with beads, and their naked shoulders were streaked and daubed with red paint.

The Konzas, one thousand five hundred and sixty souls, reside sixty or eighty miles from this place, on the Konzas River, fifty miles above its union with the Missouri from the west.

This tribe undoubtedly sprung from the Osages, as their personal appearance, language, and traditions clearly prove. They live adjoining the Osages at this time, and although a kindred people, sometimes have deadly warfare with them. The present chief is known by the name of The White Plume, a very urbane and hospitable man, of good portly size, who speaks some English and makes himself good company for all white persons who travel through his country.

The Konzas shave their heads and ornament them with a crest of deer's hair; so do the Osages, the Pawnees, the Sacs, the Foxes, and the Ioways. The custom is uniformly adhered to by every man in the nation; except in some few instances along the frontier, where efforts are made to imitate white men by allowing the hair to grow out.

The hair is cut as close to the head as possible, except a tuft of two inches in length, the size of the palm of the hand, on the crown of the head, which is left. In the center, the tuft is fastened by a beautiful crest made of hair of the deer's tail (dyed red) and horse-hair, and often surmounted with a war-eagle's quill. In the center of the patch of hair is preserved a small lock, which is never cut, but cultivated to the greatest length possible and uniformly kept in braid. It is passed through a piece of carved bone, which lies in the center of the crest, and spreads it out to its uniform shape, which they take great care to preserve. Through this little braid, and outside of the bone, passes a small wooden or bone key, which holds the crest to the head. This little braid is called the "scalp-lock," and is scrupulously preserved in this way, and offered to their enemy if they can get it, as a trophy.

With the exception of these few, all the other tribes in North America cultivate their hair to the greatest length they possibly can, preserving it to flow over their shoulders and backs in great profusion, and quite unwilling to spare the smallest lock of it for any consideration.

All of these tribes, as well as the many semi-civilized remnants of tribes that have been thrown out from our settlements, have missionary establishments and schools, as well as agricultural efforts among them. They furnish evidence as to the success those philanthropic exertions have met, contending (as they have had to do) with the contaminating influences of whisky-sellers and other mercenary men.

Baptiste and Bogard have paddled, and I have steered, and we have dodged our little craft through snags and sawyers, until at last we landed the humble little thing among the huge steamers and floating palaces at the wharf of St. Louis.

First of all, I must relate the fate of my little boat. She had borne us safe over two thousand miles of the Missouri's boiling current, with no fault except in two or three instances when the waves became too saucy. Then, like the best of boats of her size, she went to the

266

bottom, and left us soused, paddling our way to shore to drag out our things and dry them in the sun.

When we landed at the wharf, my luggage was all taken out and removed to my hotel. I returned a few hours afterwards to look for my little boat. Some mystery or medicine operation had relieved me from any further anxiety or trouble about it—it was gone. It had safely laid weeks and months at the villages of red men, with no laws to guard it. It had often been taken out of the water, carried up the bank, and turned against my wigwam; and then again safely carried to the river's edge when I was ready to take a seat in it.

St. Louis is destined to be the great emporium of the West—the greatest inland town in America. I have made it *my* starting-point, and place of deposit, to which I send from different quarters my packages of paintings and Indian articles, minerals, and fossils as I collect them in various regions, to be stored until my return.

Pawnee: The Buffalo Bull.

The Blistered Foot, Ioway Medicine Man.

Konza: The Man of Good Sense.

Konza: No Fool.

Omahas: The Big Elk, a famous warrior.

Peoria: The No English, a tribal dandy, or beau.

Ottoes: He-Who-Strikes-Two-at-Once, a brave.

Plate I. Buffalo chase in the Great American Desert.

Plate II. White Cloud, called The Prophet, adviser to Black Hawk.

Plate III. Black Hawk, fought by militiaman Abraham Lincoln.

Plate IV. White Cloud spoke: ". . . it is to keep our sons and our sons' sons free. . . . His way is his own."

Plate V. Wun-Nes-Tow, The White Buffalo, Blackfoot Medicine Man.

Plate VI. Wi-jun-jon, The Pigeon's Egg Head, going to and returning from Washington.

Plate VII. "O-kee-pa": hung by rawhide thongs tied to skewers run through their flesh.

Plate VIII. Kee-o-kuk, The Running Fox, Chief of the Sauk and Fox.

Belle Vue, on the west bank, about nine miles above the Platte.

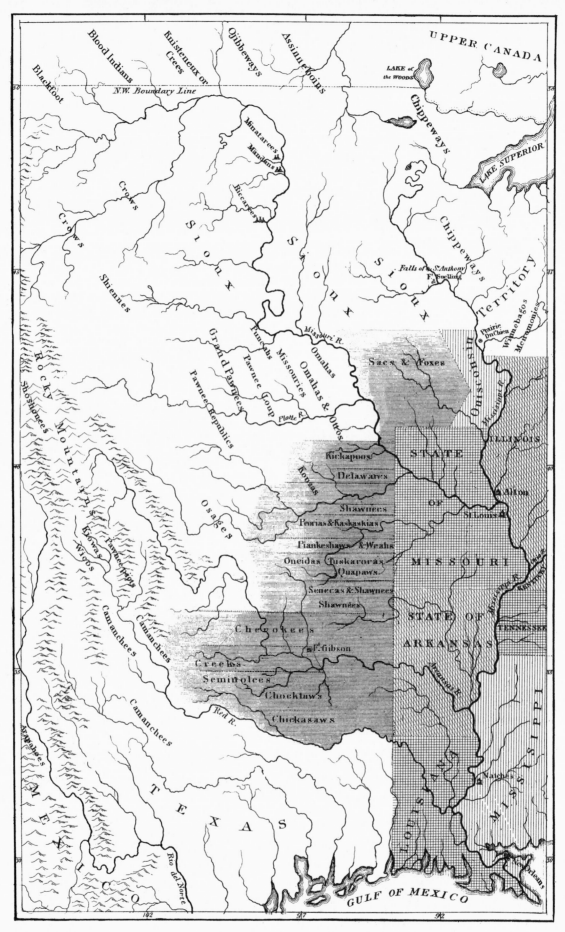

Map of United States frontier in 1840 showing the positions of the tribes that had been removed west of the Mississippi. Drawn by George Catlin.

XV

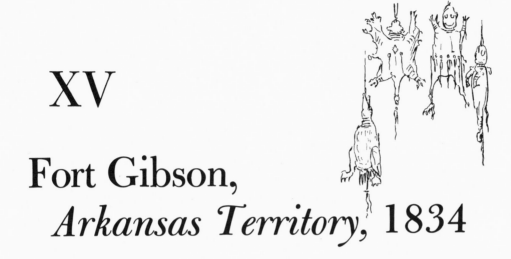

Fort Gibson,
Arkansas Territory, 1834

FROM PENSACOLA, Florida, I travelled to New Orleans, and from there up the Mississippi several hundred miles to the mouth of the Arkansas, then up the Arkansas seven hundred miles to this place. We steamed our way up on the riverboat "Arkansas" until we were within two hundred miles of this post. Then we ran aground. The water fell fast, leaving the steamer nearly on dry ground. Hunting and fishing, and whist, and sleeping and eating were our principal amusements to pass the time while waiting for the water to rise. We lay two weeks without prospect of further progress. But at last with higher water we reached our destined goal, and here we are.

Fort Gibson is the extreme south-western outpost on the United States frontier, situated on the banks of the river in the midst of an extensive prairie. It is at present occupied by the 7th regiment of United States infantry, heretofore under the command of General Arbuckle, one of the oldest officers on the frontier, and the original builder of the post.

I obtained permission from the Secretary of War to accompany the regiment of the United States dragoons in their summer campaign. I reported myself at this place two months ago, where I have been waiting ever since for their organization. After many difficulties, they have at length all assembled. The *natives* are again "to be astonished," and I shall probably again be a witness of the scene.

The regiment of eight hundred men with whom I am to travel will be a protection against any attacks made by Indians. It is composed principally of young men who would act from feelings of pride and honor in addition to those of the common soldier.

The day before yesterday the regiment of dragoons and the 7th regiment of infantry stationed here were reviewed by General Leavenworth, who has arrived at this post, superseding Colonel Arbuckle in the command.

Both regiments were drawn up in battle array, in fatigue dress, and passing through a number of the maneuvers of battle, of charge and repulse, presented a thrilling scene on the prairie to the thousands of Indians and others who had assembled to witness the display.

Each company of horses has been selected of one entire color. There is a company of bays, a company of blacks, one of whites, one of sorrels, one of grays, one of cream color. The colors render the companies distinct, and the effect is pleasing. The regiment goes out under the command of Colonel Dodge. From his well-testified qualifications, and from the beautiful equipment of the command, there can be little doubt that they will do credit to themselves and honor to their country—so far as honors can be gained and laurels can be plucked from their wild stems in a savage country.

The object of the campaign seems to be to cultivate an acquaintance with the Pawnees and Comanchees. These are two extensive tribes of roaming Indians who have not yet recognized the United States in treaty. They have struck frequent blows on our frontiers and plundered our traders traversing their country. For this I cannot so much blame them, for the Spaniards are gradually advancing upon them on one side and the Americans on the other, fast destroying the furs and game of their country, which God gave them as their only wealth and means of subsistence.

The troops are starting too late in the season for their summer's campaign, by two months. The journey is a very long one. Although the first part of it will be picturesque and pleasing, the later part will be fatiguing in the extreme. As they advance to the west, the grass (and consequently the game) will gradually diminish, and water become scarce. The troops will be obliged to subsist for themselves a great part of the way. It will be extremely difficult to hold themselves in readiness, with half-famished horses and men nearly exhausted, and contend with a numerous enemy who are at home, on the ground on which they were born, with horses fresh and ready for action.

I have been industriously at work with my brush and my pen, recording the looks and the deeds of the Osages, who inhabit the country on the north and the west of Fort Gibson.

The Osage, or (as they call themselves) *Wa-saw-see,* are a tribe of about five thousand two hundred in number, inhabiting and hunting over the head-waters of the Arkansas, and Neosho or Grand rivers. Their present residence is three villages, constituted of wigwams built of barks and flags or reeds about seven hundred miles west of the Mississippi River. One of these villages is within forty miles of this Fort, another within sixty, and the third about eighty miles. Their chief place of trade is with the settlers at Fort Gibson, and there are constantly more or less of them encamped about the garrison.

The Osages may justly be said to be the tallest race of men in North America, either of red or white skins. Few of the men are less than six feet in stature, and many of them six and a half, and others seven feet. They are at the same time well-proportioned in their limbs, and good-looking. They are rather narrow in the shoulders, and like most all very tall people, a little inclined to stoop. Their movement is graceful and quick. In war and the chase I think they are equal to any of the tribes about them.

Though living near the borders of the civilized community, they have studiously rejected every civilized custom. They are dressed in skins of their own making. They maintain their primitive looks and manners without the slightest appearance of innovations, except their use of blankets instead of buffalo robes, which are now getting scarce among them.

The Osages are one of the tribes who shave the head, as do the Pawnees and Konzas, and they decorate and paint it with great care and considerable taste. There is a peculiarity in the heads of these people which is very striking to the eye, produced by artificial means in infancy. Their children, like those of all the other tribes, are carried on a board and slung upon the mother's back. The infants are lashed to the boards, with their backs upon them, apparently in a very uncomfortable condition. With the Osages, the head of the child bound down so tight to the board forces in the occipital bone and creates more than a natural elevation of the top of the head. They told me they practiced this custom because "it pressed out a bold and manly appearance in front." From observation, I think this is more imaginary than real. I cannot see that they exhibit any extraordinary development in front, though they show a striking deficiency on the back part, and also an unnatural elevation on the top of the head, which is, no doubt, produced by this custom.

These people, like all those tribes who shave the head, cut and slit their ears; and suspend from them great quantities of wampum and tinsel ornaments. Their necks are generally ornamented also with a profusion of wampum and beads. Because they live in a warm climate, there is not so much necessity for warm clothing as among the more northern tribes. Their shoulders, arms, and chests are generally naked, and painted in a great variety of picturesque ways, with silver bands on the wrists, and often a profusion of rings on the fingers.

The head-chief of the Osages is a young man by the name of Clermont, the son of a very distinguished chief of that name who recently died, leaving his son to be his successor, with the consent of the tribe. I painted him at full length, in a beautiful dress, his leggings fringed with scalp-locks, and in his hand his favorite war-club.

By his side I also painted his wife and child. She was richly dressed in costly clothes of civilized manufacture, an almost solitary instance among the Osages, who studiously reject every luxury and every custom of civilized people. Even the use of whisky, which is on all sides tendered to them, is almost uniformly rejected! This is an unusual and unaccountable thing. Perhaps the influence which the missionary and teacher have exercised over them has induced them to abandon the destructive habit of drinking to excess. From what I can learn, the Osages were fond of whisky, and like all other tribes who have had the opportunity, they were in the habit of using it to excess.

For years several exemplary men have been exerting their greatest efforts, with those of their families, among these people. They have established schools and agricultural

Osage: Clermont, head chief.

The Black Dog, seven-foot Osage chief.

experiments among them. And I believe that this decided anomaly in the Indian country has resulted from the devoted exertions of these few pious and good men.

Among the chiefs of the Osages, and probably the next in authority and respect in the tribe, is Tchong-tas-sab-bee (The Black Dog). I also painted him at full length, with his pipe in one hand and his tomahawk in the other, his head shaved and ornamented with a beautiful crest of deers' hair, and his body wrapped in a huge mackinaw blanket.

He is blind in the left eye, and one of the most conspicuous characters in all this country because of his huge size. His height is seven feet I think. His limbs are full and rather fat, making his bulk formidable, and he weighs perhaps some two hundred and fifty or three hundred pounds. He is chief of one of the three bands of the Osages, which are divided into three villages called "Clermont's Village," "Black Dog's Village," and "White Hair's Village."

The Osages were until quite recently a powerful and warlike tribe. They carried their arms fearlessly through all these realms. They were ready to cope with any foes they were liable to meet. Now the case is quite different. They have been repeatedly moved and jostled along from the head waters of the White River and even from the shores of the Mississippi, to where they now are. They were reduced by every war and by every move. The small-pox has taken its share of them two or three different times, and the Konzas, once a part of the Osages, seceded from them and reduced their strength. Their decline has been very rapid, though still preserving their valor as warriors, which they show off as bravely and as professionally as they can. They must wage incessant war with the Pawnees and the Comanchees, but the Osages are the principal sufferers in the incidents in which they fearlessly persist, as if they were actually bent on their self-destruction.

Great efforts have been made among these people to civilize and Christianize them, but I believe with little success. Agriculture they have caught but little of; and of religion and civilization still less. One good result has, however, been produced by these faithful laborers: the conversion of these people to temperance.

Here I must leave the Osages for the present, because I am to start in a few days, in company with the 1st regiment of dragoons, in the first grand *civilized foray* into the country of the wild and warlike Comanchees.

Osage braves: The Big Crow, The Man of the Bed, He-Who-Is-Not-Afraid.

The Little Spaniard.

XVI

Mouth of the False Washita, *Red River*

UNDER THE protection of the United States dragoons, I arrived at this place three days ago. We are on the banks of the Red River, having Texas under our eye on the opposite bank. Our encampment is on the point of land between the Red and False Washita rivers, at their junction. The country about us is a panorama too beautiful to be painted with a pen. It is composed of prairie and timber, alternating in the most delightful shapes and proportions the eye of a connoisseur could desire. The verdure is everywhere of the deepest green, and the plains about us are literally speckled with buffalo. Fort Gibson is now about two hundred miles behind us, a distance we accomplished in ten days.

A great part of the way the country was prairie, gracefully undulating, well watered, and beautified by copses and patches of timber. On our way, my attention was attracted by the tops of some prairie bluffs. I rode to the top of one of these mounds with my friends Lieutenant Wheelock and Joseph Chadwick. From the top, the horizon all around us was bounded by mountain streaks of blue, softening into azure as they vanished. The pictured intermediate vales deepened into green as the eye returned from its roamings. Beneath us, and winding through the waving landscape, we could see the "bold dragoons" forming a train

279

a mile in length. Baggage wagons and Indians *(engagés)* helped to lengthen the procession. From the point where we stood, the line looked like a huge black snake gracefully gliding over a rich carpet of green.

Scarcely a day passed that we did not cross oak ridges several miles in breadth, with a sandy soil and scattering timber. The ground was covered with vines, producing the greatest profusion of delicious grapes, of five-eighths of an inch in diameter and hanging in endless clusters. The next hour we would be trailing through broad valleys of green prairies. Then we might find our progress completely arrested by hundreds of acres of small plum-trees, of four or six feet in height, so closely woven and interlocked together as entirely to dispute our progress and send us several miles around. Every bush was so loaded with the weight of its delicious wild fruit, it was bent quite to the ground. Among these, in patches, were intervening beds of wild roses, wild currents, and gooseberries. Underneath and about them, and occasionally interlocked with them, were huge masses of prickly pears, and wild flowers that sweetened the atmosphere above. An occasional huge yellow rattlesnake, or a copper-head, could be seen gliding over or basking on the tendrils and leaves.

We have halted for a few days to recruit horses and men, after which the line of march will be resumed. If the Pawnees are as near to us as we have reason to believe from their recent trails and fires, it is probable that within a few days we shall "thrash" them or "get thrashed," unless through their sagacity and fear, they elude our search by flying before us to their hiding-places.

The prevailing policy among the officers seems to be that of flogging them first and then establishing a treaty of peace. If this plan were morally right, I do not think it practicable. As enemies, I do not believe they will stand to meet us; but as friends I think we may bring them to a talk, if the proper means are adopted.

We are encamped on the ground on which Judge Martin and servant were butchered, and his son kidnapped by the Pawnees or Comanchees only a few weeks ago. The moment they discover us in a large body, they will presume we are relentlessly seeking revenge, and they will probably be very shy of our approach. We are over the Washita—the "Rubicon is passed." We are invaders of a sacred soil.

The cruel fate of Judge Martin and family has been published in the papers. It is the objective of the regiment of dragoons to demand the surrender of the murderers, and get some authentic account of how this horrid outrage was committed.

Judge Martin was a very respectable and independent man, living on the lower part of the Red River. He was in the habit of taking his children and a couple of black men-servants every summer, with a tent to live in, into the prairie. He would spend several months killing buffaloes and other wild game for his own private amusement. A few weeks before we started, the news came to Fort Gibson that he had been set upon by a party of Indians and destroyed. A detachment of troops was speedily sent to the spot. They found his body horridly mangled, and also of one of his Negroes. It is supposed that his son, a fine boy nine years of age, has been taken by them to their villages, where they still retain him and where it is our hope to recover him.

I have been detained here with the rest of the cavalcade from an extraordinary

280

sickness that is afflicting the regiment and threatening to arrest its progress. Nearly one-half of the command and several officers, including General Leavenworth, have been thrown upon their backs with the prevailing epidemic, a slow and distressing bilious fever. The horses of the regiment are also sick, in about equal proportion, and seemingly suffering with the same disease. They are dying daily, and men are still falling sick. General Leavenworth has ordered Colonel Dodge to select all the men and all the horses that are able to proceed and be off tomorrow at nine o'clock upon the march towards the Comanchees. He hopes thereby to preserve the health of the men and still advance towards the destination.

General Leavenworth has reserved Colonel Kearney to take command of the remaining troops and the little encampment. He promises Colonel Dodge that he will be well enough himself in a few days to proceed with a party on his trail and overtake him at the Cross Timbers.

Instead of the eight hundred men the regiment of dragoons was supposed to contain when we started from Fort Gibson, there were only four hundred men. Now half of these are sick, leaving only two hundred effective men to penetrate the untried regions of the hostile Comanchees. All has been bustle and confusion this day, packing up and preparing for the start tomorrow morning. My canvas and painting apparatus are prepared and ready for the packhorse, which carries the goods of my esteemed companion Joseph Chadwick and myself. We shall be the only two guests of the procession, and the only two who will be at liberty to gallop about where we please, despite military rules and regulations.

Mr. Chadwick is a young man from St. Louis for whom I have the highest regard. He has stood by me as a faithful friend, and I rely implicitly on his society during this campaign for much good company. Though I have an order from the Secretary of War to the commanding officer to protect and supply me, I have, with my friend Joe, laid in my own supplies for the campaign, not putting the Government to any expense on my account.

I am writing this in General Leavenworth's tent, where he has invited me to take up my quarters during our encampment here. The General lies pallid and emaciated on his couch, with a dragoon fanning him. He breathes forty or fifty breaths a minute, and writhes under a burning fever, although he is yet unwilling even to admit that he is sick. He looks very feeble now, and I very much fear the result of the fever that has set in upon him. We take up our line of march at bugle-call tomorrow.

In the morning, the part of the regiment that was not sick was in motion at nine o'clock. And with them my friend "Joe" and I went, with our provisions laid in and all snugly arranged on our packhorse, which we alternately led or drove between us.

Our course was about due west, on the divide between the Washita and Red rivers, with our faces looking towards the Rocky Mountains. The country over which we passed from day to day was inimitably beautiful: one continuous prairie of green fields, with occasional clusters of timber and shrubbery. All seemed gay and buoyant at the fresh start, which all trusted was to liberate us from the fatal miasma that we conceived was hovering about the mouth of the False Washita.

On the fourth day of our march, we discovered many fresh signs of buffaloes, and at last immense herds of them grazing on the hills. Indian trails were daily growing fresher, and

General Leavenworth.

their smokes were seen in various directions ahead of us. On the same day at noon, we discovered a large party several miles away, sitting on their horses and looking at us. From the glistening of the blades of their lances, which blazed as they turned them in the sun, it was at first thought they were Mexican cavalry who had advanced to contest their territory with us. On drawing a little nearer, however, and scanning them closer with our spy-glasses, they were soon ascertained to be a war-party of Comanchees.

The regiment was called to a halt and after the requisite preparations made and orders issued, we advanced in a direct line towards them until we were within two or three miles of them. Then they suddenly disappeared over the hill, but soon after showed themselves on another mound farther off and in a different direction. The course of the regiment was then changed, and another advance towards them was commenced. Once again they disappeared and showed themselves in another direction. After several such ineffectual efforts, Colonel Dodge ordered the command to halt. He rode forward with a few of his staff and an ensign carrying a white flag. I joined this advance, and the Indians stood their ground until we had come within half a mile of them and could distinctly observe all their numbers and movements. We then came to a halt, and the white flag was sent a little in advance, and waved as a signal for them to approach. One of their party galloped out in advance of the war-party on a milk-white horse, carrying a piece of white buffalo skin on the point of his long lance.

All eyes, both from his own party and ours, were fixed upon the maneuvers of this gallant little fellow, and he well knew it. The distance between the two parties was perhaps half a mile. For a quarter of an hour, he reined and spurred his maddened horse, gradually approaching us by tacking to the right and the left, like a vessel beating against the wind. At length he came prancing and leaping along until he met the flag of the regiment, which he leaned his spear against, looking the bearer full in the face. Then he wheeled his horse and dashed up to Colonel Dodge, with his hand extended, which was instantly grasped and shaken.

We all had him by the hand in a moment. The rest of his party, seeing him received in this friendly manner, started under "full whip" in a direct line towards us, and in a moment gathered around us like a black cloud. The regiment then moved up in regular order, and a general shake of the hand ensued, each warrior riding along the ranks, shaking the hand of everyone as he passed. This necessary form took up considerable time.

During the whole operation my eyes were fixed upon the little fellow who bore us the white flag on the point of his lance. He rode a spirited wild horse as white as the drifted snow, with an exuberant mane and a long and bushy tail sweeping the ground. In his hand he tightly drew the reins upon a heavy Spanish bit. At every jump, he plunged a huge pair of spurs into the animal's sides, until they were in a gore of blood. The eyes of the horse seemed to be squeezed out of its head. Its fright and its agitation had brought to its skin a perspiration fretted into a white lather.

The warrior's quiver was slung on his back, and his bow grasped in his left hand, ready for instant use. His shield was on his arm; and across his thigh, in a beautiful cover of buckskin, his gun was slung. In his right hand he had a lance fourteen feet long.

We soon understood they were a war-party in search of their enemy. We dismounted, and the pipe was lit and passed around. And then a "talk" was held in which we were aided by a Spaniard we luckily had with us who could converse with one of the Comanchees who spoke some Spanish.

Colonel Dodge explained to them the friendly motives with which we were penetrating their country: that we were sent by the President to reach their villages and see the chiefs of the Comanchees and Pawnee Picts; to shake hands with them and to smoke the pipe of peace; and to establish an acquaintance, and consequently a system of trade that would be beneficial to both.

They listened attentively, and taking Colonel Dodge at his word, they informed us that their great town was within a few days' march. Pointing in its direction, they offered to abandon their war-excursion and turn about and escort us to it. We were on the march by afternoon. They led us over hill and dale, encamping by the side of us at night, and resuming the march each morning.

We had with us about thirty Osage and Cherokee, Seneca and Delaware Indians,

The Dragoons meet the Comanche.

employed as guides and hunters for the regiment. With the war-party of ninety or a hundred Comanchees, we formed a picturesque scene passing over the prairies. We were now out of bread stuffs and subsisted entirely on buffalo meat. The Indians of the different tribes, anxious to show their skill and prove the mettle of their horses, took infinite pleasure in dashing into every herd we approached. As a result, the regiment was abundantly supplied with fresh meat.

The tract of country over which we passed between the False Washita and this place is stocked not only with buffaloes but with many bands of wild horses. There is no other animal on the prairies so difficult to come up with as the horse. So remarkably keen is their eye that they will generally run "at the sight" when they are a mile away. They seem able to distinguish the character of the enemy approaching at that distance. Once started, they seldom stop short of three or four miles. I have made many attempts to approach them by stealth when they were grazing, without ever having been able to succeed.

284

The usual mode of taking wild horses is by throwing the *laso* while pursuing them at full speed. Dropping a noose over their necks soon checks them, and they are "choked down." The laso is a thong of rawhide some ten or fifteen yards in length, twisted or braided, with a noose fixed at the end of it. When the coil of the laso is thrown out, it is dropped with great skill over the neck of the animal, which is then soon conquered.

The Indian coils his laso on his arm, starts off under full whip, until he can enter the herd. He soon gets it over the neck of one. He instantly dismounts, leaving his own horse, and runs as fast as he can, letting the laso pass out gradually through his hands, until the horse falls for want of breath and lies helpless on the ground. The Indian advances slowly towards the horse's head, keeping his laso tight upon its neck, until he fastens a pair of hobbles on the animal's two forefeet. He loosens the laso (giving the horse chance to breathe), and gives it a noose around the under jaw, by which means he gets great power over the frightened animal, which is rearing and plunging. He advances hand over hand towards the horse's nose. He is able to prevent the horse from throwing itself over its back, at the hazard of its limbs. He gradually advances until he is able to place his hand on the animal's nose and over its eyes. Finally he breathes in its nostrils. It becomes docile and conquered. He removes the hobbles from its feet, and leads or rides it into camp. Great care is taken, however, not to subdue the spirit of the animal, although they use them with great severity, being, generally speaking, cruel masters.

While on our march we met with many droves of these beautiful animals. Several times we had the opportunity of seeing the Indians pursue them, and take them with the laso.

The horses that were caught were by no means very valuable specimens, being rather of an ordinary quality. I saw to my satisfaction that the finest of these droves can never be obtained in this way because they take the lead at once when they are pursued, and in a few moments will be seen half a mile or more ahead of the bulk of the herd.

After many hard days of travel, we were at last told by our Comanchee guides that we were near their village. They led us to the top of a gently rising elevation on the prairie and pointed to their village several miles away, in the midst of one of the most enchanting valleys that man's eyes have ever looked upon. The general course of the valley is from N. W. to S. E., several miles wide, with a magnificent range of mountains rising in the distance beyond. In the midst of this lovely valley, we could just discern among the scattering shrubbery that lined the banks of the watercourses, the tops of the Comanchee wigwams, and the smoke curling above them. The valley seemed speckled with horses and mules grazing in it. The chiefs of the war-party requested the regiment to halt until they could ride in and inform their people who were coming.

We dismounted for an hour or so. We could see them busily running and catching their horses. At length, several hundred braves and warriors came out at full speed to welcome us. They wheeled their horses, rapidly formed in a line, and "dressed" like well-disciplined cavalry.

The regiment was drawn up in three columns, with a line formed in front by Colonel Dodge and his staff. In the center of our advance was a white flag. The Indians answered it with one which they sent forward and planted by its side.

The Comanche braves formed a line in front of the regiment.

The two lines were drawn up face to face within twenty or thirty yards of each other, as if inveterate foes that never had met. To the everlasting credit of the Comanchees, they had all come out without a weapon of any kind to meet a war-party bristling with arms, and trespassing in the middle of their country. They had every reason to look upon us as their natural enemy. Yet instead of arms or defenses, or even of frowns, they galloped out and looked us in our faces without an expression of fear or dismay, and evidently with expressions of joy and impatient pleasure to shake us by the hand, on the bare assertion of Colonel Dodge that "we came to see them on a friendly visit."

After we had sat and gazed at each other in this way for half an hour or so, the head chief of the band came galloping up to Colonel Dodge, and having shaken him by the hand, he passed on to the other officers in turn, and then rode alongside of the different columns, shaking hands with every dragoon in the regiment. He was followed in this by his principal chiefs and braves, which altogether took up nearly an hour longer. Then the Indians retreated slowly towards their village, escorting us to the banks of a fine clear stream and a good spring of fresh water, half a mile from their village, which they designated as a suitable place for our encampment. We were soon bivouacked.

A fine-looking Indian hung about my tent very closely for several days. He continually scanned an old and half-worn cotton umbrella, which I carried over me to keep off the sun, as I was suffering with fever and ague. Finally he proposed to purchase it with a neat limbed and pretty pied horse which he was riding. He proposed at first that I should give him a knife and the umbrella, but I was not disposed for the trade. The umbrella was a useful article to me, and I did not want to part with it, not knowing whether there was another in the regiment. He came a second time and offered me the horse for the umbrella alone, which offer I still rejected. He then went back to the village and returned with another horse of a much better quality, supposing that I had not considered the former one equal to the umbrella.

With this he endeavored to push the trade. I had great difficulty making him understand that I was sick, and could not part with it. He turned and rode back towards the village, and in a short time returned again with one of the largest and finest mules I had ever seen, which I also rejected. He disappeared again.

In a few moments my friend Captain Duncan, in whose hospitable tent I was quartered, came in. The tale was told to him and he instantly sprang to his feet, and exclaimed, "D——mn the fellow! Where is he gone? Here, Gosset! Get my old umbrella out of the pack. I rolled it up with my wiper and the frying-pan—get it as quick as lightning!"

With his umbrella in his hand, the worthy Captain soon overtook the young man and escorted him into the village, returning in a short time not with the mule, but with the second horse that had been offered to me.

The Mountain of Rocks.

XVII

Great Comanchee Village

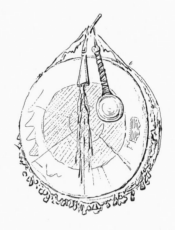

THE VILLAGE of the Comanchees is composed of six or eight hundred skin-covered wigwams made of poles and buffalo skins, like those of the Sioux and other Missouri tribes. In changing their encampments, each horse drags his load, and each dog that will do it (and there are many that will *not)* drags his wallet on a couple of poles; also, each squaw has her load. All together (notwithstanding their burdens) cherish their pugnacious feelings, which often bring them into general conflict. It usually starts among the dogs, and is sure to result in fisticuffs between the women. The men, riding leisurely on the right or the left, take infinite pleasure in watching these desperate conflicts. They are sure to have a laugh, and just as sure never to lend a hand.

The Comanchees, like the Northern tribes, have many games, and in pleasant weather seem to be continually practicing them on the prairies back of their village. In their ball-plays, and some other games, they are far behind the Sioux, but in racing horses and riding they are not equalled by any other Indians on the Continent. Racing horses, it would seem, is an almost incessant exercise, and their principal mode of gambling. A more finished set of jockeys are not to be found.

Among their feats of riding, there is a strategem of war practiced by every young man in the tribe. A Comanchee is able to drop his body over the side of his horse, effectually screening himself from his enemies' weapons as he lays in a horizontal position behind the body of his horse. His heel hangs atop the horse's back, and he can throw himself up again and change to the other side of the horse if necessary. He can hang while his horse is at full gallop, carrying with him his bow and his shield, and his long lance of fourteen feet in length, all or either of which he can wield upon his enemy as he passes. He can rise and shoot his arrows over the horse's back, or with equal ease and equal success under the horse's neck.

The young men have been showing off this astonishing feat for our amusement, while galloping about in front of our tents. I coaxed a young fellow up within a little distance of me by offering him a few plugs of tobacco. I found that a short hair halter was passed around under the neck of the horse, and both ends tightly braided into the mane, on the withers. A loop is left to hang under the neck and against the breast. It makes a sling into which the elbow falls, taking the weight of the body on the middle of the upper arm. Into this loop the rider drops suddenly and fearlessly, leaving his heel to hang over the back of the horse to steady him, and also to restore him when he wishes to regain his upright position on the horse's back.

In stature, the Comanchees are rather low, often approaching corpulency. In their movements, they are heavy and ungraceful. On their feet, they are one of the most unattractive and slovenly-looking races of Indians I have ever seen. But the moment they mount their horses, they seem at once metamorphosed—with ease and elegance in their movements. A Comanchee on his feet is out of his element and almost as awkward, comparatively, as a monkey on the ground, without a limb or a branch to cling to. The moment he lays his hand upon his horse, his face even becomes handsome, and he gracefully flies away like a different being.

The head chief of this village, who is represented to us as the head of the nation, is a pleasant-looking gentleman, without anything striking or peculiar in his looks. He dresses in a humble manner, with few ornaments upon him, and his hair carelessly falling about his face and over his shoulders. His name is Ee-shah-ko-nee (The Bow and Quiver). A couple of beautiful shells worn in his ears, and a boar's tusk attached to his neck and worn on his breast are his ornaments.

When we first arrived at this place, a huge mass of flesh, Ta-wah-que-nah (The Mountain of Rocks) was put forward as head chief of the tribe. All honors were paid to him by the regiment of dragoons, until The Bow and Quiver arrived from leading a war-party. When he arrived, The Mountain of Rocks, who is the largest and fattest Indiant I ever saw, stepped into the background, giving way to this admitted chief, who seemed to have the confidence and respect of the whole tribe.

The Mountain of Rocks must have weighed three hundred pounds or more. He was a perfect personation of Jack Falstaff in size and in figure, with an African face and a beard on his chin of two or three inches of length. His name, he tells me, he got because he conducted a large party of Comanchees through a secret passage in the mountain of granite rocks which lies back of their village. He thereby saved them from a powerful enemy, who had "cornered them up." The mountain through which he conducted them is called Ta-wah-que-nah (the

290

Comanche feats of horsemanship: sham battle.

mountain of rocks); and he has taken his name from it, which would certainly have been far more appropriate if it had been a *mountain of flesh*. Yet corpulency is exceedingly rare in any of the tribes, probably because of the exposed and active lives they lead.

Ish-a-ro-yeh (He Who Carries a Wolf), and Is-sa-wah-tam-ah (The Wolf Tied with Hair) are also chiefs of some standing in the tribe, and evidently men of great influence, for they were put forward by the head chiefs for their likenesses to be painted. The first of the two seemed to be leader of the war-party that we met. In escorting us to their village, he took the lead and piloted us the whole way, for which Colonel Dodge presented him a fine gun.

His-oo-san-ches (The Spaniard), a gallant little fellow, is represented to us as one of the leading warriors of the tribe. He is one of the most extraordinary men. He is half Spanish and, being a half-breed (for whom they generally have the most contemptuous feelings), he has been all his life thrown into the front of battle and danger. Nevertheless, he has distinguished himself and commands the highest respect of the tribe for his daring and adventurous career. He was the man who dashed out from the war-party and came to us with the white flag raised on the point of his lance. I have represented him as he stood for me, with his shield on his arms, with his quiver slung, and his lance of fourteen feet in length in his right hand. He seemed to be all bone and muscle, and exhibited immense power by the curve of the bones in his legs and arms.

From what I have seen of the Comanchees, I am convinced they are a numerous and powerful tribe, equal in numbers and prowess to their reputation. It is impossible at present to

291

Comanche village: women dressing buffalo robes and drying meat.

make a correct estimate of their numbers, but taking their own account of villages south of the banks of the Red River, as well as those that lie farther west and north of its banks, I think I am able to say, from estimates that the chiefs have made me, that they number some thirty or forty thousand—being able to show some six or seven thousand warriors, well mounted and well armed. I do not offer this estimate as conclusive, for so little is yet known of these people.

They speak much of their allies and friends, the Pawnee Picts who live some three or four days' march to the west. We are going to visit there in a few days, then return to this village and "bend our course" back to Fort Gibson. Every preparation is now making to be off, but so many men and officers are sick that the little command will be much crippled. We shall have to leave about thirty sick, and about an equal number of well to take care of and protect them. We are constructing a fort, with a sort of breastwork of timbers and bushes, which will be ready in a day or two. The sound part of the command is prepared to start with several Comanchee leaders who have agreed to pilot the way.

All hands, except those who were too sick, left for the Pawnee village. Before the hour of start I was too sick to mount. I have got well enough again to write, and I will render some account of the excursion, which is from the report of my friend Joe Chadwick, who went with them.

They travelled over beautiful country for four days, most of it prairie, and along the base of a range of mountains of reddish granite, in many places piled up to an immense height without tree or shrubbery on them. The Pawnee village, on the bank of the Red River,

292

The Pawnee village on the banks of the Red River, its wigwams looking like beehives.

about ninety miles from the Comanchee town, was surrounded by these mountains. The dragoon regiment drew up within half a mile or so of the village and camped in a square, where they remained three days. The village contained some five or six hundred wigwams, all made of long prairie grass thatched over poles that are fastened in the ground and bent in at the top; giving to them, at a distance, the appearance of straw bee-hives.

To their great surprise, they found these people cultivating extensive fields of corn (maize), pumpkins, melons, beans, and squashes. With these and an abundant supply of buffalo meat, they may be said to live very well.

The day after their arrival, Colonel Dodge opened a council with the chiefs, in the chief's lodge, where he had most of his officers around him. He first explained to them the friendly views with which he came to see them; and the wish of our Government to establish a lasting peace with them, which they seemed at once to appreciate and highly estimate.

The head chief of the tribe was a very old man, and he replied to Colonel Dodge in an eloquent manner, assuring him of the friendly feelings of his chiefs and warriors towards the pale-faces.

After Colonel Dodge had explained in general terms the object of his visit, he told them that he would expect from them some account of the foul murder of Judge Martin and his family on the False Washita, which the Comanchees had said was done by the Pawnee Picts. The Colonel also told them he had learned from the Comanchees that they had the little boy, the son of the murdered gentleman, in their possession. He expected them to deliver him up, as an indispensable condition of the friendly arrangement they were now making. They

293

Wee-ta-ra-sha-ro, head chief of the Pawnee Picts.

Sky-se-ro-ka, second chief of the Pawnee Picts.

positively denied all knowledge of it, insisting they knew nothing of the murder or of the boy. The demand was repeatedly made and as often denied.

Finally a Negro man was discovered living with the Pawnees who spoke good English. He came into the council-house and said that such a boy had recently been brought into their village, and was now a prisoner among them. This excited great surprise and indignation in the council. Colonel Dodge then informed the chiefs that the council would rest. Certainly nothing further of a peaceable nature would transpire until the boy was brought in.

All remained in gloomy silence for a while. Then Colonel Dodge further informed the chiefs that as an evidence of his friendly intentions towards them, he had, on starting from Fort Gibson, purchased at a very great price, from their enemies the Osages, two Pawnee and one Kiowa girls. They had been held by the Osages for some years as prisoners. Colonel Dodge said he had brought them the whole way home, and was ready to deliver them to their friends and relations. But he certainly would never give them up until the little boy was produced.

He also made another demand for the restoration of a United States ranger by the name of Abbé, who had been captured by them the summer before. They acknowledged the seizure of Abbé, and all solemnly declared that he had been taken by a party of the

294

Thighs, Pawnee girl who was prisoner of the Osages.

Wild Sage, second Pawnee prisoner of the Osages.

Comanchees, over whom they had no control, and carried beyond the Red River into the Mexican provinces, where he was put to death.

They held a long consultation about the boy. Seeing their plans defeated by the evidence of the Negro, and being convinced of the friendly disposition of the Colonel, they sent out and had the boy brought in from the middle of a corn-field, where he had been secreted.

He was an intelligent boy of nine years of age, and when he came in he was entirely naked, as they keep their own boys at that age. There was a great excitement in the council when the little fellow was brought in. As he passed among them, he looked around and exclaimed with some surprise, "What! Are there white men here?" To which Colonel Dodge replied by asking his name. He promptly answered, "My name is Matthew Wright Martin."

He was then received into Colonel Dodge's arms. An order was immediately given for the Pawnee and Kiowa girls to be brought forward. In a few minutes they were brought into the council-house. They were at once recognized by their friends and relatives, who embraced them with the most extravagant expressions of joy and satisfaction.

The heart of the old chief was melted at this evidence of white man's friendship. He rose to his feet and took Colonel Dodge in his arms. Placing his left cheek against the left cheek of the Colonel, he held him for some minutes without saying a word. Tears were flowing from his eyes. He then embraced each officer in turn in the same silent and affectionate manner, which took more than half an hour before it was completed.

From this moment the council, which before had been a very grave and uncertain one, took a pleasing and friendly turn. The old man ordered the women to supply the dragoons with something to eat, as they were hungry.

295

The White Weasel and The Thunderer, her brother; Kiowas purchased by the Dragoons.

The dragoons had eaten up their last rations twelve hours before. They were gladdened by the approach of the women, who brought "back-loads" of dried buffalo meat and green corn, and threw it down among them. The meat seemed a providential deliverance, for the country between this Pawnee village and the Comanchee village was destitute of game.

The council proceeded pleasantly for several days. Warriors of the Kioways and Wicos, two adjoining and friendly tribes living farther to the west, arrived, as did other bands of Comanchees. Two thousand wild fellows were assembled, and all looking into a pitiful little encampment of two hundred men, in a state of starvation with nearly half the number too sick to make any resistance if attacked.

The command returned to the Comanchee village after fifteen days, in a destitute condition, with scarcely anything to eat, or chance of getting anything. Colonel Dodge almost instantly ordered preparations to be made for a move to the head of the Canadian River, a distance of an hundred or more miles, where we could get enough to eat, and, lying by awhile, could restore the sick, who were occupying a great number of litters.

Some days have elapsed, however, and we have not been able to start. Meanwhile, continual parties of Pawnee Picts, Kioways, and Comanchees from other villages have come to get a look at us.

Six days of severe travelling have brought us from the Comanchee village to the

296

north bank of the Canadian. We are encamped on a beautiful plain, in the midst of countless buffaloes, and have halted a few days to restore our horses and men to dry meat for the remainder of our journey.

Many are now too sick to ride, and are carried on litters between two horses. Nearly every tent belonging to the officers has been converted into hospitals for the sick. Sighs and groaning are heard in all directions. From the Comanchee village to this camp, the country was entirely prairie; most of the way dry ground, without water, for which we have sometimes suffered very much. From day to day we have dragged along exposed to the sun, without a cloud to relieve its intensity, a bush to shade us, or anything to cast a shadow, except the bodies of our horses. The grass, for a great part of the way, was dried up, scarcely affording a bite for our horses. Sometimes the only water we could find was in stagnant pools, in which the buffaloes had been lying and wallowing like hogs in a mud-puddle. Sometimes we drove the wallowing buffaloes from these dirty lavers, and then our dying horses ran and plunged their noses in them, sucking up the poisonous draught until they fell dead in their tracks. The men also would spring from their horses and drink to almost fatal excess, fill their canteens, and suck the bilious contents during the day.

We found many deep ravines, in the bottom of which were the marks of powerful streams. But in this season they were all dried up. Occasionally we found them dashing along in the coolest and clearest manner. But then, to our great agony, so salty that even our horses could not drink from them. We had the tantalizing pleasure of hearing the roar of the clearest and most sparkling streams, but the dire necessity of drinking from stagnant pools, their waters poisonous.

This indigestible water seems the cause of the sickness of the horses and men. Both appear to be suffering from the same disease, a slow and distressing bilious fever which seems to terminate in a fatal infection of the liver.

I have suffered severely. My friend Joe Chadwick has been constantly by my side, dismounting and filling my canteen for me, or doing other kind offices for me. I am too weak to mount my horse without aid.

During this march we have picked up a number of horned frogs. In our portmanteau we had a number of tin boxes in which we carried Seidlitz powders. We caged a number of them safely, hoping to carry them home alive. Several remarkable specimens have horns of a half to three-fourths of an inch in length, and very sharp at the points. Joe's fancy for horned frogs has grown into a sort of *frogmania,* and his eyes are strained all day, gazing in the grass and pebbles as he rides along.

An express arrived from the encampment we left at the mouth of False Washita, with the melancholy tidings of the death of General Leavenworth, Lieutenant McClure, and ten or fifteen of the men. This has cast a gloom over our little encampment here, and seems to be received as a fatal foreboding by those who are sick with the same disease.

The General had followed on our trail a few days after us to the "Cross Timbers," a distance of fifty or sixty miles. There his disease at last overcame him.

He had said to me: "It was a very lucky thing, Catlin, that you painted the portrait of me before we started, for it is all that my dear wife will ever see of me."

Charley was saddled. With his sketch book slung on his back, and a compass, Catlin set off.

XVIII

Fort Gibson,
Arkansas Territory

I AM in comfortable quarters with friends about me. I am sick and feeble, and have been for several weeks—since I was brought in from the prairies. I am slowly recovering, and able to use my pen or my brush.

We left the camp on the Canadian with a great number sick and carried upon litters—with horses giving out and dying by the way. Our progress over the long route to Fort Gibson was slow. Fifteen days of constant toil and fatigue brought us here, but in a most crippled condition. Many of the sick were left by the way with attendants to take care of them. Others were buried from the litters on which they breathed their last. Others were brought in to this place merely to die and have the privilege of a decent burial.

There were not enough well ones to take care of the sick. Many were left out upon the prairies. Of those that have been brought in and quartered in the hospital, a number are buried daily. I have the mournful sound of "Roslin Castle," with muffled drums, passing six or eight times a day under my window to the burying ground. I can lay in my bed and see every poor fellow lowered down into his silent grave. The day before yesterday, no less than eight solemn processions visited that insatiable ground. Among them was the corpse of my much-loved friend Lieutenant West, who was aide-de-camp to General Leavenworth on this disastrous campaign. He leaves a distracted widow with her little ones to mourn him.

After leaving the head waters of the Canadian, my illness continually increased. I lost strength every day. I soon had to be lifted on and off my horse. Finally I could not ride at all. I was then put into a baggage wagon which was going back empty, except for several sick soldiers. Eight days, most of the time in a delirious state, I rode lying on the hard planks of the wagon, jarred and jolted until the skin from my elbows and knees was literally worn through. At length we reached this post, and I was taken to a bed in comfortable quarters.

Since we came in from the prairies, and the sickness has a little abated, we have had a bustling time with the Indians. Colonel Dodge sent runners to the chiefs of all the contiguous tribes, with an invitation to meet the Pawnees in council. Seven or eight tribes flocked to us, on the first day of the month, and the council commenced. It continued for several days, and gave the semi-civilized sons of the forest a fair opportunity of shaking hands with their wild and untamed red brethren of the West.

Colonel Dodge, Major Armstrong (the Indian agent), and General Stokes (the Indian commissioner) presided at the council. For several days free vent was given to fearlessly asserting their rights, their happiness, and friendship for each other. The vain orations of the half-polished Cherokees and Choctaws, with all their finery and art, found their match in the brief and jarring gutturals of the wild and naked Indians of the West.

After the council had adjourned, and the fumes of the peace-making calumet had vanished, Colonel Dodge made additional presents to the Pawnees for their departure.

We had brought with us to Fort Gibson, from the Canadian, three of the principal chiefs of the Pawnees, fifteen Kioways, one Comanchee, and one Wico chief. The group was one of the most interesting ever to visit our frontier. I have portraits of all of them, as well as seven of the Comanchee chiefs who came part of the way with us and turned back.

Although the council was a handsome one, and at first sight a great benefit, yet I have my doubts whether it will better their condition, unless they can be protected in the rights to which they are entitled.

At Fort Gibson there is already a company of eighty men fitted out to start tomorrow. They will overtake these Indians a few miles from here and accompany them home. They have a large stock of goods, with traps for catching beavers, and they plan to build a trading-house in Indian territory. They calculate they will amass an immense fortune quickly, because they are the first traders and trappers in that part of the country.

I have travelled too much among Indian tribes, and seen too much, not to know the evil consequences of such a system. Goods are sold at such exorbitant prices that the Indian gets a mere shadow for his peltries. The Indians see no white people but traders and sellers of whisky, and of course judge us all by them. They consequently hold us, and always will, in contempt. In the circumstance they have reason to: They neither fear nor respect us. If the Government would promptly prohibit such establishments, and invite the Indians to our frontier posts, they would bring in their furs, their robes, horses, and mules where there is a good market for them all. They would get the full value of their property where there is some competition, and they would get four or five times as much for their articles of trade as they would get from a trader in their village, out of the reach of competition.

The Indians have cost the United States a vast sum of money as well as the lives of

300

valuable officers and men. For the honor of the American name, I think we ought, in forming an acquaintance with these numerous tribes, to adopt and *enforce* some different system from that which has been generally practiced beyond our frontiers.

During my illness my friend Joe Chadwick has been constantly by my bedside. He had administered every aid and every comfort that lay in his power to bring. Such tried friendship as this I shall ever recollect. It will often lead my mind back to retrace the first part of our campaign, which was pleasant. Many of its incidents I will preserve to the end of my life.

But I had hope that the end of my life was not yet near. I had grown into such a dread of Fort Gibson that I resolved to be off as soon as I had strength to get on my horse and balance myself upon his back. One fine morning, Charley was brought up and saddled, a bear-skin and a buffalo robe spread upon his saddle, and a coffee-pot and tin cup tied to it also. With a few pounds of hard biscuit in my portmanteau, with my fowling-piece in my hand, my pistols in my belt, my sketch-book slung on my back, and a small pocket compass in my pocket, I took leave of Fort Gibson. No argument could contend with the fixed resolve of my mind that if I could get out upon the prairies and move continually northward, I should daily gain strength, and save myself, possibly, from the jaws of that voracious burial-ground which lay in view of my room. For months I had imagined myself going with the other poor fellows, whose mournful dirges were played under my window every day. No one can imagine the dread I felt for that place; nor the pleasure when Charley was trembling under me, and I had turned him around on the top of a prairie bluff a mile from the Fort to take a last look upon it, and to thank God that I was not to be buried there. I said to myself that to die on the prairie, and be devoured by wolves, or be scalped by an Indian, would be far more acceptable than the lingering death.

So, alone with my affectionate horse Charley, I turned north and commenced on my long journey, with confidence that I would gain strength daily. No one can ever know the pleasure of the boundless sea of waving grass as I commenced my course to the Missouri.

Day by day I galloped along through waving grass and green fields, occasionally dismounting and lying an hour or so until the grim shaking and chattering of an ague chill had passed off. At night I slept on my bear-skin, with my saddle for my pillow, and my buffalo robe drawn over me for my covering. Charley was picketed near me at the end of his laso, which gave him room for his grazing. Every night gangs of sneaking wolves sniffed at our little encampment, but were a safe distance from us at sun-rise in the morning—gazing at us and impatient to pick up the crumbs and bones left when we moved away from our feeble fire that had faintly flickered through the night. In the absence of timber, I used dried buffalo dung.

I generally halted on the bank of some little stream while there was still half an hour of sunlight, where feed was good for Charley, and where I could get wood to kindle my fire and water for my coffee. The first thing was to undress Charley and drive down the picket to which he was fastened, so he could graze over the circle inscribed by the end of his laso. One evening he slipped the laso over his head, and took his supper wherever he chose to stroll. When night approached, I took the laso in my hand and endeavored to catch him. I soon saw he was determined to enjoy a little freedom. He evaded me until dark, when I abandoned my pursuit, making up my mind that I should inevitably lose him and be obliged to perform the rest of my journey on foot. He led me a chase of half a mile or more. I left him busily grazing, returned to my solitary bivouac, and laid myself on my bear-skin and went to sleep.

In the middle of the night I awakened. I was lying on my back, and through half-open eyes, I thought I saw the huge figure of an Indian standing over me, ready to take my scalp! Horror paralyzed me for a moment, until I saw there was no need to scramble. Charley had moved up, from feelings of pure affection, or from instinctive fear, or possibly from a due share of both, and taken his position with his forefeet on the edge of my bed and his head hanging directly over me. He was standing fast asleep.

In the morning I had another half-hour of fruitless endeavors to catch Charley. He seemed mindful of his success on the evening before, and continually tantalized me by turning around and around and keeping out of reach. So I packed up my things and slung the saddle on my back, trailing my gun in my hand, and started on my route. After I had walked a quarter of a mile, I looked back. I saw him standing with his head and tail very high, looking alternately at me and at the spot where we had been encamped, and where a little fire still burned.

He stood and surveyed the prairies for a while. I continued on. Finally he walked to the camp, and seeing everything gone, began to neigh very violently. He started off at full speed, overtook me, and passing within a few paces of me, wheeled about at a few yards away, trembling like an aspen leaf.

I called him, walked up to him with the bridle in my hand, and put it over his head, which he held down for me. I put the saddle on his back, and he actually stooped to receive it. I was soon arranged and on his back. We started off upon our course as if he was pleased, like his rider, with the maneuver that had brought us together again. I took good care after that night to keep him under my strict authority, resolving to avoid further experiments till we got to the land of cultivated fields and steady habits.

That night Charley and I stopped in one of the most lovely little valleys: an enchanting lawn of five or six acres, on the banks of a cool and rippling stream, and alive with fish. Every now and then a fine brood of young ducks would settle in.

With a broiled duck and a delicious cup of coffee, I made my supper. After this I strolled about this paradise, which I found was chosen not only by myself, but by the wild deer. They were rising from their lairs and bounding out and over the swells of the prairies.

The Indians had also loved this spot once, and left it: Here and there were their deserted graves, which told of former haunts and sports; and perhaps of wars and deaths that once echoed through this now silent vale.

I laid down upon my back and looked awhile into the blue heavens over me. Pure milk-white clouds were passing. The sun was just setting and the moon rising, renewing the impressions of my own insignificance. I trembled at the dangerous expanse of my thoughts, and turned them to more comprehensible things. One of the first was a newspaper, which I had brought from the Fort: *The National Intelligencer* of Washington.

I remember the sensation I produced among the Minatarees on the Upper Missouri a few years ago, when I took from among my painting apparatus an old number of the *New York Commercial Advertiser*. The Minatarees thought I was mad when they saw me sit

302

for hours with my eyes fixed upon its pages. They had various conjectures about it. The most popular was that I was looking at it to cure my sore eyes, and they called it the *"medicine cloth for sore eyes!"*

Eventually I read passages from it, which were interpreted to them, and the purpose of a newspaper fully explained. After this, it was looked upon as much greater mystery than before. Several liberal offers were made for it, which I was obliged to refuse, having already received a beautifully garnished robe for it from the hands of a young brave who told me that if he could employ a good interpreter to explain everything in it, he could travel about among the Minatarees, Mandans, and Sioux and exhibit it after I was gone. He would get rich with presents, and add greatly to the list of his medicines. The newspaper would make him a great medicine-man. I left the poor fellow his painted robe, and the newspaper. Just before I left the Upper Missouri, I saw him unfolding it to show to some of his friends. He took from around it eight or ten folds of birch bark and deer skins, all of which were carefully enclosed in a sack made of the skin of a pole cat, and undoubtedly destined to become, and to be called, his mystery or medicine bag.

With such pleasant memories I slept upon the ground each night. My health improved daily. I was now moving along cheerfully and hoping to reach the end of my journey soon. I still had vast prairies to pass over and occasional difficulties: Deep sunken streams, like ditches, occasionally presented themselves when I was within a few steps of plunging into them. Their perpendicular sides were overhung with long wild grass and almost obscured from sight. The bearings of my compass told me that I must cross them, and the only alternative was to plunge into them and get out as well as I could. They were often muddy, and I could not tell whether they were three or ten feet deep until my horse was in them. Sometimes he went down head foremost, and I with him, to scramble out on the opposite shore in the best condition we could. In one of these canals, which I had followed for several miles in the vain hope of finding a ford, I plunged, with Charley, where it was about six or eight yards wide. God knows how deep it was, for we did not go to the bottom. I swam him to the opposite bank, on to which I clung. It was perpendicular and of clay, and three or four feet higher than the water, an insurmountable difficulty to Charley. I led him at least a mile, as I walked on the top of the bank with the bridle in my hand, holding his head above the water as he swam. At times I was almost inextricably entangled in the long grass that was often higher than my head. Hanging over the brink, and woven together, were ivy and wild pea vines. Just before I was ready to drop the rein of faithful Charley in hopeless despair, we came to an old buffalo ford, where the banks were graded down. The exhausted animal at last got out, and was ready and willing to take me and my luggage on our journey again.

Our journey was about five hundred miles, and at last brought us out at Boonville on the western bank of the Missouri. From Boonville I crossed the river to New Franklin, where I laid by several days, on account of stormy weather. From there I proceeded to Alton, Illinois, where I now am, under the roof of friends, with my dear wife, who has patiently waited one year to receive me back, a wreck, as I now am. In a few days we will start for the coast of Florida, fourteen hundred miles south of this, to spend the winter in patching up my health and fitting me for future campaigns. We take a steamer for New Orleans tomorrow.

Kickapoo: The Cock Turkey, a disciple of The Prophet, counting his prayers on his stick.

XIX

Saint Louis

A LONG winter has passed, which I whiled away on the Gulf of Mexico and about the shores of Florida and Texas. My health was restored by the congenial climate, and my dear wife was my companion the whole way. We visited the different posts, and all that we could find to interest us in those delightful realms. We took a steamer from New Orleans to St. Louis, and arrived just a few days ago.

I have resolved to sit down awhile before I go further, and open my sketch-book, in which I have a great many entries that I have not as yet showed for want of proper opportunity.

In opening my sketch-book, I can turn over leaf after leaf and describe tribe after tribe and chief after chief without the tediousness of travelling too minutely over the intervening distances.

About a year ago I made a visit to the

KICKAPOOS

At present a small tribe, numbering six or eight hundred, the Kickapoos are the remnant of a once numerous and warlike tribe. They reside within the State of Illinois, near the south end

The Foremost Man, usually called The Shawnee Prophet.

Potawatomi: The Sauk, praying.

of Lake Michigan, and live in a miserable condition, although they have one of the finest countries in the world. They have been reduced in numbers by whisky and small-pox, and because the game has been destroyed in their country. They have little inclination to work, so they are exceedingly poor and dependent. In fact, there is very little inducement for them to build houses or cultivate their farms. They own so large and so fine a tract of land—now completely surrounded by civilized settlements—that they know from experience they will soon be obliged to sell their land for a trifle and move west. This system of moving has already commenced with them, and a considerable party have located on a tract of lands offered to them on the west bank of the Missouri River, a little north of Fort Leavenworth.

The Kickapoos have lived in alliance with the Sacs and Foxes, and speak a language so similar they seem almost to be one family. The present chief is Kee-an-ne-kuk (The Foremost Man), usually called The Shawnee Prophet, a very shrewd and talented man. When he sat for his portrait, he took an attitude of prayer. I soon learned he was a devoted Christian, regularly holding meetings in his tribe on the Sabbath, preaching to them, and exhorting them to a belief in the Christian religion, and to abandon the fatal habit of whisky-drinking. He represented whisky as the bane that was to destroy them all. How far his efforts have succeeded in Christianizing, I cannot tell, but it is quite certain that his exemplary and constant endeavors have completely abolished the practice of drinking whisky in his tribe.

306

Ah-ton-we-tuck (The Cock Turkey) is another Kickapoo of distinction, and a disciple of The Prophet. I also painted him in an attitude of prayer. He is reading from characters cut upon a stick he holds in his hands. The story is told by the traders (though I am afraid to vouch for the whole truth of it) that a Methodist preacher solicited permission to preach in his village. The Prophet refused the privilege, but secretly took the Methodist aside and supported him until he learned from the preacher his creed, and his system of teaching it to others. Then he discharged the preacher and commenced preaching to his people himself.

He pretended to have had an interview with some superhuman mission. Apparently he had decided that if there was any honor or influence to be gained by preaching, he might as well have it as another person.

He commenced preaching and invented a prayer, which he ingeniously carved on a maple-stick an inch and a half in breadth, in characters somewhat resembling Chinese letters. He has introduced these prayer-sticks into every family of the tribe, and into the hands of every individual. He is the sole manufacturer, and he sells them at his own price, thus adding lucre to fame and augmenting his influence in his tribe with both money and faith.

Every man, woman, and child in the tribe says their prayers from this stick when going to bed at night and when rising in the morning. They place the fore-finger of the right hand under the upper character, repeat a sentence or two, and then slip the finger down to the next, and the next, and so on, to the bottom of the stick. Altogether their prayers require about ten minutes, sung in a sort of chant.

Many people have called all this an ingenious piece of hypocrisy on the part of The Prophet. Whether that be so or not, I cannot decide. Yet one thing I can vouch to be true: that whether his motives and his life are as pure as he pretends, or not, his example has done much towards correcting the habits of his people, and has effectually turned their attention from the destructive habits of dissipation and vice, to temperance and industry in the pursuits of agriculture and the arts. His influence has arrested the miseries of dissipation in the descending prospects of a nation who have long had the white-skin teachers of vice and dissipation among them.

WEAHS

These are also the remnant of a once powerful tribe reduced by the same causes to about two hundred. They once lived in the State of Indiana, but have been moved with the Piankeshaws to a position forty or fifty miles south of Fort Leavenworth.

POTAWATOMIES

Once numerous and warlike, these Indians are now reduced by whisky and small-pox to not more than twenty-seven hundred. They may be said to be semi-civilized. They have lived a long time in contiguity with white people, with whom their blood is considerably mixed, and

Kaskaskias: The Little Chief.

Peorias: The Man Who Tracks.

whose manners they have copied. They were once part of the Chippewas or Ottawas living near them, in the north. They live within the State of Michigan, and own a rich and valuable tract of land. Like the Kickapoos, they are selling out to the Government and are about to move to the west bank of the Missouri. A part of the tribe has already gone and settled in the vicinity of Fort Leavenworth. Of this tribe I have painted the portraits of On-saw-kie in the attitude of prayer, and Na-pow-sa (The Bear Travelling in the Night). These people have for some time lived somewhat under the influence of the Kickapoos. Many of the tribe have become zealous disciples of the Kickapoo prophet, using his prayers most devoutly.

KASKASKIAS

They once owned a vast tract of country lying east of the Mississippi, between its banks and the Ohio, and now forming a considerable portion of the State of Illinois. The banes of whisky and small-pox, and the unexampled cruelty of neighboring hostile tribes who struck at them in their adversity, helped to erase them from existence.

Perhaps no other tribe on the Continent so suddenly disappeared. The remnant merged into the tribe of Peorias of Illinois. I doubt whether one dozen of them now exist. When the few remnants die in a few years, a beautiful language, distinct from all others about it, will disappear.

Piankeshaws: The Left Hand.

Delawares: The Answer.

PEORIAS

Another tribe, inhabiting a part of Illinois, and also a remnant, but civilized. They number about two hundred and, like other remnants on the frontier, are under contract to move west of the Missouri. Of this tribe I painted the portrait of Pah-me-cow-e-tah (The Man Who Tracks), and Kee-mo-ra-ni-a (No English).

PIANKESHAWS

Another remnant tribe, in Illinois and Indiana, who have also recently sold out their country to the Government, and are under contract to move west of the Missouri, in the vicinity of Fort Leavenworth. Ni-a-co-mo (To Fix with the Foot), a brave of distinction, and Men-son-se-ah (The Left Hand), a fierce-looking warrior with a stone-hatchet in his hand, are fair specimens of this enfeebled tribe, which do not number more than one hundred and seventy persons.

DELAWARES

The name of these Indians once carried terror wherever it was heard. They originally occupied a great part of the eastern border of Pennsylvania, and parts of New Jersey and

309

Delaware. No other tribe on the Continent has been moved and jostled about so much by civilized invasions. None have retreated so far, or fought their way so desperately. They have honorably and bravely contended for every foot of ground they have passed over. From the banks of the Delaware to the lovely Susquehanna, my native valley, over the Alleghany Mountains to the Ohio River, to the Illinois and the Mississippi, and at last west of the Missouri, they have been moved by treaty after treaty with the Government.

The mere handful of them that are left have been assigned a tract of land, as has been done a dozen times before, in *fee simple, for ever*. In every move they have made, they have been thrust against their wills from the graves of their fathers and their children. They have been planted as they are now, on the borders of new enemies. Every time their first occupation has necessarily been to take up their weapons in self-defense, and fight for the ground they have been assigned.

Continued exertions have been made for their conversion to Christianity. Ever since the zealous Moravian missionaries first began, these pious efforts have been in vain because of bad faith with which they were so often treated by white people.

This scattered tribe that once contained some ten or fifteen thousand now numbers only eight hundred. For the past fifty or sixty years, most of them have resided in Ohio and Indiana. But their reservations have been gradually surrounded by white people, and their lands have become too valuable for Indians—and the certain consequence has been that they have sold out and been moved to lands west of the Mississippi.

The wild frontier on which they are now placed affords them a fine opportunity to indulge in both war and hunting. They will wander in little and desperate parties over the vast buffalo plains, exposed to their enemies, until finally the new country which has been given to them in "fee simple, for ever" is destitute of game. Then they, like most of the removed remnants of tribes, will be destroyed. Yet the faith of the Government will seem preserved, having offered *this* as their *last move*, and these lands as *theirs in fee simple*, for ever.

MO-HEE-CON-NEUHS, or MOHEGANS
(THE GOOD CANOEMEN)

There are four hundred of this once powerful and still famous tribe residing near Green Bay, on a rich tract of land given to them by the Government, in the territory of Wisconsin, near Winnebago Lake. They are living comfortably, having brought with them from Massachusetts a knowledge of agriculture.

They are the remains of the once powerful and celebrated tribe of Pequots of Massachusetts. In their wars with the whites, a considerable portion of the tribe moved off under the command of a rival chief and established a separate tribe or band, and took the name

Mohegans: Both Sides of the River, a psalmbook in one hand, a cane in the other.

Oneida: Bread.

of Mo-hee-con-neuhs, which they have preserved until the present day. The rest of the tribe has long since been extinct.

The chief of this tribe, Ee-tow-o-kaum (Both Sides of the River), I painted with a psalmbook in one hand and a cane in the other. He is a shrewd and intelligent man, and a professed Christian. Waun-naw-con (The Dish), John W. Quinney in civilized dress, is a civilized Indian, well educated, speaking good English, and a Baptist missionary preacher.

ONEIDAS

This tribe is now a remnant destroyed by wars with the whites, and by whisky and small-pox. They number about five or six hundred, and live in the most miserable poverty on their reserve in New York, near Utica and the banks of the Mohawk River. They were one of the confederacy called the Six Nations. Their present chief is *Bread*, a talented man, well educated, and handsome.

TUSKARORAS

The Tuskaroras are another of the Six Nations, once numerous but now reduced to five hundred. They live on their reserve, a fine tract of land near Buffalo, New York, surrounded by civilized settlements. Many of them are good farmers, and raise fine crops.

The chief is a dignified man by the name of Cu-sick. His son, of the same name, is a talented man—educated for the pulpit in our public institutions, and now a Baptist preacher.

SENECAS

The Senecas are one thousand two hundred in number, now living on their reserve near Buffalo, within a few miles of Niagara Falls. They once lived near the Seneca and Cayuga lakes, but like all the other tribes who have stood in the way of the "march of civilization," have repeatedly bargained away their country, and been removed.

They once contained some eight or ten thousand. Because of their position in the center of New York, they held an important place in its history. The Senecas were one of the most effective tribes, creating the compact called the "Six Nations," a confederacy formed to gain strength and to resist the incursions of white people in their country. The confederacy consisted of the Senecas, Oneidas, Onondagas, Cayugas, Mohawks, and Tuskaroras. Until the arrival of white people, with their destructive engines of war, and with whisky and small-pox, they held sway in their country, carrying victory, and consequently terror and dismay wherever they warred. Their war-parties were fearlessly sent into Connecticut and Massachusetts, to Virginia, and even to the Carolinas, and victory everywhere crowned their efforts. Their combined strength, however, in all its might was not enough to withstand the flood that advanced upon them.

The Senecas had an aged and distinguished chief by the name of Red Jacket. I painted his portrait from life and indulged him in the wish he expressed, "that he might be seen standing on the Table Rock, at the Falls of Niagara, about which place he thought his spirit would linger after he was dead."

Red Jacket was the head chief of the scattered remnants of the Six Nations. Part reside on reservations in the vicinity of the Senecas, in all amounting perhaps to about four thousand, and owning some two hundred thousand acres of fine lands.

The Mohawks and Cayugas emigrated to Canada some fifty years ago, leaving the Senecas, Tuskaroras, Oneidas, and Onondagas in the State of New York, on fine tracts of lands but completely surrounded by white population. The whites, by industry and enterprise, are making the Indian lands too valuable to be long in Indian possession. They will no doubt be induced to sell out to the Government.

Red Jacket was one of the greatest orators of his day, more distinguished for his eloquence and his influence in council than as a warrior. The greater part of his life was spent with his tribe during its downfall. Instead of the horrors of Indian wars, they had a more

Seneca: Red Jacket.

destructive enemy to encounter: the insidious encroachments of pale-faces. He exerted his eloquence and all his talents to resist. He remonstrated with both the Governor of New York and the President of the United States against the encroachments of white people. He represented the whites as using every endeavor to wrest from the Indian his lands—destroying their game, introducing vices of a horrible character. Most vehemently of all, he continually remonstrated against the preaching of missionaries in his tribe, alleging that the "black coats" (as he called the clergymen) did more mischief than good in his tribe by creating doubts and dissensions among his people. They were destructive of peace and dangerous to the success and even the *existence* of his tribe.

Like many other great men who endeavor to soothe broken and painful feelings by

313

Iroquois: The Thinker.

the kindness of the bottle, Red Jacket long since took up whisky-drinking. Much of his time, he lay drunk in his cabin, or under the corner of a fence, or wherever else the *kindness* of whisky required him to drop his helpless body. He was as great a drunkard as some of our most distinguished law-givers and law-makers.

There are no better people to be found than the Seneca Indians—none that are by Nature more talented and ingenious, nor any that would be better neighbors if the arts and abuses of white men and whisky could be kept away from them. They have laid down their hunting habits and become efficient farmers, raising fine crops of corn, a great abundance of hogs, cattle, and horses, and other necessaries and luxuries of life.

IROQUOIS

The Iroquois are one of the most powerful tribes that ever existed, and now one of the most completely annihilated. They occupied a vast tract of country on the River St. Lawrence, between its banks and Lake Champlain. At one time, they actually over-ran the whole country, from Lake Champlain to the shores of Lakes Erie, Huron, and Michigan. But continual wars with the French, the English, and other Indians, and dissipation and disease, have almost entirely annihilated them. The few remnants have long since merged into other tribes.

The whole of the Six Nations has been said by some writers to be Iroquois. How correct this may be, I am not quite able to say. One thing is certain: the Iroquois tribe did not all belong to the Confederacy. Their original country was on the shores of the St. Lawrence, and although one branch of their nation—the Mohawks—formed a part, and the most effective portion of the compact, yet the other members of it spoke different languages. A great part of the Iroquois moved their settlements farther north and east, instead of joining in the continual wars carried on by the Six Nations. It is of this part of the tribe that I am speaking when I mention them as nearly extinct.

Of this tribe I have painted only one, Not-o-way (The Thinker). I had much conversation with him, and became very attached to him. He seemed to be quite ignorant of the early history of his tribe, as well as of the position and condition of its few scattered remnants. He told me, however, that he had always believed that the Iroquois had conquered nearly all the world. But the Great Spirit was offended at the great slaughters committed by his favorite people and resolved to punish them. He sent a dreadful disease among them that carried most of them off; all the rest that could be found were killed by their enemies. Though he was an Iroquois, which he was proud to acknowledge because I was to "make him live after he was dead," he wished it to be generally thought that he was a Chippewa, so that he might live as long as the Great Spirit would allow.

The history of this once powerful tribe is closely connected with that of the United States and the Revolutionary War. The tribe once inhabited parts of Pennsylvania, New Jersey, and for the last sixty years, a part of Ohio and Indiana, to which they had removed. Now they occupy a tract of country several hundred miles west of the Mississippi, which was conveyed to them by the Government in exchange for their lands in Ohio.

This tribe and the Delawares were neighbors on the Atlantic coast and alternately allies and enemies. They retreated together and fought their enemies united; they fought each other until the few who outlived their nation's calamities settled as neighbors together in the West. Now the sweeping hand of death will soon relieve them from further necessity of warring or moving.

In their long and disastrous pilgrimage, both of these tribes laid claim to, and alternately occupied, the beautiful and renowned valley of Wy-ô-ming, Pennsylvania. After strewing the Susquehanna's banks with their bones, they both fled to the banks of the Ohio. Necessity soon came again, and again, and again, until the great "Guardian of all red children" placed them where they now are.

About one thousand two hundred remain. Some are agriculturists, and are industrious, temperate, and religious. But the great proportion of them are miserably poor and dependent, having little ambition to labor or to hunt, and a passion for whisky-drinking that sinks them.

The great Tecumseh was chief of this tribe, and perhaps the most extraordinary Indian of his age.

The present chief of the tribe, Lay-law-she-kaw (He Who Goes Up the River), is a very aged but extraordinary man, with a fine head. His ears are slit and stretch down to his shoulders, a custom highly valued in this tribe. It is done by severing the rim of the ear with a knife and stretching it down by wearing heavy weights, to elongate it as much as possible, making a large orifice through which, on parades, they often pass a punch of arrows or quills to wear as ornaments. In this instance (which was not an unusual one), the rims of the ears were so extended down that they touched the shoulders, making a ring through which a whole hand could easily be passed.

The daughter of this old chief, Ka-te-qua (The Female Eagle), was an agreeable-looking girl, fifteen years of age and much thought of by the tribe. Pah-te-coo-saw (The Straight Man) was a warrior who sat for his picture with his face painted in a very curious manner with black and red paint.

Ten-squa-ta-way (The Open Door), called The Shawnee Prophet, is perhaps one of the most remarkable men on the frontier. He is a brother of the famous Tecumseh, and equal in his medicines or mysteries to what his brother was in arms. He is blind in his left eye. With his medicines he made his way through most of the North Western tribes, enlisting warriors wherever he went to assist Tecumseh in effecting his great scheme of forming a confederacy of all the Indians on the frontier. They would drive back the whites and defend the Indians' rights. He told them there was no other way to protect themselves. His plan was certainly a correct one. The Prophet exercised astonishing influence in raising men for Tecumseh, to fight battles and carry out his plans.

The Prophet started upon an embassy to the various tribes on the Upper Missouri, nearly all of which he visited with astonishing success. He exhibited his mystery fire, and used a sacred string of beans. Every young man who was willing to go to war was to touch the beans, thereby taking the solemn oath to start when called upon and not to turn back.

This ingenious man entered the villages of even his inveterate enemies, and of others who had never heard of the name of his tribe. He made his medicines a safe passport for him to all villages. He enlisted from the different tribes some eight or ten thousand warriors who solemnly swore to return with him on his way back, and to assist in the wars that Tecumseh was to wage against the whites on the frontier. I found on my visits to the Sioux, the Puncahs, the Riccarees, and the Mandans that he had been there.

Everywhere he assured them of the potency of his mysteries. He carried with him a life-sized image of a dead person, ingeniously made of some light material, and kept concealed under bandages of thin white muslin. He got his recruits to swear by it, and by touching the sacred string of white beans which he had hung around its neck.

With extraordinary cunning he carried terror into the country everywhere he went. Ten thousand men would have been on their way with him, if a couple of political enemies from his own tribe had not followed his track, pronouncing him an impostor to whom anybody would be a fool to listen.

To save his life, he had to dispose of his medicines as quickly as possible, and sneak home to his own tribe. The opposition of his enemies had killed his prospects, and with the death of Tecumseh he was doomed to live the rest of his days in silence, and a sort of disgrace. In Indian communities all men who pretend to great medicine in any way, and fail, are disgraced. Indians think such failure an evidence of the displeasure of the Great Spirit, who always judges right.

He now lives respected, but silent and melancholy. I conversed with him a great deal about his brother Tecumseh, of whom he spoke frankly and, seemingly, with great pleasure; but of himself and his own great schemes, he would say nothing. He told me that Tecumseh's plans were to embody all the Indian tribes in a grand confederacy, from the province of Mexico to the Great Lakes, to unite their forces in an army that would be able to meet and drive back the white people who were continually advancing on the Indian tribes, and forcing them from their lands towards the Rocky Mountains; he said, too, that Tecumseh was a great general, and that nothing but his premature death defeated his grand plan.

The Shawanos, like most other remnants of tribes in whose countries the game has been destroyed, have been reduced to poverty and absolute want. They have become, to a certain degree, agriculturists. They raise corn and beans, potatoes, hogs, and horses. If they could possess a country that they could be certain of holding as their own, they might plant and raise their own crops and necessaries of life. But the Government agreed with these people, as with most of the other dispersed tribes, to an arrangement by which they are to

Cherokee: John Ross.

Cherokee: Tuchee, called "Dutch."

remove west of the Mississippi, to lands assigned them; on which they have been solemnly promised a home *for ever*. The uncertain definiton of that important word, time and circumstances alone will determine.

CHEROKEES

The Cherokees are now living in the vicinity of Fort Gibson on the Arkansas. They originally inhabited a considerable part of the State of Georgia. Under a treaty, they have been removed to Fort Gibson, where they are settled on a fine tract of country. They were advanced in the arts and agriculture before they started, and they live well, cultivating their fields of corn and other crops with great success.

These people, from their former solemn treaties with the United States Government, were acknowledged a free and independent nation with powers to make and enforce their own laws. But the State of Georgia could not admit such a Government within her sovereignty. It was thought expedient by the Government of the United States to propose to them, for the fourth or fifth time, to enter into treaty stipulations to move again. By so doing they would settle the difficult question with the State of Georgia and, at the same time, would

318

gain possession of a large tract of fine country, where they would for ever be free from the continual trespasses and abuses which it was supposed they would be subjected to if they were to remain in the State of Georgia.

John Ross, a civilized, highly educated, and accomplished gentleman, is the head-chief of the tribe. Several of his leading subordinate chiefs have sternly and steadily rejected the proposition of still another move. The great majority of the nation remain on their own land in Georgia, although some six or seven thousand of the tribe did move several years ago to the Arkansas, under the guidance of a chief by the name of Jo-lee.

The Cherokees amounted in all to about twenty-two thousand. Of these, sixteen thousand have been living in Georgia under their chief, John Ross. For many years he devotedly opposed the treaty stipulations for moving from Georgia, despite the bitter invective that has been heaped upon him by his political enemies.

The Government has finally succeeded in removing the remainder of the Cherokees beyond the Mississippi where they have taken up residence alongside their old friends, who emigrated several years ago under Jo-lee. The Government has now removed nearly every remnant of every tribe west of the Mississippi so that there remain only a few hundred red men east of the Mississippi.

CREEKS (or MUS-KO-GEES)

Twenty thousand Creeks used to occupy an immense tract of country in the states of Mississippi and Alabama. But by arrangement with the Government, they have exchanged their possessions there for a country adjoining the Cherokees, on the south side of the Arkansas. They have already all moved. Like the Cherokees, they are laying out fine farms and building good houses surrounded by immense fields of corn and wheat. There is scarcely a finer country on earth than that now owned by the Creeks. In North America, no Indian tribe is more advanced in the arts and agriculture than they are. It is no uncommon thing to see a Creek with twenty or thirty slaves at work on his plantation, having brought them from slave-holding country.

CHOCTAWS

They are another tribe of fifteen thousand removed from the northern parts of Alabama and Mississippi, and now occupying a rich tract of country south of the Arkansas and the Canadian rivers, adjoining the country of the Creeks and Cherokees. They are equally civilized, and living in much the same manner.

These people seem, even in their troubles, to be happy. They have preserved their different games, which they are everlastingly practicing. While I was staying at the Choctaw agency, it seemed to be a sort of season of amusements, a kind of holiday. The whole tribe were assembled around the agency, and day after day we were entertained with some game or feat: horse-racing, dancing, wrestling, foot-racing, and ball-playing. The most beautiful was decidedly ball-playing. This wonderful game is the favorite among all the tribes.

He-Who-Drinks-the-Juice-of-the-Stone, champion ballplayer of the Choctaw.

It is common for six hundred, eight hundred, or a thousand young men to engage in a game of ball, with five or six times that number of spectators—men, women, and children —surrounding the ground and looking on. I have made it a uniform rule to attend every ball-play I hear of. My usual custom on such occasions has been to straddle the back of my horse to be able to see to the best advantage. I have sat, and almost dropped from my horse's back with irresistible laughter at the succession of droll tricks and kicks and scuffles which ensue in the almost superhuman struggles for the ball. Play generally commences at nine o'clock in the morning. I have more than once balanced myself on my pony from nine until sundown, without more than one minute of intermission before the game was decided.

While at the Choctaw agency one day, it was announced there was to be a great play, and I attended. Monday afternoon, at three o'clock, I rode out to a pretty prairie, the ball-play-ground of the Choctaws. Several thousand Indians were encamped. There were two points of timber about half a mile apart, in which the two parties for the play, with their respective families and friends, were encamped. Lying between them was the prairie on which the game was to be played.

* During the afternoon, we loitered about among the different tents and shantees of the two encampments, and afterwards, at sundown, witnessed the ceremony of measuring out the ground and erecting the goals which were to guide the play. Each party had their goal made with two upright posts, about twenty-five feet high and six feet apart, set firm in the ground, with a pole across at the top. These goals were about two hundred and fifty yards apart. At a point just half way between was another small stake driven down, where the ball was to be thrown up at the firing of a gun.

All preparations were made by some old men who were selected to be the judges. They drew a line from one goal to the other. Immediately from the woods on both sides of the field a great concourse of women and old men, boys and girls, dogs and horses came up to the line drawn across the center of the field to place their bets. The betting was all done across this line. It seemed to be chiefly left to the women who martialled out a little of everything their houses and their fields contained: Goods and chattels, knives, dresses, blankets, pots and kettles, dogs and horses and guns. All were placed in the possession of stake-holders, who sat by them and watched them all night preparatory to the play.

The sticks with which the game is played are bent into an oblong hoop at the end, with a sort of slight web of small thongs tied across, to prevent the ball from passing through. The players hold one in each hand. By leaping into the air, they catch the ball between the two nettings and throw it, without being allowed to strike it or catch it in their hands.

It is a rule of play that no man shall wear moccasins on his feet, or any dress other than his breech-cloth around his waist, with a beautiful bead belt, and a "tail" made of white horse-hair or quills, and a "mane" on the neck, of horse-hair dyed various colors.

This game had been arranged and "made up" three or four months before the parties met to play it, in the following manner: The two champions who led the two parties chose players alternately from the whole tribe. They each sent runners with ball-sticks,

* Catlin is describing Indian "lacrosse."—Ed.

321

Hundreds of Choctaw play at once, running, tripping, fighting, throwing.

fantastically ornamented with ribbons and red paint, to be touched by each one of the chosen players, who thereby agreed to be on the spot at the appointed time and ready for the play.

Once the field was prepared, and preliminaries of the game all settled, the bettings all made and goods all "staked," night came on without the appearance of any players on the ground. But soon after dark, a procession of lighted flambeaux was seen coming from each encampment. The players assembled around their respective goals. At the beat of the drums and chants of the women, each party of players commenced the "ball-play dance." Each party danced for a quarter of an hour around their respective goals in their ball-play dress; rattling their ball-sticks together in the most violent manner, and all singing as loud as they could. Meanwhile, the women of each party, who had their goods at stake, formed into two rows on the line between the two parties of players, and also danced in a uniform step, all their voices joined in chants to the Great Spirit. In the meantime, four old medicine-men, who were to be the judges of the play, were seated at midfield. They were busily smoking to the Great Spirit, too, for their success in judging rightly between the parties in so important an affair.

The dance was repeated at intervals of every half hour all night. The players were certainly awake all the night, but prepared for play the next morning.

322

In the morning, at the appointed hour, the game commenced with the judges throwing up the ball and firing a gun. An instant struggle ensued between the players, as some six or seven hundred men mutually endeavored to catch the ball in their sticks and throw it into their opponent's goal. Hundreds ran together and leapt over each other's heads, and darted between their adversaries' legs, tripping and throwing and foiling each other in every possible manner. Every voice was raised in shrill yelps and barks. There were rapid successions of feats, and of incidents.

Every trick is used that can be devised, to oppose the progress of the ball. These obstructions often meet desperate resistance, which terminate in a violent scuffle, and sometimes in fisticuffs. Sticks are dropped, and the parties are unmolested as they settle it between themselves.

Every weapon, by rule of all ball-plays, is laid by in their respective encampments. No man is allowed to go for one. The sudden broils that take place are presumed to be as suddenly settled without any probability of much personal injury. No one is allowed to interfere in any way with contentious individuals.

At times, when the ball is on the ground, such a confused mass rushes around it, and knocks their sticks together, there is no possibility of anyone seeing it. The condensed mass of ball-sticks, and shins, and bloody noses, travels around the different parts of the field for a quarter of an hour at a time. Since no one can see the ball, several minutes may pass while the mob struggles even though the ball is being played over another part of the field.

Each time the ball passes between the stakes of either party, one point is counted for game, and there is a halt of about one minute. Then play is started again by the judges. The struggle continues until the successful party gets to one hundred, which is the limit of the game. It was not finished until an hour before sunset. The winners take their stakes. Then, by previous agreement, a number of jugs of whisky were produced, which sent them all off merry and in good humor.

The Red Pipe-Stone Quarry of The Great Spirit.

XX

Red Pipe-Stone
Quarry, 1836

THE READER who would follow me to where I now am must start from my own native state, Pennsylvania. From there I wended my way to Buffalo, on Lake Erie, then followed the zigzag course of the Lakes from Buffalo to Detroit, to the Sault de St. Mary's, to Mackinaw, to Green Bay, and the tortuous windings of the Fox and Ouisconsin rivers, to Prairie du Chien; thence the mighty Mississippi to the Fall of St. Anthony, and the sluggish yet decorated and beautiful St. Peter's River towards its source. From there I went on horse-back across the terraces of the green plains called the "Côteau des Prairies" (the dividing ridge between the St. Peter's and the Missouri rivers). Now I am bivouacked at the "Red Pipe-Stone Quarry." The distance of such a tour would take the reader four thousand miles; but I save him the trouble by bringing him, in a moment, to the spot.

This place is great, not in history, for there is none of it, but in traditions and stories. According to Indian traditions, the mysterious birth of the red pipe happened here. It has blown its fumes of peace and war to the remotest corners of the Continent. Through its reddened stem the irrevocable oath of war and desolation has passed. And here also, the peace-breathing calumet was born, and fringed with the eagle's quills. It has soothed the fury of the relentless savage.

325

Long ago the Great Spirit called the Indian nations together. He stood on the red pipe-stone rock, broke a piece from its wall, and made a huge pipe by turning it in his hand. He smoked it over them, to the north, the south, the east, and the west. He told them that this stone was red; that it was their flesh; that they must use it for their pipes of peace; that it belonged to them all, and that the war-club and scalping knife must not be raised on its ground. At the last whiff of his pipe, his head went into a great cloud, and the whole surface of the rock for several miles was melted and glazed. Two great ovens were opened beneath, and two women (guardian spirits of the place) entered them in a blaze of fire. They are heard there yet (Tso-mec-cos-tee and Tso-me-cos-te-won-dee), answering to the invocations of the high priests or medicine-men, who consult them when they are visitors to this sacred place.

Whether it has been an Indian Eden or not, or whether the thunderbolts of the Indian Jupiter are actually forged here, it is nevertheless a place renowned in Indian heraldry and tradition. I am encamped on the very rock where "the Great Spirit stood when he consecrated the pipe of peace by moulding it from the rock, and smoking it over the congregated nations that were assembled about him."

Nothing is seen in the distance except the thousand treeless, bushless, weedless hills of grass and vivid green, which vanish into an infinity of blue and azure. Stretched on our bear-skins, my fellow-traveller, Mr. Robert Serril Wood, an Englishman travelling for his education and amusement, and I have laid and contemplated the splendid heavens. We camped night after night, and mused on our own insignificance. We have drawn our buffalo robes about us, talked of the ills of life—of friends we had lost—of projects that had failed—and of the painful steps we had to retrace.

On our way here, we were arrested by a band of the Sioux, and held captive for having dared to approach the sacred fountain of the pipe. We had halted at the trading-hut of "Le Blanc," at a placed called Traverse des Sioux on the St. Peter's River, about one hundred and fifty miles from the Red Pipe. A cloud of warriors and braves gathered around the house. One of them began an agitated and insulting harangue, announcing that we were prisoners, and could not go ahead.

About twenty of them spoke in turn. We were doomed to sit the whole afternoon, without being allowed to speak a word in our behalf, until they had all got through. We were compelled to keep our seats like culprits, and hold our tongues, until all had brandished their fists in our faces, and vented all the threats and invective that could flow from Indian malice, grounded on the presumption that we had come to trespass on their dearest privilege—their religion.

Perhaps their anger was justified. We were persisting in a determination to visit their greatest medicine (mystery) place—a place they had resolved no white man should ever be allowed to go. They took us to be "officers sent by the Government to see what this place was worth."

Since "this red stone was part of their flesh," it would be sacrilegious for a white man to touch it or take it away. "A hole would be made in their flesh, and the blood could never be made to stop running."

We were here in a fix, one that demanded the use of every energy we had about us.

Astounded at so determined a rebuff, we were more than ever excited to go ahead and see what was to be seen at this strange place.

The grave council was opened in the following manner: Te-o-kun-hko (The Swift Man) rose first and said: "My friends, I am not a chief, but the son of a chief. I am the son of my father. He is a chief, and when he is gone away, it is my duty to speak for him. He is not here, but what I say is the talk of his mouth. We have been told that you are going to the Pipe-Stone Quarry. We come now to ask for what purpose you are going, and what business you have to go there.

"Brothers, we look at you and we see that you are Che-mo-ke-mon captains (white men officers). We know that you have been sent by your Government to see what that place is worth, and we think that the white people want to buy it.

"Brothers, we have seen always that when white people see anything in our country, they want to send officers to value it, and then if they can't buy it, they will get it some other way.

"Brothers, I speak strong, my heart is strong, and I speak fast. This red pipe was given to the red men by the Great Spirit—it is a part of our flesh, and therefore is great medicine.

"Brothers, we know that the whites are like a great cloud that rises in the East, and will cover the whole country. We know that they will have all our lands. But if ever they get our Red Pipe Quarry, they will have to pay very dear for it.

"Brothers, we know that no white man has ever been to the Pipe-Stone Quarry, and our chiefs have often decided in council that no white man shall ever go to it.

"Brothers, you have heard what I have to say, and you can go no farther, but you must turn about and go back.

"Brothers, you see that the sweat runs from my face, for I am troubled."

Then I commenced to reply in the following manner: "My friends, I am sorry that you have mistaken us so much, and the object of our visit to your country. We are not officers and we are not sent by anyone. We are two poor men travelling to see the Sioux, and shake hands with them, and examine what is curious or interesting in their country. This man who is with me is my friend; he is a *Sa-ga-nosh* (an Englishman)."

All rose and shook hands with him, and a number of them took out and showed British medals that they carried in their bosoms.

"We have heard that the Red Pipe Quarry is a great curiosity; we have started to go to it, and we will not be stopped."

Here I was interrupted by a grim and black-visaged fellow who shook his long shaggy locks as he rose, with his sunken eyes fixed in direct hatred on me, and his fist brandished within an inch of my face. "Pale Faces! You cannot speak till we have all done; you are our *prisoners*—our young men are about the house, and you must listen to what we have to say. What has been said to you is true, you must go back.

"We heard the word *Sa-ga-nosh,* and it makes our hearts glad; we shook hands with your brother. His father is our father—he is our Great Father—he lives across the big lake. His son is here, and we are glad. We wear our Great Father the Sa-ga-nosh on our bosoms, and we keep his face bright. We shake hands, but no white man has been to the red pipe and none shall go.

"You see (holding a red pipe to the side of his naked arm) that this pipe is a part of our flesh. The red men are a part of the red stone.

"If the white men take away a piece of the red pipe-stone, it is a hole made in our flesh, and the blood will always run. We cannot stop the blood from running.

"The Great Spirit has told us the red stone is only to be used for pipes, and through them we are to smoke to him.

"Why do the white men want to get there? You have no good object in view. We know you have none, and the sooner you go back the better."

Muz-za (The Iron) spoke next: "My friends, we do not wish to harm you. You have heard the words of our chief men, and you now see that you must go back.

"Tchan-dee-pah-sha-kah-fee (The Red Pipe-Stone) was given to us by the Great Spirit, and no one need ask the price of it, for it is medicine.

"My friends, I believe what you have told us. I think your intentions are good. But our chiefs have always told us that no white man was allowed to go there—and you cannot go."

Another: "My friends, you see I am a young man; you see on my war-club two scalps from my enemies' heads; my hands have been dipped in blood, but I am a good man. I am a friend to the whites, to the traders, and they are your friends. I bring them three thousand muskrat skins every year, which I catch in my own traps.

"We love to go to the Pipe-Stone and get a piece for our pipes; but we ask the Great Spirit first. If the white men go to it, they will take it out, and not fill up the holes again, and the Great Spirit will be offended."

Another: "My friends, listen to me! What I am to say will be the truth.

"I brought a large piece of the pipe-stone and gave it to a white man to make a pipe; he was our trader and I wished him to have a good pipe. The next time I went to his store, I was unhappy when I saw that stone made into a dish!

"'This the way the white men would use the red pipe-stone, if they could get it. Such conduct would offend the Great Spirit, and make a red man's heart sick.

"Brothers, we do not wish to harm you. If you turn about and go back, you will be well, both you and your horses. You cannot go forward.

"I have no more to say."

These and a dozen other speeches to the same effect having been pronounced, I replied in the following manner: "My friends, you have entirely mistaken us. We are not officers, nor are we sent by anyone. The white men do not want the red pipe. It is not worth their carrying home so far, if you were to give it all to them. Another thing: They don't use pipes. They don't know how to smoke them.

"My friends, I think as you do, that the Great Spirit has given that place to the red men for their pipes.

"I give you great credit for the course you are taking to preserve and protect it. And I will do as much as any man to keep white men from taking it away from you.

"'But we have started to go and see it, and we cannot think of being stopped."

328

The Mississippi by canoe: Madame Ferrebault's Prairie above Prairie du Chien.

I made a few more remarks stating that we should go ahead, which we did the next morning, by saddling our horses and riding off through the midst of them. In this emergency, Mr. Wood and I mutually agreed to go ahead, even if it should be at the hazard of our lives. Perhaps our own speeches were our safeguard.

The position of the Pipe-Stone Quarry is nearly three hundred miles west from the Fall of St. Anthony, on the summit of the dividing ridge between the St. Peter's and the Missouri rivers, about equidistant from either. This dividing ridge is called by the French the "Côteau des Prairies," and the Pipe-Stone Quarry is situated near its southern extremity and consequently not exactly on its highest elevation, as its general course is north and south, and its southern extremity terminates in a gradual slope.

Our approach to it was from the east, and the ascent, for fifty miles, was over an almost imperceptibly rising succession of slopes and terraces. There is not a tree or bush to be seen from the summit of the ridge. The eye may range endlessly east or west over a surface covered with a short grass which is green at one's feet, but changes to blue in the distance, like the vast blue of the ocean.

On the top of this ridge, we found the quarry of the Red Pipe. The most striking feature is a perpendicular wall of close-grained, compact quartz, twenty-five and thirty feet in elevation, running nearly north and south with its face to the west, on a front nearly two miles in length. It then disappears at both ends by running under the prairie, which probably covers it for many miles both north and south. The depression of the brow of the ridge has been caused by the wash of a little stream, produced by several springs on the top, a little back from

Eastern Sioux: The Black Dog, Chief of the O-hah-kas-ka-toh-y-an-te Band.

the wall. It has gradually carried away the earth, and bared the wall for two miles. Then it leaps from the top of the wall into a deep basin below, and from there to the Missouri, forming the source of a noted tributary called the Big Sioux.

This wall is horizontal, and stratified in several distinct layers of light gray and rose- or flesh-colored quartz. For most of the way, both on the front of the wall and for acres of its horizontal surface, it is highly polished or glazed as if by ignition.

At the base of this wall there is a level prairie half a mile in width and running parallel to it. In all parts of it, the Indians procure the red stone for their pipes by digging through the soil and several slaty layers of the red stone, to a depth of four or five feet.

330

At the base of the wall, and within an hundred yards of it, is a group of five stupendous boulders of gneiss, leaning against each other. The smallest of these is twelve or fifteen feet in diameter, and the largest twenty-five feet. Altogether they weigh several hundred tons. These blocks are composed chiefly of feldspar and mica, of an exceedingly coarse grain, the feldspar often occurring in crystals an inch in diameter. The surface of these boulders is in every part covered with a gray moss, which gives them an extremely ancient appearance, and their sides and angles are rounded by attrition. It is under these blocks that two holes, or ovens, are seen. In these, according to the Indian superstition, two old women, the guardian spirits of the place, reside.

I broke off specimens and brought them home. They certainly bear as high a polish and lustre on the surface as a piece of melted glass. I was strongly inclined to believe that the Pipe-Stone, which differs from all known specimens of lava, was a new variety of steatite and would be found to be a subject worthy of careful analysis.

In Stillman's *American Journal of Science,* Vol. xxvii, p. 394, will be seen the following analysis of this mineral, made by Dr. Jackson of Boston, one of our best mineralogists and chemists. I sent him some specimens for the purpose and he pronounced it "a new mineral compound, not steatite, harder than gypsum, and softer than carbonate of lime."

Chemical Analysis of the Red Pipe-Stone, brought by George Catlin from the Côteau des Prairies in 1836.

Water	8.4	Carbonate of lime	2.6
Silicia	48.2	Peroxide of iron	5.0
Alumina	28.2	Oxide of manganese	0.6
Magnesia	6.0		
			99.0
	Loss (probably magnesia)		1.0
			100.0

The red pipes are found in almost every tribe on the Continent; and in every instance have, I venture to say, been brought from the Côteau des Prairies. The stone from which they are all manufactured is of the same character exactly, and different from any known mineral compound ever yet discovered in any part of Europe or in other parts of the American Continent.

Within a few years, the Sioux have claimed the entire quarry, probably at the instigation of the whites, who have told them that by keeping off other tribes and manufacturing the pipes themselves, and then trading them to other adjoining nations, they can acquire much influence and wealth. The quarry is in the center of their country. They are more powerful than any other tribe, and they are able to prevent any access to it.

The quarry was visited for centuries in common by all tribes. They hid the war-club as they approached it and stayed the cruelties of the scalping-knife. They feared the ven-

Eastern Sioux: The Blue Medicine, a Medicine Man of the Ting-ta-to-tah Band.

geance of the Great Spirit, who overlooks it. The *totems* and *arms* of the different tribes who have visited this place for ages are deeply engraved on the quartz rocks.

I am aware that the neutrality preserved at the Pipe-Stone Quarry may be opposed by subsequent travellers, who will find nobody but the Sioux here. I refer them to Lewis and Clark's tour thirty-three years ago, before the influence of traders had deranged the system and truth of things in these regions. I have often conversed with General Clark in St. Louis on this subject. He told me explicitly that every tribe on the Missouri told him they had been to this place, and that the Great Spirit kept the peace among his red children on this ground, where they had smoked with their enemies.

332

Among the many traditions of Pipe-Stone is the following one related to me by a Knisteneaux on the Upper Missouri, four years ago:

"In the time of a great flood, which took place many centuries ago and destroyed all the nations of the earth, all the tribes of the red men assembled on the Côteau des Prairies to get out of the way of the waters. After they had gathered here from all parts, the water continued to rise, until at length it covered them all in a mass, and their flesh was converted into red pipe-stone. Therefore, it has always been considered neutral ground—it belonged to all tribes alike, and all were allowed to get pipe-stone and smoke it together.

"While they were all drowning in a mass, a young woman, K-wap-tah-w (A Virgin), caught hold of the foot of a very large bird that was flying over, and was carried to the top of a high cliff, not far off, that was above the water. Here she had twins, and their father was the war-eagle, and her children have since peopled the earth.

"The pipe-stone, which is the flesh of their ancestors, is smoked by them as the symbol of peace, and the eagle's quill decorates the head of the brave."

The tradition of the Upper Missouri Sioux is a different one:

"Before the creation of man, the Great Spirit (whose tracks are yet to be seen on the stones at the Red Pipe in the form of the tracks of a large bird) used to slay the buffaloes and eat them on the ledge of the Red Rocks, on the top of the Côteau des Prairies, and their blood running onto the rocks turned them red. One day when a large snake had crawled into the nest of the bird to eat his eggs, one of the eggs hatched out in a clap of thunder, and the Great Spirit catching hold of a piece of the pipe-stone to throw at the snake, molded it into a man. This man's feet grew fast in the ground where he stood for many ages, like a great tree, and therefore he grew very old; he was older than an hundred men at the present day; and at last another tree grew up by the side of him, when a large snake ate them both off at the roots, and they wandered off together. From these have sprung all the people that now inhabit the earth."

Among the Sioux of the Mississippi, and those who live in the region of the Red Pipe-Stone Quarry, I found the following and not less strange tradition on the same subject:

"Many ages after the red men were made, when all the different tribes were at war, the Great Spirit sent runners and called them all together at the 'Red Pipe.' He stood at the top of the rocks, and the red people were assembled in infinite numbers on the plains below. He took out of the rock a piece of the red stone and made a large pipe. He smoked it over them all. He told them that it was part of their flesh; that though they were at war, they must meet at this place as friends; that it belonged to them all; that they must make their calumets from it and smoke them to him whenever they wished to appease him or get his good-will. The smoke from his big pipe rolled over them all, and he disappeared in its cloud. At the last whiff of his pipe a blaze of fire rolled over the rocks and melted their surface. At that moment two squaws went in a blaze of fire under the two medicine rocks, where they remain to this day, and must be consulted and propitiated whenever the pipe-stone is to be taken away."

The following is the speech of a Mandan, made to me in the Mandan village four years ago, after I had painted his picture:

"My brother, you have made my picture and I like it much. My friends tell me they can see the eyes move, and it must be very good—it must be partly alive. I am glad it is done, though many of my people are afraid. I am a young man, but my heart is strong. I have jumped onto the medicine-rock. I have placed my arrow on it, and no Mandan can take it away."

The medicine (or leaping) rock is a part of the precipice severed from the main part, standing about seven or eight feet from the wall, just equal in height, and about seven feet in diameter. It stands like an immense column, thirty-five feet high, and is highly polished on its tops and sides. It requires a daring effort to leap onto its top from the main wall, and back again, and many a heart has sighed for the honor of the feat without daring to make the attempt. Some have tried it with success, and left their arrows standing in its crevice, several of which are seen there at this time. Others have leapt the chasm and fallen from the slippery surface, and suffered instant death upon the craggy rocks below. Every young man in the nation is ambitious to perform this feat. Those who have successfully done it are allowed to boast of it all their lives.

A distinguished young man was killed about two years before I was there. His sad fate was related to me by the Sioux chief who was the father of the young man. He was visiting the Red Pipe-Stone Quarry with thirty others of his tribe when we were there, and he cried over the grave as he related the story of his son's death.

The Mandan chief resumed his story: "The red stone is slippery, but my foot was true—it did not slip. My brother, this pipe which I give to you, I brought from a high mountain. It is towards the rising sun. Many were the pipes that we brought from there. And we brought them away in peace. We left our *totems* or marks on the rocks. We cut them deep in the stones, and they are there now. The Great Spirit told all nations to meet there in peace, and all nations hid the war-club and the tomahawk.

"The Dahcotahs, our enemies, are very strong. They have taken up the tomahawk, and the blood of our warriors has run on the rocks. My friend, we want to visit our medicines. Our pipes are old and worn out. My friend, I wish you to speak to our Great Father about this."

The chief of the Puncahs, on the Upper Missouri, also made the following allusion to this place, in a speech which he made to me on the occasion of presenting me a very handsome pipe about four years ago:

"My friend, this pipe, which I wish you to accept, was dug from the ground, and cut and polished as you now see it, by my hands. I wish you to keep it, and when you smoke through it, recollect that this red stone is a part of our flesh. This is one of the last things we can ever give away. Our enemies, the Sioux, have raised the red flag of blood over the Pipe-Stone Quarry, and our medicines there are trodden under foot by them. The Sioux are many, and we cannot go to the mountain of the red pipe. We have seen all nations smoking together at that place—but, my brother, it is not so now."

On my return from the Pipe-Stone Quarry, one of the old chiefs of the Sacs, on seeing some specimens of the stone which I brought with me from that place, observed as follows:

334

"My friend, when I was young, I used to go with our young men to the mountain of the Red Pipe, and dig out pieces for our pipes. We do not go now. And our red pipes, as you see, are few. The Dahcotahs have spilled the blood of red men on that place, and the Great Spirit is offended. The white traders have told them to draw their bows upon us when we go there. They have offered us many of the pipes for sale, but we do not want to smoke them, for we know that the Great Spirit is offended. My mark is on the rocks in many places, but I shall never see them again. They lie where the Great Spirit sees them, for his eye is over that place. He sees everything that is there."

Kee-o-kuk, chief of the Sacs and Foxes, when I asked him whether he had ever been there, replied: "No, I have never seen it. It is in our enemies' country. I wish it was in ours. I would sell it to the whites for a great many boxes of money."

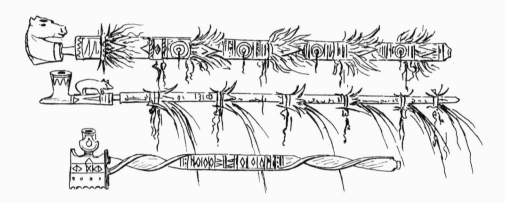

Kee-o-kuk, The Running Fox, chief of the Sauk and Fox. See Plate VIII, following page 270.

XXI

Rock Island, *Upper Mississippi*

I AM again wending my way towards home. Our neat little dugout has brought us safely to Rock Island—the river, the shores, and the plains are alive with plumes, with spears, and with war-clubs of yelling red men. We heard that the whole nation of Sacs and Foxes were to meet Governor Dodge here in treaty. We reached here in time to see the parades and ceremonies of an Indian community transferring the rights and immunities of their soil to the insatiable grasp of pale-face voracity.

The treaty was signed yesterday. Today is one of revel and amusements—shows of war-parades and dances. The whole of the Sacs and Foxes are gathered here, and their appearance is thrilling. These people have sold so much of their land lately that they have the luxuries of life to a considerable degree, and may be considered rich. They look elated and happy.

Kee-o-kuk (The Running Fox) is their chief. At the close of the "Black Hawk War" in 1833, waged with disastrous effects by a Sac chief of that name, Kee-o-kuk was acknowledged chief of the Sacs and Foxes by General Scott, who held a treaty with them at Rock Island. His appointment as chief was in consequence of the friendly position he had taken during the war. He held two-thirds of the warriors neutral, which was the cause of the successful termination of the war, and the means of saving much bloodshed. Black Hawk and his two sons, as well as his principal advisers and warriors, were brought into St. Louis in chains, and Kee-o-kuk was appointed chief with the assent of the tribe.

There is no Indian chief on the frontier better known or more highly appreciated for his eloquence than Kee-o-kuk. He has repeatedly visited Washington and our other Atlantic towns, and made his speeches before thousands. He has contended for his people's rights in their stipulations with the United States Government and in the sale of their lands.

The Sacs and Foxes were once two separate tribes, but with a language very similar. At some period not very long ago, they united into one, and go by the amalgam name of "Sacs and Foxes." They shave and ornament their heads, like the Osages and Pawnees. They are among the tribes who have relinquished their tracts of lands and are moving west of the Mississippi River. Their numbers are not more than five or six thousand, yet they are a warlike and powerful tribe.

Muk-a-tah-mish-o-kah-kaik (The Black Hawk) was defeated by General Atkinson, and held a prisoner of war. He was sent through Washington and other Eastern cities, with a number of others, to be gazed at.

His name carried terror through the country when it was mentioned, but he was more distinguished as a speaker or counsellor than as a warrior. I believe it has been pretty generally admitted that "Nah-pope" and "The Prophet" were in fact the instigators of the war. Both of them held much higher claims to the name of warrior than Black Hawk ever had.

When I painted Black Hawk he was dressed in a plain suit of buckskin, with strings of wampum in his ears and around his neck. He held his medicine-bag, which was the skin of a black hawk from which he had taken his name, and the tail of which made him a fan, which he was almost constantly using.

After I had painted the portrait of Kee-o-kuk, he said to me that he wished me to paint him on horse-back. So I prepared my canvas in the door of the hospital which I occupied, in the dragoon cantonment. He flourished about for a considerable part of the day in front of me, until the picture was completed. The horse he rode was an extraordinary animal: a fine blooded horse, for which he had paid three hundred dollars, a price he could afford because he controlled the distribution of fifty thousand dollars in annuities annually, among his people. He made a great display on this day, and hundreds of the dragoons and officers were about him, and looking on during the operation. His horse was beautifully caparisoned, and his scalps were carried attached to the bridle-bits.

About two years after the portrait was painted, I was giving lectures on the customs of the Indians in the Stuyvesant Institute in New York. Kee-o-kuk and his wife and son, with twenty chiefs and warriors of his tribe, visited the City of New York on their way to Washington City. They were present one evening at my lecture, amid an audience of fifteen hundred persons. During the lecture, I placed a succession of portraits on my easel before the audience, and they were successively recognized by the Indians as they were shown. Finally I placed this portrait of Kee-o-kuk before them. They all sprung up and hailed it with a piercing yell. After the noise had subsided, Kee-o-kuk arose and addressed the audience in these words: "My friends, I hope you will pardon my men for making so much noise, as they were very much excited by seeing me on my favorite war-horse, which they all recognized in a moment."

Many persons had questioned the correctness of the picture of the horse. Some had said no Indian on the frontier rode so good a horse. This was explained to Kee-o-kuk by the interpreter. He arose again quite indignant, and assured the audience "that his men knew the horse the moment it was presented; further, he wished to know why Kee-o-kuk could not ride as good a horse as any white man?" He received a round of applause.

The Sacs and Foxes have a society, which they call the "slaves." It is composed of a number of young men from the best families in the tribe. They volunteer to be slaves for a term of two years, and perform any menial service the chief may order, no matter how humiliating or how degrading it may be. After serving their two years, they are exempt for the rest of their lives, on war-parties or other excursions, or wherever they may be, from all labor or degrading occupations, such as cooking, making fires, and so on.

Smoking horses is another curious custom of this tribe. I arrived at Kee-o-kuk's village just in time to see this amusing scene take place on the prairie back of the village. The Foxes, who were making up a war-party to go against the Sioux, did not have enough suitable horses by twenty. They sent word to the Sacs the day before that they were coming at a certain hour to "smoke" twenty horses.

At the hour, the twenty young men who were beggars for horses were on the spot. They seated themselves on the ground in a circle and began smoking. The villagers flocked around them in a dense crowd.

Soon after, half a mile away, an equal number of young men of the Sac tribe, who each had agreed to give a horse, came galloping up. They went around in a circle, coming in nearer to the center until they were close around the ring of young fellows seated on the ground. While dashing around the circle, each one, with a heavy whip in his hand, as he came within reach of the group on the ground, selected the one to whom he decided to present his horse. As he passed him, he gave him the most tremendous cut with his lash over his naked shoulders, with a violent "crack!" until the blood could be seen trickling down over naked shoulders. Then he dismounted and placed the bridle and whip in his hands, saying: "Here, you are a beggar—I present you a horse, but you will carry my mark on your back."

In a little while they were each "whipped up," and each had a good horse to ride into battle. Necessity was such, each could afford to take the stripes and the scars as the price of the horse, and the giver could afford to make the present for the satisfaction of putting his mark upon the other, and of boasting of his liberality, which he has always a right to do, when going into the dance, or on other important occasions.

Dance to the Berdashe is a funny scene which happens when a feast is given to the "Berdashe," as he is called in French (or I-coo-coo-a in their own language). He is a man dressed in woman's clothes, as he is known to be all his life, and for the extraordinary privileges which he gains, he is driven to the most servile and degrading duties, which he is not

Smoking Horses.

allowed to escape. Since he is the only one of the tribe submitting to this disgraceful degradation, it is looked upon as medicine and sacred, and a feast is given to him annually. Before it, a dance by those few young men of the tribe who can dance forward and publicly make their boast (without the denial of the Berdashe) that Agh-whi-ee-choos-cum-me hi-anh-dwax-cumme-ke on-daig-nun-chow ixt. Che-ne-a'hkt ah-pex-ian I-coo-coo-a wi-an-gurotst whow-itcht-ne-axt-ar-rah, ne-axt-gun-he h'dow-k's dow-on-daig-o-ewhicht nun-go-was-see.

Precious few in the tribe have legitimately gained this singular privilege, or are willing to make a public confession of it. The society consists of quite a limited number of "odd fellows."

The Dance to the *Medicine of the Brave* is a custom well worth recording for the beautiful moral which is contained in it. When a party of Sac warriors have returned victorious from battle, with the scalps they have taken from their enemies, but have lost one of their own party, they appear and dance in front of his wigwam. For fifteen days in succession they dance about an hour. The widow hangs his medicine-bag on a green bush which she erects before her door, under which she sits and cries. The warriors dance and brandish the

340

Dance to the Berdashe.

scalps they have taken, and at the same time recount the deeds of bravery of their deceased comrade in arms. At the same time, they throw presents to the widow to heal her grief and afford her the means of a living.

The Sacs and Foxes are already drawing an annuity of twenty-seven thousand dollars for thirty years to come, in cash. By the present treaty, that amount will be enlarged to thirty-seven thousand dollars per annum. This treaty with the Sacs and Foxes, held at Rock Island, was for the purchase of a tract of land of two hundred and fifty-six thousand acres, lying on the Ioway River, west of the Mississippi; a reserve which was made by the tract of land conveyed from the Government by treaty after the Sac War, and known as the "Black Hawk purchase." The treaty has been completed by Governor Dodge, stipulating on the part of the Government to pay seventy-five cents per acre for the reserve, amounting to one hundred and ninety-two thousand dollars.

Thirty thousand dollars to be paid in specie next June at the treaty-ground, and ten thousand dollars annually for ten years to come. The remaining sixty-two thousand was assigned in the payment of their debts. The American Fur Company was their principal

Dance to the Medicine of the Braves.

creditor, for goods advanced on credit, they admitted, to the amount of nearly fifty thousand dollars. It was stipulated by an article in the treaty that one-half of the Company's demands should be paid in cash as soon as the treaty was ratified, and that five thousand dollars should be appropriated annually, for their liquidation, until they were paid off.

The price paid for this tract of land is a liberal one, comparatively speaking. The usual price heretofore paid for Indian lands has been one and a half or three-quarter cents (instead of seventy-five cents) per acre.

But even one dollar per acre would not have been too much to have paid for this tract, for every acre of it can be sold within one year for much more to settlers. These very people sold to the Government a great part of the rich states of Illinois and Missouri, at the same low rates. This tract is the last they have to part with.

As evidence of the immediate value of the land to the Government, and as a striking instance of the overwhelming torrent of emigration to the West, Governor Dodge addressed

342

a few sentences to the chiefs after the treaty was signed and witnessed. He finished by requesting them to move their families and all their property from this tract within one month, which time he would allow them to make room for the whites. His suggestion created a hearty laugh, which was soon explained:

"My father, we have to laugh. We require no time to move—we have left the lands already, and sold our wigwams to Chemokemons (white men)—some for one hundred and some for two hundred dollars, before we came to this treaty. There are already four hundred Chemokemons on the land, and several hundred more on their way moving in. And three days before we came away, one Chemokemon sold his wigwam to another Chemokemon for two thousand dollars, to build a great town."

With an old frock coat and brown hat on, and a cane in his hand, Old Black Hawk stood outside the group the whole time in dumb and dismal silence, with his sons by the side of him, and also his *quondam* aide-de camp, Nah-pope, and The Prophet. They were not allowed to speak, nor even to sign the treaty.

Osceola, The Black Drink.

XXII

Fort Moultrie, *South Carolina,* January 1837

TWO HUNDRED and fifty Seminolees and Euchees, prisoners of war, are being kept here at Fort Moultrie. They will be transferred to the country assigned them, seven hundred miles west of the Mississippi and fourteen hundred from here. The famous Os-ce-o-la is among the prisoners; also Mick-e-no-pah, the head chief of the tribe; and Cloud, King Philip, and several other distinguished men of the nation, who have celebrated themselves in the war that is now waging with the United States Government.

There is scarcely any need of my undertaking to give a full account of the disastrous war now waging with the United States Government. The Indians have held an invading army in their country for four or five years. The Government is attempting to dispossess them and compel them to remove to the West. These are matters of history, and I leave them to the hands of those who will do them more complete justice.

For those who know nothing of the Seminolees, they are a tribe of three or four thousand occupying the peninsula of Florida, and speaking the language of the Creeks, once a part of the same tribe.

The word Seminolee is a Creek word signifying runaways. The name was given to

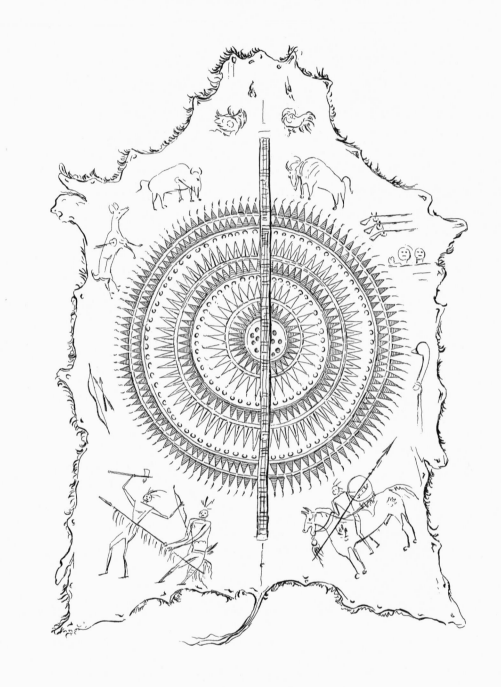

a part of the Creek nation that emigrated in a body into Florida, where they have lived to the present day. They extended their dominions by overrunning the once numerous tribe that occupied the southern extremity of the Florida Cape, called the Euchees. whom they have at last nearly annihilated, and taken the remnant of them in as a part of their tribe.

With this tribe the United States Government has been engaged in deadly and disastrous warfare for four or five years, endeavoring to remove them from their lands in compliance with a treaty stipulation, which the Government claims to have been justly made, and which the Seminolees aver was not.

Thirty-six million dollars have already been expended in the Seminolee War, as well as the lives of twelve or fourteen hundred officers and men, and defenseless inhabitants, who have fallen victims to the violence of the enraged savages. The war is being prosecuted at this time with vigor. The best troops in our country, and the lives of our most valued officers, are being jeopardized in the deadly swamps of Florida, with little certainty of a speedy termination of the war.

Much more will doubtless be yet spent before the Seminolees can be removed from their impenetrable swamps and hiding-places. From these hiding-places they will be enabled to make continual sallies upon the defenseless inhabitants of the country, venting their relentless feelings of vengeance on the unoffending and innocent.

The prisoners who are held here, to the number of two hundred and fifty men, women, and children, were captured during the recent part of this warfare. Among them the most conspicuous is Os-ce-o-la, commonly called Powell as he is generally supposed to be a half-breed, the son of a white man (by that name) and a Creek woman.

I painted him precisely in the costume in which he stood for his picture, even to a string and a trinket. He wore three ostrich feathers in his head, and a turban made of a vari-colored cotton shawl. His dress was chiefly of calicoes, with a handsome bead sash or belt around his waist, and his rifle in his hand.

He is looked upon by the Seminolees as the master spirit and leader of the tribe, although he is not a chief. From his boyhood, he led an energetic and desperate sort of life, which secured for him a conspicuous position in society. When war came to his country, he took a conspicuous and decided part. In some way, whether he deserved it or not, he acquired an influence and a name that soon sounded to the remotest parts of the United States, especially among the Indian tribes.

This gallant fellow was captured a few months ago and brought in to Fort Mellon, Florida. Then he was sent to this place for safe-keeping, where he is grieving with a broken spirit and ready to die, cursing white men, no doubt, to the end of his breath.

The Great Chief, a Menominee boy.

XXIII

The Frontier

I HAVE now a little leisure, and no particular tribes before me to speak of. I hope the reader will allow me to glance my eye over the whole Indian country for a while, both along the frontier and beyond it, taking a brief survey of them and their prospects in the aggregate.

By the policy of the Government, one hundred and twenty thousand of these people, who had just got initiated into the mysteries of civilized life, surrounded by examples of industry and agriculture which they were beginning to adopt, have been removed to the West, to meet a second siege of the whisky-sellers and traders in the wilderness. They will have to pay ten times their accustomed price for their goods. They must scuffle for a few years upon the plains with the wild tribes and white men, for the flesh and the skins of the last of the buffaloes. Their carnage, but not their appetites, must stop in a few years, and with the ghastliness of hunger and despair, they will find themselves gazing at each other upon a vacant waste.

The lucky white man will return to his comfortable home with no misfortune, save that of deep remorse and a guilty conscience. There is plenty enough to claim his pity and engage his whole soul's indignation at the wholesale and retail system of injustice which has been, from the very first landing of our forefathers, visited upon these poor, unoffending, and untrespassing people.

In the cruel policy of removing the tribes west of the Mississippi, I respect the motives of the Government—and the feelings and opinions of those worthy Divines, whose advice and whose services were instrumental in bringing it about. They were, no doubt, of the opinion they were effecting a plan that would redound to the Indian's benefit. Such was once my own opinion. Until I went through every one of those tribes removed. At home they had learned to use the ploughshare. They had contracted a passion and a taste for civilized manufactures. Then they were moved west, to a wild and lawless region, where their wants were to be supplied by the traders, at eight or ten times the prices they have been in the habit of paying; where whisky was easily sold to them without the restraints that had been successfully put upon the sellers of it in their civilized neighborhoods; and where also they were allured from the use of their ploughs by the herds of buffaloes and other wild animals on the plains.

I believe the system is one calculated to benefit the interests of the voracious land-speculators and Indian traders: the first of whom are ready to grasp at lands as soon as they are vacated; and the traders at the annuities of one hundred and twenty thousand extravagant customers. I believe the system is calculated to aid these, and perhaps to facilitate the growth and wealth of the civilized border. But I believe, like everything else that tends to the white man's aggrandizement, and the increase of his wealth, it will have a rapid tendency to destroy the poor red men.

The system of trade, and the small-pox, have been the great destroyers of these people, from the Atlantic Coast to where they are now found. And no one but God knows where the voracity of the one is to stop, short of the acquisition of everything that is desirable to money-making man in the Indian's country. Or when the mortal destruction of the other is to be arrested, while there is still untried flesh for it to act upon.

The Government of the United States has always held out every encouragement to the fur traders, whose traffic has uniformly been looked upon as beneficial, and a source of wealth to nations. Thousands are selling whisky and rum and useless gewgaws to the Indians on the United States, the Canada, the Texian, and the Mexican borders. In addition, there are hardy adventurers in the Rocky Mountains and beyond, one thousand armed men, in the annual employ of the United States fur companies. All of them pervade the countries of the wildest tribes they can reach, with guns and gunpowder in their hands, to terrify and coerce the Indian to favorable terms in trade. In all instances, they assume the right (and prove it, if necessary, by the superiority of their weapons) of hunting and trapping the streams and lakes of the Indian countries.

These traders, in addition, carry into these remote realms, at the muzzles of their guns, whisky and small-pox. And they are continually arming tribe after tribe with fire-arms. In this wholesale way, tribe after tribe sink their heads before the next and succeeding waves of civilization flow over them.

Small-pox is the infallible plague that follows, sooner or later, the introduction of trade and whisky-selling to every tribe. Numerous tribes have already disappeared. Those that have been traded with all the way to the Rocky Mountains have had this exotic disease in their turn—and lost half or more of their numbers. This appalling disease has several times run like a wave through the western tribes, over the Rocky Mountains, and to the Pacific Ocean—thinning the ranks of the Indians to an extent which no knowledge, save that of the overlooking eye of the Almighty, can justly comprehend.

So long as the present system of trade and whisky-selling is tolerated, there is little hope. I have closely studied the Indian character in its native state, and also in its secondary form along our frontiers. I have seen it in every phase, and although there are many noble instances to the contrary—many of whom I am personally acquainted with—yet the greater part of those who have lingered along the frontiers have been kicked about like dogs by white men, and have been beaten into a sort of civilization which is very far from being civilized by the examples of good and moral people.

The present system brings that small part of these poor unfortunate people who outlive the first calamities of their tribes to a degraded and pitiable condition. Most of them end their days in wretchedness. Standing on the soil which they have occupied from their childhood, and inherited from their fathers, the greater part of their friends and connections in the grave, they have no better prospect than the dreary one of living a few years longer and then sinking into the ground themselves. They surrender their lands and their fair hunting-grounds to the enjoyment of their enemies; and their bones are dug up and strewed about the fields, or labelled in our museums.

For the Christian, there is enough, I am sure, in the character, condition, and history of these unfortunate people, to engage his sympathies. For the nation, there is an unrequited account of sin and injustice that sooner or later will call for national retribution. For the American citizens, who live, everywhere proud of their growing wealth and their luxuries, over the bones of these poor fellows, there is a lingering terror for reflecting minds: Our mortal bodies must soon take their humble places with their red brethren, under the same glebe; to appear and stand, at last, with guilt's shivering conviction, amid the myriad ranks of accusing spirits at the final day of resurrection.

Appendix

The following brief vocabularies of several different Indian languages have been carefully written by the Author from the lips of the Indians as they pronounced them. I have endeavored to convey with the simplest use of the English alphabet conclusive proof of the radical difference that actually exists among a vast number of the languages spoken by the North American Indians.

ENGLISH.	MANDAN.	BLACKFOOT.	RICCAREE.	SIOUX.	TUSKARORA.
I	Me	Nistoa	Nan to	Mi a	Ee
You	Ne	Cristoa	Kag hon	Nia	Eets
He	E	Amo	Wite	Dai	Rawonroo
She	Ea	....	Sapatish	Hai chay	Unroo
It	Ount	....	Tihai	Dai Chay	Hay
We	Noo	Ne stoa pinnan	Aps	On kia	Dinwuh
They	Eonah	Maex	Arrish	Ni a pe	Ka ka wen roo
Great Spirit	Mah ho peneta	Cristecoom	Te wa rooh teh	Wakon shecha	Ye wunni yoh
Evil Spirit	Mahho penkheka	Cristecoom sah	Ka ke wa rooh teh	Wakon tonka	Katickuhraxu
Medicine (Mystery)	Hopeneche [che	Nahtova	Wa rooh teh	Wa kon	Yunnu-kwat
Mystery-man	New mohk hopene-	Nah tose	So nish wa rooh teh	We chasha wakon	Yunnu kwat haw
Sacrifice	Wa pa shee	Kits tah kee	....	We oh pa	Yunnu wonus
Drum	Bereck hah	Ogh tum	....	Chon che a ha	Ye nuf hess

353

ENGLISH.	MANDAN.	BLACKFOOT.	RICCAREE.	SIOUX.	TUSKARORA.
Rattle	Eeh na de	....	....	Waga moo	Wuntits u runtha
Sun	Menahka	Cristeque ahtose	Sha-koona	Wee	Hiday
Moon	Esto menahka	Cogue ahtose	We-tah	On wee	Autsunychaw
Stars	H'ka ka	Ca cha tose	Sa ca	We chash po	Ojisnok
Rain	H'ka hoosh	Shotta	Tas sou	Ma how jea	Wara
Snow	Cop caze	Cane	Tah hah	Wah	Wun
Night	Estogr	Caquay	Ee nahght	On ha peo	Autsunyo
Day	Hampah	Cristoque	Sha cona	On pah	Yor huh uh
Dark	Ham pah eriskah	Skaynatsee	Te ka tistat	Ee ohk pa zec	Yor wets a yuh
Light	Edayhush	Cristequenats	Sha koona	O jan jee	Yoohooks
Heavy	T'kash	Socoay	Tah tash	Te kay	Wau wis na
Not heavy	Ho hesh	Mahts coay	Kak a tash	Ka po jel la	Wau ri yos
Yes	K'hoo	Ah	Nee coo la	How	Unhuh
No	Megosh	Sah	Ka ka	Ea	Gwuss
Good	Shusu	Ahghsee	Toh nee	Wash tay	Wa gwast
Bad	K'he cush	Pah kaps	Kah	Shee cha	Wa shuh
Very bad	Keks-cusha	Eehcooa pah kaps	Koo nah hee	Shee cha lahgeha	Array wa shuh
How do you do?	Tush kah thah mah kah [hush?	How ne tucka?	Chee na se nun?	How ke che wa?	Dati yoot hay its?
Very well	Mah shuse	Neet ahkse	Ah teesh te	Tran wou an	Array as gu nuh
I am sick	Me au gana bush	Estse no stum	Na too te rate	Mah koo je	Ee wak nu wax
Are you tired?	E da e teache?	Cho hetta ke tesistico?	Kah ka nee now a?	Won ne too ka?	Was na ra huh?
I am not tired	Wah ee wah ta hish	Nemah tesistico	....	Won ne tooka shee noe	Grons a runk na rahouk
Look there	Etta hant tah	Essummissa	Hay nah ho too tayrick	Wi a ka	Tsotkathoo
Come here	Roo hoo tah	Pohks a pote	Shee sha	Ta ha na dah pe	Ka jee
Hot	Dsa shosh	Ea cristochis	Tow war ist	Mush ta	Yoo nau ri hun
Cold	Shinee hush	Stuya	Teep se	Sinnee	Aut hooh
Long	Hash kah	Innuya	Tac chess	Honska	Ee wats
Short	Sonnah ka	Sah kee	Nee hootch	Pe tah cha	Di wats a
War Eagle	Mah sish	Pehta	Nix war roo	Wa me day wah kee	Akwiah
Buffalo	Ptemday	Eneuh	Wa tash	Pe tay	Hohats
Elk	Omepah	Ponokah	Wah	Opon	Joowaroowa
Deer	Mah man a coo	Ouacasee	A noo nach	Teh cha	Awgway
Beaver	Warrapha	....	Chee tooghs	Chapa	Jonockuh
Porcupine	Pahhee	Ponokah meta	Pan hi e	....	Onhatau
Horse	Ompah meneda	Aihahwa	Ha wah rooh te	Shon ka wakon	Tyanootsruhuh
Robe	Mah he toh	Itseekist	Sa hooche	Shee na	Otskiyatsra
Moccasins	Hoompah	Kekstakee	Hooche	Hong pa	On ok qua
Shirt	Ema shotah	Assokas	Kraitch	O ken dee	....
Leggings	Hoh shee	Ahtsaiks	Kah hooche	Hons ka	Oristreh
Bow	Warah e noo pah	Netsinnam	Nache	Eta zee pah	Awraw
Quiver	Eehkticka	....	Nish kratch	O ju ah	Yonats ronarhoost pah
Arrow	Mahha	Ohpsis	Neeche	Wonhee	Kanah
Shield	Wah kee	....	....	Woh ha chon k	Yununay nahquaw
Lance	Monna etorook shoka	Sapa pistats	Na se wa roo	Wow oo ke za	....
Wigwam	Ote	Moeese	Acane	Wah kee on	Onassahunwa
Woman	Meha	Ahkeea	Sa pat	Wee on	Kau nuh wuh
Wife	Moorse	Netohkeaman	Tah ban	We noh cha	....
Child	Sookhomaha	Pohka	Pe ra	Chin cha	Yetyatshoyuh
Girl	Sook meha	Ahkeoquoin	Soo nahtch	Wee chin cha	....
Boy	Sook numohk	Sah komape	Wee nahtch	Okee chin cha	Kunjookwher
Head	Pan	Otokan	Pahgh	Pah	Otahra

354

ENGLISH.	MANDAN.	BLACKFOOT.	RICCAREE.	SIOUX.	TUSKARORA.
Arms	Arda	Otchist	Arrai	Ees ta	Orunjha
Legs	Doka	Ahcatches	Ahgha	Hoo	Orusay
Eyes	Estume	Owopspec	Chee ree coo	Ustah	Ookaray
Nose	Pahoo	Ohcrisis	....	Pah soo	Oojyasa
Mouth	Ea	Mah oi	....	Poo tay	Oosharunwa
Face	Estah	Oestocris	....	Ee tay	Ookahsa
Ears	Nakoha	Ohtokiss	Tickokite	Noh ghee	Ookahnay
Hand	Onka	....	Teho nane	Non pay	Ohahna
Fingers	On ka hah	Ohkitchis	Pa rick	....	Oosookway
Foot	Shee	Ahocatchis	Ahgh	See	Oosa
Hair	Pah hee	Otokan	Pa hi	Pay kee	Auwayrah
Canoe	Menanka	Ahkeosehts	Lah kee hoon	Wahta	Oohuwa
River	Passah ah	Naya tohta	Sa hon nee	Wah ta pah	Kinah
Paddle	Manuk pah sho	....	Natoh-catogh	Eee chah bo ka	Okawetsrch
Fish	Poh	Mummea	....	Oh hong	Runjiuh
Vermilion	Wah sah	Ahsain	Pa hate	....	Yout kojun ya
Painter	Wah ka pooska	Ahsainahkee	....	Ee cha zoo kah ga	Ah ah
Whisky	Men e pah dah	Nah heeoh kee	Te son nan	Me ne wah ka	Wis ky
Pipe	E hudka	Ahquayneman	Laps	Tchon de oopa	Yet jy arhoot hah
Tobacco	Mannah sha	Pistacan	Lapscon	Tchondee	Jarhooh
Gun	Eroopah	Nahma	Tnan kee	Mon za wakon	Au naw
A man runs	Numohk p'tahush	Ohks kos moi nema	Sa rish ka tar ree	We chasha ee onka	....
He eats	E roosh toosh	Oyeet	Te wa wa	U tah pee	Yusyhoory
I think	Wah push e dah hush	Neetasta	Nanto te wiska	Ee me doo ke cha	Kary
I am old	Wah k'hee hush	Neetashpee	Nanto co nahose	We ma chah cha	Auk hoor
She is young	Ea sook me hom mehan	Mahto mahxim	Tesoonock	Ha chee na tum pee	Akatsah
Scalp	Pon dope khee	Otokan	San ish pa	Wecha sha pa	....
Scalp dance	Pon dope khee na pish	Otokan epascat	Pah te ra ka rohk	Wah kee ta no wah	Onahray na yun kwah
War dance	Keeruck sah nah pish	Soopascat	....	....	Ne yunk wah
White buffalo	Woka da	Eneuh quisix sinunum	Toh n hah tah ka	Ta his ka	Owaryakuh
Raven	Ka ka	Mastoa	To kah ka	Kong hee	....
Bear	Mahto	Keahyu	Koo nooghk	Matto	Jotakry yukuh
Antelope	Ko ka	Saw kee owa kasee	Annoo notche	Tah to ka no	Ojiruk
Spirits, or Ghosts	Mounoh he ka	Ah eene	....	Wa nough hgee	Oonowak
Wolf	Harratta	Ahpace	Steerich	....	Tskwarinuh
Dog	Mones waroota	A meeteh	Hahtch	Shon ka	Jir
A brave	Numohk harica	Mahtsee	Too ne roose	O eet e ka	....
A great chief	Numohk k'shese k'tich	Ahecooa nin nah	Nay shon tee rehoo	We chasha on ta pe ka	Yego wa nuh
Old woman	Rokah kah ksee ha	Kee pe tah kee	Sooht sabat	Wa kon kana	Kaskwary
Fire	Wareday	Steea	Te ki eeht	Pah ta	Yoneks
Council-fire	Kaherookah Waraday	Nahto steea	Ki eeht te warooht	Pah ta wah ka	....
Council-house	Kaherookah kahar	Nahto yeweis	Warooht ta ko	Te pe wah ka	Yunt kunis ah thah
Good-bye	....	How	....	How ke che wa	Tyowits nah na
One	Mah han nah	Jeh	Asco	On je	Unji
Two	Nompah	Nah tohk	Pit co	Non pa	Nexty
Three	Namary	No oks kum	Tow wit	Hi ami ni	Au suh
Four	Tohpa	Nee sooyim	Tchee tish	Tau pah	Hun tak
Five	Kakhoo	Ne see tsee	Tchee hoo	Za pe tah	Wisk
Six	Kemah	Nahoo	Tcha pis	Shah pai	Ooyak
Seven	Koo pah	E kitch ekum	To tcha pis	Shah co	Jarnak
Eight	Ta tuck a	Nah ne suyim	To tcha pis won	Shah en do hen	Nakruh

ENGLISH.	MANDAN.	BLACKFOOT.	RICCAREE.	SIOUX.	TUSKARORA.
Nine	Mah pa	Paex o	Nah e ne won	Nen pe che onca	Ni ruh
Ten	Perug	Kay pee	Nah en	Oka che min en	Wutsuh
Eleven	Auga mahannah	Kay pee nay tchee kopochee	Ko tchee te won	Oka on je	Unjits kahar
Twelve	Auga nompah	Kay pee nah kopochee	Pit co nah en	Oka nonpa	Nexty tskahar
Thirteen	Auga namary	Kay pee nay ohk kopochee	Tow wit nah en	Oka hiamini	Au su tskahar
Fourteen	Auga tohpa	Kay pee nay say kopochee	Tchee tish nah en	Oka tau pah	Untak tskahar
Fifteen	Ag kak hoo	Kay pee ne see tchee kopochee	Tchee hoo nahen	Oka za petah	Wisk tskahar
Sixteen	Ag kemah	Kay pee nay kopochee	Tch a pis nahen	Oka shah'pai	Ooyok tskahar
Seventeen	Ag koopah	Kay pee eh kee chie kopochee	To tcha pis nahen	Oka shahko	Jarnak tskahar
Eighteen	Aga tah tucka	Kay pee nan e sic kopochee	To tcha pis won nahen	Oka shah en do hen	Nakruh tskahar
Nineteen	Aga mahpa	Kay pee paex sic kopochnee	Nah ene won maker	Oka nen pe chi on ka	Nirut tskahar
Twenty	Nompah perug	Natchip pee	Weetah	Oka chiminen non pa	Na wots huh
Thirty	Namary amperug	Ne hippe	Sah wee	Oka chiminen hiamini	Au tuh tiwotshuh
Forty	Toh pa amperug	Ne sippe	Nachen tchee tish	Oka chiminen taupah	Huntak tiwotshuh
Fifty	Kah hoo amperug	Ne se chippe	Nahen tchee hoo	Oka chiminen za petah	Wisk tiwotshuh
Sixty	Keemah amperug	Nah chippe	Nahen tchee pis	Oka chiminen shah pai	Ooyak tiwotshuh
Seventy	Koopah amperug	O kitch chippe	Nahen to tcha pis	Oka chiminen shahco	Janak tiwotshuh
Eighty	Ta tuck amperug	Nahne sippe	Nah en to tcha pis won	Oka chiminen sha hen do hen	Naknuh tiwotshuh
Ninety	Mah pa amperug	Paex sippe	Nah en nah e ne won	Oka chiminen nen pe chee on ca	Ninuh tiwotshuh
One hundred	Ee sooc mah hannah	Kay pee pee pee	Shoh tan	O pounkrai	Kau yaustry
One thousand	Ee sooc perug	Kay pee pee pee pee	Shoh tan tera hoo	Kaut o poun krul	Wutsu-kau yaustry

356

Acknowledgments

My greatest debt in editing and introducing George Catlin's *Letters and Notes* is quite obviously to George Catlin himself—not only to his *Notes* in themselves, not only to his paintings and sketches, but also to the example of his character. In attempting to understand his achievements, I incurred a schedule of additional debts.

Although the major intellectual debts are listed in the Selected Bibliography, I would like to single out and express my thanks to certain scholars. Of these, Bernard DeVoto heads the list. I could not have understood either the geography or history of the West without his instruction. He was a master teacher and master writer, the author of grand designs. I came to be wholly dependent upon his work, and the trails he had cut comforted me in what turned out to be a much longer adventure than I had at first imagined.

Of course, if my version of Catlin's life and circumstance contains errors, the errors are mine, not DeVoto's. In the same sense I wish to single out, and to thank, but to absolve, other companions and teachers: John C. Ewers, Alvin M. Josephy, Jr., and his editors, Lloyd Haberly, Marvin C. Ross, and Harold McCracken. Their works on the West, on the Indian, and on George Catlin were source, guide, example, and comfort.

357

To these intellectual debts I must add a schedule of personal thanks—incomplete because it cannot salute all those who were companions of the voyage. Of these, Clarkson N. Potter heads the gang sheet. This edition bears his imprint, but only after a serpentine history in the gathering of the idea, the traipsing of the West, the preparation of manuscript, and the vagaries of the publishing trade. From my first acquaintance with Catlin's work six years ago, the "edited" Catlin has been steadfastly supported by Clarkson Potter, and it is only a sweet irony that he has become its publisher. I am indebted to his encouragement and his habitual generosity of spirit.

I also owe special thanks to another patient and enthusiastic companion. Exploration is romantic in both prospect and in memory. Yet tracing Catlin's routes, and camping the landscapes of Indian meeting grounds, and following the trails of fur trade routes are also dusty and dirty ventures—subject to stifling heat, icy sleeping bags, soaking rainstorms, bilious campfire food, insatiable mosquitoes, long boring drives, and fatigue. Christopher B. Mooney never exhausted his curiosity, his energy, his laughter.

I am embarrassed that I cannot list all those who responded with patience. It would be a long list: officers of the Corps of Engineers, archivists, anthropologists, curators, and librarians—especially librarians in eleven states and the District of Columbia. They searched, found, led, and gave directions. To those who responded with patience I want to add my thanks to those whose diligence was outstanding: copy editor Carol O'Neill, production editor Diane Girling, and editor Jane West. Finally, in addition to teachers, guides, companions, the patient, and the diligent, I am indebted to companions in spirit—men who like Clark Potter kept reminding me to continue: William C. MacMillen, and John and Alan; brothers of the tribe who live in the interstices of the provident, and blood brothers.

M.M.M.

Selected Bibliography

Brown, Dee. *Bury My Heart at Wounded Knee.* Holt, Rinehart & Winston, New York, 1970.

Catlin, George. *Catlin's North American Indian Portfolio. Hunting Scenes and Amusements of the Rocky Mountains and Prairies of America.* Published by the author at Egyptian Hall, London, 1844.

———. *Last Rambles Amongst the Indians of the Rocky Mountains and the Andes.* D. Appleton and Company, New York, 1867.

———. *Letters and Notes on the Manners, Customs, and Conditions of the North American Indians.* Published by the author at Egyptian Hall, London, 1841.

———. *Life Amongst the Indians—A Book for Youth.* D. Appleton & Co., New York, 1857.

———. *Notes of Eight Years' Travel and Residence in Europe.* Published by the author at his Indian Collection, No. 6, Waterloo Place, London, 1848.

———. *O-Kee-pa: A Religious Ceremony.* Trubner and Co., London, 1867.

———. *Souvenir of the North American Indians.* Unpublished portfolio, manuscript, and drawings, dated 1852, The Newberry Library, Chicago.

Curry, Larry. *The American West, Painters from Catlin to Russell.* The Viking Press, Inc., in association with the Los Angeles County Museum of Art, New York, 1972.

DeVoto, Bernard. *Across the Wide Missouri.* Houghton Mifflin Company, Boston, 1947.

———. *The Course of Empire.* Houghton Mifflin Company, Boston, 1952.

———. *The Journals of Lewis and Clark,* edited and interpreted by Bernard DeVoto. Houghton Mifflin Company, Boston, 1953.

Donaldson, Thomas C. "The George Catlin Indian Gallery." In *U.S. National Museum Annual Report, 1885,* Washington, D.C., 1886.

Drinnon, Richard. *White Savage: The Case of John Dunn Hunter.* Schocken Books, New York, 1972.

The Editors of American Heritage, Editor in Charge, Alvin M. Josephy, Jr. *The American Heritage Book of Indians.* American Heritage Publishing Co., Inc., New York, 1961.

The Editors. "George Catlin, Sketching up the Missouri River in 1832." *American Scene Magazine,* Vol. V, No. 3, The Thomas Gilcrease Institute of American History and Art, Tulsa, Oklahoma, 1964.

Ewers, John C. *Early White Influence upon Plains Indian Painting: George Catlin and Carl Bodmer among the Mandan, 1832–34.* Misc. Col., Vol. 134, No. 7., pub no. 4292, The Smithsonian Institution, Washington, D.C., 1957.

———. "George Catlin, Painter of Indians and The West." From the *Smithsonian Report for 1955,* pp. 483-528, The Smithsonian Institution, Washington, D.C., 1956.

———. "Folk Art in the Fur Trade of the Upper Missouri," Prologue: *The Journal of the National Archives,* Summer 1972, Washington, D.C.

Ewers, John C., editor. *O-Kee-pa, by George Catlin, A Religious Ceremony and Other Customs of The Mandans,* by George Catlin, with an introduction by John C. Ewers. Yale University Press, New Haven and London, 1967.

Garrard, Lewis H. *Wah-to-yah & The Taos Trail.* American West Publishing Company, Palo Alto, California, 1968.

Getlein, Frank. *Images of the old West painted while it was still there.* The Smithsonian Institution, May 1972, pp. 36–43, Washington, D.C.

Haberly, Lloyd. *Pursuit of the Horizon.* The Macmillan Company, New York, 1948.

Halpin, Marjorie. "Catlin's Indian Gallery: The George Catlin Paintings in the United States National Museum," pamphlet, 36 pp. The Smithsonian Institution, Washington, D.C., 1965.

Hunt, David C. "Portraits and Portfolios." *American Scene Magazine,* Vol. XI, No. 1, The Thomas Gilcrease Institute of American History and Art, Tulsa, Oklahoma, 1968.

McCracken, Harold. *George Catlin and the Old Frontier.* The Dial Press, New York, 1959.

Monaghan, Jay, editor. *The Book of The American West.* Bonanza Books. Julian Messner, Inc., New York, 1963.

Parsons, Elsie Clews, editor. *American Indian Life.* A Bison Book, University of Nebraska Press, Lincoln, 1967. Copyright 1922, B. W. Huebsch, Inc.

Quaife, Milo Milton, editor. *The Commerce of the Prairies,* by Josiah Gregg. A Bison Book, University of Nebraska Press, Lincoln, 1967. Copyright 1926, Lakeside Press.

Ross, Marvin C., editor. *George Catlin: Episodes from Life Among the Indians and Last Rambles.* University of Oklahoma Press, Norman, 1959.

Rossi, Paul A., and Hunt, David C. *The Art of The Old West.* From the Collection of The Gilcrease Institute. Alfred A. Knopf, New York, 1971.

Sandoz, Mari. *Love Song to the Plains.* A Bison Book, University of Nebraska Press, Lincoln, 1966. Copyright 1961, Harper & Row.

Thomas, Phillip Drennon. "George Catlin: Pictorial Historian of Aboriginal America." *Natural History,* December 1972, pp. 30–43, The American Museum of Natural History, New York.

Washburn, Wilcomb E., editor. *The Indian and the White Man,* edited with an Introduction by Wilcomb E. Washburn. Documents in American Civilization Series, Anchor Books, Doubleday & Company, Inc., Garden City, New York, 1964.

———. (Catalogue) *Faces and Places, Changing Images of 19th Century America.* Hirschl & Adler Galleries, Inc., New York, 1972.

Index